THE CAMBRIDGE COMPANION TO MEDIEVAL BRITISH MANUSCRIPTS

The scholarship and teaching of manuscript studies has been transformed by digitization rendering previously rarefied documents accessible for study on a vast scale. *The Cambridge Companion to Medieval British Manuscripts* orientates students in the complex, multidisciplinary study of medieval book production and contemporary display of manuscripts from *c.* 600 to 1500. Accessible explanations draw on key case studies to illustrate the major methodologies and explain why skills in understanding early book production are so critical for reading, editing, and accessing a rich cultural heritage. Chapters by leading specialists in manuscript studies range from explaining how manuscripts were stored, to revealing the complex networks of readers and writers which can be understood through manuscripts, to an in-depth discussion of the Wycliffite Bible.

Orietta Da Rold is University Lecturer in the University of Cambridge and Fellow of St John's College. Her publications include *The Dd Manuscript: A Digital Edition of Cambridge University Library, MS Dd. 4. 24 of Chaucer's Canterbury Tales* (2013), and *Paper in Medieval England: From Pulp to Fictions* (2020).

Elaine Treharne is Roberta Bowman Denning Professor of Humanities, Professor of English, and Robert K. Packard University Fellow in Undergraduate Education at Stanford University, and a Fellow of the Society of Antiquaries, the Royal Historical Society, the English Association, and the Learned Society of Wales. A qualified archivist, she has published more than thirty books and sixty articles on early medieval literature and the History of Text Technologies.

THE CAMBRIDGE COMPANION TO
MEDIEVAL BRITISH MANUSCRIPTS

EDITED BY

ORIETTA DA ROLD
University of Cambridge

ELAINE TREHARNE
Stanford University

CAMBRIDGE
UNIVERSITY PRESS

University Printing House, Cambridge CB2 8BS, United Kingdom

One Liberty Plaza, 20th Floor, New York, NY 10006, USA

477 Williamstown Road, Port Melbourne, VIC 3207, Australia

314–321, 3rd Floor, Plot 3, Splendor Forum, Jasola District Centre,
New Delhi – 110025, India

79 Anson Road, #06–04/06, Singapore 079906

Cambridge University Press is part of the University of Cambridge.

It furthers the University's mission by disseminating knowledge in the pursuit of
education, learning, and research at the highest international levels of excellence.

www.cambridge.org
Information on this title: www.cambridge.org/9781107102460
DOI: 10.1017/9781316182659

© Cambridge University Press 2020

This publication is in copyright. Subject to statutory exception
and to the provisions of relevant collective licensing agreements,
no reproduction of any part may take place without the written
permission of Cambridge University Press.

First published 2020

A catalogue record for this publication is available from the British Library.

ISBN 978-1-107-10246-0 Hardback
ISBN 978-1-107-50014-3 Paperback

Cambridge University Press has no responsibility for the persistence or accuracy of
URLs for external or third-party internet websites referred to in this publication
and does not guarantee that any content on such websites is, or will remain,
accurate or appropriate.

CONTENTS

List of Illustrations	*page* vii
List of Contributors	ix
Acknowledgements	xii
List of Abbreviations	xiii

Introduction: The Matter of Manuscripts and Methodologies — 1
ORIETTA DA ROLD AND ELAINE TREHARNE

PART I HOW DO WE STUDY THE MANUSCRIPT?

1 Describing and Cataloguing Medieval English Manuscripts: A Checklist — 13
RICHARD BEADLE AND RALPH HANNA

2 Reading a Manuscript Description — 39
DONALD SCRAGG

3 Reading and Understanding Scripts — 49
JULIA CRICK AND DANIEL WAKELIN

4 Working with Images in Manuscripts — 76
BEATRICE KITZINGER

5 The Sum of the Book: Structural Codicology and Medieval
Manuscript Culture — 106
RYAN PERRY

PART II WHY DO WE STUDY THE MANUSCRIPT?

6 Networks of Writers and Readers — 129
ELAINE TREHARNE AND ORIETTA DA ROLD

v

CONTENTS

7 The Written Word: Literacy across Languages 149
JANE GILBERT AND SARA HARRIS

8 The Wycliffite Bible 179
ELIZABETH SOLOPOVA

9 Editing Medieval Manuscripts for Modern Audiences 187
HELEN FULTON

10 Where Were Books Made and Kept? 214
TERESA WEBBER

PART III   WHERE DO WE STUDY THE MANUSCRIPT?

11 Charming the Snake: Accessing and Disciplining the Medieval Manuscript 237
SIÂN ECHARD AND ANDREW PRESCOTT

12 The Curation and Display of Digital Medieval Manuscripts 267
SUZANNE PAUL

13 Medieval Manuscripts, the Collector, and the Trade 284
A. S. G. EDWARDS

Guide to Further Reading 295
Index 308
General Index 310

vi

ILLUSTRATIONS

1.1	Example of a reconstructed collation	24
3.1	Oxford, Bodleian Library, MS Bodley 264, fol. 67r	63
3.2	Cambridge, University Library, MS Dd.14.30, fol. 10r	65
3.3	Cambridge, University Library, MS Gg. 4. 27, fol. 457v	70
4.1	Crucifixion, psalter with canticles and litanies, and additional texts (the 'Arundel Psalter'). Probably Winchester, fourth quarter of the eleventh century (*c* 1073) with twelfth-century additions. 320 × 220 mm. London, British Library, Arundel MS 60, fol. 12v	82
4.2	Crucifixion, Arundel Psalter. London, British Library, Arundel MS 60, fol. 52v	83
4.3	Calendar: month of August, Arundel Psalter. London, British Library, Arundel MS 60, fol. 5v	90
4.4	Crucifixion and Psalm 1, Arundel Psalter. London, British Library, Arundel MS 60, fols. 12v–13r	92
4.5	Crucifixion and Psalm 51, Arundel Psalter. London, British Library, Arundel MS 60, fols. 52v–53	94
4.6	Crucifixion, psalter with additional texts (the 'Tiberius Psalter'). Winchester, third quarter of the eleventh century with twelfth-century additions. 345 × 250 mm (binding). London, British Library, Cotton MS Tiberius C. vi, fol. 13r	99
5.1	Manchester, John Rylands Library, MS Eng. 895	107
7.1	Oxford, Bodleian Library, MS Bodley 340, fol. 169v	152
7.2	Paris, Bibliothèque nationale de France, MS hébreu 113, fol. 2v	157
7.3	Oxford, Bodleian Library, MS Ashmole 328, fol. 195r	160
7.4	Rome, Vatican Library, MS Ottobonianus Latins 1474, fol. 2r	164
7.5	Cambridge, Trinity College, MS R. 17. 1, fol. 207r	167

vii

LIST OF ILLUSTRATIONS

7.6	Cambridge, University Library, MS Dd. 3. 53, fol. 213v	170
7.7	Oxford, Bodleian Library, MS Bodley 264, fol. 67r	173
9.1	Stemma for 'In Praise of Sir Hywel' (from gutorglyn.net, poem 70)	202
9.2	Archives and Special Collections, Bangor University, Gwyneddon MS 4, p. 238	203
9.3	Aberystwyth, National Library of Wales, MS 3049D, p. 194	204
9.4	Aberystwyth, National Library of Wales, MS 8497B, fol. 43v	205

CONTRIBUTORS

RICHARD BEADLE is Emeritus Professor of Medieval English Literature and Palaeography at the University of Cambridge, and a Fellow of St John's College.

JULIA CRICK is Professor of Palaeography and Manuscript Studies at King's College, University of London. Her publications include *The Historia regum Britannie of Geoffrey of Monmouth, IV. Dissemination and Reception in the Later Middle Ages* (1991) and *Charters of St. Albans* (2007).

ORIETTA DA ROLD is University Lecturer in the University of Cambridge and Fellow of St John's College. Her publications include *The Dd Manuscript: A Digital Edition of Cambridge University Library, MS Dd. 4. 24 of Chaucer's Canterbury Tales* (2013), and *Paper in Medieval England: From Pulp to Fictions* (2020).

SIÂN ECHARD is Professor at the University of British Columbia. Her publications include *Printing the Middle Ages* (2008), and she is the General Editor, with Robert Rouse, of *The Encyclopedia of Medieval Literature in Britain* (2017).

A. S. G. EDWARDS, FSA, FEA, is Honorary Visiting Professor at the University of Kent and University College, London, and Deputy Editor of *The Book Collector*.

HELEN FULTON is Professor of Medieval Literature at the University of Bristol. She specializes in literary and political engagements between medieval Wales, England, and Europe, and is the editor of a corpus of medieval Welsh poetry. She has published widely in the areas of medieval literature, manuscript transmission, and urban culture.

LIST OF CONTRIBUTORS

JANE GILBERT is Senior Lecturer in French at University College London. She has published on medieval French and English literature both separately and comparatively. She is currently completing a co-authored monograph arising from the AHRC-funded research project, Medieval Francophone Literary Culture Outside France.

RALPH HANNA is Professor of Palaeography Emeritus and Emeritus Fellow of Keble College, Oxford. He hangs out a lot in libraries.

SARA HARRIS is the author of *The Linguistic Past in Twelfth-Century Britain* (2017).

BEATRICE KITZINGER is Assistant Professor of Medieval Art in the Department of Art and Archaeology at Princeton University. She is the author of *The Cross, the Gospels, and the Work of Art in the Carolingian Age* (2019).

SUZANNE PAUL is the Keeper of Rare Books and Early Manuscripts at Cambridge University Library, and is closely involved in international digitization efforts for manuscripts.

RYAN PERRY is Senior Lecturer in Late Medieval Literature at the University of Kent at Canterbury. He specializes in the material contexts of vernacular manuscript corpora, and especially Middle English religious textual culture.

ANDREW PRESCOTT is Professor of Digital Humanities in the School of Critical Studies at the University of Glasgow. He was formerly a curator in the Department of Manuscripts at the British Library and was one of the collaborators in 'Electronic Beowulf', edited by Kevin S. Kiernan. He was AHRC Theme Leader Fellow for the 'Digital Transformations' theme from 2012 to 2019.

DONALD SCRAGG is Professor of Anglo-Saxon Studies Emeritus at the University of Manchester, and the founding Director of the Manchester Centre for Anglo-Saxon Studies. He is the author of numerous books and articles on Old English homiletic prose, *The Battle of Maldon*, and, most recently, *A Conspectus of Scribes in Anglo-Saxon England*.

ELIZABETH SOLOPOVA is Research Fellow at the University of Oxford, and Lecturer at Christ Church College and Harris Manchester College. Her publications include *The Wycliffite Bible: Origin, History and Interpretation* (2017). She is the Principal Investigator of the 'Towards a New Edition of the Wycliffite Bible' Project, funded by the Arts and Humanities Research Council (2016–19).

LIST OF CONTRIBUTORS

ELAINE TREHARNE, FSA, FRHISTS, FEA, and FLSW, is Roberta Bowman Denning Professor of Humanities and Professor of English at Stanford University, where she also directs the book historical/digital projects – Stanford Text Technologies, Stanford Global Currents, and CyberTexts. She has published widely on Old and Middle English manuscripts and literary culture, and is currently completing *The Phenomenal Book*.

DANIEL WAKELIN is Jeremy Griffiths Professor of Medieval English Palaeography at the University of Oxford. Among his publications are *Scribal Correction and Literary Craft: English Manuscripts 1375–1510* (2014) and *Designing English: Early Literature on the Page* (2017).

TERESA WEBBER, FBA, is Professor of Palaeography at the University of Cambridge. Among her publications are *Scribes and Scholars at Salisbury Cathedral c. 1075–c. 1125* (1992), with A. G. Watson, *The Libraries of the Augustinian Canons*, CBMLC 6 (1998), and, with E. Leedham-Green, *The Cambridge History of Libraries in Britain and Ireland*, Volume I: to 1640 (2006).

xi

ACKNOWLEDGEMENTS

We should like to extend our thanks to our contributors, who have patiently assisted in the process of getting this volume to press. Our gratitude goes to Linda Bree and our editors at Cambridge University Press.

We should also like to offer heartfelt thanks to the librarians and manuscript curators at Special Collections' repositories from Cambridge, London, Oxford, Paris, and elsewhere; their professional contribution, support, and kindness enriches the research of all manuscript scholars in fundamental ways. Similarly, thank you to St John's College for supporting our formative workshop and to the teams of digitizers and image processors in small and big libraries alike, from Trinity College Cambridge, to the British Library, and to Stanford University Libraries: without your collaboration, contemporary scholarship would be much impoverished.

ABBREVIATIONS

BL	British Library
DDBL	A. G. Watson, *Catalogue of Dated and Datable Manuscripts c. 700–1600 in the British Library*, 2 vols. (London, 1979)
DDCL	P. R. Robinson, *Catalogue of Dated and Datable Manuscripts c. 737–1600 in Cambridge Libraries*, 2 vols. (Cambridge, 1988)
DDLL	P. R. Robinson, *Catalogue of Dated and Datable Manuscripts c. 888–1600 in London Libraries*, 2 vols. (London, 2003)
DDOL	A. G. Watson, *Catalogue of Dated and Datable Manuscripts c. 435–1600 in Oxford Libraries*, 2 vols. (London, 1984)
f., fol.	folio
ff., fols.	folios
OE	Old English
OI	Old Irish
MS(S)	Manuscript(s)
r	recto
v	verso

xiii

ORIETTA DA ROLD AND
ELAINE TREHARNE

Introduction: The Matter of Manuscripts and Methodologies

Over the last twenty years, the study of medieval manuscripts has flourished on an unprecedented scale. Once considered to be ancillary disciplines, codicology or palaeography were studied as part of historical, classical, and literary fields, and taught as part of a regime of foundational training for medievalists. Now these core components of Manuscript Studies have been further developed as part of a field in its own right. Manuscript Studies has become, then, a capacious field with such a multitude of research possibilities, practices, trajectories, and potential that it is difficult to trace a full survey of its scholarly reach across continents, languages, and geographical locales.[1] Different methodologies – ranging from quantitative to qualitative approaches – different terminological systems for scripts, and distinctive ways of displaying dates have created a notable set of issues for manuscript specialists, particularly as we move through the digital era, when metadata is created without focused regard for consistency and interoperability. Still, rightly, medieval Manuscript Studies is a major area of research, scholarship, teaching, and public outreach. In the case of the former, tens of thousands of curious and informed citizens engage in browsing manuscripts through social media and the internet; and one of the most successful and widely publicized heritage events in recent years has been the 'Anglo-Saxon Kingdoms' exhibition held at the British Library in the winter of 2018–19, in which manuscripts from all over Europe were reunited, some for the first time in centuries.

As knowledge of manuscript collections grows through improved and more discoverable cataloguing, through increased access to library and online materials, and through the impact of the flourishing field of Book, Cultural and Social History, the study of the medieval manuscript itself takes on greater import both in university curricula globally and in the consciousness of a more popular appreciation of cultural heritage. In order to provide a scholarly foundation for this interest in manuscripts, this volume, comprising new specially commissioned texts, offers a sequence of thoughtful overviews of key areas of investigation in the field. Each chapter gives substantial information about its topic, and can be regarded as an initial theoretical training in or introduction to the specialized areas of investigation that make up Manuscript Studies. Case studies anchor the descriptive and analytical research, so that readers can see the application of approaches.

In our work with students and colleagues in Medieval Studies (as in other disciplines), scholars have recourse to that most critical of reflections: 'What methodology are you thinking of using in order to answer your research question?' For all researchers, at every stage of our academic exploration, there is a clear need to be explicit about the process or processes which underpin our study, and it is essential that we identify, understand, and discuss our approach early on in our work on manuscripts.

Working with manuscripts is an inductive experience, although it is possible, of course, to work deductively with the objects of study from a set of assumptions or hypotheses. Inductively, we begin with the evidence in front of us and scrutinize it for what it might reveal in the light of our specific topic. But the matter is not as simple as it may appear. What evidence do we look up? How do we gather the evidence? How do we make sense of what we are looking up?

Multiple potential methodologies present themselves to manuscript scholars and book historians, ranging from the specifically textual to the principally material. Methodologically, for example, it is possible to study only the text – the words on the page – from the perspective of textual dissemination. One might gather every witness to a literary work, like the later fourteenth-century English text *Piers Plowman*, and transcribe every manuscript version of this complex alliterative poem to see how each instantiation differs, and what the relationships between the versions might be. There is little doubt that the answers to these questions are generated by the type of research questions which a student has identified. But then *method* has to be informed by a clear *methodology*: two slightly different processes. Of course, the methodology is what guides the principles underpinning the research. It can include the chosen approach, which can be interdisciplinary in scope and can be borrowed from other cognate or non-cognate disciplines. The method is the practical application of that methodology – the tools which are employed to carry out the study.

The contributors in this book show that there is not one set of tools which may be considered above any other; they demonstrate that a codicological, palaeographical, art historical, or textual understanding of the object under discussion is a good starting point. If codicology can be defined as a branch of scholarship which studies the manuscript book in its structural as well as in its broader cultural and historical contexts,[2] then palaeography is the

Introduction: The Matter of Manuscripts and Methodologies

discussion of scripts and all that is entailed in scribal practice broadly.[3] Manuscript Studies itself as a field extends beyond the realm of books;[4] a manuscript is something handwritten, and such source materials include historical records which are not held together in books, such as charters, inventories, and letters, and also handwritten material in rolls, fascicles, and loose quires.

Historically, this interest in the materiality of books started with the interest in editing classical texts and philological investigations into language and the morphological make-up of all kinds of textual production. The study of the book as a cultural manifestation of literary, social, and historical synergies was also developed from this interest. Friedrich Ebert, in his *Zur Handschriftenkunde* (1825), ambitiously argued for this contextualized approach to Manuscript Studies. Henry Bradshaw, Librarian of Cambridge University Library, also adopted similar ideas in shaping the way in which scholars ought to study books. Richard Beadle has demonstrated how influential the work of this humble Cambridge librarian has been on the development of the study of books in his Sandars Lectures, and returns to some of these issues in the following chapter.[5] Other scholars have written copiously on the relation between manuscripts and disciplinary specialism. A close perusal of the 'Guide to Further Reading' at the end of this book will offer many possible directions of research within the study of medieval manuscripts, and invites students of manuscripts not to compartmentalize one approach against the other, but instead to reflect on the significance of each of them.

This *Companion* thus aims not only to engage students in a well-established field of enquiry, but also to challenge expectations. The combination of different threads offers the opportunity to create innovative dialogue within the core paradigms of medieval Manuscript Studies. This *Companion* also proposes different ways of looking at the primary material; that is, it provides detailed analysis of a manuscript's significance from its moment and place of production, its subsequent history and use, its place within a broad textual and generic dissemination, its collection and description, to its contemporary display and reception, including as photographic and digital media.

The production and use of medieval manuscripts in Britain are particularly notable, because of the significant concatenation of major events and historical processes affecting the manuscripts' creation and interpretation: in early England, the rise of the English vernacular in the ninth and tenth centuries created a precocious body of texts alongside the Latin textual tradition; the Celtic manuscript tradition, already so important by the eighth century, the Scandinavian influences on language, literature, and ornament, and the

3

tremendous impact of the Norman Conquest all combined to create a dynamic and rich culture of textuality and literacy from the late sixth to the late fifteenth centuries. This history brought about a truly multicultural turn in the written word, supported by different agencies from secular and monastic institutions, to royal households, to heterogeneous lay audiences. Traditionally, scholars look at these phenomena of place, time, and context of production *within* disciplinary, temporal, and linguistic boundaries. The *Companion* brings together scholars from different disciplinary and linguistic backgrounds to enhance what can be learned by looking at British Manuscript Studies *supra-partes*. Contributors have worked on case studies and textual examples that contain English, French, Latin, Welsh, and other languages; that is, the focus is the manuscript copied at any centre in Britain, and not simply the language in which the text is written.

The chapters have been grouped in sections that encourage the reader to think further about 'How do we study the manuscript?' 'Why do we study the manuscript?' and 'Where do we study the manuscript?' These recognizable labels aim to provide a clear sense of direction. Within this organizational structure, contributors offer both a survey of their field and a clear statement of how their own topic can be challenged and advanced by new research in the future. Naturally, some of these areas of investigation complement each other very closely, and not every conceivable aspect of Manuscript Studies has been covered, but what is in the chapters should offer a very good start as an introduction to the field.

In Chapter 1, Richard Beadle and Ralph Hanna provide a detailed account of the process of manuscript description, demonstrating that descriptive analysis 'is now recognized as capable of being a sophisticated type of hermeneutic activity in its own right'. Their checklist – covering shelfmarks, dating, contents, and materials, for example – reminds scholars that each manuscript is unique and should be an accurate reflection of scribal production, and, for each element of manuscript description, best practice is recommended. This chapter is fundamental reading, too, for the methods of membrane preparation; uses and arrangement of medieval paper manuscripts; how to collate quires; how to describe decorative features of the *mise-en-page*; scribal characteristics, including abbreviation and correction; and binding practices.

Donald Scragg's Chapter 2 shows how scholars can interpret a manuscript from the way in which it is described in a catalogue, with a particular focus on the booklet as the key unit of manuscript production. Using an early English manuscript as his main example, Scragg demonstrates the complexity of collation formulae, and the care and attention that is required to reconstruct the physical manuscript from the details provided by

Introduction: The Matter of Manuscripts and Methodologies

cataloguers. He shows that close reading of descriptions can provide sufficient evidence to re-evaluate the history and transmission of early medieval manuscript books.

Julia Crick and Daniel Wakelin's Chapter 3 on how we are to understand script methodologically also sees in the evaluation of written materials the potential for greater apprehension of culture and society. They comment on the idiosyncrasy and craft of scribal hands, irrespective of the model script; on the uniqueness of each instantiation of a scribe's endeavour; and on the ways in which scripts spread across geographical space and through time. Various scripts' biographies are overviewed, showing the diversity of possible scripts in early medieval Europe: their longevity and functionality. A focus on Insular, Caroline, and Welsh minuscules emphasizes the variety of writing styles and the prevalence of one over the other demonstrates the ideological and cultural roles that script plays. In the later period, too, the uses of particular scripts for particular functions indicate not only the significance of nuance in considering handwriting in this long period, but also how teams of scribes operated, how important the patron or commissioner of a volume of texts would be, and how scribal production was so often a commercialized activity, where motivations for particular choices can reveal a tremendous amount about attitudes to books and textual communities.

Beatrice Kitzinger's focus in Chapter 4 is on the art historical component of the manuscript: how we can describe images; what materials and techniques were used; the limitations of facsimile and digital editions; and how images affect our perception of the manuscript and its contexts of production. Concerned particularly with what *method* can reveal, Kitzinger discusses one major case study in detail – the Arundel Psalter – to illustrate that there are many levels upon which one can investigate the artistic component of the medieval codex. Here, the images of the Crucifixion represent different artistic choices, with significant consequences for theological and intellectual strategies and traditions, and these are traced through a number of their most important networks and contexts.

In Chapter 5, Ryan Perry considers the physical make-up of manuscript books: their divisions into quires and booklets, and the manner of putting the parts of the book together. Ranging from pre-Conquest books to late medieval books, and complementary to Scragg's chapter, Perry assesses the evidence for the manufacture of flexible assemblages of texts, considering the portability of loose-bound or unbound booklets and the independent circulation of works in these formats. Evidence of stationers' sales of *pecia* – books copied in 'pieces' – in the later medieval period suggests the commercialization of manuscript facture, and Perry discusses the

5

important phenomenon of professional scribes, whose work was in great demand from increasingly literate consumers. Perry also offers timely comments on how modern scholars are meant to classify manuscripts produced – perhaps over time – with a wide variety of genres, complex networks of transmission, and potential uses, well beyond their own period of production.

Continuing the theme of networks and transmission, in Part II, 'Why Do We Study the Manuscript?', Chapter 6 leads with Elaine Treharne and Orietta Da Rold adding to Perry's discussion of historical manuscripts by focusing almost entirely on that longstanding genre to show how writers worked with a broad and important sense of their place within a tradition. From Bede to Brut, they show the complex relationships of writers and readers of history in English, Latin, and French. Issues of known authorship and anonymity are raised alongside institutional and collective programmes of manuscript production to show that what was copied, adapted, translated, and rewritten both contributed to and reflected particular forms of writerly identity.

Translation and adaptation inform Chapter 7 by Jane Gilbert and Sara Harris, who discuss the prominence of multilingual expertise and practice in the written record, problematizing obvious classifications, such as 'What constitutes an *English* manuscript?' The questions they raise of the nature of linguistic skillsets in the later Middle Ages are critical to understanding the appearance of particular vernacular and Latin texts – often incorporated in manuscripts as additions or glosses – and categorized by scholars in ways that do not fully recognize the broad spectrum of linguistic possibility and permeability in this period. By considering the changing nature of what constituted 'book languages' and what did not, Gilbert and Harris reveal the dynamic and rich linguistic environment of the eleventh and twelfth centuries, ranging from liturgical texts, to Orrm's lengthy poetic homilies, the *Prophecies of Merlin*, to the later *Treatise on the Astrolabe* by Chaucer. Throughout the chapter, the significance of translation for indicating knowledge transfer becomes clear, while the ostensibly simple task of labelling linguistic presentation within medieval manuscripts is shown to be complicated and worthy of a great deal more research.

A major movement, inspired by John Wyclif, had important repercussions in the High Middle Ages for the English vernacular and the copying of manuscripts, and Elizabeth Solopova elucidates the history and tradition of the Wycliffite Bible in Chapter 8. The origins, dissemination, and nature of this English Bible and its many manuscripts – especially in the first half of the fifteenth century – can be shown to be, in part, supported by the nobility, certainly aimed at erudite readers, who were interested in complex

Introduction: The Matter of Manuscripts and Methodologies

explication in the commentaries and paratext that accompanied the biblical text, and meticulously produced, often within major centres.

In Chapter 9, Helen Fulton deals with the history and major movements in the editing of medieval texts, with a detailed case study that permits a step-by-step explication of how one can go about editing a text that exists in more than one instantiation. Acknowledging the profound complexity of the editorial role, especially in relation to the often-perceived dominance of the author-figure, Fulton reveals the various modes of engagement that are available to editors, from the re-creation of an *ur*-text that pre-dates the earliest extant textual witnesses to the intentional privileging of the work of scribe-copyists themselves. At the heart of all medieval scholarship is mediation – whether because of the necessity of translation, or because of access to texts only through the work of traditional and digital editors. Fulton's chapter makes clear the significance and influence of this editorial role, and also demonstrates how readers can approach the edited text, understanding the decisions, methods, and components included in the publication.

In Chapter 10, Teresa Webber addresses the nitty-gritty of book production: when, where, and why books were produced. Her examination of the field of research reminds us all about the tenuousness of a great deal of the evidence upon which assumptions are made and theories constructed. Deeply cognizant of the limits and variety of the evidence offered by the medieval manuscripts themselves, Webber discusses how palaeographers date and localize books, introducing the complex make-up of specific case studies to show how every piece of information must be folded into the assessment of a manuscript's history, and that speculation and hypothesis do not constitute proof. This chapter also tackles the core question of where books were produced in the long medieval period: explaining terminology, such as 'scriptorium' and 'workshop', Webber highlights the difficulties encountered by manuscript specialists in ascertaining places of origin, a difficulty that extends to localizing book production based on script or contents or *ex libris* marks of ownership. Still, so much more research remains to be done, and Webber's chapter provides the foundation upon which students of manuscripts can build.

From studying manuscripts to accessing manuscripts, Part III, 'Where Do We Study the Manuscript?', introduces the places and sites where manuscripts can be discovered. Siân Echard and Andrew Prescott begin Chapter 11 with an account of what it is like to order a manuscript in one of the largest and most significant manuscript repositories in the world: the British Library in London. Brief accounts of how these institutional manuscript collections and archives emerged, and how some of the idiosyncratic systems in place within these establishments were created, will help to anchor the new

7

manuscript scholar. These accounts, together with the information provided here revealing the complicated and non-standardized manner of describing the books and documents in repositories, and detailing the staff who conserve and curate them, remind readers of the sometimes rarefied world in which medieval textual materials reside. Echard and Prescott aim to demystify the process of description, cataloguing, accessing, and exhibiting manuscripts for scholars, students, and interested citizens alike by recounting the processes involved in discovering and examining manuscripts both in person and at a distance. Indeed, distance from primary sources is less significant now – or seemingly so – given the benefit of access via photographic reproduction of many manuscripts, and, latterly, digitization, even though so much more remains to be done, particularly with regard to imaging and the provision of standardized metadata.

Suzanne Paul offers a curatorial perspective on the current state of digitization and the implications for scholars of digital mediation of manuscript holdings in Chapter 12. From highlighting the professionalization of the procedure for photographing and processing images, Paul also evaluates the international initiatives afoot to create images that are interoperable, with linked data that enhances discoverability, and seeks to ensure sustainability. The choices informing what gets digitized and the concomitant costs create pressure on textual heritage providers, but the benefits to scholarship are shown to be inestimable. Paul surveys the new tools, new approaches, and new discoveries that are emerging from the accessibility of the literary and historical record (despite the fact that many scholars do not acknowledge their online resources).

A. S. G. Edwards closes the volume in Chapter 13 by investigating a fundamentally important aspect of Manuscript Studies that is rarely the subject of sustained research: the trade in and commodification of medieval books and fragments, both in the Middle Ages and through to the present day. Careful examination of the meagre evidence shows books, especially, were often highly valued from the fifteenth century onwards, for example, and collecting began in earnest in the sixteenth century leading to the development of catalogues, the foundation of major repositories, and, by the seventeenth century, the sale of books at auction. Modern auctions are analysed here, including the processes and personnel involved, as well as pertinent advice about why it is important to know about the sale of medieval books, and where to obtain the scattered information that does exist.

The editors and contributors hope that these chapters will facilitate students', interested citizens', and scholars' understanding and interpretation of the medieval British manuscript, no matter how it is accessed. The Guide to Further Reading section, together with all the embedded links to sites and

Introduction: The Matter of Manuscripts and Methodologies

resources on the internet, will assist in consolidating and augmenting the introductions provided throughout the volume. Studying medieval manuscripts is a deeply rewarding pursuit, and it is our aim to encourage an appreciation of, and interest in, these unique textual objects.

Notes

1. See O. Da Rold and M. Maniaci, 'Medieval Manuscript Studies: A European Perspective', in A. Conti, O. Da Rold, and P. Shaw, eds., *Writing Europe 500–1450, Essays and Studies*, 68 (Woodbridge: Boydell and Brewer, 2015), 1–24.
2. O. Da Rold, 'Codicology', in S. Echard and R. Rouse, eds., *The Encyclopaedia of Medieval British Literature*, 4 vols. (Oxford: Wiley-Blackwell, 2017), 531–38.
3. D. Wakelin, 'Palaeography' and E. Treharne, 'Manuscript Studies', in S. Echard and R. Rouse, eds., *The Encyclopaedia of Medieval British Literature*, 4 vols. (Oxford: Wiley-Blackwell, 2017).
4. L. M. J. Delaissé, 'Towards a History of the Mediaeval Book', *Miscellanea André Combes* (Rome: Pont. Università Lateranense, 1967), 28–39; E. Treharne, 'Manuscript Studies', in S. Echard and R. Rouse, eds., *The Encyclopaedia of Medieval British Literature*, 4 vols. (Oxford: Wiley-Blackwell, 2017), IV, 2071–8.
5. R. Beadle, *Henry Bradshaw and the Foundations of Codicology: The Sandars Lectures 2015* (Cambridge: Langham Press, 2017).

PART I

How Do We Study the Manuscript?

I

RICHARD BEADLE AND
RALPH HANNA

Describing and Cataloguing Medieval English Manuscripts: A Checklist

Procedures for describing medieval manuscripts have developed gradually, over several centuries, and have come to vary from one region and country to another in response to differing intellectual and scholarly traditions.[1] Descriptions appear in a variety of places: the formal catalogues of institutional and private collections; philological works devoted to particular medieval authors or to writings in particular genres; the introductions to editions of medieval texts; and monographs and scholarly articles. Though such descriptions may differ in arrangement, emphasis, and detail, according to the opinions and purposes of the compilers, their underlying requirements remain essentially the same.

What follows here may be regarded as a brief, discursive checklist of the main points to be observed by anyone engaged in assembling a description of a medieval manuscript book and presenting it in print, bearing in mind that mastery of several important sections of it assumes careful study of technical literature cited in the footnotes, supplemented by ample practical experience of working with manuscripts themselves. In other words, it is the tip of an iceberg. Every manuscript codex is a one-off, entirely *sui generis*, and describing it involves knowing how to recognize and present to others, in a succinct, coherent, and systematic form, the basic features that define the individual book. In the context of such an enquiry, it is worth reflecting that most palaeographers and codicologists of note have, at some stage in their career, compiled at least one 'collection catalogue' that describes a numerous and varied assemblage of books. Only through sustained and habituated investigation of such a congeries does anyone discover those features that define and are pervasively important in the study of medieval books, against which the divagations of the individual copy might be measured. Thus, these features will guide any researcher in recognizing the salient aspects of whatever book is of primary interest to them.

Speaking generally, a formal description offers, as an ordered sequence of categories, a synthesis of numerous details that are initially observed synchronically in the process of examining a book. In doing so, the primary object of a description is to offer information that reconstructs the scribe's activity in producing it. The categories that such a description imposes are those that centuries of manuscript scholars have identified as most basic to the production of any volume. Published descriptions thus formalize observation, and provide, with greater or lesser explicitness depending on how they are organized, an account of how scribes went about making such objects. In addition, descriptions conventionally offer further, post-production information. Such information is seldom confined to strictly palaeographical or codicological data, and extends towards providing the rudimentary facts of 'book-history', usually including information about a manuscript's provenance, and its engagement with successive owners and readers. Ideally (though in practice this is very seldom possible), these observations document the book's history from its inception in the hands of its medieval scribe to its presence in some library or collection in the present day. Formerly thought of as an activity subordinate, or ancillary to the supposedly higher forms of scholarly activity associated with philology, the descriptive analysis of manuscripts as culturally significant objects, irrespective of whatever text they might contain, is now recognized as capable of being a sophisticated type of hermeneutic activity in its own right.

The checklist offered here reflects Anglophone tradition. It descends ultimately from descriptive practices that were first conceived and developed by Henry Bradshaw (1831–86) of the University Library, Cambridge, in the course of his investigations into that library's manuscript collections. Most of Bradshaw's manuscript descriptions remain unpublished, but towards the turn of the nineteenth century his methods were adopted and displayed on a large scale by his disciple Montague Rhodes James, in the great series of what he termed 'descriptive catalogues' of manuscripts in Cambridge and other British libraries.[2] During the mid-twentieth century, James's procedures were further elaborated and systematized by N. R. Ker and others (notably R. A. B. Mynors and A. C. de la Mare), most notably in Ker's monumental *Medieval Manuscripts in British Libraries*. The 'sixteen points' to be observed in describing manuscripts that he sets out in the introduction have since been followed by most practitioners in English Manuscript Studies, with certain refinements suggested by Ker's immediate successors in the field, M. B. Parkes and A. I. Doyle.[3]

Headings and Preliminary Information

Most formal manuscript descriptions begin with a heading that identifies the manuscript and its location, and gives a brief indication of its contents and date. Various conventions need to be followed when making reference, especially a first reference, to a manuscript in this or any other context, and best practice for offering dates should be carefully observed. All manuscripts should be referred to by the geographical location of the repository where they are held, then by the name of the library or other form of collection within which they are housed, and finally by their shelf mark or call number, which, in the case of larger repositories, commonly includes the name of a particular subcollection or *fonds*. In a list of manuscripts all these elements should, within their respective categories, be placed in alphabetical and numerical order. The contents may be indicated by quoting the binding title (if it is adequate), or by giving some other commonly understood identification of the principal text; where they are varied or miscellaneous, more generalized means may be necessary, which may also call for reference to the different languages that may be encountered in the book.

Care must be taken over the date assigned to a manuscript in the heading, since it may well go on to be quoted summarily by others who do not make use of the exact evidence, discussed within the full description itself, for arriving at it. If a manuscript is not *dated* (e.g., in a colophon), nor generally *datable* via other forms of internal or external evidence, then only an approximate dating can be given, and this is usually a matter of synthesizing information from various parts of the extended description, notably the handwriting, *mise-en-page*, decoration, and (in manuscripts written on paper) watermarks.[4] Calendar years should thus only be used to refer to manuscripts that are dated, or datable; a different system of reference, not using the calendar, is required for approximate datings.

If a manuscript concludes with a reliably dated colophon (e.g., not one manifestly copied from an exemplar), or contains some other precise indication of the date of writing that pertains to the principal contents, this may be given as a calendar year. If a manuscript is only generally datable within a reasonably narrow time span, it is conventional to give (with any necessary discussion and documentation) the earliest and latest externally verifiable dates after which and before which it must have been written, known respectively as the *terminus ante quem non* and the *terminus post quem non*. The many illustrated albums of dated and datable European manuscripts published under the auspices of the Comité International de Paléographie Latine (listed on its website, www.palaeographia.org) provide abundant examples.

For manuscripts that are not dated or datable by means such as these, an approximate or presumed dating, based on palaeographical and codicological evidence, may be offered. Since the interpretation of such evidence is subjective, a matter of informed opinion, mention of calendar years should be avoided. A statement attributing a manuscript to a particular half-century, or even a slightly more restricted period, is sometimes possible, and such refinements can be expressed succinctly in the type of system suggested by N. R. Ker in *Medieval Manuscripts in British Libraries* (where 's.' stands for *saeculo*): s. xv in. (*ineunte*) for 'early fifteenth century'; s. xv¹ for 'first half of the fifteenth century'; s. xv med. (*medio*) for 'around the middle of the fifteenth century'; s. xv² for 'second half of the fifteenth century'; s. xv ex. (*exeunte*) for 'late fifteenth century'; and s.xv/xvi for 'around the turn of fifteenth century'.[5] Such statements should be supported by further discussion under one or more of the appropriate headings in the description that follows, and (in respect of handwriting in particular) are made on the understanding that a scribal career might last up to thirty years or more.

Contents

Procedures for describing the contents of manuscripts are generally straightforward, up to the point where the texts concerned have to be identified and documented bibliographically. Many medieval texts have complicated histories of transmission, or have been repeatedly edited, and may call for quite extensive documentation, which sometimes bears upon aspects of one's understanding of elements of a manuscript's codicology. Other texts may be only sparsely or inadequately documented, or may even be unknown to previous scholarship. In any event, a description of the contents of a manuscript should distinguish clearly between information derived from the manuscript itself, and external information supplied by the describer to identify the text and author.

Information derived from the manuscript should include the heading (if any) of each distinct text, and the numbers of the first and last folios that it occupies, distinguishing between the *recto* (the front) and the *verso* (the back) of the leaf. In texts laid out in columnar fashion, the columns should be designated *a* and *b*: thus fol. 4v^b means the second column on the back of the fourth leaf. It is usually convenient to combine the folio numbers with the text's *incipit* (the first line in verse, and up to about a dozen words in prose), and its *explicit* (the corresponding components at the end of a text); if a colophon is present at the end, it should also be quoted here. This information should be presented separately from any received modern identification of the work and its author. Thereafter, it is customary to give bibliographical references to the text and (if known) the author, derived from standard *incipitaria* and *repertoria* or other comparable resources, as appropriate. Likewise, one should refer to the work's appearance in print, taking care to indicate whether the manuscript being described has provided the base text

Describing and Cataloguing Medieval English Manuscripts

of the printed version, or has been used as the source of collations in a printed edition, or has not been consulted at all by editors. The nature and extent of such references is too varied and ramified to be pursued further here, for the reasons given above.

In a manuscript containing more than one work, the separate texts should normally be numbered in the order of their appearance. Items added later (e.g., in the margins, or on pages or parts of pages left blank by the original scribes) can be recorded as they appear, though some cataloguers have preferred to group them as 'Later additions' at the end of the main sequence of contents.[6] The list of contents may be subdivided if the disposition of the texts correlates markedly with the physical structure of the manuscript; for example, if it is made of units of differing date, or material (see following sections 'Collation' and 'Booklets and Fascicles'). If the text is visibly subdivided, mention should be made of the number and type of divisions it displays (books, chapters, fitts, etc.; see in the following section 'Presentation of the text'). The integrity of a text is likely to be of concern to many users of a manuscript description, and it may therefore be necessary to adduce information derived from comparison with the text as printed in a critical edition. Where no such edition exists, comparison with other manuscript copies or early printed editions may be called for. Omissions or later additions of scribal origin should be carefully distinguished from textual anomalies caused by lost or damaged leaves, or leaves substituted or added by others, matters which are in any case considered when examining the materials of which the leaves themselves were made, and the collational structure of the manuscript. The technical description of a manuscript normally follows a summary account of its contents of the kind suggested here, and it begins with a statement of the material, or materials, of which it is composed.

Materials

Membrane

The various kinds of animal skin from which medieval manuscripts were made is best described as membrane. In the absence of scientific analysis of the substance, it is not possible to be certain of the animal concerned. In any case, the traditional terms for such materials have been too loosely and inconsistently applied to be useful, because vellum and parchment have sometimes been intended or taken to mean, respectively, 'calf skin' and 'sheep skin'. Moreover, one soon finds that there are major libraries whose catalogues describe their manuscripts written on membrane by only one or other of these terms.[7]

Medieval English manufacturers of such materials called themselves *parcheminers*, parchmentmakers (Lat. *membranarius*), and the trade is still practised in a few places today. An understanding of the processes involved (studied and illustrated in detail in several technical works on the subject) is often relevant to codicological analysis and the description of manuscripts.[8] Animal skins were first soaked in lime and water, and then stretched on a rack to be scraped with a knife to remove hair and flesh residues, before being dried and finished by rubbing with pumice or chalk, to provide a smooth writing surface. Sometimes, in high-quality membranes, the hair and flesh sides of the skin become indistinguishable to the naked eye through these processes, but usually it is still possible to see which was which. The differences are often quite marked in poorly produced examples: the flesh side tends to be smoother and paler, while the hair side has a darker tinge, is rougher to the touch, with the follicles visible. Quires tended to be made up of bifolia (conjoint leaves) derived from a single skin, and symmetries in textures, colourings, follicular patterns, and thickness, together with defects in the manufacturing process, can provide important clues to their format and make-up.[9] Wherever possible, note should always be taken of the distribution of hair sides and flesh sides of the leaves within quires, and whether a quire begins with one or the other. Most scribes were trained in a convention whereby a flesh side always faced a flesh side, and a hair side a hair side, across openings, but it was neither universally nor punctiliously observed, especially in later periods. Where it was, anomalies in the pattern can often indicate irregularities in the progress of copying, which in turn may be relevant to issues of textual integrity.

Paper

Paper began to be imported into England around the turn of the thirteenth century and at first its use as a medium for writing seems to have been largely restricted to documentary purposes. During the second half of the fourteenth century (and especially, it seems, in the north) it was also adopted as a suitable material for other forms of book production – the inception of R. J. Lyall's 'paper revolution'. This is an area of great potential usefulness, one so far inadequately exploited, indeed calling out for research, and not simply for descriptive purposes. This man-made product was not manufactured in England until *c.* 1500, so where did paper used in England come from? Were there specific and repeated sources of supply? How was the product imported, marketed, and distributed? And so on.[10]

Like membrane, the natural product that it imitates, paper comes in large sheets, usually folded to produce the desired book size. But for a manuscript student, paper is a good deal more interesting and useful than membrane, which, as we have seen, is relatively anonymous in its origins. In contrast, papermakers advertised their craft through the product itself; they affixed their house trademarks into the moulds used to make the material. In later periods paper became much more widely used than parchment, particularly in legal, administrative, and epistolary environments, and consequently there is extensive evidence, mainly in archival repositories, of datable examples of these individual trademarks (the 'watermarks' left in the produced sheets). When studied minutely, and circumspectly, watermarks can potentially offer a more precise tool for dating a manuscript than does the handwriting of its scribe. Competent palaeographers may feel secure in dating the latter to a quarter-century, but, as Irigoin[11] has shown, paper evidence has, in some cases, the potential to reduce this space to under a decade. In general, however, and for a variety of sound reasons, it is unwise to rely solely on watermark evidence when offering a date for a manuscript.

Any degree of precision in dating, however, depends upon an accurate identification of the mark concerned. The two great repertories of dated watermarks, Briquet and Piccard, provide indispensable aids for this procedure. There, one will find numerous images of recorded marks, arranged by headings grouping similar images; for example, anchor, the letter 'P', bull's head. One has to trace out and measure the dimensions of the mark carefully, with attention to its details (being made of wire, they could change their appearance over time with use and wear), and to its position in relation to the chain lines in the paper. This is more straightforward in books in folio format, where the sheet is only folded once, and the watermark is usually found near the centre of the leaf. In quartos and other small format books, where the sheet has been folded at least twice, the process is usually only approximative, since the mark will appear in the book's gutter, split between two or more leaves, with parts often invisible. One then seeks to identify what one has seen with one of Briquet and Piccard's 'types', compares the manuscript's forms with their images, and looks for a match. In this procedure, pursuit of the commonest kinds of marks often leads only to frustration, but books on more than one paper stock, or on infrequently recorded examples, sometimes allow narrower conclusions. Recording what one has observed, even if it is only the type of mark, offers an important contribution to a much-needed general study of papers commonly used in England in the fourteenth and fifteenth centuries. Fortunately, various scientific methods of reproducing watermarks are gradually replacing what can be achieved with the naked eye, and Briquet's century-old tracings.

Paper does, however, have its downside: it is a weaker and more perishable substance than membrane, especially susceptible to moisture. It tears easily, is more difficult to bind securely in the longer term, and more susceptible to wear in use, so that the leaves constituting bifolia in paper manuscripts are more apt to become loose and part company than those made of membrane. Sometimes scribes encased their paper sheets within parchment ones (the inner and outer bifolia of such quires thus appear as membranes) precisely to mitigate this problem. On the whole, paper manuscripts routinely display a great deal more damage and disruption than those made on membrane. However, watermarks again prove to be of assistance here: because these are imposed on the sheets symmetrically in manufacture, they will appear in symmetrical sequences in any produced book. Thus, even if the whole binding has disintegrated and one has been left with only a pile of loose leaves, the form of the original production can often be reconstructed.[12]

In any description of the material support of a manuscript, it is relevant to comment on the quality of its original manufacture, and its present condition, which often gives clues to how the book has been used or treated over its lifetime. Obvious defects and signs of wear and tear should be noted, including places where liquids or other substances have defaced the leaves. In well-used manuscripts the top and bottom right-hand corners of the rectos are often grimier and thinner than the remainder of the leaf. An entire recto or verso that is dirtier and more worn than those that precede or follow it, especially at the beginning or the end of a quire, may point to its having had a separate existence, or lain unbound at some time (see following section 'Booklets and fascicles').

Dimensions

The reader of a manuscript description needs to know the dimensions of the leaves, which reveal the format of the book, and should also be given information that will enable them to picture the extent of the written space in relation to the size of the page. Quite often manuscripts contain leaves of differing sizes: if they differ significantly something must be said to the effect, but if not, the maximum and minimum dimensions and an average derived from a sampling should suffice. The dimensions of the written space can be approached likewise. Suspiciously narrow margins, or attenuation of marginal annotation, or even of the text-block itself, are signs that the book has been cropped, a process that might have occurred more than once. Cropping was usually the work of binders: when quires were re-sewn into a new binding the outer edges of the leaves would usually stand out at different levels, and in former times binders would often plane the heads, feet, and fore edges to create a smooth appearance. Catchwords and quire and leaf signatures (see following section 'Collation'), which scribes often placed as close to the foot of the leaf as possible, were often casualties of this process, perhaps intentionally so in some cases.

The average dimensions of the leaves, height followed by width, are conventionally given in millimetres. It is often convenient to give the dimensions of the written space or the ruled frame around the text in brackets after the dimensions of the leaf, thus: 295 × 210 mm (230 × 145 mm).

Number of Leaves

The other dimension of a manuscript that needs to be accurately established and conventionally expressed is its extent in terms of the number of leaves that it contains. Here it is necessary to distinguish between the number of quired leaves (i.e., those that were prepared by the scribe to receive text) and the flyleaves, which, strictly speaking, are a component of the binding that protects the text-bearing section of the book. The number of quired leaves is given in Arabic numerals and the flyleaves at the front and back of the book are numbered in Roman; for example, iv + 263 + iii. Flyleaves often differ in material and date from the quired leaves, and should be distinguished by further explanation (usually in the context of binding; see following section 'Binding') as necessary. Older flyleaves that have been physically incorporated into the binding by being pasted to the back or front boards (pastedowns) should be counted as flyleaves; modern conservators sometimes detach them from the binding and return them to their former role ('raised pastedowns').

The number of leaves in the above formula should be given without regard to any foliation that may have been inserted, or any enumeration of the flyleaves, irrespective of whether they are accurate or not; deviations between the actual number of leaves and those represented in the foliation should be noted. It is important to count the number of leaves in a manuscript carefully, one by one, because the number given will need to tally with the total implied in the collational formula, which shows how they are disposed in the structure of the book (see following section 'Collation'). Foliations attributable to the original scribes are relatively rare in English manuscripts, and those that have been added may date from any subsequent period, depending on whose hands a book has passed through. Many manuscripts bear more than one foliation; and if, as is very occasionally the case, a manuscript has been paginated, it is still important to count and refer to its leaves as a folio sequence. Most manuscripts in modern institutional collections now bear a pencilled foliation at the top right-hand corners of the leaves, usually the work of a librarian or cataloguer. As far as possible the dates of any foliations should be noted, and their accuracy established.

Collation

Having dealt with the materials and dimensions of a manuscript, the next step is to establish its collation, which in this context means a succinct formulaic statement of its quire structuring. Working out the collation is the core element in any bibliographical description, because it effectively puts one in the position of the person who originally constructed and wrote the manuscript. The quire was the basic unit of medieval book production: professional scribes were paid by the quire, and it is not too much to say that scribes thought in quires, as it were, when they were estimating the extent and construction of a manuscript. Establishing the collation also puts one in possession of essential information about the progress of the copying, and can thus be crucial to an understanding of the integrity or otherwise of the text. The first modern bibliographer to have grasped these points was Henry Bradshaw, who conceived and developed the collational formula now almost universally found in technical descriptions of both manuscripts and printed books in Anglophone scholarship; and it was he who began systematically to apply the terms 'collate' and 'collation' (in the context of bibliographical description) to the procedures involved. As Bradshaw saw it, collation in this sense is a matter of establishing the number of leaves that a book contains; explaining how it comes to have that number of leaves; and being able to account for each leaf individually in terms of the book's overall structure.[13]

The process of collating a manuscript usually involves coordinating several different sources of information about the construction of the quires, and about the relationship of each quire to its immediate neighbours, while simultaneously attending to the continuity and disposition of the text borne by the leaves. The actual availability of all these possible sources of information will depend on the date of the manuscript, the method used in the construction of the quires and the tightness of the binding; and even if all the necessary evidence is visible, it may not lend itself to a definitive interpretation. Ideally, the thin cords used by the binder to attach each quire to the spine of the book should be visible, and will normally signify its centre (see following section 'Binding'). If the quire is intact, and unaltered by the removal or addition of any leaves, there will be an equal number of leaves on either side of the strings, with the text running continuously from one leaf to the next. Any anomalies or discontinuities will need to be accounted for separately. In English manuscripts dating from *c.* 1300 onwards, one can also look for the quire and leaf signatures, often faint, worn, or minute, that many scribes inserted at the bottom right-hand corners of the recto side of the leaves in the first half of a quire (i.e., on the first leaf of each constituent bifolium), which can also serve as evidence of its structure. Finally, in English manuscripts from the twelfth century onwards, a catchword is normally found towards the foot of the verso of the last leaf of a quire, quoting the first few words from the recto of its successor in the quire sequence. More is said about these features later.

Quires (or gatherings) were effectively small booklets, whose extent could vary, made up of conjoint leaves (bifolia) derived from the folding and cutting up of parts of a larger sheet of membrane or paper. The numerous issues surrounding the original size of the sheets, the different methods of folding and cutting them, the various quire and book formats that result from these processes, and the sequence in which scribes inscribed the text on the leaves are often very complex. They were painstakingly investigated by a succession of bibliographers and codicologists during the twentieth century, and their work should be carefully studied prior to embarking on collation.[14] The overt evidence for the structure of quires is nonetheless relatively simple: four sheets piled on top of one another and then folded down the centre to constitute bifolia (the most straightforward method, but not the only one) made up an eight leaf quire, which was the commonest structure; six similarly handled would form a twelve, which was also favoured in some periods; and so on. Paper, a more pliable material, and more tractable to the binder, arrived from the manufacturer in large packages, and was sometimes used to form much larger quires than those normally found in membrane manuscripts.

The collation of a manuscript is conventionally given as a formula, listing the quires in their order of appearance as a numerical or alphabetical sequence. A method of doing so that is less likely to lead to confusion than some is that adopted by M. B. Parkes in his descriptions of the manuscripts of Keble College, Oxford, reproduced in the examples here; it uses uppercase Roman numerals to list the quires. The number of leaves of which they are made up, or were originally made up, are inserted as Arabic superscript figures, as shown in Figure 1.1. Anomalies or disturbances in the structure should be carefully noted, and reference to them incorporated in the formula. Not all of those potentially possible can be described in detail here, but typical variations on the basic quiring structure arise either from leaves that have been accidentally or intentionally removed or from leaves that have been added, singly or themselves in quired form. Attention to the continuity of the text is normally required. For missing leaves which appear to have carried away a section of text (which may or may not leave visible stubs in the gutter), one might, for example, enter 'IV^8 (wants 2, 3, after fol. 25)', which means that the second and third leaves of the fourth quire, originally an eight, are absent. Where a leaf appears to be missing (again, a stub may or may not be visible) but the text appears to read continuously, it may be suspected that the scribe was responsible for its removal – that is, that he or she 'cancelled' it for some reason in order to make a fresh start; here one might enter 'V^8 (7 cancelled, after fol. 54)', which means that the seventh leaf of the fifth quire, originally an eight, is absent, but that the text reads uninterruptedly across from the verso of the sixth leaf to the recto of the eighth. To avoid confusion, insertions into an existing quire of a single leaf (a singleton), a conjoint pair of leaves (a bifolium), or even a small additional quire should be entered by enumerating the inserted leaves in words, rather than by numerals; for example, 'IX^8 + four (fols. 67–70, inserted after 5)' would mean that four additional leaves have been inserted after the fifth leaf of the ninth quire, originally an eight. In particularly difficult cases it may be helpful to draw a diagram of a quire, as if one were looking at it from the bottom edges, with the leaves fanned out so as to show where the bifolia are joined. Figure 1.1 shows the disposition of the leaves in an imaginary manuscript whose collation would thus read: I–III^8, IV^8 (wants 2, 3, after fol. 25), V^8, VI^{10}, VII^8 (7 cancelled, after fol. 54, stub visible), VIII^6, IX^8 + four (fols. 67–70, inserted after 5).

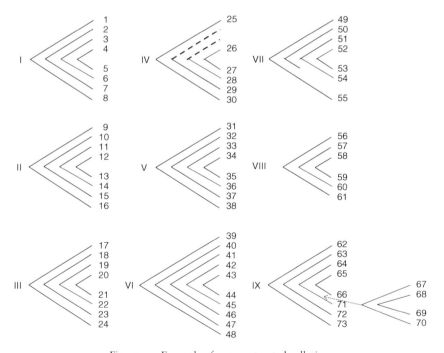

Figure 1.1 Example of a reconstructed collation

The disposition of the hair and flesh sides in membrane manuscripts, or the distribution of watermarks or chain-line patterns in paper quires, can sometimes provide important clues to the make-up of quires, and anomalies within them, and can on occasion shed light on the likely date of a manuscript. In many manuscripts, the size of the quire remains constant throughout; the sudden appearance of a shorter or longer one in an otherwise regular sequence is always worth investigating, since it is frequently found to correlate in some way with the progress of copying, or the state of the text. In manuscripts that are composites of manifestly different sections, often varying in date, it is usually helpful to collate the individual units separately, and to indicate them in the formula by introducing spaced vertical bars (|) into the numerical sequence (see following section Booklets and Fascicles).

Quire and Leaf Signatures and Catchwords

In manuscripts dating from before *c.* 1300, scribes did not habitually sign the individual leaves in the first halves of their quires, but numbered each quire as a whole, usually at the foot of the final verso, the numeral sometimes accompanied by the letter *q* (for *quaternio*). Thereafter, primarily in order to be sure of placing and keeping their piles of completed bifolia in the correct order, they began to insert quire and leaf signatures in the manner described above. If these signatures remain visible – and often they do not, because they were easily cropped away by the binder – their hand, inking, and positioning should be noted. The form and sequencing of quire and leaf signatures in English manuscripts have yet to be studied in detail. From the fourteenth century onwards, a very common pattern is an alphabetical cum Roman-numerical sequence (*a j–a ij–a iij–a iiij, b j–b ij–b iij–b iiij*, and so on), but various other kinds of sequence using numerals in conjunction with arbitrary symbols, or the forms of some Latin abbreviations, had already been in existence for some time, and continued in use. Sometimes a first quire in alphabetical sequences was left unsigned, and the sequence begins with the second. It is not unusual to discover more than one sequence, either wholly or partially preserved, since both those overseeing the construction of multi-scribe manuscripts and binders sometimes found it necessary to re-insert signatures in the course of their work.

Catchwords first appeared in English manuscripts in the post-Conquest period.[15] Like quire and leaf signatures they served as an aide-memoire to the scribe, this time for keeping the finished quires in the correct order, but, equally importantly, they also constituted a message to the same effect to the binder after a pile of unbound quires had left the scribe's hands. Many manuscripts, however, were kept unbound, often in folders or wrappers made of membrane, and the catchwords naturally continued to be functional in such an environment. Whereas quire and leaf signatures were often inserted as close as possible to the foot of the leaf (perhaps even with the intention that they should eventually be cropped away), catchwords tended to be placed somewhat higher, and were sometimes rubricated, or placed within scrolls or cartouches to signify their intended permanence as a feature of the book. Their form and disposition should be noted.

Pricking and Ruling

In manuscripts produced with any degree of formality, it was usual to prick and rule the sheets at some stage in one of the various processes whereby quires were manufactured. Frames and columns within which the writing was to be contained were laid out by piercing small holes around the edges of the sheets with a sharp instrument. These served as guides for the straight edge used to rule the bounding lines. Lines to guide the writing within the frames could also be ruled according to prickings down the sides of the sheet that would eventually become the fore edges of the book when the sheets were folded; occasionally (in earlier periods) they may also be observed down the inner margins, against the fold. Prickings were often made as near the edges of the sheet as possible, with the intention that they should in due course be cropped away by the binder, but in many cases they are still visible. If the sheets have been pricked and ruled, one should try to infer the instruments and materials used, and the practices involved.[16] The lines themselves were ruled using a variety of methods and substances: ruling in dry point (an uninked pen, stylus or other sharp instrument, the norm before third quarter of the eleventh century) was sometimes favoured because it tended to fade to near-invisibility; later, ruling with plummet (lead, with a pencil-like appearance) and brownish crayon became very common. Ruling in ink, either of a similar colour to that of the text or occasionally in some contrasting shade, is unusual before the turn of the fourteenth century.

The dimensions of the frame as a whole should be given in millimetres, height followed by width (see previous section Dimensions); more detailed measurements for columnar layouts can be given separately. For complex patterns of ruling (e.g., those that include provision for headings, running titles, marginal glosses, commentaries, annotation), a diagrammatic copy of the page layout is likely to be more helpful to the reader than a verbal description. Significant variation in pricking and ruling from quire to another should be noticed, because it is often found to correlate to other factors, such as a change of scribe, or some feature of the continuity of the text, or 'booklet'/fascicular construction (see the next section). The relation of the writing to the frame and ruled lines may be worth observing for similar reasons; for example, whether it begins above or below the top line, or whether it sits on the line, or floats above it. The number of lines to the page should also be recorded, if necessary as an average in cases where it varies.

Booklets and Fascicles

Producing a printed book requires a considerable amount of planning in advance ('how much paper do we need to have on hand for 500 copies?' for example) and consequently a good deal of fixity in the end product. Such considerations do not obtain to anything like the same extent with manuscript books. A manuscript, and particularly the kind of composite or miscellaneous book that characterizes the later stages of medieval book production, is potentially never finished. Even the optional stage that would seem to conclude production, imposing a binding, is never final. Books can be disbound and rebound to include additional contents; owners may decide to consolidate their libraries by binding together separate books, some perhaps produced decades or even centuries apart. P. R. Robinson first brought this well-nigh ubiquitous feature of manuscripts to scholarly attention, and defined the criteria for identifying and describing books that present themselves in this form; others have refined them since.[17] A great many factors, sometimes working together in relation to one another, need to be taken into account in analysing manuscripts composed of 'booklets' or fascicles: abrupt variations in the quality or sources of the membrane or paper, or in the dimensions of the leaf; pages that are noticeably grimier than those that precede or follow; the distribution of different handwritings across the volume; differences of scribal practice as to pricking and ruling, quire and leaf signatures, and catchwords; different schemes of decoration; and so on.

Any description needs to take some account of this fluidity, at the very least by marking off portions of a volume that reflect separate origins. But the problem is complicated by the fact that two separate forces are at work here. Owners treat books as they wish, and may make thoroughly arbitrary collocations of materials, the subject of Robinson's initial intervention, and the sort of information descriptions also treat under Provenance (see following section 'Marginalia, Later Additions and Provenance'). However, it is equally and perhaps more powerfully the case that in this activity owners merely imitate practices already present in producing complicated volumes. That is, because the limits of a manuscript book are usually undefined, and because constructing miscellanies draws unpredictably on what may be numerous sources, medieval books are very frequently discontinuous from the outset, loosely planned agglomerations of smaller units. While the quire, as we have indicated, remains basic to description, between 'quire(s)' and 'books as a whole' there are many other possible divisions and segments of production to account for.

In general, there is one ready way to recognize such fascicular production. At certain points in any such volume, textual boundaries will correspond with quire boundaries. This will often be found at points where anomalies occur, where the book's quiring varies from that normal elsewhere, where leaves have been left blank, or where leaves appear to be missing. Such moments mark the breaks in the production process that reveal the volume as something other than a pre-planned and continuous whole.

One common place to spot such mediate units is in books produced by multiple hands. These divisions, although they may initially appear gross, need not be separate from one another in production. Splitting a book among a group of scribes is a production economy; five hands can come up with a finished volume in a fraction of the time one could, though note that this case presupposes that such labour transpired with a sense of a whole, final product in mind. Such communal products quite readily betray the single motivation that underlay all their perhaps disparate units. However different the hands of the various scribes involved may look, they may, for example, all approximate the same script-type, or all use the same page-format (rough agreement in size of the writing area, number of lines to the page, etc.), or share a common decorating hand. Particularly important in such productions are the signature systems, and whether individual activities of this sort have been accommodated to a single unified system by a contemporary hand that has consolidated dispersed signatures into an ordered whole; or whether the volume shows signs of a contemporary continuous foliation.

Group-copying, however, is scarcely the only situation that might stimulate fascicular production. In a world in which many people might have had libraries of but a single volume, a single scribe – indeed, perhaps the owner himself – might construct a variegated collection from a number of sources. At least one feature that fascicles can but do not necessarily encourage is intellectual organization, the ability to group items of interest as they come into the scribe-compiler's hands. They typically exist as collections less extensive than 'the whole book', tending to consist of what are judged by some standard to be 'like materials', or ordered groupings of material; for example, elementary treatments first, more sophisticated ones later.

Any thoughtful description obviously should notice these signs of fascicular production. The disparate portions of the volume, the constituent fascicles, should be clearly distinguished; this is accomplished most effectively by centred headings of the type 'Booklet 3 = fols. 125–41'. Such marking is important as indicating to readers that although this manuscript may share texts *x* and *y* with another book, here they seem to have entered the production independently, and that any apparent connections between the volumes may be only incidental.

Presentation of the Text (*mise-en-page*)

An account of the presentation of a manuscript text to its reader (often called its *mise-en-page*, the 'page design' of the print era) calls for attention to a wide variety of features, both verbal and non-verbal, some of them already implied in the foregoing sections. The format of the book and the relation of the text-block to the overall size of the page is an important determinant, and many variations in the layout of the text on the page are created by different patterns of ruling. Beyond that, one should note different types or grades of script that are chosen for different headings or different sections of the text, or for different languages. The handwriting, inking, decoration, and general disposition on the page of running titles, rubrics, headings, subdivisions of the text, and marginal apparatus in the hand of the text (e.g., glosses, indexing or concording symbols, and so on) should all be observed, noticing their relation to the text-block. Other paratextual features that contribute to the *mise-en-page* (and which may appear either within the texts itself or in the margins) include paraphs, capitulum marks, line fillers, versals (ornate capitals marking verses) and other *litterae notabiliores*, rhyme brackets, underlining or boxing of parts of the text, and colour touching of selected letters, words, or phrases (other aspects of some of these features may also be dealt with in more detail, or from a different point of view in the next section 'Decoration'). Scribal directions to rubricators, flourishers, and illuminators (some executed and some not) are occasionally visible, and should be recorded.

Though observing all these features is primarily an end in itself in the description of a manuscript, it is also worth considering how far they appear to reflect a pre-ordained plan on the part of the scribe, and the sources from which he or she may have derived it; and, at the same time, in what ways the layout might be thought to act directively upon the reader, or even to bear upon the interpretation of the text. A useful way of attuning oneself to these issues is to compare the presentation of the same text as it appears in several different manuscripts, while bearing in mind that not only the verbal substance of a text but also the features of its disposition on the page are potentially inherited from the scribe's exemplar, liable to be carried over from exemplar to copy in the course of scribal activity.[18] The historical circumstances within which many of the phenomena described in this section were first widely and systematically used were described in an influential article by M. B. Parkes, first published in 1976, 'The Influence of the Concepts of *Ordinatio* and

Compilatio on the Development of the Book'.[19] The Latin terms used in the title have unfortunately been appropriated, misunderstood, and misapplied in discussions of *mise-en-page*, mostly by literary and cultural critics only rudimentarily versed in Manuscript Studies, and interested primarily in vernacular texts; nowadays they should be invoked with caution.[20]

Decoration

Several features of decoration in manuscripts have been touched on in the previous section: the use of different coloured inks within the text, the flourishing of certain letters and some paratextual items with coloured penwork, and the painting or gilding of initial letters. More elaborate decoration includes the painting of full or partial decorative borders to the page, and the inclusion of paintings and drawings of particular subjects, some within letters that form parts of the text, some in the margins, and some free-standing in larger areas of the page, within their own decorative frames. In-depth study of many decorative motifs, involving their dating, localization, attribution to particular artists, and the more technical aspects of their execution and iconography, is the province of those with special training as art historians, especially those with extensive experience in the field, whose opinions may be sought and quoted. The manuscript describer's task is to document what can be seen, in straightforward terms, and to relate the decoration to the material evolution of the book in hand, and (where appropriate) to the text that it contains.[21]

Flourished or illuminated letters may be defined descriptively by the number of text lines that they occupy, and the presence of gold or silver leaf in them, which commonly extends into border decoration, can be taken as a measure of the quality and value of the manuscript. The colouring and description of floral, zoomorphic, and anthropomorphic ornamentation attached to initials or miniatures, or appearing in the margins, also calls for comment. The content and basic iconography of historiated initials and miniatures, together with any associated inscriptions, should be noted, and likewise the appearance of heraldic devices, which can offer clues to early ownership and dating. The prices charged by flourishers and illuminators with a note of the extent of their work may occasionally be found, usually in minute writing, either on a text page (often the final verso of a quire) or a flyleaf.

Handwriting

The account of the handwriting found in a manuscript should identify the *script*, which is best thought of as the generic or abstract model which the

Describing and Cataloguing Medieval English Manuscripts

scribe might have had in mind, or which he or she had been taught; and then, in terms of that model, attention should be drawn to those details of its execution that characterize the *hand* – that is, what actually appears on the page.[22] An estimate of the scribe's level of expertise and consistency may also be called for, and the appearance of the same hand in other manuscripts should be noted. Some English scribes identified themselves by name, but the great majority did not, and where the work of more than one appears in a manuscript, it is customary for their hands to be numbered or lettered in order of appearance; the extent of their stints can then be indicated by folio and line numbers. Places where there are marked changes of pen or inking, or in the scale or aspect of the hand, can be worth noting, since they may be found to correlate with the physical structure of the manuscript, or with the state of the text.

Abbreviation and Punctuation

A limited range of abbreviated forms of words were incorporated into the copying of Latin texts from early times, but from the thirteenth century, with the rise of scholastic philosophy (generating many long and compendious texts), the establishment of universities (creating the student habit of rapid note-taking in lectures), and the widespread proliferation of cursive hand-writing in administrative and documentary environments, innumerable new ways of shortening words and economizing on the copying process were devised. As well as enabling scribes to write more quickly, abbreviations also reduced the space on the page occupied by the text, making for more economical use of the materials from which manuscripts were made. In some thirteenth- and fourteenth-century Latin manuscripts, it can often seem that more words are abbreviated than not, by means of contraction (like the modern 'Dr'), suspension (like 'Rev.'), special signs (there were many ancestors of the modern printed '&'), and the use of superscript letters (preserved in ordinal numerals like '7ᵗʰ'). Many thousands of abbreviations are listed and illustrated in standard dictionaries and reference works, and (though the subject has yet to be systematically and exhaustively studied) some of them are temporally and regionally distinctive, or characteristic of certain genres of writing.[23] The great majority of scribes confine themselves to standard abbreviations, but a few personalize either their form or their deployment of them in unusual or eccentric ways, and a manuscript description can usefully draw attention to such features.

However unhelpful abbreviated forms may seem to us, scribes also offer reader-friendly signals to their readers, namely, punctuation. In the Middle Ages, as the great student of punctuation M. B. Parkes demonstrates, the purpose of such pointing differed from our own.[24] In contrast to our 'grammatical' parsing of sentences through such signs, scribes emphasize 'rhetorical' features. Thus, manuscript markings may routinely fail to 'map onto' any modern representation; for example, the medieval scribe routinely uses the 'punctus' (.) to mark, not a thoroughly complete utterance (our 'sentence'), but a rhetorical 'period' (hence the modern American name for the sign). The later Middle Ages has a widespread and conventional set of such markings, from lightest to heaviest, the 'virgule' (rod), 'slant bar', or 'solidus' (/) to indicate light pauses (our 'comma'); the 'punctus elevatus' (⁊) to mark major clausal breaks (typically conditional statements or contrasts), and the already mentioned 'punctus'; some scribes distributed or combined these marks in idiosyncratic ways, which are worth noting. Parkes offers a rich variety of other techniques and traces their development through time, together with a useful glossary of terms.

Correction

Copying by hand sooner or later results in error, and all manuscripts contain evidence of the measures taken to correct errors, either by the scribes themselves or by others who subsequently paid close attention to the text. It is helpful if a manuscript description gives some impression of the frequency and nature of such corrections; a short list of representative examples will normally suffice. The form and function of corrections (matters which have recently been productively studied in later medieval English vernacular manuscripts) have substantial implications for editors and textual critics, whose task it is to study them in detail.[25] Various kind of deletion, substitution and alteration were practised, some of which are naturally characteristic of longhand writing in any period. Cancellations and deletions, erasures and rewritings, expunctions, superimpositions, insertions, both interlinear and marginal, with or without the *caret* mark (∧), are all common. Less frequently, a longer passage written in error may or may not be crossed through, but will be marked *vacat* (sometimes with *va* at the beginning and *cat* at the end), signifying 'it [this section] is void'. Scribes sometimes reproduced lines of verse in the wrong sequence and subsequently indicated the correct order in which to read them by means of small letters placed to the left of each one (for *cba* read *abc*). The correct place to read passages that were more drastically misplaced, for example by a page or more, were indicated by special symbols, often devised *ad hoc* by the scribe, and sometimes rubricated for greater clarity. Some manuscripts show signs of having been 'proofread', with marginal corrections entered faintly in plummet or crayon by another hand, before being handed back to the scribe for emendation within the text.

Describing and Cataloguing Medieval English Manuscripts

The presence from time to time in a manuscript of abbreviated marginal notes in the form *Cor'* or *Ex'* (probably signifying *Corrigitur* and *Examinatur*) are generally taken to signify that someone has progressively corrected or examined the text.

Binding

As indicated earlier, the binding of a book in this period is always super-erogatory. Numerous medieval manuscript catalogues tell us that their owners, most often institutions, had works 'in quaternis', that is, as loose quires, in some unbound form. Binding meant passing on a manuscript in this form to another book-artisan, a specialist, and added cost to any book. The primary reason for binding is protection. It preserves the book from dirt and other damage, and most importantly, it secures all its constituent parts and renders them as a single unit. For this reason, very simple structures often seem to have been sufficient – a heavy parchment wrapper around the text pages, for example. More frequently, however, one finds elaborate examples, typically in the form of leather over heavy wooden boards.

This procedure begins with sewing; each of the quires is sewn, through its centre, to two or several bands. Usually at this stage, the outer pages of the text-block are protected by sewing to the bands one or more flyleaves at either end of the book, to prevent the covers from abrading the facing text-leaves. Then, the bands are drawn through channels bored into the wooden boards, tautened, and anchored there by small dowels. The sewing, now fixed, may be further supported by pasting parchment leaves (often discarded manuscript waste, but frequently just the outmost flyleaf), the pastedowns, over the channels. The outside of the whole assemblage is then covered with leather, pasted directly onto the boards and their inner edges and to the spine with the bands. Covers may be decorated, with stamps or rolls, and they may be equipped with leather ties or metal clasps to hold the fore-edges closed. Medieval bindings tend relatively to be quite tight across the spine, as a result of tautening the bands, and most books that survive in bound form are distinctly trapezoidal, splaying along the leading edge. In institutional libraries, many books were chained to the reading lecterns; this process regularly leaves scars and rust marks on the boards, sometimes on the paste-downs or inner leaves.

If the binding of a manuscript in hand is original, or at least early, details of the appearance, structure, and especially any decoration should be given. One should pay particular attention to separating the flyleaves, which are not part of the book produced by the scribe but have been supplied by the binder,

33

from the text sections. Note that some libraries which have rebound their older manuscripts preserve the original bindings separately for inspection. Binding fragments (usually strips of membrane, inserted by binders to strengthen the spine or pad the boards) are likewise sometimes preserved separately, and occasionally give clues as to date or provenance. Binding is a highly technical procedure, and there are very few experts in the field, but nonetheless it is possible to offer a serviceable general description on one's own, noting the shaping of the boards, the number of bands, and the presence of decoration and of clasps.[26] However, even skilled cataloguers routinely seek an expert to confirm their opinions about bindings, and the identification of the handiwork of specific binders.

Marginalia, Later Additions and Provenance

Few medieval manuscripts remain pristine, untouched by any writing but the scribe's. Marginalia are inscriptions by later hands in the areas of the page left blank after the copying of the main text. Wherever possible one should try to distinguish inscriptions that appear to relate to the text from more casual insertions that do not. Casual insertions in margins and on flyleaves often consist of no more than pen-trials, such as alphabets, standard documentary formulae ('Sciant presentes et futuri...') or random biblical phrases; their existence may be briefly noticed (mentioning the hand and its likely date), but otherwise they may generally be ignored. However, if such later additions include personal names, place names, or dates, they may have an important part to play in establishing a manuscript's history and provenance, and should be carefully noted.

Like those who habitually mark their books nowadays, early owners tended to be drawn to and to emphasize items they considered important. Activity of this kind most frequently occurs in the margins, around the text, but can appear within the text-block itself with interlinear inscriptions and underlining. It may be quite full, consisting of marks exclaiming 'Nota', 'Memorandum', manicules (hands pointing at the text), and many types of personal sign. Sometimes one finds inscriptions capable of some 'reader-response' analysis, such as marked divisions, notations of important subjects, and names of 'authorities'. Moreover, owners scarcely felt restricted to offering annotation only. In medieval books, no space left blank is sacred, and is always capable of receiving additional texts, provided by the book's successive users. The originally blank flyleaves supplied by the binder are especially favoured target areas, and often contain short items of practical use, such as brief theological exhortations, medical recipes, short Latin verses (especially mnemonics), and the like.

34

Likewise, flyleaves have always been the places (although far from exclusive ones) where owners leave notices of possession. From such information – typically someone's signature accompanied by 'verus possessor huius libri' or 'Iste liber pertinet' – one can derive information about a book's provenance. Descriptions routinely track, so far as it is possible, where the manuscript has belonged and been used through time. Frequently, new owners have sealed their ownership by erasing marks left by their predecessors. Such information is often recoverable, and a careful examination of any manuscript should include scanning flyleaves and the first and last text-leaves under ultraviolet light, which can reveal detail otherwise invisible, and (with luck) may render what has been erased legible.

The most fully developed tools for tracing past owners are devoted to books once in institutional collections, which for the most part means religious houses.[27] Such books are often conspicuously marked as communal property, first by shelf- or pressmarks (most simply of the type 'B.39'), indicating where a book was shelved in an earlier library, and sometimes much fuller inscriptions ('liber domus...'), often with donors' names and occasionally with curses on those who might think of removing the volume. The *secundo folio* (or *dicta probatoria*), consisting of the first two or three words on fol. 2r of Latin manuscripts that have been or are suspected of having been in institutional ownership, may conveniently be cited here; its usefulness to the modern bibliographer has recently been ably expounded.[28] Tracing non-institutional owners of books in the late medieval and early modern periods, especially those who were not of high status, or identifiable in academic or professional environments, is usually more difficult. It is also time-consuming, and apt to be inconclusive, leading some researchers into fruitless realms of speculation involving suppositious and unverifiable connections between manuscripts, and persons or places whose names appear in additions in margins or on flyleaves. However, there are plenty of good examples of what can be achieved, and the main points of entry into what is effectively a separate field of historical and prosopographical enquiry have been well set out in a useful handbook.[29]

An account of provenance also needs to bring the record of the book from the medieval and early modern period to the present. In this respect manuscripts will themselves embody all sorts of random information: rebindings (sometimes associated with known individuals in the trade), successions of old library numbers and shelfmarks, notations of sale prices, lot numbers, pasted-in sale catalogue descriptions, bookplates, late signatures, traces of the activities of nineteenth-century editors, and so forth. A full account of a book's provenance arranges these details chronologically in an ongoing narrative, and may be rounded off with a bibliography of published discussions, editions, facsimiles, exhibition appearances, and the like.

Notes

1. A. Petrucci, *La Descrizione del Manoscritto: Storia, Problemi, Modelli* (Rome: Carocci, 1984).
2. See R. Beadle, *Henry Bradshaw and the Foundations of Codicology* (Cambridge: Langham Press, 2017), 85–98.
3. N. R. Ker, *Medieval Manuscripts in British Libraries* (Oxford: Oxford University Press, 1969), I, vii–xiii; M. B. Parkes, *Medieval Manuscripts of Keble College Oxford* (London: Scolar Press, 1979). We are indebted to the late Dr Doyle for the opportunity to consult his unpublished teaching materials on the subject. Ker's 'Elements of Medieval English Codicology (1944)', edited by Doyle in 2008, should be carefully studied as regards historical developments in the arrangement of quires and in the deployment of catchwords, quire and leaf signatures, and ruling in English manuscripts.
4. See introduction to *DDCL*, I, 1–12.
5. Ker, *Medieval Manuscripts in British Libraries*, I, viii. Many of Ker's datings do not go beyond specifying a century as a whole.
6. See the alternative method of listing adopted by Parkes, *Medieval Manuscripts of Keble College*, xix.
7. W. L. Ustick, '"Parchment" and "Vellum"', *The Library*, 4th Ser., 16 (1936), 439–43.
8. See, for example, R. Reed, *Ancient Skins, Parchments and Leathers* (London and New York: Seminar Press, 1972), and P. Rück, ed., *Pergament: Geschichte–Struktur–Restaurierung–Herstellung* (Sigmaringen: Jan Thorbecke Verlag, 1991).
9. See especially J. P. Gumbert, 'Skins, Sheets and Quires', in D. Pearsall, ed., *New Directions in Manuscript Studies* (Woodbridge: Boydell and Brewer, 2000), 81–90.
10. It is important to be aware that the study of paper in book production has generally been led by those concerned with early printing, rather than manuscripts. For preliminary orientation, see P. Gaskell, *A New Introduction to Bibliography* (Oxford: Clarendon Press, 1972), 55–77 and E. Heawood, 'Sources of Early English Paper Supply', *The Library*, 4th ser., 10 (1929–30), 282–307, 427–54. Recent work on paper in manuscripts is surveyed in O. Da Rold, 'Materials', in A. Gillespie and D. Wakelin, eds., *The Production of Books in England* (Cambridge: Cambridge University Press, 2011), 22–5.
11. J. Irigoin, 'La Datation des papiers italiens des XIIIe et XIVe siècles', *Papiergeschichte* 18 (1968), 18–21.
12. Technical studies should begin with A. Stevenson, 'Watermarks Are Twins', *Studies in Bibliography*, 4 (1951–2), 52–91 and ' Paper as Bibliographical Evidence', *The Library*, 5th ser., 17 (1962), 197–212; S. Spector, 'Symmetry in Watermark Sequences', *Studies in Bibliography*, 31 (1978), 162–77; G. T. Tanselle, 'The Bibliographical Description of Paper', *Studies in Bibliography*,

Describing and Cataloguing Medieval English Manuscripts

24 (1971), 27–67; M. Bat-Yehouda, *Le Papier au Moyen Âge: Histoire et Techniques* (Turnhout: Brepols, 1999).

13. P. Needham, *The Bradshaw Method* (Chapel Hill, NC: Hanes Foundation, 1988), Appendix, 24–33, 'Henry Bradshaw and the Development of the Collational Formula'; Beadle, *Henry Bradshaw and the Foundations of Codicology*, 66, 73–80.

14. G. Pollard, 'Notes on the Size of the Sheet', *The Library*, 4th Ser., 22 (1941), 105–37; L. Gilissen, 'La Composition des Cahiers, le Pliage du Parchemin et l'Imposition', *Prolégomènes à la Codicologie* (Ghent: Éditions Scientifiques Story-Scientia, 1977), 21–44; J. P. Gumbert, 'Sizes and Formats', in M. Maniaci and P. F. Munafò, eds., *Ancient and Medieval Book Materials and Techniques*, Studi e Testi 357 (1993), 227–63, and his 'Skins, Sheets and Quires'.

15. J. Vezin, 'Observations sur l'Emploi des Réclames dans les Manuscrits Latins', *Bibliothèque de l'Ecole des Chartes*, 125 (1967), 5–33.

16. L. W. Jones, 'Pricking Manuscripts: The Instruments and Their Significance', *Speculum*, 21 (1946), 389–403; J. P. Gumbert, 'Ruling by Rake and Board: Notes on Some Late Medieval Ruling Techniques' in P. Ganz, ed., *The Role of the Book in Medieval Culture* (Turnhout: Brepols, 1986), 41–54.

17. P. R. Robinson, 'The "Booklet": A Self-contained Unit in Composite Manuscripts', *Codicologica: Essais typologiques*, 3 (1980), 46–69; R. Hanna, 'Booklets in Medieval Manuscripts: Further Considerations', *Studies in Bibliography*, 39 (1986), 100–11.

18. See, for example, H. J. Martin and J. Vezin, *Mise-en-page et Mise-en-texte du Livre Manuscrit* (Paris: Éditions du Cercle de la librairie – Promodis, 1990), and D. Wakelin, *Designing English: Early Literature on the Page* (Oxford: Bodleian Library, 2018).

19. M. B. Parkes, 'The Influence of the Concepts of *Ordinatio* and *Compilatio* on the Development of the Book' (1976), repr. in *idem*, *Scribes, Scripts and Readers: Studies in the Communication, Presentation and Dissemination of Medieval Texts* (London: Hambledon, 1991), 35–70.

20. R. H. Rouse and M. A. Rouse, '*Ordinatio* and *Compilatio* Revisited', in M. D. Jordan and K. Emery, eds., *Ad Litteram: Authoritative Texts and Their Medieval Readers* (Notre Dame: University of Notre Dame Press, 1992), 113–34, includes important qualifications.

21. See M. Rickert, *Painting in Britain: The Middle Ages*, 2nd edn (London: Penguin Books, 1965), 209–14 (glossary of terms); K. L. Scott, 'Limning and Book-producing Terms and Signs *in situ* in Late Medieval English Manuscripts: A First Listing', in R. Beadle and A. J. Piper, eds., *New Science Out of Old Books: Studies in Manuscripts and Early Printed Books in Honour of A. I. Doyle* (Aldershot: Scolar Press 1995); S. Scott-Fleming, *The Analysis of Pen-Flourishing in Thirteenth-Century Manuscripts* (Leiden: Brill, 1989); K. L. Scott's *Dated and Datable English Manuscript Borders, c.1395–1499* (London: British Library, 2002).

22. See M. B. Parkes, *English Cursive Book Hands, 1250–1500* (Oxford: University Press, 1969), for standard nomenclature; also J. Roberts, *Guide to Scripts Used in English Writings up to 1500* (London: British Library, 2005).

23. See A. Cappelli, *Dizionario di Abbreviature latine ed italiane*, 6th edn (Milan: Hoepli, 1967), introduction translated in *The Elements of Abbreviation in*

Medieval Latin Palaeography, trans. D. Heimann and R. Kay (Lawrence, KA: University of Kansas Libraries, 1982); A. Pelzer, *Abréviations latines médiévales: Supplément au Dizionario di Abbreviature Latine ed Italiane de Adriano Cappelli*, 2nd edn (Louvain: Publications Universitaires, 1966); C. T. Martin, *The Record Interpreter*, 2nd edn (London: Stevens, 1910).

24. M. B. Parkes, *Pause and Effect: An Introduction to the History of Punctuation in the West* (Aldershot: Ashgate, 1992).

25. See D. Wakelin, *Scribal Correction and Literary Craft: English Manuscripts 1375–1510* (Cambridge: Cambridge University Press, 2014), esp. 101–27.

26. See G. Pollard, 'Describing Medieval Bookbindings', in J. J. G. Alexander and M. T. Gibson, eds., *Medieval Learning and Literature: Essays Presented to R. W. Hunt* (Oxford: Clarendon Press, 1976); A. Gillespie, 'Bookbinding', in Gillespie and Wakelin, eds., *The Production of Books in England*, esp. 157.

27. N. R. Ker's *Medieval Libraries of Great Britain*, 2nd edn (London: Offices of the Royal Historical Society, 1964) and A. G. Watson's *Supplement to Medieval Libraries of Great Britain* (London: Royal Historical Society, 1987) are available online, edited by J. Willoughby. 'The Corpus of British Medieval Library Catalogues project', under the general editorship of R. Sharpe, has published fifteen volumes to date.

28. J. Willoughby, 'The Secundo Folio and Its Uses, Medieval and Modern', *The Library*, 7th Ser., 12 (2011), 237–58.

29. D. Pearson, *Provenance Research in Book History: A Handbook* (London: British Library, 2004). For examples of sound practice see S. Cavanaugh, 'A Study of Books Privately Owned in England 1300–1450' (PhD thesis, University of Pennsylvania, 1980); C. M. Meale, 'Patrons, Buyers and Owners: Book Production and Social Status', in J. Griffiths and D. Pearsall, eds., *Book Production and Publishing in Britain 1375–1475* (Cambridge: Cambridge University Press, 1989), 201–38; K. Harris, 'Patrons, Buyers and Owners: The Evidence for Ownership and the Role of Owners in Book Production and the Book Trade', in Griffiths and Pearsall, eds., *Book Production and Publishing*, 163–200; A. G. Watson, *Medieval Manuscripts in Post-medieval England* (Aldershot: Ashgate, 2004).

2

DONALD SCRAGG

Reading a Manuscript Description

Anyone seeking to understand the scholarship surrounding a manuscript or a group of manuscripts should begin with its description in the most recent catalogue of the holding library. Most libraries today have up-to-date catalogues of their holdings, including those with extensive medieval holdings in Britain, where we find descriptions of their codicology, palaeography, and contents. This chapter seeks to explain how to interpret the information supplied in such a descriptive catalogue of manuscript materials. The work chosen is Neil Ker's *Catalogue of Manuscripts Containing Anglo-Saxon*,[1] one of the most enduring works of reference for English of the early period, and the example selected for close analysis is his number 332, shelfmark Oxford, Bodleian Library, MS Hatton 115. It follows that this chapter will be best understood when read in conjunction with Ker, pages 399–403. Another manuscript will be analysed at the end of the chapter to show how the procedure identified with respect to MS Hatton 115 can be used to extend our knowledge of the history of other items.

Ker's arrangement for main entries is the same throughout. Each begins with a heading, which briefly summarizes the contents of the manuscript together with a broad indication of its date. This is followed by a paragraph outlining its contents and design more fully, with cross-references to other manuscripts that have the same or similar composition, and then by a more detailed, numbered list of its items. Principal entries then have, in smaller type, a collation of quires and the arrangement of the leaves by which they are made up, together with a summary of scribal hands. The entry concludes with a history of the book where known.

Ker's description of MS Hatton 115 begins with the heading '*Homilies, &c*' and with the date 's[aeculo] XI², XII med.', which the passage of the Introduction on dating[2] explains as signifying about the middle of the second half of the eleventh century and about the middle of the twelfth. In other words, the book principally contains homilies, but also some other related material, copied in the second half of the eleventh century and in the twelfth.

It should be noted, however, that dating refers to the date of copying, not to composition. The first sentence of the paragraph of contents also includes a note that the majority of articles in the manuscript 'are miscellaneous homilies and admonitions ... [in] quires 1–9 and 27–33' (p. 399). Since his collation on page 403 lists, as we shall see, only twenty-two quires in the manuscript, this statement must be wrong. The first lesson we should learn from any work of reference, then, is that books, however seminal, are the work of fallible human beings, and they contain errors which have the potential to mislead. In fact, '27–33' refers not to quires but item numbers, the significance of which we shall see later in the chapter. Slips like this are occasionally overlooked in subsequent revisions of the book and additions to it, and this fact should make readers even more on their guard.[3]

The most difficult part of the description of a manuscript for a beginner is the collation where a number of unfamiliar codes are used. A detailed analysis of the collation in Ker's description of MS Hatton 115 is therefore an appropriate place to begin.[4] It starts with the foliation, endleaves used in the binding being numbered with Roman numerals, leaves which are written as part of the original manuscript with Arabic. His foliation of MS Hatton 115 reads: 'Ff. v + 156 + iii, foliated i–v, 1–139, 139a, 140–58'. This plainly needs some explanation. Ker's numbering of a folio between 139 and 140 as '139a' suggests that whoever foliated the manuscript (at some time from the sixteenth century onwards) failed to give a number to that folio. The reason can be found in the description of items where we are told of the end of his item 33 that there are only two lines of writing on fol. 139 verso, with lines 3–27 remaining blank, while the following leaf, in his numbering 139a, is blank and lacks its outer half; in other words, someone cut down that blank leaf vertically and used the excised parchment elsewhere. This explains why whoever numbered the folios failed to give a number to the partial folio, now called 139a. It is necessary, then, to read the collation in conjunction with the list of items in order to form a full picture of the manuscript as it now exists.

Pre-Conquest English manuscripts are regularly made up of eights; that is, four sheets of membrane (bifolia) folded to make a quire of eight leaves, as described by Beadle and Hanna in Chapter 1. This arrangement is conventionally signalled in Ker by a superscript figure 8 after the quire number. Hence in relation to MS Hatton 115, Ker's collation begins with '1–7[8]', which means that the first seven quires are eights, and that tells us that the first fifty-six leaves of the manuscript are in regular quires of eight. Next, however, Ker lists '8[6] + 1 leaf after 4 (f. 61)', indicating that the eighth quire is a six rather than an eight, with a single leaf (also known as a singleton) after the fourth leaf, and as a further help to the reader he gives the folio number of

40

that extra leaf. The first four leaves then are fols. 57–60 (each of which is one half of a bifolium), followed by the singleton fol. 61, and there are then two more leaves, fols. 62 and 63 (which again are parts of bifolia).

The next quire, Quire 9, Ker describes as 'four half-sheets (ff. 64–67), the second, fol. 65, being a later insertion'. A quire consisting only of half-sheets is clearly very vulnerable, and the reader would therefore be wise to consult the list of items to ascertain if there is a disturbance of text indicating the loss of leaves. At the end of the description of item 20, which covers fols. 66r to 67v, Ker notes that 'Lines 25–27 on the verso [of the last leaf] are blank'; in other words, instead of items following one another with no more than a line or two of blank lines between them, this item has three blank lines at the end of a page. This suggests that the missing folios after 67 were also blank, which perhaps caused their removal at some unknown date. If we link this with Ker's opening statement about the composition of the manuscript, we find that the first nine quires, excluding the late addition of fol. 65, are described as 'miscellaneous homilies and admonitions', and the quiring suggests that these nine items formed a 'booklet', independent of the rest of the manuscript.

The term 'booklet' comes from Pamela Robinson.[5] Robinson takes MS Hatton 115 as a typical example of manuscripts containing independent self-contained units,[6] and assumes that there are a number of booklets in this manuscript, the first of them ending at fol. 64 at the conclusion of Ker's item 17, fol. 64v, before the inserted leaf (fol. 65). She starts the second booklet at fol. 68, assuming the two leaves before this were written by the same scribe who wrote booklets 1 and 2, for 'a homily on St Alban on two singleton leaves (fols. 66 and 67)'. This means that she has taken Ker's description of his item 20 'Skeat 1881–1900, I 424 (no. 19, St Alban, ll. 155–258)' to mean that the item is indeed a homily on St Alban, whereas that section of Ælfric's homily is in fact an appendix on the suffering of criminals, including an account of Absalom and Achitophel. This, as John Pope has pointed out,[7] is then like the preceding items in MS Hatton 115, Ker's articles 11–17 (18 and 19 being on the inserted leaf), being 'all short and decidedly miscellaneous' (p. 55). Since there is only one empty line at the foot of fol. 64v (where the scribe would presumably have been reluctant to begin a fresh item) and since the half-sheets of Quire 9 are unlikely to have been made as a quire of half-sheets, it would seem to me that the first booklet did not end with the first leaf of Quire 9 but continued to the end of Ker's item 20 (fol. 67v). At this point there are three blank lines, while the rest of the quire has been removed, presumably because its leaves were blank. In other words, since the final leaf of item 17 ends on the first leaf of Quire 9, that quire was prepared with material to follow item 17 in mind. I therefore place the end of the first booklet at fol. 67, as Ker, by implication, does. Robinson did not consider the collation in conjunction with the manuscript's items as this chapter is at pains to stress readers should always do.

This booklet is followed by another, smaller one. Ker's collation shows that Quires 10 and 11 are eights although the second of these lacks its final leaf (after fol. 82), but Quire 12 he describes as three half-sheets, with one lost before the first. So, two leaves are lost after fol. 82, and this is confirmed by the description of items where item 24 lacks its conclusion, while item 25 begins in the middle of a homily. However, in a series of notes updating his *Catalogue* published in 1976,[8] he changed his view of Quire 12, which is now described as a regular eight, because of the discovery, two years after Ker's *Catalogue* was published, of another leaf of Quire 12 which originally followed the surviving three half-sheets, but is now found pasted into the binding of a printed book in the University of Kansas Library at Lawrence, Kansas.[9] Such discoveries, especially ones to be found in bindings, are a constant source of encouragement for those working with manuscripts, and reference books regularly become outdated because of them. Readers therefore need to be on their guard to ensure that the information supplied in the reference work has not been superseded. Quire 12 is now seen as a regular eight, following two other regular quires of eight, which means that this section of MS Hatton 115 was not unusual when it was first made, but has later been greatly disturbed by the loss of leaves. Quire 13, which follows Quire 12 that has been so confused in this way, is a regular eight with an extra half-sheet, in Ker's words, 'after 7'. Why the scribe should have made a nine-leaf quire becomes apparent when the end of that enlarged quire is considered, since a long block of lines at the end of the verso of fol. 94, the last of the quire, is blank (nine lines out of a total of twenty-seven), the next piece (item 27) beginning at the top of the first leaf of the following quire. Since such a large space between items is unusual, it indicates that Quires 10–13 again constituted a booklet, with its final quire enlarged so that all the text either available to the scribe or that he intended to copy, could be accommodated. This booklet contains the last six items from Ælfric's Second Series of Homilies,[10] all of which could be modified to be preached on a variety of occasions. Incidentally, Ker's *Catalogue* has useful appendices which map Ælfric's First and Second Series *Catholic Homilies* to the manuscripts in which they are found (p. 412–15), and these show the pattern of homilies in all manuscripts very clearly.

A third booklet follows, largely consisting of eights. Quires 14 to 18 remain as eights, but Quire 19 Ker describes as a four with two leaves added after the opening leaf. The last remaining full leaf, fol. 139, has only two lines of writing on the verso, and the following leaf (139a) is, as we have

Reading a Manuscript Description

seen, only the inner half and blank, with much of the parchment having been cut away. The booklet also consists wholly of Ælfric pieces, largely written not as homilies but adapted to make them suitable for preaching. Thus, we may conclude that MS Hatton 115 up to this point consisted of three booklets all written by a single scribe (except for the added leaf fol. 65 which was written by other scribes a generation later), and all containing items by Ælfric alone and modified, where necessary, to make them suitable for preaching on any occasion. They differ, however, in that whereas what is now the middle of the three booklets contains items from the Second Series which Ælfric wrote as homilies, both the first and the last contain other Ælfric material which has been adapted to make it appropriate for preaching. This may be inferred from Ker's introduction to the manuscript, although it is not stated explicitly.

Quire 20 is different from its predecessors, although again it is an eight. It has one more line per page than the earlier quires, it is written by a scribe of a slightly earlier date than the Ælfric scribe, and it contains one item only, a variant version of a known early anonymous homily which also survives in the Vercelli Book (Vercelli, Biblioteca Capitolare CXVII) and elsewhere.[11] Its last leaf, fol. 147, has only nine lines of writing on the recto while the verso is blank. This quire then constitutes a fourth booklet, and Ker offers no opinion on when it was added to those which now go before it in the manuscript.

The two final quires are perhaps best described as belonging to or made for a different manuscript and added to the rest of MS Hatton 115 at the end of the twelfth century or the beginning of the thirteenth. Quires 21 and 22 are both fours, an arrangement unknown in the rest of the manuscript. Quire 22 is noticeably different: its parchment is described by Ker as soft and thick (presumably in contrast to that of other parts of MS Hatton 115), and it has different dimensions, being considerably shorter in length than the rest of MS Hatton 115 (218 mm against 248 mm) although the width (perhaps created by the binder) is the same, and the written area is different in shape being both shorter and wider (167 × 115 mm against approximately 197 mm × 100 mm). These two quires are ruled in pencil while the rest of the book is ruled in dry point. They are written by a twelfth-century scribe, more than half a century later than the rest of the book (except for the inserted leaf, fol. 65), and contain prognostications as against the homiletic pieces found in the rest the volume. It would appear that these sections are quite unrelated to the book as a whole, and were presumably added to it at a late stage for safekeeping.

MS Hatton 115 therefore consists of four originally independent booklets, largely made up of quires of eight leaves, plus added material on an inserted leaf, fol. 65, as well as unrelated material on the last two quires which are in themselves very different in their make-up. The first three

43

booklets are by a single scribe and contain works by Ælfric, and although it is possible that its scribe put these booklets together himself to form an Ælfric collection, this is by no means certain, nor can we be sure that they were either written or put together in the order in which they now survive. In his description of the Ælfric scribe, Ker notes (p. 403) that his hand is 'very like that of' London, British Library, Cotton MS Faustina A. x, which contains a copy of Ælfric's Latin Grammar and its associated Glossary. It would seem that all these works by Ælfric were collected together as a conscious act. The fact that an extra leaf, fol. 65, written by two later scribes, was inserted into Quire 9 at an unknown date suggests that alterations continued to be made to the Ælfric booklets after the main scribe had completed his work on them. It has been shown that Quire 9 consisted solely of half-sheets after blank leaves had been removed from the end to form the first of three Ælfric booklets, and it is therefore reasonable to assume that the addition of the late half-sheet, which is now folio 65 between two Ælfric items (Ker's 17 and 20), took place after the blank leaves had been removed since this would have involved a half-sheet being added to other half-sheets. Fol. 65 also was inserted between two Ælfric items so that it did not disturb the earlier copying. The fourth booklet in MS Hatton 115 containing a single item – a homily, but not one composed by Ælfric – is here copied by an otherwise unknown scribe of a slightly earlier date than that of the first three booklets, and it can be shown that this quire existed separately for some time, before being added to MS Hatton 115 (see below). Finally, the last two quires, written by a much later scribe, were added to the collection last, and contain material which is neither by Ælfric nor has any association in terms of content with anything else in the volume. All this can be deduced through a close reading of Ker's description, but it must be stressed that although Ker gives the basic information, the significance of his account has to be extrapolated from the facts he supplies.

Ker gives no indication of the way in which the material was put together nor of the probable date of the creation of the manuscript as a whole, although he does note that the table of contents on fol. v recto, which was 'written *c*. 1200' (p. 402), contains only his items 1–33, which would suggest that as late as that date, only the Ælfric items were together; in other words, that booklet 4 and the last two quires were not at that time added. Ker does not note that the items on the inserted folio 65 plus the short items on either side were added to the table of contents by the Tremulous Hand of Worcester,[12] presumably because the table of contents is in Latin, and Latin material, although noted briefly throughout the *Catalogue*, is not his main concern. It would seem, then, that MS Hatton 115 as we know it is a thirteenth-century creation.

44

Reading a Manuscript Description

As this account suggests, through a careful reading of Ker's collation together with his description of items, a student may make new discoveries about the history of manuscripts containing Old English since this chapter has shown how MS Hatton 115 is made up of a series of booklets, something implied by Ker but not specifically stated by him. Another useful example is supplied by the double volume of homilies now shelfmark Cambridge, Corpus Christi College, MSS 419 and 421, Ker's manuscript numbers 68 and 69. This double volume was written by a single scribe somewhere in the south of England in the first half of the eleventh century. The first book contains fifteen homilies plus an originally blank initial leaf, on the reverse of which has been copied, perhaps by the same hand, a seventeen-line prayer which also occurs elsewhere in Old English. This leaf has now been moved to the opening of the second volume. All this information is reported by Ker, *Catalogue*, p. 115–17. The second book has eight homilies in the hand which wrote Corpus MS 419, plus a further seven items written half a century later by three scribes who use, in Ker's words, 'an "Exeter" type of script' (p. 118).[13] On his pages 117 and 118, Ker reports the number of lines per page: nineteen throughout the original items in Corpus MS 419 and also those written by the same scribe in MS 421. The Exeter scribes conformed exactly to this format in the five items, which he added and which are now at the beginning of 421 (p. 3–98; see Ker, p. 118), but not in the two items now in the middle of the book (Ker's items 10 and 11), which, as Ker reports, occupy twenty-five lines (Ker, p. 118). Ker also notes that his items 10 and 11 were once adjacent to his item 5 (Ker, p. 118); in other words, all the added 'Exeter' items were at one time together.[14]

The importance of reading Ker very carefully is revealed by considering a change in the number of lines per page in items 10 and 11, in conjunction with the note at the end of Ker's item 11 that pages 225 and 226 in the manuscript which follow these items are blank. Why should a scribe increase the number of lines per page for items 10 and 11 only, as against the number of lines in the other additions in the book? We may assume that he did so because he knew that the two items that he wished to copy would occupy more space in a single quire than was available with the nineteen-line page layout of the rest of the book. But the significant increase to the number of lines per page seems to conflict with the blank leaf which follows. The solution lies in fuller consideration of Ker's collation. Quire 15, which is the one that uniquely has twenty-five lines per page, is an eight; in other words, it has sixteen pages. Since the collation makes it clear that Quire 14 now ends with page 208, the sixteen pages of Quire 15 are pages 209 to 224. Hence, the blank pages 225 and 226 constitute the opening leaf of Quire 16, even though in Ker's description of items the note that these pages are blank

45

occurs at the end of his details on item 11 (i.e., Quire 15). If we look back at the companion volume, Corpus MS 419, we see that it originally had a blank leaf at the beginning of the book, now furnished with a prayer on what was the verso, which in the present binding has become the recto and moved to the opening of Corpus MS 421. So we can speculate that pages 225 and 226 originally constituted the opening leaf of Corpus MS 421 also, and that both 419 and 421 each originally had a blank opening leaf. This is something not hitherto noticed by the many scholars who have worked on this manuscript.[15] Furthermore, it also implies that Ker's item 12 of Corpus MS 421, Ælfric's item *In Letania maiore* from his First Series of Catholic Homilies (Clemoes XVIII),[16] was originally the first item in the manuscript. This piece is followed (items 13–15) by three more successive items from the First Series (Clemoes XIX, XX, and XXI), each presented in its manuscript context in exactly the same way: each has no break between the end of one text and the Latin heading of the next, but there is one blank line between that Latin heading and the start of the Old English text, and the Old English itself begins in large capitals preceded by an ornamental letter. It is likely that this block of items was copied continuously from a single source text. Unfortunately, the last item ends imperfectly in Corpus MS 421, five lines of it in Clemoes's edition (taken from other manuscripts) being lost. The surviving incomplete conclusion of the last item is written on all that remains of a new quire. Since it is unlikely that this quire was otherwise blank, we must assume that the rest of the quire was removed because it was wanted elsewhere or, more probably, that it was removed by someone who decided that the next item in the First Series (Clemoes XXII, set for Pentecost) was inappropriate in this context, an obvious reason being that the same piece for Pentecost is now the first item of Corpus MS 421, copied by one of the Exeter scribes. It may be that this excision happened late in the history of the manuscript, even as late as the sixteenth century when the book was in the possession of Matthew Parker.[17] Only the existence of the blank page and the oddity of its position as reported by Ker is found in the *Catalogue* itself. The rest is typical of information that can be deduced from following up on what seem to be discrepancies in Ker's account.

For my final point, I return briefly to MS Hatton 115. The third sentence of the collation in Ker's description reads: 'Ff. iv v[erso] are parchment leaves ruled like the rest of the manuscript: they are half-sheets and were, no doubt, taken from one of the quires with now missing blank leaves, e.g., quire 9.' In fact, careful examination of these two folios in the manuscript shows that there is little likelihood that they were taken from Quire 9 itself. The four folios now missing from Quire 9 have been roughly cut, with linking parchment still in place to hold the remaining leaves. The irregular cutting does not

Reading a Manuscript Description

match the edge of folios iv and v, and therefore it is unlikely that they came from Quire 9. It is probable – indeed, highly likely given the fact that, as Ker states, the ruling of fols. iv and v matches that of the manuscript as a whole – that they came from one of the other quires which has had leaves removed. In other words, these folios came from one of the final quires of a booklet, but we have no way of knowing which one, nor indeed how many booklets there were originally, simply that only three now remain. On a different point, Quire 20, which is the independent quire containing a single item only, an anonymous homily, described previously as the only item in booklet 4, not only has a different number of lines from the rest of the manuscript, as Ker reports, but each page has a clear crease across the middle, which Ker failed to note. This shows that while it was an independent 'booklet', this quire was folded, presumably for ease of carriage, and the homily it contains was at some time in the hands of an itinerant preacher. There are, then, two sins in Ker's account, a minor one of commission and a more serious one of omission. The first is the suggestion that the flyleaves originated in Quire 9, which is almost certainly wrong, and the second is the failure to note the creased leaves in Quire 20. The lesson to be drawn from these examples is that there is no substitute for examining original manuscripts before arriving at conclusions. Facsimiles, however seemingly perfect the reproduction, can never supply as much information as a first-hand encounter with the text, while descriptions, such as those in reference books like Ker's, can be no more than a starting point for further investigation. Nevertheless, it is hoped that this chapter has shown that real advances in scholarship can be achieved by a careful reading of printed descriptions which are readily available, even to those without access to manuscript-holding libraries, and that from them much new information may be derived.

Notes

1. N. R. Ker, *Catalogue of Manuscripts Containing Anglo-Saxon* (Oxford: Clarendon Press, 1957, repr., 1990).
2. Ker, *Catalogue*, xx–xxi.
3. Ker addended and corrected his work in 'A supplement to *Catalogue of Manuscripts Containing Anglo-Saxon*', *Anglo-Saxon England*, 5 (1976), 121–31, with more additions and corrections in M. Blockley, 'Addenda and Corrigenda to N. R. Ker's "A Supplement to *Catalogue of Manuscripts Containing Anglo-Saxon*"', *Notes and Queries*, 29 (1982), 1–3, revised and reprinted in 'Further Addenda and Corrigenda to N. R. Ker's Catalogue', in M. P. Richards, ed., *Anglo-Saxon Manuscripts: Basic Readings* (New York: Garland Publishing, 1994), 79–85. In no case is the opening statement of MS Hatton 115 corrected.

4. See Ker, 'Introduction', *Catalogue*, xxii.
5. P. R. Robinson, 'Self-contained Units in Composite Manuscripts of the Anglo-Saxon Period', *Anglo-Saxon England*, 7 (1978), 231–8.
6. Robinson, 'Self-contained Units', 235–8.
7. J. C. Pope, ed., *Homilies of Ælfric: A Supplementary Collection*, EETS 259–60 (London: Oxford University Press, 1967–8).
8. See previous note 3.
9. R. L. Collins, *Anglo-Saxon Vernacular Manuscripts in America* (New York: Pierpont Morgan Library, 1976), no. 7.
10. M. Godden, ed., *Ælfric's Catholic Homilies: The Second Series: Text*, EETS ss 5 (London: Oxford University Press, 1979). MS Hatton 115 is there referred to with the siglum P. A siglum is a shorthand identifier for a manuscript, used by textual editors.
11. See D. G. Scragg, ed., *The Vercelli Homilies and Related Texts*, EETS 300 (Oxford: Oxford University Press, 1992), item 9.
12. See C. Franzen, *Worcester Manuscripts*, Anglo-Saxon Manuscripts in Microfiche Facsimile, vol. 6 (Tempe, AZ: Medieval & Renaissance Texts and Studies, 1998), 47.
13. On the Exeter additions, see E. Treharne, 'The Bishop's Book: Leofric's Homiliary and Eleventh-century Exeter', in S. Baxter et al., eds., *Early Medieval Studies in Memory of Patrick Wormald* (Farnham, Surrey: Ashgate, 2008), 522–37.
14. Ker, *Catalogue*, 117, notes that an 'offset on p. 98 is of writing on p. 209': the latter page has been pressed so hard against the blank p. 98 that an imprint of the writing on p. 209 may be seen.
15. Listed by J. Wilcox in the bibliography to *Wulfstan Texts and Other Homiletic Materials*, Anglo-Saxon Manuscripts in Microfiche Facsimile, vol. 8 (Tempe, AZ: Medieval & Renaissance Texts and Studies, 2000), 12–13.
16. P. Clemoes, ed., *Ælfric's Catholic Homilies: The First Series: Text*, EETS ss 17 (Oxford: Oxford University Press, 1997).
17. Ker reports (*Catalogue*, 117) that Parker's table of contents on a flyleaf 'states that a homily **De duodecim abusiuis** . . . began on p. 356', that is, with at least one folio unaccounted for between what is now the end of Clemoes XXI and Parker's final item.

3

JULIA CRICK AND
DANIEL WAKELIN

Reading and Understanding Scripts

First and foremost, manuscripts – whether books, booklets, documents, bills posted, or rolls – are objects which carry writing. The appearance of the writing contributes to the other tasks that books do in a society: communicating knowledge, forging relationships, expressing attitudes, pleasing the eye, reinforcing or subverting relationships with the past and in the present. It is among the tasks of palaeography to understand scripts, by training us not only to decode their content through transcribing and reading archaic handwriting, but also to interpret the significance of their form or letterforms. Scribes belonged to a 'graphic system', as it has been called, which involved readers as well as writers, and the consequent relationship between text, the page, and the scribe has inspired much palaeographical work and reflection in the last century.[1]

This chapter will introduce some important scripts and historical shifts in their use, in approximately chronological order; but it will do so in part because sometimes different questions about understanding scripts arise from different moments in their history. The main aim of this chapter is to think methodologically about ways to understand script, and some ways in which understanding script might illuminate other aspects of cultural history.

The style of lettering in which a manuscript is written is what we call the *script*. Across the millennium of handwritten documents and books up to the 1400s, there was a wide range of scripts with their own connotations and social functions.[2] To understand handwriting, we must remember two essential differences between typefaces and scripts. Unlike typefaces, a script did not need to have any physical form before it appeared on the page of a book. It existed often as a design or scheme in the mind's eye, even primarily, perhaps, as a motor memory.[3] It could be taught by training but then it had to be held in the mind for future use. There were sheets advertising scripts, which paid scribes could produce or writing masters could teach, such as one from Oxford in the early 1300s.[4] The users of books also

49

practised their letters on flyleaves or blank margins, or tested their pens by trial alphabets.[5] But this evidence is erratic in occurrence and unsystematic in form, so that we cannot assume that such alphabets were direct models for the handwriting we see in finished books. While most scribes produce letterforms like those of other scribes and sometimes will have copied what they found in their exemplars, often what they shared a notional script, an idea, or a learned practice, rather than a set of direct physical models. There is, then, something artificial and anachronistic about the way that palaeographical textbooks give sample 'alphabets' of each script: these are useful for recording what we see and teaching us what to look for, but they codify scripts and the scribal practices associated with them in a way which few scribes did at the time. Scribes were less predictable than palaeographers might like.

This is manifest in the second difference between typefaces and scripts. Each time a person tries to write a particular script, the reproduction is not exact. In rendering a script, each letter can differ by microscopic movements of the hand. This could be a disadvantage, as haste, incompetence, and the mistransmission that occurs in passing on skills might result in unintended variation and, over time, change. It probably explains why some scripts changed so dramatically; for instance, why Caroline minuscule of the 800s slowly morphed, generation by generation, into the apparently unlike Gothic *textualis* of the 1300s. But that variability could also be an advantage, as a scribe might not reproduce a learned example strictly but might modify it to suit his or her needs: greater ease and speed, more calligraphic showing-off, a harmonization with the page design. Unlike a typeface, a script can be handwritten more or less slowly, with more or fewer calligraphic details, on different occasions and so can be revealing evidence for the occasions and motives for writing.

As the exercise of handiwork which can change, moment to moment, script constitutes a form of craft.[6] The practitioner was trained to use familiar tools and material. The shapes and proportions of the letterforms, their disposition on the page, the relationship between individual letters, between words, the size of the script, the distance of the ruled lines, and the size of the page all illustrate the traditions within which the maker was trained, his or her personal skills and limitations, and the connections and resources, both economic and cultural, of the place of writing. Arabic script, for example, reached right across the Muslim world in the Middle Ages, from Africa into Eurasia, as far as China. Within that wider tradition, local practices modified the manner of making books and of writing them, and Arabic-based scripts were used for writing local vernaculars.[7] Likewise, the Latin tradition which came to dominate writing in the medieval West from Ireland to the Balkans, from Iceland to southern Spain, permitted local differences and exchanges of influence. The evidence suggests that most Western scribes who had received any degree of formal training could write multiple scripts: display script, a text hand, and a more informal hand for note-writing. Drawing on a repertoire of examples inculcated by years of physical repetition, the skilled scribe exercised his or her training as the commission dictated. As such, in committing writing to the page each scribe consciously and unconsciously recorded a relationship with both past and present models and traditions: habits taught and learned, the aesthetic choices made, the emulation or rejection of influences and exemplars, the exercise and limits of the individual's own skill. Script bears particularly eloquent witness to the dynamic fields of contact and influence within which the writers and readers of medieval Britain were situated and in which they chose to situate themselves. These dynamics can be detected both at the relatively elevated social level of literary production where politics and processes of patronage are articulated in written texts and at the level of the mundane and quotidian, where low-level instruction or record was replicated in unknown circumstances by anonymous hands.

What a scribe produces attests to the conjunction of three components – the scribe's own skill along with the exemplar and page – which illustrate a unique negotiation between very variable, sometimes disparate and unfamiliar items. The exemplar, and sometimes the page as well, lay beyond the scribe's control. The exemplar frequently presented difficulty: the text written on one of a great variety of possible media, such as wax tablets, papyrus, crumbling or decaying parchment, and in challenging scripts, perhaps foreign, ancient, highly abbreviated, or rendered unintelligible by speed. The job of making meaning rested with the scribe. The success of the operation could and can be judged according to a variety of factors: intelligibility, textual fidelity, and calligraphy being foremost among them. On each occasion the scribe must simultaneously improvise in response to a different exemplar. For an illustration of how this relationship worked in practice we can examine repairs and additions made by native scribes to imported books. A scribe working in later tenth-century England took it upon himself to replace the first sixteen folios of a copy of the poems of the sixth-century bishop of Poitiers, Venantius Fortunatus. London, British Library, MS Add. 24193 had been made on the Continent in the early ninth century and presumably lacked these opening pages, or, more likely, had sustained physical damage to them, prompting the recopying by an English scribe who mimicked the preparation of the page, layout, script, and initial capitals of the antique import in order to render the volume complete. In the later eleventh century, a liturgical book from Germany, the Germano-Roman pontifical (London, British Library,

Cotton MS Tiberius C. i, 43–203) was extended by a series of scribes working at Sherborne, Dorset, first an Englishman clearly taking care to match to the work of the German scribe both in the layout of the text and the vermilion colour of the ink of his rubrics.

In the earlier Middle Ages, the creation of the copy almost never took the form of exact replication. For new texts the scribe might work from notes recorded in informal hands on scraps of parchment, or wax tablets; and for old ones, which formed the bulk of copying, the scribe had to negotiate an exemplar distant from the present in time and space. Thus, copying taxed the scribe both physically and cognitively.[8] Scholars can rarely identify the precise exemplar of a particular manuscript and so the fundamental skill of the scribe in transposition, in setting out the page, of deciding how the text is to be organized, is hidden. Sometimes, as in The Book of Kells (Dublin, Trinity College, MS 58), the tensions between exemplar and copy become manifest. Here, in a manuscript of the highest calligraphic and artistic contrivance, whose polychrome illustration extends to almost every page, the scribe failed to fit his text into the space available. The mismatch between the length of lines in the exemplar and the size of his own script and the length of line available to him caused him time after time to let the text spill over to the line above.

The scribe sits quite literally at the intersection of meaning: it is his or her task to convey information and knowledge across time and space, and equally failure in this task will have corrupted meaning and generated nonsense. The understanding and capacity of scribes, their ability to execute the systems of writing within which they were trained, and their facility to understand those of their exemplars are of critical importance in the production of a usable text.

Arguably, the cultural distance between scribe and exemplar gaped widest in post-Roman Britain where the broken connection between the colonial language (Latin) and the seat of empire (Rome) left a fragile and vulnerable remnant, ostentatiously shunned by the English-speaking conquerors of lowland Britain. Literate culture had, at the very least, to be reinfused from outside. Despite the particular importance of remembered, spoken and performed texts, not just for basic catechism, but for the conduct of law in the Old English and Old Welsh vernaculars, medieval Britain more than the continental core of the Roman Empire had to acquire *Romanitas* from books.[9] It depended on books for most complex texts, with the initial exception of systems of governance and information, for complex knowledge, personal salvation, and later, as elsewhere, for the scholastic texts of philosophy, medicine, and law which ended the cultural hegemony of late antiquity so dominant in religious life in Britain until the eleventh century.

Thus, in Britain, Latin texts were constantly being imported,[10] and the imports would often have been the products of different script systems.

In the first millennium, throughout western Europe, the uses of script were set by the writing practices of the pagan Roman Empire, and overlaid by those of the Christian past and present. In Britain, the generally fractured inheritance from Rome made the relationship with western tradition particularly unstable. One consequence was variegation across Britain: different parts of sub-Roman Britain related differently to this inheritance. The writings of Patrick in the fifth century and Gildas in the sixth attest to the survival in western Britain of educational and ecclesiastical structures presumably derived from Roman origins. In the east, meanwhile, the institutions of the church appear to have ceased to function almost entirely. Certainly, the scripts written in eastern Britain after the establishment of a continuous Christian tradition in the seventh century are characterized by an impressionability, a susceptibility to external influence through the influence of imported models, new and antique, or by the movement of people and ideas. As many as ten identifiable types of script were written there in the half-millennium following the conversion of the English kingdoms to Christianity in the seventh century, a figure surely unusually high in the post-Roman West.[11]

The habits of script styles, of orthography and training, together with the preparation of the page, vary across Europe in different centuries. Four main zones, including Insular, are recognized as direct heirs to the script traditions of the western Roman Empire, all with some common or shared features, but each with a unique combination of practices. Such systems were not necessarily mutually intelligible. Scribes regularly failed to decode the abbreviations and letterforms of older or foreign script systems with which they were unfamiliar, mistranscribing them, copying them uncomprehendingly, or simply omitting difficulties.[12] But the post-Roman script systems share a common Roman inheritance, differently preserved. So, the letterforms of late Roman cursive are clearly replicated in the round-backed **d** and in the long **r** and **s** preferred by Insular scribes; likewise, the shorthand system of the Roman Empire, Tironian *notae*, is perpetuated in the characteristic Insular abbreviations for *autem, enim, est*, and *et*, this last co-opted into vernacular writing in English (OE *ond*) and Gaelic (OI *ná*). The characteristic ligatures of high-**e** with following consonants (i.e., strokes shared between two letters) have continental counterparts, and also the ligatures of **i** following **f, m, n, t**, found across the Insular zone but also in Beneventan script in southern Italy.[13] This operation of intersecting systems lends scripts their fascination, their practical value as criteria for dating and localizing manuscripts, and their significance as cultural markers.

The information which script encodes is pelagic in its scope and complexity, particularly in situations in which datable contexts are lacking; for example, in the post-Roman centuries when multiple scripts were written in Britain, or in large parts of Britain beyond the few identifiable and relatively well-studied centres. In early medieval Britain, until the second millennium at least, script was written in places whose material culture was richer and more eclectic than that of the hinterlands in which they were situated, although the steepness of the cultural gradient between places of writing and their localities gradually moderated over the period. Extant evidence for this period can never represent more than the flotsam and jetsam of complex systems now lost to us; individual pieces can only be understood using a process of detailed reconstruction, an option only possible when suitable contextual information also survives. Despite the sometimes fragmentary and ambivalent quality of the evidence, distinct processes are in play in the period and surprising patterns can be detected. Continuity, rupture, and reform characterize the period between 600 and 1200 across Ireland and Britain. These three processes create an interplay between the universal and the local: influences flowing from and to the European continent, the product of conquest, migration, or religious alignment. Sometimes the circumstances simply support received historical argument; sometimes they run counter to it. In Britain they amount to a statement of the cultural and educational complexity of a politically fractured island.

Britain was not a palaeographical unit at any point in the early or later Middle Ages any more than it was a political or cultural one. Rather, Britain represents an intersection of opposing influences. The Insular zone was an area of cultural experimentation and invention in the early Middle Ages: a living system of scribal practices which makes visible a series of cultural connections extending across Ireland and Britain to the monasteries of Germany and the Rhineland founded under the influence of Gaelic- and English-speaking clerics in the seventh and eighth centuries. Ultimately one of the four major script zones of post-Roman Europe, elements of its codicology, letterforms, and abbreviations can be compared with late Roman traditions, although the channels of the influence remain deeply controversial.[14] The domains within the Insular zone, arrayed across two seas, were populated by Gaelic-, Brittonic-, and Germanic-speaking peoples connected with the Roman world at best at second hand. For them Latin was a foreign language. Their institutions of learning were plantations, consciously created in order to foster a faith whose books, assumptions, and language belonged to an alien culture. Writing constituted the primary mechanism by which that culture was instantiated, perpetuated, and furthered. Memorized texts of Holy Scripture were paraded and chanted by

Reading and Understanding Scripts

missionaries to the English; books were acquired from Gaul and Italy; their texts were studied, glossed, copied. The conversion process generated new texts: letters from the missionaries back to Rome; and, if we accept their claims to be contemporary, the texts in the name of St Patrick in fifth-century Ireland; in England, the lawcode of Æthelberht, king of Kent (ob. 616), followed by charters recording land tenure and then hagiography.[15] The mechanics of the recording process in the first generations after conversion are lost to history: without surviving contemporary manuscripts we have no means of knowing who did the writing and how they wrote. But when Insular writing does start to survive, from the sixth century in Ireland, from the seventh in England, and the ninth in Wales, it tells its own surprising story.[16]

After Rome: Ireland, Britain and the Continental Tradition

Irish scripts are ultimately indebted to two sources, neither visible now: Roman cursive, manifested in Insular minuscule, and half-uncial, a script of late antiquity, whose presence in Ireland, an island never subject to Roman authority but Christianized from Britain in the fifth century, suggests cultural entente with the rest of Christendom.[17] The set of graphic traditions which were the fruit of these two elements predominated in the island of Britain until the Norman Conquest, and in Ireland well after partial colonization from England in the late twelfth century, in both islands proving much more tenacious in vernacular writing than in Latin.[18] Indeed, paradoxically it was in Ireland, incontrovertibly beyond the Roman frontier, that continuity with the Roman way of writing is attested earliest and endured longest. The writing traditions of Roman Britain are well known from casual 'cursive' writing preserved on the lead curse tablets and waxed wooden writing tablets which continue to be unearthed from urban and rural sites.[19] In Ireland, the discovery of an early writing tablet, from Springmount Bog, and a piece of papyrus, used to line the cover of the Faddan More Psalter, indicates the perpetuation of Roman-derived traditions outside the Empire. Similarly striking is the adoption in Ireland of half-uncial, the most serviceable book-hand in use in the Roman West in Late Antiquity, widely written, including in North Africa. This script offered a clear, legible, and relatively rapid means of committing text to the page, a forerunner of the simplified bookhand known as Caroline minuscule, which came to dominate writing in nearly all parts of the Latin West between the eighth and the eleventh centuries. Half-uncial involved a trade-off between clarity – lack of ligature, a propensity to form letters carefully and deliberately, like straight-backed **d** – and features which assisted rapid writing, such as the adoption of the simplified

55

letterforms of cursive writing (3-shaped **g**, long **r** and **s** rather than the capital 'majuscule' forms **G**, **R**, and **S**) and longer descending and ascending strokes.

In its offshore home, half-uncial shifted shape. Once used to convey lengthy patristic texts, in the hands of Insular craftsmen half-uncial was pressed into service for short texts, including documents, and most strikingly in the short biblical inscription incised on the gilded strip from the Staffordshire hoard. Half-uncial was adopted as a script of Insular epigraphy, manifest on inscribed stone monuments across eastern and western Britain and in Ireland. The practice is strikingly counter-intuitive, both because the rounded letterforms resist easy cutting on stone, and because pre-existing epigraphic traditions, whether those of Rome or of the Irish and Germanic worlds (ogam and runes), all employ straight-sided characters. Nevertheless, it chimes with contemporary continental practice.[20] In its use as a script for writing books, Insular scribes again transformed the raw material. Half-uncial, from the earliest known script of Latin manuscripts from Ireland, was elevated to a distinguished bookhand, employed in gospel books across Britain and Ireland. English scribes had largely abandoned half-uncial as a text script by the ninth century, as had continental scribes, but it was maintained as a display script as late as the tenth and even eleventh centuries in Ireland and Wales. The counterpoint to the adoption of half-uncial (a rounded script) for incising on stone is the use of an unnamed and highly stylized straight-sided display script commonly seen in early Insular gospel books, whose tendency to be regimented into compartments on the manuscript page has been likened to the traditions of Insular metalwork.[21] Its presence signals the pan-Insular horizons of the craftsmen who participated in this graphic tradition over several centuries in Ireland, in England, and on the Continent.

Contact with the Continent extended across western Britain and Ireland in the early Middle Ages, as exchanges of texts, personnel, and religious practices attest, but England provides strongest evidence that scribes responded to influence from contemporary writing styles from the Continent.[22] The first recognizably English writing suggests dual influences: contact with the cursive writing of the sort employed by Irish scribes; and initially unconvincing imitation of Roman uncials, the rounded majuscule script of late antiquity, notably in the form that was used in Rome during the pontificate of Gregory the Great, patron of the English mission. Uncial was deployed apparently for the weight of the symbolic associations which it embodied, used in centres in which the authority of the Roman church was particularly cultivated and for specific purposes. It was used for solemn texts: *liturgica*, the Rule of St Benedict, and Latin diplomas recording the first land-grants to the new churches planted by monks from Rome.[23] In its most sophisticated

Reading and Understanding Scripts

manifestations uncial was used as part of a hierarchy of scripts, as a texthand in copies of the Bible whose rubrics were written in that other antique script, Rustic capitals, as in the three gigantic Bibles made in Northumbria before 716; or used alongside Rustic capitals to pinpoint papal formulae in Bede's *Ecclesiastical History*.[24]

Insular minuscule was itself another displacement from continental antiquity: from a script used in the Empire for practical communication, often by inexpert writers on wax or unbaked clay, to a bookhand capable of carrying the text of the Bible. The first datable appearance of Insular minuscule is from England: the letter addressed by Bishop Wealdhere of London to the Archbishop of Canterbury in 704 or 705; but this represents a single fixed point in a fluid and resilient chain of associations which in England extended into the beginning of the second millennium CE in Latin and, in the vernacular, to the end of the Middle Ages.[25] The round-backed **d**, 3-shaped **g**, long **f**, **r**, and **s**, were all derived from cursive writing but, even when cursively written, the script could look calligraphic and elegant: the wedged tops to **h** and **l** counterbalancing the tapering strokes on and descending below the baseline, an impression of fluency derived from the frequent use of ligatures and run-ons and the restraint and rhythm of expert execution.[26] Insular minuscule gave scribes trained in the Insular tradition a medium for experimentation. It offered alternative letterforms, a set of abbreviations and ligatures, a tradition of high aesthetic standards, and an appreciation of the manuscript page. While the calligraphic potential of the script could be realized in cursive performances, scribes could slow the script down or dress it up, whether the effect was the emulation of monumental liturgical half-uncial (compare the Royal Bible, or the Book of Nunnaminster) or, in the hands of the brilliant calligraphers of eighth-century Wearmouth-Jarrow, a lucid bookhand displaying classicizing symptoms and clear visual cues for the reader.[27] Likewise, the clearly compartmentalized Insular minuscule seen in southern England in the ninth century may owe something to the newly reformed script adopted in the Carolingian Empire.[28]

The Reconfiguration of Insular Writing, 850 to 1100

The Insular script zone crossed political and linguistic boundaries. It is difficult to differentiate between English and Irish minuscule in the seventh century or between Insular and continental-Insular script in the eighth and early ninth centuries. But the pan-Insularity characteristic of the period before 850 did not outlive the Viking wars of the ninth century. The most obvious and dramatic developments in writing in Britain in the quarter-millennium after 850 pertain to relationships across the North Sea, where we see the progressive dominance of the reformed script of the Carolingian Empire, Caroline minuscule. Caroline minuscule had displaced Insular writing in the monasteries of the continental missionary zone by the mid-ninth century at the latest. The script was known in England, perhaps as early as the ninth century, and an important new style of Insular minuscule known as Square minuscule, which emerged in the early decades of the tenth century, can be viewed as an English response to Caroline: royal, reformed, compartmentalized, eschewing the full gamut of ligatures which had proliferated in the past. Caroline minuscule was known, read, and written at the court of the newly ascendant kings of Wessex, the future kings of England. An imported gospel book (London, British Library, Cotton MS Tiberius A. ii) now contains a praise poem in continental Caroline celebrating Æthelstan, king of Wessex from 924 to 939 on f. 15r, and, on the verso, a Latin inscription in Square minuscule entered by one of the court scribes recording the king's gift of the book to Christ Church Canterbury. Square minuscule was used for many texts associated with the royal court, both English and Latin, both old and new, including the *Anglo-Saxon Chronicle*, the Laws of Alfred, royal diplomas, and the collection of medical texts known as *Bald's Leechbook*. However, the style was short-lived. In the third quarter of the tenth century, English scribes started writing Caroline minuscule for specific purposes: for copying Latin diplomas and for texts pertaining to the reform of English monastic life undertaken under the auspices of the king and queen; by the start of the eleventh century English Caroline minuscule was the script for Latin. A typically English idiom, developed in the 1020s, marked the development of English Caroline minuscule written right through to the twelfth century.[29] Meanwhile, Insular minuscule lived on as the medium for writing in English, but mutated again, adopting rounder proportions and a greater diversity of styles.[30] All through the eleventh century, most particularly from the middle onwards, both Latin and English script proved susceptible to outside influence, notably from French and Flemish churchmen active in England both before and after the Norman Conquest.

Let us stop for a moment to consider developments in Wales. In western Britain, and specifically beyond the jurisdiction of the West Saxon king of England, in the Welsh kingdoms, no identifiable manuscripts survive from the first four centuries after Christianization: they date only from the ninth century, although there is epigraphic evidence of no determinable date, but presumed to be earlier.[31] The first identifiable Welsh writing shows affiliation with Insular practices seen also in the writing of English and Irish scribes, with a tendency to local variation: a marked propensity to use ligatures, to emphasize the top of the line of writing by the use of exaggerated wedged strokes to give a flat-topped effect, and for the topmost extremity of b, h, and l to carry a flag-like wedge, features seen in the earliest Irish half-uncial. It is possible that Welsh influence, as well as the imprint of Caroline minuscule, explains the particular aesthetic which produced the English style known as Square minuscule. Only about a dozen manuscripts from pre-Norman Wales have been identified, and only a few carry indications of dating. Manuscripts from other Brittonic-speaking areas, notably Cornwall and Brittany, do survive, and exhibit some of the same features, but with few examples extant and no clear evidence about context, reconstructing relationships and institutional structures is fraught with difficulty.

On the other hand, recent research on the palaeography of western and northern Britain demonstrates the existence of an Irish-Sea or Late Celtic Zone which retained a common system of abbreviation and letterforms and flourished into the late eleventh and even twelfth centuries, 250 years after the implosion of the Insular system of scripts as classically defined. One example is Cambridge, Corpus Christi College, MS 199, a copy of Augustine's *De Trinitate* made at the Welsh *clas* of Llanbadarn Fawr on the eve of its appropriation by the Normans, by Ieuan ap Sulien, the younger son of the Welsh bishop of St David's, Sulien. The circumstances of the family are well attested through the Latin poetry written by Sulien's other sons, notably Rhigyfarch's *Lament* on the atrocities inflicted by the Norman conquerors on the Welsh, but Ieuan's calligraphy demonstrates his training and intellectual pedigree. Folio 1v shows the opening of the text: the quality and Irish influence of the initials (in orange, yellow, and black) and the intricately abbreviated script, deeply indebted to Insular models, the exaggeratedly flagged wedges on the top of ascenders and minim-strokes seen in Irish script of the tenth century and later and the horizontal equivalent at the left-hand approach to the top of **t**. The multiple subscript letters (*si*), and flat-toppedness seen in ninth-century Welsh examples, older abbreviations derived from Tironian *notae*, and rare or no longer current on the European continent, the flared v-shaped **u** in *ut* and likewise the two supra-script commas above **g** and **t** to represent the suspension of *–ra* are both now identified as Late Celtic features;[32] likewise, the Insular *–tur* abbreviation.

The Gothic System of Scripts

A major transformation befell Caroline minuscule from the late 1000s.[33] By the start of the 1200s it had become quite different in appearance: it had angles instead of curves; was narrower in proportions; had calligraphic treatments of the tops and bottoms of minims and ascenders, and a few distinctive new letterforms such as so-called 'round r', really zetoid, or shaped like *z*. Specimens from the late 1100s onwards are usually described with a different name: *textura* or Gothic *textualis*. These differences create the 'black letter' script, which to later eyes seems so alien and stereotypically 'medieval'. Though these differences of Gothic *textualis* arose gradually, the more calligraphic aspects of Gothic *textualis* look like stylistic affectations: the serifs or ticks at the top and bottom of minims and the way in which letters began to overlap or 'bite'. It is sometimes suggested that its fussiness reflects the growing number of skilled scribes who wrote as paid employment and chose to display their professional virtuosity.[34] Yet another context is clear. From the 1200s onwards, the volume of writing that survives increases significantly, and while recency is on the side of survival, the volume of writing produced does seem to have increased. Universities, new trends in copying the Bible and the mass of liturgical and paraliturgical books, including Books of Hours for the pious laity, led to ever more books being made, often outside of monastic settings and professionally, for money. Many singly and cumulatively bulky Bibles and scholastic texts were written in *textualis*. The script's narrowness allowed more words to fit the page.

But this same growth in book production also led to another script becoming common from the 1200s onwards, in parallel with *textualis*. This was the adoption of cursive scripts, sometimes with the adaptation of them, as acceptable scripts for books. The term *cursive* (or the Latin *cursiva*) needs clarifying. Cursive scripts are made not with the separately formed, often vertical strokes of *textualis*, but with a flow of the pen with fewer interruptions horizontally across the page. In contrast with the set execution of Gothic *textualis*, cursive writing was written more quickly, sometimes very currently, and often more sloppily; and as it took less time and care, it had less prestige than *textualis*. The use of cursive for copying documents and then books was driven by the need for faster, less difficult production. From the 1200s to the late 1300s, the variety of cursive script used in England known as *anglicana* helped optimize the proliferation of bureaucracy there. Malcolm Parkes relates the spread of cursive scripts to the need to produce documents in ever greater quantities for ever more people, often by an ever wider range of people with ever more variable skills. This has been called the age of 'the literacy of the laity' or 'pragmatic literacy'.[35]

From at least the 1260s to the late 1400s, scribes in England borrowed *anglicana* for the copying of books. The use of cursive script, and the use of paper as a writing support, created what Erik Kwakkel called 'a new kind of book for a new kind of reader'.[36] *Anglicana* facilitated the making of books by people trained in other kinds of writing, such as lawyers and legal scriveners – it is common in books of the law in the 1300s, for instance – and university scholars and clergy making books for their own use. It also made the task of copying quicker, with a lower level of skill required, so that

60

the amount one would have to pay somebody to write a book in such script was less. It was a crucial tool for disseminating religious, historical, and scientific learning in French and English in the late 1200s and 1300s; all these genres were often copied in *anglicana* script. Literary manuscripts of English verse, such as Oxford, Bodleian Library, MS Digby 86 or London, British Library, MS Harley 2253, are only the most famous examples of an extension of book production that *anglicana* made possible. *Anglicana* was exported with English colonization to Ireland, where it coexisted alongside Insular script.

This parallel development of *textualis* and then *anglicana* meant that from the late 1200s to the late 1400s, England had a clear system of scripts in coexistence regulated by differences of speed and prestige. Scribes often had a choice of script; and the option of combining elements from more than one script. The choices among scripts are simpler to describe than the mixtures. Conventions were established in some genres for the suitability of one script or another, resulting in a perceived hierarchy between scripts. The hierarchy might be abstracted thus: *textualis*, with various grades of execution, the grandest often known as *textura*; certain 'bastard' or hybrid scripts mixing features of *textualis* with other scripts to form bastard *anglicana* or bastard secretary; a more effortful kind of *anglicana*, known as *anglicana formata*, which often seems a distinct script of its own; and two fully cursive scripts – *anglicana* and, from the 1370s onwards, secretary. The hierarchy is immediately visible when more than one script is used on the page, with one in the more prominent position of headings or for more prestigious passages, such as quotations from Latin authorities within vernacular works; then those prominent or prestigious words are often in a script higher in the hierarchy. The conventional hierarchy of script, however, was not a fixed one, and texts could climb up and down it. For instance, elaborately statuesque or calligraphic styles of *textualis* were conventional for Latin liturgical and paraliturgical books such as Psalters, often visibly the work of a highly trained scribe working in an orderly system with the collaboration of skilled painters or limners. Yet it was, of course, possible to use a lower grade of script, say, to copy a liturgical calendar in *anglicana*. Such surprising appearances were often brought about by limitations in the training of the scribe. Striking examples are additions to Books of Hours by later users or readers, which are seldom modelled on the *textualis* used for the Book of Hours itself but on a cursive script, hurried in execution, sometimes with problems in orthography and layout.[37]

As well as choosing among scripts, scribes could also modify and mix the scripts they employed. The people copying books at this time increasingly often worked outside orderly establishments which would encourage a homogenizing style, such as religious houses. Monastic production did continue but was less predominant as a share of book production, and even within religious orders, many members made books for their own use.[38] Elsewhere, many laypeople made books for money 'freelance' in urban communities of artisans who might collaborate in ad hoc ways.[39] The fifteenth century in particular saw many people copying books for themselves as so-called 'amateurs': although, being trained to write for professional purposes, such as law or administration, they need not be amateurish; they just were not as well trained to make books for payment for other people.[40] Those who primarily earned their living as scribes might be encouraged to experiment or excel while impressing clients, following fashion, or, in the late 1400s, outdoing print.[41] All these contexts for making books might license or even encourage scribes not only to choose a script carefully from a rich tradition but also to rework the traditions they inherit.

Some of this creativity can be seen in the *textualis* used in fourteenth- and fifteenth-century England. The specimens of this script can be difficult to date, due to slowness in shifts of fashion, and different scribes' contributions can be hard to distinguish. It is possible, though, to discern a variety of calligraphic styles that flourish in the 1300s and 1400s in England. The vertical strokes of *textualis* of the 1200s often have a slight curving or tapering and were spindly at the ends, but in the 1300s the strokes become broader and straighter, making the letters increasingly statuesque, especially in liturgical books, and there was a tendency in the late 1300s and 1400s for the script to become increasingly calligraphic. Scribes might have been encouraged to elaborate this script by analogous changes in the styles of other arts, such as the floridity of ecclesiastical Latin, the aureate English literary style of the fifteenth century, or even by other cultural practices, such as affective piety and funereal display. In particular, from the 1370s *textualis* became the lettering used for inscriptions in churches and on artefacts, replacing the Lombardic capitals favoured earlier. It is possible that the kinds of strokes manageable when engraving set the fashion for similar strokes in writing books.[42] The contrast between generations of *textualis* can be seen in an older Franco-Flemish copy of *Le roman d'Alexandre* from 1338 with materials added in French in England in the early 1400s and a note in English added in the later 1400s (Figure 3.1). The older French text is in *textualis* of rounded execution and with less effortful breaking of the strokes of the pen. The later English writing is more rigidly upright, so that even strokes that might be curved or diagonal (**e** or *z*-shaped so-called 'round' **r**) are formed in neat parallel verticals. Elegant hairline strokes decorate **h, l, w,** and, disambiguating it from **i,** the *z*-shaped **r.** These decorations befit a book of high quality owned, at or close to the time when this English writing was

Reading and Understanding Scripts

Figure 3.1 Oxford, Bodleian Library, MS Bodley 264, fol. 67r. Reproduced by permission of the Bodleian Library.)

added, by Richard Woodville, Earl Rivers, a person connected to the royal family.[43] Even this conventional script allowed for a display of scribal skill for a wealthy patron.

As well as being reshaped by creative effort, the choice of script is determined not only by the scribe's skill but also by the text he is copying and the page onto which he writes. Other varieties of *textualis* were attempted where the length of the text or the smallness of the page made more calligraphic handwriting too time-consuming or too spacious. Even this most prestigious script, *textualis*, had various levels of execution across the centuries. (Continental European scholarship, by calling these all Gothic *textualis* and then distinguishing them by grade, can account for these slightly less-formal varieties which scholars of English manuscripts have sometimes overlooked.[44]) The ergonomics of writing or practicality might overcome ideology. Notably, in most Bibles, whether of the complete Vulgate in Latin from the 1220s onwards, or of parts of the English Wycliffite translations of the Bible from the 1390s and beyond, the enormous number of words to be copied was often accommodated on more pages of smaller size, and these practical constraints made it tricky to adopt the smartest grades of *textualis*. Instead, the script of Bibles was often smaller to fit in the space, and rounder in formation, with less calligraphic penwork.[45] Such *textualis* was also used among Wycliffites for other writings, such as a set of sermons circulated for reading (Figure 3.2). Such script could be written more quickly than higher grades of *textualis* and looked less polished. In the sermons, letters are formed inconsistently with broken strokes or quicker rounded ones: o varying from word to word; hairline flourishes on only a few letters (such as final s on 'dedis', line 9); and decorative features such as the split top of l and h done only intermittently (compare l in 'lettris', line 10, and 'poul', line 17). But one would have to look closely for these irregularities, and overall the aspect of the page evokes a tradition of Scriptural study. Nor does this script look overpompous in these sermons which claim to be passed from hand to hand illicitly and which criticize worldly vanities.[46] Even the script at the top of the hierarchy could be adapted for practical conditions – and perhaps ideological ones.

Gothic Cursives

Conversely, the cursive script, *anglicana*, could be executed more formally. It is common in the history of script for people to take the less prestigious cursive scripts and use them for books to make them more neatly formed, and sometimes more calligraphic, as befits more important or impressive kinds of writing. Such attention to formality was identified in different grades of

Reading and Understanding Scripts

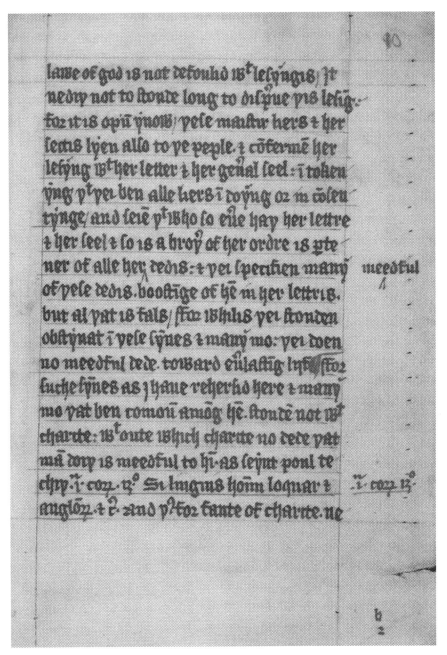

Figure 3.2 Cambridge, University Library, MS Dd.14.30, fol. 10r. Reproduced by kind permission of the Syndics of Cambridge University Library.

Insular minuscule in the previous millennium. Likewise, *anglicana* did not have the gravitas appropriate for all kinds of texts, so its current varieties were 'upgraded' to copy authoritative works in books. A more neatly formed *anglicana – anglicana formata –* was notably common for the works of authors in English, who were newly prestigious, after various subtle shifts in literary and political attitudes to the English language from the late 1300s onwards. For the works of courtly poets and learned translators, such as Geoffrey Chaucer and John Trevisa, a hurried *anglicana* might have seemed too casual but *textualis* too grand, redolent of Scripture and liturgy. What resulted was a combination of the letterforms from *anglicana* but made with the careful execution otherwise used on *textualis*. The normally current shapes of *anglicana* were mimicked by separate, definite strokes: so the loops which hastily joined the tops of letters such as **b, h,** and **l,** in the flow of *anglicana*, became instead hooks which were added to the tops deliberately. The formality is not sustained throughout; it is often more prominent in minims, the upright strokes in **i, m,** and **n,** than in more rounded letters. But by the later 1300s it settled into conventions recurrent enough that it seems like a separate script.[47] Early works copied in *anglicana* often have this *formata* execution for titles and *incipit*s or opening words, done at a larger size: the use in such prominent positions suggests the prestige of this slightly more effortful writing. But soon, throughout the 1300s and 1400s, it was used to copy whole works, including the proliferating copies in the early 1400s of Chaucer, Trevisa, and also William Langland and John Gower. One suspects that for those copying English literature around and just after 1400 the choice of *anglicana formata* as a model became conventional or was even copied from exemplars.

That identification of *anglicana formata* as a convention for certain works raises questions about how we identify and distinguish the scribes who adopted it. As was noted, the scribe's work reflects not only his or her training but also the exemplars from which the copy is made and the broader traditions in which they fall. As such, one can ask about the degree of scribal individuality evident in such copying. Some important palaeographical research has focused on identifying individual scribes of copies in *anglicana formata* of English poetry. Our knowledge of these scribes is growing richer by various suggestions and debates.[48] Others, notably Simon Horobin, have examined the kinds of evidence needed for making such identifications.[49] One remaining question, though, is *why* the scribes are so alike that it makes such identifications difficult, or unalike enough that it makes individualization possible. Their creativity inheres in part in producing books in a conventional script, sometimes even in directly copying, or only lightly modifying the layout including the script. In such imitation, would the

Reading and Understanding Scripts

scribes have wanted to be identified? In a study of monastic scribes of the first millennium, Patrick Conner noted how copyists matched their handwriting to the 'house style', so to speak, of their religious house.[50] The motives of urban scriveners or text-writers around 1400 are likely different, but their culture still held the Christian ideals of humility and communality, and perhaps there is a perennial impulse in craft to 'unselfing', sublimating one's individuality by serving the needs of tradition.[51]

Yet scribes of the 1300s and 1400s were also able to innovate by adopting or adapting new scripts. Scripts can proliferate in other ways that might seem less hierarchical, like blending *anglicana* letterforms and *textualis* execution, than horizontal. Script varied from place to place, and English script was shaped by books, scribes, and models of writing which moved freely across the seas. Early in the Gothic period, from the 1200s onwards, English script traditions moved abroad to Iceland.[52] Conversely, England and Scotland made copious use of one major cursive script, or series of related cursive scripts, from France and the Low Countries, known after its adoption in English-speaking regions as *secretary*, a name attested as early as the 1500s, by which point this script was one of the main models for writing there.

The models and antecedents for secretary would have been read in England in letters and books from French and papal territories throughout the 1300s, but the earliest records of it in English-allied milieux are the handwriting of bureaucrats governing England's territory in south-west France in the later 1300s, and then in documents made in London. It appears in books made in England datable from the 1390s and in books produced by scribes connected to the royal writing offices late in the 1300s, and such a style might sometimes reveal a scribe's training as a bureaucrat. It then spreads to books from monasteries and universities. It starts with heavier penstrokes, in features such as the tail of **g**, but by the mid-1400s it was used in a tightly curled and flattened sloping form, which suggests a faster movement across the page. At that time in the mid-1400s, some kinds of secretary enjoyed a second wave of cross-channel influence, as the formal and calligraphic styles of northern France and then the Low Countries were borrowed afresh, whether by imitation of script or by the arrival of scribes. The occasions seem to be England's failed attempt to conquer Normandy, abandoned after 1453, and the trade in books with the cities of Flanders. Some specimens of writing in English show scribes with elegant styles of secretary but some uncertain spelling for English; for instance, little grasp of English's distinctive **w**, less common in French. Style was evidently one goal, when scribes borrowed the smarter varieties of secretary from France and Flanders, as though to refresh their look, and to imitate an international courtly chic. This is evident in the work of scribes such as Ricardus Franciscus, the

67

'hooked **g**' scribes and others like them, whose letterforms were elaborate and whose page design included fanciful flourishes on letters at the edge of pages, creating decorative patterns in black on the white margins.[53] Simultaneously, secretary was used for writing Older Scots in documents from the late 1300s and books from the 1400s, and became the main script for that language into the 1500s.[54] Scotland's variety of secretary developed its own distinctive characteristics. The use of secretary script, in its various forms, exemplifies the energizing influence on script of social trends: war, but also the free exchange of paperwork, people, trade, literature, and fashion. It is an index of the role of the British Isles in a shared European culture and economy, of their international political ambitions, and of their internal political divisions.

It is not clear whether the scribes and readers themselves were always interested in secretary script for its origins overseas, in a form of cultural emulation. The use of secretary was not as obviously programmatic a change as were the introduction of uncial or Caroline minuscule. Older textbooks before the influence of Parkes's work do not identify secretary as a separate script but describe instead a 'reform' in documentary handwriting in the late 1300s; a change in execution with more broken strokes for a more calligraphic look.[55] That older description might capture the perspective of many scribes and their readers: for people who took literary, artistic, and political models from other countries unselfconsciously, it might not have been seen as a distinct genre with 'foreign' cultural cachet, but as a chance to diversify one's practice in more individualistic, *sui generis* ways. After all, as people adopted secretary for documents and books of scholarly or literary sorts, they used it interchangeably with England's distinctive script *anglicana*. One example is a copy of John Gower's *Confessio amantis* from the early 1400s, in Cambridge, Trinity College, MS R. 3. 2, in which several widely attested scribes collaborate, some in *anglicana formata*, some in secretary. Other copies of English poetry continued to be made collaboratively by scribes using both *anglicana* and secretary, as in Oxford, Bodleian Library, MS Rawl. Poet. 163. Moreover, scribes could adopt letterforms from one script into the other. For instance, some scribes of secretary in the early 1400s still use *anglicana*'s longer **r**. Conversely, from as early as the 1380s but of greater longevity is the tendency of scribes of *anglicana* to borrow secretary's **a** with one compartment, presumably because it was simpler to write than *anglicana*'s **a** with two compartments. Likewise, from the outset and especially later in the 1400s, many scribes made more thorough mixes between *anglicana* and secretary scripts. In the unpredictable mixtures and experiments of fifteenth-century scribes, each instance of handwriting tells a story of competing influences, ambitions, and constraints.

The mixing and adapting of scripts in these centuries raises the question of how far people perceived distinctions between scripts, and if they did, whether those distinctions were seen to inhere in distinct repertoires of letterforms or in modes of execution, or perhaps in other features such as the styles of page layout which certain scripts tended to accompany. Vexingly, people seldom left written comment on this, so much of their understanding must be deduced, by wary interpretation, from their practice. Most striking are moments when one scribe attempts to continue the work of another, and we might infer the second scribe's response to an earlier scribe's work in his or her choice of script. Often, scribes left blank space for passages which were missing or indecipherable in their exemplars, and others filled the gaps.[56] Often those later people wrote in disregard of the original script, as in Cambridge, University Library MS Ii. 3. 26, but others tried to imitate features of it, as though they recognized what made it different. This could be unconscious, like the socio-linguistic phenomenon of 'assimilation', in which speakers slowly adopt the dialect of the their interlocutors; but it could be more conscious mimicry, perhaps to conceal the 'join'. That seems likely in some additions to a copy of Chaucer's poems in writing modelled on *anglicana formata* from the first quarter of the 1400s (Figure 3.3). The third of the four stanzas on the page is added by a second hand. In that added stanza, there are a few features typical of secretary script of the mid-1400s: the simpler **w** (except in the first word 'Nowe'), the open tail of **g**, the single-compartment **a** once only (in the short word 'a' in line 17). Moreover, there is a pervasive slope in **f** and **s**, a subtler feature of secretary script that a copyist might not even have recognized as typical of his work. These few clues suggest that the scribe of this added stanza was more accustomed to secretary script. But in much of the added stanza, he tried to mimic the letterforms of *anglicana formata*. It often looks as though he is trying too hard: while in *anglicana formata* there are hooks on the ascending strokes on **b, h, k,** and **l,** here those hooks are added ineptly, often not attached to the ascender, or are overly large. There is also 'biting' or overlapping between **d** and **e,** which in fact is not typical of *anglicana formata* but of the *textualis* script which influenced it. The imperfection and effort suggest that a scribe trained in secretary script is self-consciously trying to mimic another style.

The lines added are a roundel set to a tune 'makid' or composed in France sung by the birds in Chaucer's *The Parliament of Fowls* as they settle their discordant parliamentary debate. Hitherto, they have spoken at cross-purposes, some aristocratic birds in Frenchified courtly tones and some lowly ones in earthy vernacular slang, but at the end they sing together in harmony: 'By euene a cord'. The poem might serve us as a mnemonic for the complex script worlds of the British Isles across this millennium. Writing,

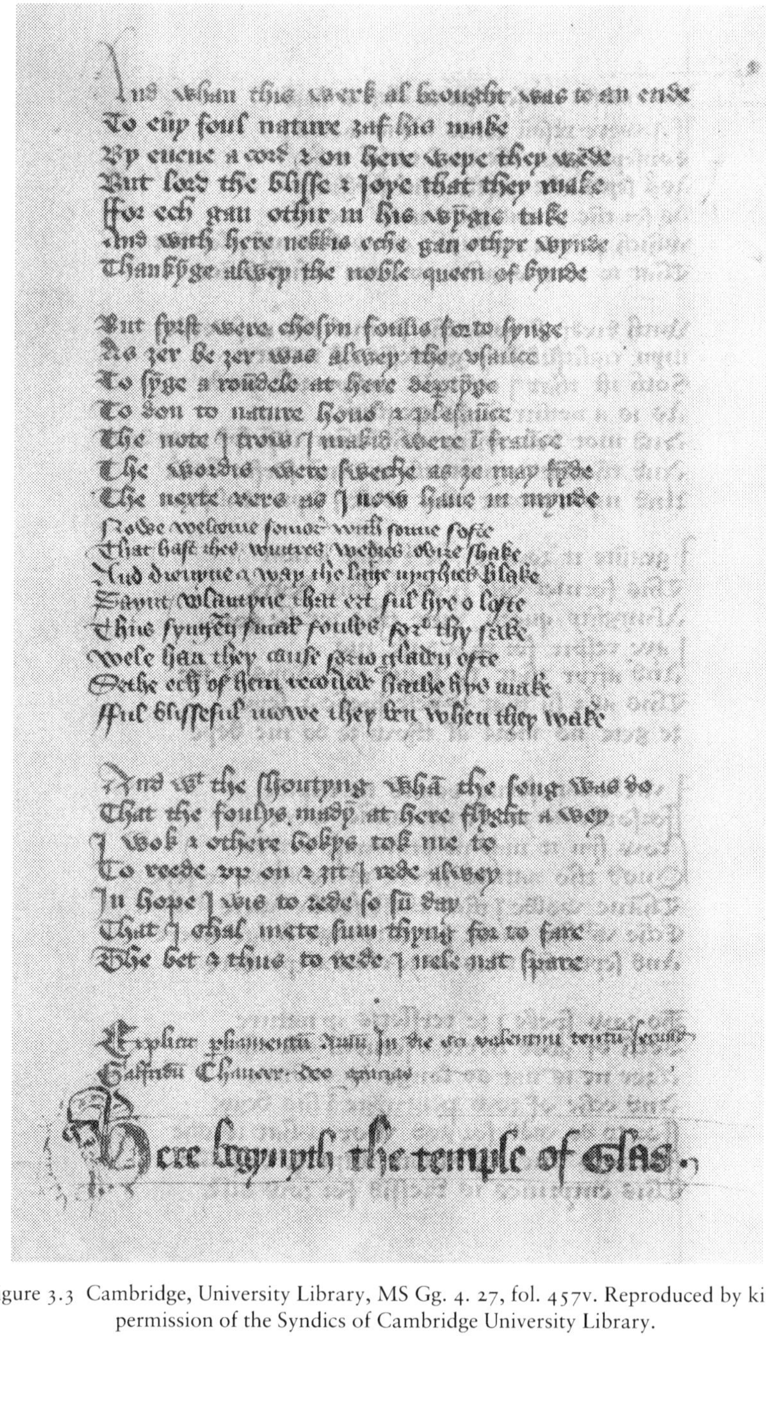

JULIA CRICK AND DANIEL WAKELIN

Figure 3.3 Cambridge, University Library, MS Gg. 4. 27, fol. 457v. Reproduced by kind permission of the Syndics of Cambridge University Library.

Reading and Understanding Scripts

like these birds' words, conveyed social origins or social pretensions, betrayed both trans-European influences and local styles, differentiated people, and saw people seek to subordinate their identity to communal communication. These are only some of the vectors along which script was ranged, and the exact placement of each script, let alone particular books, along those vectors, or others, remains to be better understood. Palaeography is an under-researched field, only now being opened for all to study by the digitization of manuscripts. Like Chaucer's narrator at the end of *The Parliament of Fowls*, we still have lots to learn from 'othere bokys' about the script of the British Isles: '*and ʒit* I rede alwey'.

Notes

1. M. B. Parkes, *Their Hands before Our Eyes: A Closer Look at Scribes* (Aldershot: Ashgate, 2008), 57–69.
2. See C. Sirat, *Writing as Handwork: A History of Handwriting in Mediterranean and Western Culture* (Turnhout: Brepols, 2006); J. Mallon, *De l'écriture: recueil d'études publiées de 1937 à 1981* (Paris: Éditions du Centre national de la recherche scientifique, 1986); S. Morison, *Politics and Script: Aspects of Authority and Freedom in the Development of Graeco-Latin Script from the Sixth Century BC*, ed. N. Barker (Oxford: Clarendon Press, 1972); A. Petrucci, *Public Lettering: Script, Power and Writing*, trans. L. Lappin (Chicago: University of Chicago Press, 1993); Parkes, *Their Hands before Our Eyes*.
3. See Sirat, *Writing*; E. Clayton, 'Workplaces for Writing', in M. Gullick, ed., *Pen in Hand: Medieval Scribal Portraits, Colophons and Tools* (Walkern: Red Gull Press, 2006), 1–17.
4. Oxford, Bodleian Library, MS e Musaeo 198*, discussed by S. J. P. Van Dijk, 'An Advertisement Sheet of an Early Fourteenth-century Writing Master at Oxford', *Scriptorium*, 10 (1956), 47–64.
5. See Oxford, Bodleian Library, MS Digby 26, fols. 6v, 64v, 139r, described by D. Thomson, *A Descriptive Catalogue of Middle English Grammatical Texts* (New York: Garland, 1979), 268–76.
6. D. Ganz, 'Risk and Fluidity in Script: An Insular Instance', in P. R. Robinson, ed., *Teaching Writing, Learning to Write* (London: King's College London Centre for Late Antique & Medieval Studies, 2010), 17–23, at 18; M. T. Hussey, 'Anglo-Saxon Scribal *Habitus* and Frankish Aesthetics in an Early Uncial Manuscript', in J. Wilcox, ed., *Scraped, Stroked and Bound: Materially Engaged Readings of Medieval Manuscripts* (Turnhout: Brepols, 2013), 15–37, at 15–16, 31; D. Wakelin, *Scribal Correction and Literary Craft: English Manuscripts 1375–1510* (Cambridge: Cambridge University Press, 2014), 63–4, 97, 101, 123, 127, 156.
7. F. Sobieroj, 'Arabic Manuscripts on the Periphery: Northwest Africa, Yemen and China', in J. B. Quenzer, S. Bondarev, and J. U. Sobisch, eds., *Manuscript Cultures: Mapping the Field*, Studies in Manuscript Cultures, 1 (Berlin: De Gruyter, 2014), 79–112; D. Bondarev, 'Multiglossia in West African

Manuscripts: The Case of Borno, Nigeria', in Quenzer et al., eds., *Manuscript Cultures*, 113–55.

8. J. Crick, 'Historical Literacy in the Archive: Post-Conquest Imitative Copies of Pre-Conquest Charters and Some French Comparanda', in M. Brett and D. A. Woodman, eds., *The Long Twelfth-Century View of the Anglo-Saxon Past* (London: Routledge, 2015), 159–90.

9. M. Richter, *The Formation of the Medieval West: Studies in the Oral Culture of the Barbarians* (Dublin: Four Courts Press, 1994); T. O. Clancy, 'Gaelic Literature in Ireland and Scotland, 900–1500', in C. A. Lees, ed., *The Cambridge History of Early Medieval Literature* (Cambridge: Cambridge University Press, 2013), 637–59.

10. R. McKitterick, 'Exchanges between the British Isles and the Continent, c.450–c.900', in R. Gameson, ed., *The Cambridge History of the Book in Britain, vol. I: c.400–1100* (Cambridge: Cambridge University Press, 2012), 317–37; R. Gameson, 'The Circulation of Books between England and the Continent, c.871–c.1100', in Gameson, ed., *The Cambridge History of the Book*, 344–72.

11. Rustic and Square capitals, uncials; half-uncial; hybrid, set and cursive grades of minuscule; Square minuscule; Insular minuscule; Anglo-Caroline; and Anglo-Norman Caroline minuscule.

12. M. Lapidge, 'The Archetype of *Beowulf*', *Anglo-Saxon England*, 29 (2000), 5–41.

13. E. A. Lowe, *The Beneventan Script: A History of the South Italian Minuscule* (Oxford: Clarendon Press, 1914), 140–8.

14. J. Bately et al., eds., *A Palaeographer's View: The Selected Writings of Julian Brown* (London: Harvey Miller, 1993); D. N. Dumville, *A Palaeographer's Review: The Insular System of Scripts in the Early Middle Ages*, vol. 1 (Osaka: Institute of Oriental and Occidental Studies, Kansai University, 1999); W. O'Sullivan, 'Insular Calligraphy: Current State and Problems', *Peritia*, 4 (1985), 346–59.

15. Bede, *Historia Ecclesiastica*, I, xvii, xxix, xxix, xxxi.

16. J. Crick, 'The Art of Writing: Scripts and Scribal Production' in C. A. Lees, ed., *The Cambridge History of Early Medieval Literature* (Cambridge: Cambridge University Press, 2013), 50–72.

17. A. Orchard, 'Latin and the Vernacular Languages: The Creation of a Bilingual Textual Culture, in T. Charles-Edwards, ed., *Britain after Rome* (Oxford: Oxford University Press, 2003), 191–219; J. M. H. Smith, 'Writing in Britain and Ireland, c. 400 to c. 800', in C. Lees, ed., *The Cambridge History of Early Medieval Literature*, 19–49.

18. T. O'Neill, *The Irish Hand: Scribes and Their Manuscripts from the Earliest Times* (Cork: Cork University Press, 2014); J. Roberts, *Guide to Scripts Used in English Writings up to 1500* (London: British Library, 2005), 104–7, 140–3.

19. R. S. O. Tomlin, 'The Book in Roman Britain', in Gameson, ed., *The Cambridge History of the Book*, 375–88.

20. C. Tedeschi, 'Some Observations on the Palaeography of Early Christian Inscriptions in Britain', in J. Higgitt et al., eds., *Roman, Runes and Ogham:*

Medieval Inscriptions in the Insular World and on the Continent (Donington: Shaun Tyas, 2001), 16–25.

21. L. Webster, 'Encrypted Visions: Style and Sense in the Anglo-Saxon Minor Arts A.D. 400-900', in G. Hardin Brown and C. E. Karkov, eds., *Anglo-Saxon Styles* (Albany, NY: State University of New York, 2003), 11–30.

22. McKitterick, 'Exchanges'; M. B. Parkes, *Scribes, Scripts and Readers: Studies in the Communication, Presentation and Dissemination of Medieval Texts* (London, 1991), 93–120.

23. E. A. Lowe, *English Uncial* (Oxford: Clarendon Press, 1960); R. Gameson, *The Earliest Books in Canterbury Cathedral* (London: The Bibliographical Society and The British Library, in association with the Dean and Chapter of Canterbury, 2008); C. Breay and J. Story, eds., *Anglo-Saxon Kingdoms: Art, Word, War* (London: British Library, 2018), nos. 19, 21, 32, 33, 38, 122.

24. E. A. Lowe, 'A Key to Bede's Scriptorium: Some Observations on the Leningrad Manuscript of the *Historia Ecclesiastica gentis Anglorum*', in *Palaeographical Papers, 1907–1965*, ed. L. Bieler, 2 vols. (Oxford: Clarendon Press, 1972), II, 441–9; Parkes, *Scribes, Scripts and Readers*, 259–62.

25. J. Bately, M. Brown and J. Roberts, eds., *A Palaeographer's View: The Selected Writings of Julian Brown* (London: Harvey Miller, 1993), 201–20.

26. See, for example, The Book of Cerne in Breay and Story, eds., *Anglo-Saxon Kingdoms*, no. 53; The Book of Armagh: Dublin, Trinity College, MS 52.

27. Breay and Story, eds., *Anglo-Saxon Kingdoms*, nos. 52, 55.

28. M. P. Brown, 'House Style in the Scriptorium, Scribal Reality and Scholarly Myth', in Brown and Karkov, eds., *Anglo-Saxon Styles*, 131–50, at 146.

29. T. A. M. Bishop, *English Caroline Minuscule* (Oxford: Clarendon Press, 1970); D. N. Dumville, *English Caroline Script and Monastic History: Studies in Benedictinism, AD 950–1030* (Woodbridge: Boydell Press, 1993); T. Webber, 'The Norman Conquest and handwriting in England to 1100', in Gameson, ed., *The Cambridge History of the Book*, 211–24, and 'English Manuscripts in the Century after the Norman Conquest: Continuity and Change in the Palaeography of Books and Book Collections', in E. Kwakkel, ed., *Writing in Context. Insular Manuscript Culture, 500–1200* (Leiden: Leiden University Press, 2013), 185–230.

30. P. A. Stokes, *English Vernacular Minuscule from Æthelred to Cnut, circa 990–circa 1035* (Cambridge: Cambridge University Press, 2014) and 'The Problem of Grade in English Vernacular Minuscule, c. 1060 to 1220', *New Medieval Literatures*, 13 (2011), 23–47; J. Crick, 'English Vernacular script', in Gameson, ed., *The Cambridge History of the Book*, 174–86; E. Treharne, 'The Production and Script of Manuscripts Containing English Religious Texts in the First Half of the Twelfth Century', in M. Swan and E. M. Treharne, eds., *Rewriting Old English in the Twelfth Century* (Cambridge: Cambridge University Press, 2000), 11–40.

31. T. M. Charles-Edwards, 'The Use of the Book in Wales, c. 400–1100', in R. Gameson, ed., *The Cambridge History of the Book in Britain, vol. I: c.400–1100* (Cambridge: Cambridge University Press, 2012), 389–405; Helen McKee, 'The Circulation of Books between England and the Celtic Realms', in Gameson, ed., *The Cambridge History of the Book*, 338–43.

32. W. M. Lindsay, *Early Welsh Script* (Oxford: St Andrews, 1912); E. Duncan, *A History of Gaelic Script* (unpublished PhD thesis, University of Aberdeen, 2010).

33. E. Kwakkel, 'Biting, Kissing and the Treatment of Feet: The Transitional Script of the Long Twelfth Century', in E. Kwakkel, R. McKitterick, and R. M. Thomson, eds., *Turning over a New Leaf: Change and Development in the Med. MS* (Leiden: Leiden University Press, 2012), 79–125, at 103–4.

34. Parkes, *Their Hands before Our Eyes*, 103; M. B. Parkes, 'Handwriting in English Books', in N. Morgan and R. M. Thomson, eds., *The Cambridge History of the Book in Britain. Vol. II: 1100–1400* (Cambridge: Cambridge University Press, 2008), 110–35, at 120–1.

35. M. B. Parkes, *English Cursive Book Hands 1250–1500* (Oxford: Clarendon Press, 1969), xiv–xvi, xxii; Parkes, *Their Hands before Our Eyes*, 106–12; 'Parkes, The Literacy of the Laity', 1973, reprinted in *Scribes, Scripts and Readers*, 274–97.

36. E. Kwakkel, 'A New Type of Book for a New Type of Reader: The Emergence of Paper in Vernacular Book Production', *Library*, 7th ser., 4 (2003), 219–48. See now Orietta Da Rold, *Paper in Medieval England: From Pulp to Fictions* (Cambridge: Cambridge University Press, 2020).

37. E. Duffy, *Marking the Hours: English People and Their Prayers 1240–1570* (New Haven: Yale University Press, 2006).

38. A. I. Doyle, 'Book Production by the Monastic Orders in England (c.1375–1530): Assessing the Evidence', in L. L. Brownrigg, ed., *Medieval Book Production: Assessing the Evidence* (Los Altos Hills, CA: Anderson-Lovelace, 1990), 1–19.

39. See L. R. Mooney and E. Stubbs, *Scribes and the City: London Guildhall Clerks and the Dissemination of Middle English Literature, 1375–1425* (York: York Medieval Press, 2013); L. Warner, *Chaucer's Scribes: London Textual Production 1384–1432* (Cambridge: Cambridge University Press, 2018).

40. C. M. Meale, 'Amateur Book Production and the Miscellany in Late Medieval East Anglia: Tanner 407 and Beinecke 365', in M. Connolly and R. Radulescu, eds., *Insular Books: Vernacular Miscellanies in Late Medieval Britain* (Oxford: Oxford University Press, 2016), 157–73, 158–9.

41. D. Rundle, *The Renaissance Reform of the Book and Britain: The English Quattrocentro* (Cambridge: Cambridge University Press, 2019).

42. S. Morison, *'Black-Letter' Text* (Cambridge: Cambridge University Press, 1942), 27. See *DDCL* II. 183 (1397–1413).

43. See *DDOL* II, 178, the facsimile of Loreta Lucchetti, M. I. Pesce and B. C. Barker-Benfield, eds., *Il manoscritto Bodley 264: Il Romanzo di Alessandro, I Viaggi di Marco Polo: saggi e commenti* (Rome: Treccani, 2014); O. Khalaf, ed., *Alexander and Dindimus* (Heidelberg: Universitätsverlag Winter, 2017); https://digital.bodleian.ox.ac.uk/inquire/p/90701d49-5e0c-4fb5-9c7d-45af96565468 (accessed 29 November 2018).

44. J. P. Gumbert, 'A Proposal for a Cartesian Nomenclature', in J. P. Gumbert and M. J. M. de Haan, eds., *Essays Presented to G.I. Lieftinck*, 4 vols. (Amsterdam: Van Gendt, 1972–80), IV, 45–52.

45. C. Ruzzier, 'The Miniaturisation of Bible Manuscripts in the Thirteenth Century: A Comparative Study', in E. Poleg and L. Light, eds., *Form and Function in the*

Late Medieval Bible (Leiden: Brill, 2013), 105–26, at 108; R. Hanna, 'The Palaeography of the Wycliffite Bibles in Oxford', in E. Solopova, ed., *The Wycliffite Bible: Origin, History and Interpretation* (Leiden: Brill, 2017), 246–65; E. Solopova, *Manuscripts of the Wycliffite Bible in the Bodleian and Oxford College Libraries* (Liverpool: Liverpool University Press, 2016), 25, 296, e.g., *DDOL* 258 (1408).

46. A. Hudson, ed., *The Works of a Lollard Preacher*, EETS os 317 (Oxford: Oxford University Press, 2001).

47. But see the contrasting explanation by A. Derolez, *The Handwriting of Gothic Manuscript Books* (Cambridge: Cambridge University Press, 2003), 138, 140.

48. A. I. Doyle and M. B. Parkes, 'The Production of Copies of the *Canterbury Tales* and the *Confessio Amantis* in the Early Fifteenth Century', in M. B. Parkes and A. G. Watson, eds., *Medieval Scribes, Manuscripts and Libraries: Essays Presented to N.R. Ker* (London: Scholar Press, 1978), 163–210; Mooney and Stubbs, *Scribes and the City*; Warner, *Chaucer's Scribes*; and L. R. Mooney, S. Horobin, and E. Stubbs, *Late Medieval English Scribes*, www.medievalscribes.com (accessed 13 November 2016).

49. S. Horobin, 'The Criteria for Scribal Attribution: Trinity College Dublin MS 244 Reconsidered', *Review of English Studies*, 60 (2009), 371–81.

50. P. W. Conner, 'On the Nature of Matched Scribal Hands', in J. Wilcox, ed., *Scraped, Stroked and Bound: Materially Engaged Readings of Medieval Manuscripts* (Turnhout: Brepols, 2013), 39–73, at 45–8.

51. M. B. Crawford, *The Case for Working with Your Hands* (London: Viking, 2009), 63–5, 82, 99–100, 206–7.

52. G. Sigurðsson and V. Ólason, *Manuscripts of Iceland* (Reykjavík: Árni Magnússon Institute in Iceland, 2004); H. Bernharðsson, 'Scribal Culture in Thirteenth-Century Iceland: The Introduction of Anglo-Saxon "f" in Icelandic Script', *Journal of English and Germanic Philology*, 117 (2018), 279–314.

53. M. Driver, '"Me fault faire": French Makers of Manuscripts for English Patrons', in J. Wogan-Browne et al., eds., *Language and Culture in Medieval Britain: The French of England c.1100–c.1500* (York: York Medieval Press, 2009), 420–43; D. W. Mosser and L. R. Mooney, 'The Case of the Hooked-g Scribe(s) and the Production of Middle English Literature, c.1460–c.1490', *Chaucer Review*, 51 (2016), 131–50.

54. See specimens in G. G. Simpson, *Scottish Handwriting 1150–1650: An Introduction to the Reading of Documents* (Edinburgh: Tuckwell Press, 1973), nos. 8–17.

55. L. C. Hector, *The Handwriting of English Documents* (London: E. Arnold, 1958), 58.

56. D. Wakelin, 'When Scribes Won't Write: Gaps in Middle English Books', *Studies in the Age of Chaucer*, 36 (2014), 249–78.

4

BEATRICE KITZINGER

Working with Images in Manuscripts

Manuscripts brightened with colours and metals and fitted with images, embellished borders, or elaborated initials are often called 'illuminated manuscripts' – a description that derives from medieval terminology for decorated books (attested, for instance, in Chaucer). Painting and drawing form major components of manuscripts made throughout the Middle Ages. Indeed, manuscripts stage some of the finest and most inventive drawing and painting executed in the medieval period. I will describe here several paths by which to approach images and decoration within the manuscript medium. I have founded this chapter on two reciprocal premises: 1) images (and decoration generally) represent production choices that make a real difference to the character of the manuscripts that incorporate them; and 2) their execution within a manuscript makes a real difference to the character of images and decoration. The essential principle is that of symbiosis between artworks and their book contexts. Consideration of a manuscript's composition and its full contents affects the way we can interpret an image that appears within that book. While it is often fruitful to examine images in manuscripts according to research questions and methods that hold for artworks in other media (such as wall painting, embroidery, enamel, or metalwork), we gain a great deal by thinking of physical context as an integral component of how any given picture works. Conversely, the presence of images affects the way we understand a manuscript – its history, its design, and its affect. In this light, art history and book history constitute two overlapping circles of a Venn diagram – their meeting point found in the individual nature of any particular illuminated manuscript.

I aim to introduce and demonstrate lines of enquiry that may usefully be deployed in studying manuscript images across book genres and centuries. However, because my real concern here is method, I have pared to a minimum the number of variables in matters such as manuscript type and chronology: this chapter does not represent a general introduction to book painting in medieval Britain (the Further Reading suggestions at the end of this volume offers some alternatives). Following a brief treatment of some key themes in the material technique and production of manuscript decoration, I have built the discussion around one psalter painted in eleventh-century England. The psalter is an especially prominent site of painting in medieval books, and this period saw great variety and invention in the way that such psalter illumination was conceived, especially in the British Isles. Holding to one manuscript genre allows us efficiently to gauge distinctions in how illumination makes a difference to manuscripts, and how book-type itself makes a difference to the way we understand illumination. Focusing on one manuscript allows us to derive from a specific example major avenues of investigation in approaching decorated books more generally.

Material Considerations

Relative to a manuscript that includes text alone, the incorporation of images and decoration calls upon different skills in the people producing the book, and often introduces additional physical materials as well. The many possible permutations of divided labour and varying materials in distinct components of a manuscript correspond to the many different stories of production that surviving medieval books can represent. We have cases in which scribe and illuminator (whether painter or draftsperson) were clearly one and the same, and other cases in which they clearly were distinct people, sometimes of different gender, geographic origin, or social position (e.g., ecclesiastic or lay, monastic or commercial). We also have cases in which it is very hard to tell. Illuminators could work in teams, and a programme may also have been carried out in multiple stages over time. Sometimes, no inks were used for images and decoration beyond those also used for writing and rubricating, and sometimes the programme of illumination displays different colours from the text, also perhaps employing a different 'medium' (liquid base) for the pigments used to make the paint. Colours may have been derived from expensive imported mineral pigments, readily available local organic pigments, or any permutation of these categories. Gold, silver, lead, or tin may have been employed as the background for images, for the body of major initial letters, or for highlights in other patterns; these metals may have been applied as paint or as foil, burnished or left matte, tooled or left smooth. Images were sometimes rendered on membrane ruled for text, membrane was sometimes ruled for both text and images, and images were sometimes produced on specially prepared membrane – including sheets worked entirely separately from the text quires and 'tipped in' when the manuscript was bound. All these variations should be weighed when assessing a decorative programme and how it gives evidence for the history of a manuscript.

To study the materials and techniques employed in manuscript decoration may become a concatenation of people, skills, and technology in and of itself, depending on the kind of information one wishes to gather and the resources that are available to do so. Ultraviolet lamps that permit greater visibility of underdrawing (the sketch or detailed plan of a picture beneath the paint surface) are a common technology. Raman microscopes that can precision-measure pigment composition, are, at present, rarely available to many researchers, but can yield invaluable data when they are. It is a fact of modern scholarship that the study of images and decoration in manuscripts is often heavily dependent on surrogate technology – primarily photographic repro-duction, whether digital or film, made available through print publication, distribution by CD, microfilm, or the internet. Illuminated manuscripts are held in repositories all over the world, and, often for conservation reasons, they generally are not made widely available for direct study. Many famous illuminated manuscripts have been reproduced in physical facsimiles that can replicate through photography and printing the originals' codex form, size, colour values, modifications to pages (including holes and tears), and some-times even their use of reflective metal. Digital facsimiles of manuscripts have increasingly been published on repositories' websites, or in digital libraries that draw across collections. Some sites represent entire manuscripts; others represent selections. At the time of writing, digital access to illuminated manuscripts is growing by the week.

Physical and digital surrogates are invaluable for making singular manu-scripts better known and making fragile books accessible, and as sources in addressing a wide variety of research questions. At the same time, a great deal of information resides in material qualities of manuscript painting that photography cannot necessarily capture. One could never be sure about the chemistry of a manuscript's pigments, for example, without direct analysis. It can be difficult to make assertions from surrogates about aspects of painting technique such as the layering of colours, metal application, or the presence of underdrawing. The angle of photography can affect a viewer's impression of aspects such as colour and metal quality, or the use of tools that cut into membrane. On the other hand, technology such as photomicroscopy can reveal – and allow the demonstration of – physical details in painting that are not always evident to the eye alone.

All in all, it is worth noting that when considering questions of visual affect and makers' intentions in the original design of manuscripts, it is crucial to take material possibilities and limitations into account – particularly as these intersect directly with issues of social and economic history in manuscript production. Similarly, in designing research projects, it is worth evaluating the kind of information about manuscript sources that might be available or potentially available, and assessing the kinds of arguments this information might best support.

Images and Manuscripts

In the following sections, I shall focus on the illuminations of a single psalter manuscript, the 'Arundel Psalter' (London, British Library, Arundel MS 60), which was made in Winchester in the last quarter of the eleventh century (more precisely, probably *c.* 1073).[1] The medieval psalter contains, indispensably, the 150 psalms, which were traditionally attributed to the biblical King David. The most common addition to the core texts was a calendar, often marked with saints' days that may reflect local priorities, and sometimes also made the site of owners' interventions by recording the deaths of people important to their community. Many psalters were privately owned, and made at a scale that suggests individual use, but it is worth noting that devotion based around the psalms reflects the daily monastic prayer office, and that the psalms also played an essential role in more public liturgical rites. As a genre, then, even a psalter clearly conceived for personal ownership represents a kind of amalgam of the public and individualized faces of medieval Christian practice.

I shall take several tacks in surveying how one might work with the fine images that form an integral part of the Arundel Psalter. Certain issues are presented by the images if we view them primarily as pictorial compositions, isolating them from their role within the manuscript. New possibilities of interpretation open when we examine the place of the images within the immediate context of the book in which they appear, and still other kinds of questions arise when we widen the context of analysis to assess the place of a particular manuscript within categories as broad as book history, art history, religious history, cultural history, and beyond.

Images as Compositions

Any picture, whether made for a manuscript or for an entirely different medium, has a set of internal characteristics that can be differentiated and studied. These include the contents of the picture, how the elements of its content are disposed, the choices that have been made in how to render form, and the techniques that have been employed in constituting and working with the materials used. The Arundel Psalter contains two pictures of Christ on the cross ('Crucifixions') that stage a study in compositional contrasts and will be the grounds on which we work through several categories of components that constitute a manuscript image (see Figures 4.1 and 4.2; refer to colour reproductions on the British Library website).

One primary categorical distinction differentiates between compositions that are figural (in which category I include animals as well as people or things) and compositions that are not. The latter might be composed of recognizably vegetal forms, or of purely geometric patterns. Non-figural compositions are often called 'ornamental' – a designation that derives in some cases from a combination of content and placement (e.g., a geometric pattern in a bordering position).

The sides of the frame for the second Crucifixion in the Arundel Psalter (Figure 4.2) display this kind of ornament. Patterns of ornament have been given their own formal taxonomies and afforded great importance in proposing geographic and chronological groupings of manuscripts (the forms of the stylized leaves that wrap around one another and the armature of the frame, for example, provide a factor in the Arundel Psalter's localization to Winchester). Traditionally, ornament has been considered separately from figural compositions in studies that focus on 'reading' images in the light of contemporaneous cultural history. Recent approaches to early British and Irish illumination in particular, though, have emphasized the importance of not excluding ornament from analyses devoted to the representational aspects of visual programme in manuscripts. It is possible to seek out relationships between the figural and non-figural elements of pictorial composition, or even place ornament in the foreground when assessing the give-and-take between illumination and bodies of knowledge (such as theology) or investigation into the cultural experience of manuscripts.

A discussion of content in a picture weighs the identification of its subjects together with how they are depicted. This combination forms the picture's 'iconography'. The designation of common subjects for images gives rise to named types, such as Crucifixions. In the Arundel Psalter, the two Crucifixions were designed with different iconography and page compositions, which results in several substantive distinctions in how the same image type may be understood.

To begin by gathering distinctive details: both images depict a dead Christ nailed to the cross. In the first rendering (Figure 4.1), Christ's body stands straight and strong against the cross; only his closed eyes and bent head indicate that he has died. In the second image (Figure 4.2), the slumped knees and drooping thumbs compound the representation of death. In the first image Christ wears a coronet and a double-pointed beard, with his hair curling down his left shoulder. In the second picture his hands, feet, and side wound stream blood, his beard is cropped close and his hair falls to both sides of his head. Both Christs wear elaborately patterned loincloths; the cloth of the first falls rigid and straight with a V-shaped fold at the waistband, while the cloth of the second follows the bend of Christ's legs and is knotted at the right hip.

If we work out from the figure of Christ at the centre – the figure that guarantees a common type between the two pictures – the elements of pictorial content particular to one image or the other multiply further. In the first image, the cross appears as a green tree with lopped branches, planted in a strip of ground with three swellings. Above Christ's head, the Hand of God reaches down from a cloudbank. Personifications of the Sun and the Moon, labelled in Latin as *Sol* and *Luna*, flank the upper arm of the cross. Only their heads and necks are visible in the roundels, flames top their heads and Luna wears a green head covering. Beneath the transverse, the Virgin Mary stands to the proper right of the cross, and John the Evangelist to the proper left, with no ground beneath their feet. Both hold books and gesture to the centre; both are labelled with their names above their heads. In the second image, the cross appears in blue, bordered in red with white-highlighted coffers, shaped with straight sides and flared terminals, planted in a large sloping mound made up of multicoloured rounded segments. Two large trees flank the cross, both springing from the same ground. The corners of the ornamental border consist of roundels in which appear the symbols of the four evangelists, authors of the gospels: clockwise from the upper left, Matthew is represented by an angel, John by an eagle, Luke by a bull, and Mark by a lion. Matthew and John carry scrolls; Mark and Luke bear jewelled books. By contrast to the figural frame of the second Crucifixion, the first Crucifixion is framed with two sets of spare, meticulously drawn, rectangles, one red and one blue, which echo two of the three dominant colours in the drawing and firmly delineate the boundary of the scene. The more elaborate frame similarly encompasses all the figural elements within, with one exception: the upper terminal of the cross overlaps the inner border of the frame

Each detail I described represents a choice that was made in the design of these two images, determining how the scene would be represented. I shall return throughout the chapter to the question of what might be done with these individual pictorial elements and the distinctions between the two Crucifixions, but before that I will stay a little longer with the process of close looking and description, in order to bring the separate elements of form and technique into play.

In cataloguing the contents of the images, I have focused so far on *what* is represented. By attending to issues such as the position of figures relative to one another, or matters of colour and posture, I have actually already begun

Figure 4.1 Crucifixion, psalter with canticles and litanies, and additional texts (the 'Arundel Psalter'). Probably Winchester, fourth quarter of the eleventh century (c 1073) with twelfth-century additions. 320 × 220 mm. London, British Library, Arundel MS 60, fol. 12v.
Photo: © British Library Board

Figure 4.2 Crucifixion, Arundel Psalter. London, British Library, Arundel MS 60, fol. 52v. Photo: © British Library Board

another major line of analysis, which is to determine *how* the contents of an image are represented. 'Representation' is in some respects a loaded term because it anticipates issues of interpretation and argument. This anticipation is deliberate: I intend the use of the word to call for reflection on the close interlock between processes of artistic rendering and the incorporation of stories and ideas into manuscripts via their illumination. To examine the representation of the crucifixion in the Arundel Psalter more closely, we must now turn from mapping primarily the subjects of the pictures to describing their forms and execution.

Formal analysis can, on the one hand, lead to a characterization of a picture's overall qualities and affect. The first Crucifixion is executed with a limited colour palette consisting of blue, green, a light gold-brown wash, and the pink-orange known as *minium* (orange lead, and the root of the term 'miniature' often used for manuscript images). These qualities register promptly when one looks at the image – particularly in comparison to the second Crucifixion – but one can derive a description from them that moves towards interpretation. The restriction of colour and the graphic technique lends the composition a sense of rhythm and restraint that is reinforced by the clarity of the lines and the strong verticality of the composition. All the major lines in the figures were executed in dark ink with a hard, fine pen; with only a few exceptions the colour was added along these lines. Lines and blocks of shading to model the faces (particularly around John's eyes and at Mary's jawline), hands, and the details of Christ's torso were added in *minium*, as were lines, swirls, and dots to pattern the figures' robes. Long green highlights fill in the cross's horizontal beam and lower end, with small curving strokes that lend more body to the branch stumps. The colours in the first Crucifixion were all applied in isolation from one another, and as lines that work together with plain parchment to form the figures.

Continuing the comparison in this vein: colour is treated quite differently in the second Crucifixion, where in fact an only slightly wider range of pigments is in evidence. Here, colours were layered or worked in delicate proximity to one another over larger areas of the page: surface painting dominates instead of outline drawing, while the artist also employed fine pen work to describe Christ's body, details in the mane of Mark's lion or the feathers of John's eagle, and the elaborate patterning of the loincloth. White highlighting and graded colour add body to passages such as the tree trunks; light lines of minium and blue give depth to the ashy white ground used for Christ's body, while they pick out complex patterns of muscle and sinew. The same colours appear in more concentrated form to provide notes of strong, single colour in the blood, the loincloth folds, the blooming trees, and Christ's halo.

Working with Images in Manuscripts

Any one of these details may count as evidence in evaluating the Arundel images singly or comparing them to others under the banner of a particular research question. Formal analysis reveals visual relationships within a composition that often reflect priorities in the coordination of their subjects and their rendering. Parsing these priorities can move us further towards an interpretation of the image. The brightness of the blood in the second Crucifixion, for instance, ensures that this important aspect in the characterization of the Crucified does not escape attention. Similarly, the correspondence of colour between Christ's cross-halo and the cross on which he hangs indicates theological continuity between the event of the crucifixion and the nature of Christ's sanctity.

All the evangelist symbols in the corners of the frame turn their attention to the centre of the second Crucifixion – three by the direction of their heads and the twist of their bodies, Matthew primarily through the angle of his stance and the position of his hands. These vectors of attention within the picture, together with the intersecting lines of the cross itself, vertically centred in the frame, the gentle (asymmetrical) inward curve of the two trees, and the chromatic distinction of Christ's light body, all ensure that the focus of the scene in terms of story and theology – the crucified Christ – also occupies its compositional centre. Some compositions, particularly in the later Middle Ages, complicate this direct correlation of prominent subject and central position, creating a kind of game as a viewer must work out the exact relationship between subjects of a picture and their positions. In the Arundel Psalter, however, the correlation of focal composition and theology applies throughout. The first Crucifixion works along similar principles to the second in its focus of compositional attention on Christ. Several other visual relationships will prove useful shortly. Gathering information in advance, one might mark the way in which Mary and John are presented as a balanced but varied pair: both holding books, both gesturing inward, Mary wearing red over blue, while John's robes are layered blue over red. The colour of their veils and the mirrored shape of the folds falling around their heads and necks create a further visual link between Mary and Luna.

Images in Context

Equipped with the kind of visual evidence just assembled, we can begin to work out from the specifics of a composition to questions of interpretation and function. A move from description to interpretation requires contextualization along with analysis, and it is important to note that contextualization comes in different stripes. One main line of approach seeks a situation of the iconography and visual priorities in any particular image among the conventions, variations, and connotations of its type. One might seek evidence in comparison with other images of the same type (here, a Crucifixion) – in many different media and from a variety of possible geographic origins and eras, depending on the scope and research questions of the project. Textual traditions also represent deep possibilities for triangulation between images and ideas, as sources from visual and verbal culture together enhance our broader understanding of medieval artefacts – as do other types of sources, from archaeological data to music history.

Intellectual history

If we turn to the body of theological thinking about the crucifixion that has been established as active in the eleventh century on the basis of images and texts literary, exegetical, and liturgical, we gain an intellectual context in which to account for the compositional choices included in the Arundel Crucifixions. Many of the visual elements that denote these choices bespeak traditions that began to develop in recognizable form as early as the fifth century. In this, the Arundel images are part of a long story about the representation of the crucifixion, and equally part of a wide network of other compositions. At the same time, it is worth emphasizing that no other extant image I know is exactly like either one of the Arundel Crucifixions: the precise conglomeration of visual factors – style and technique plus details of iconography – belongs to each rendering alone.

The details that become 'legible' in the context of an artistic/intellectual tradition consist of different types. One consideration is the inclusion or exclusion of subjects within an established image type – the Hand of God, for example, or Mary and John – when closely related examples demonstrate the currency of other options. Christ sometimes appears alone in Crucifixions. The two thieves or soldiers tormenting him often flank the cross instead of Mary and John (compare with Figure 4.6). Similarly, angels may appear in the space above the transverse, in place of Sun and Moon. Another closely related choice to weigh, in concert with other surviving examples, is the handling of details that characterize the figures. The decision to give both Mary and John a book, for example, amounts to a choice with particular scope for interpretation when viewed in concert with Crucifixions that grant a book only to John, or render one or both witnesses weeping instead of calmly drawing attention to the Crucified. Similarly, Sol and Luna might or might not carry torches, wear fire like a crown, or indeed bear any attribute that indicates the light of these stars. The ground of Golgotha might not be emphasized (or included) at all. It might be highly abstracted, as in the second Arundel Crucifixion, or it might be shaped to reflect a deep-seated conception of the rock as trilobed, as in the first image. The cross might be

Working with Images in Manuscripts

depicted as brown wood, green wood, a precious object in gold and gems, or through plain ink lines that do not further characterize the cross beyond its essential form. These distinctions are interpretative: the choice to render the cross as wood with lopped branches, for instance, as in the first Crucifixion, associates the image with a line of thought and representation identifying the cross with the Tree of Life; the choice to render the cross with a fine border and articulated terminals, as in the second Crucifixion, embodies an alternate way of differentiating between the historical cross and the cross's role as a religious sign.

Internal composition

Colour constitutes its own category of compositional choice that can be weighed for interpretation. 'Colour symbolism' is a factor in many medieval images, but it, too, is dependent on context. Blue is often associated with divinity (not least because, in the finest form of blue pigment, made from lapis lazuli, the colour represents high material value), but the hue does not automatically denote heaven everywhere it appears. In the body of the cross – chosen instead of a wood colour that would promote attention to historical narrative – one might specifically situate blue within visual and textual traditions that characterize the cross as a sign of heavenly glory (a tradition that also includes gold crosses), just as the choice of a green colour amplifies the botanical reference in the 'living tree' variation.

Other possible ways of understanding colour are based in relations internal to an image, rather than the idea of symbolic valence inherent to a palette. Here, too, visual evidence requires balance against intellectual context, and ultimately a judgement call in how, and how heavily, to weigh an observation. The blue common to the cross and the two trees in the second Arundel Crucifixion, for instance – rendered with this commonality when we know that green was available for a more naturalistic conception of the trees – is a good candidate for such a reading. The two trees that flank the cross, bending towards it, constitute an iconography with a long history implicated, like the form of the cross with lopped branches, in the characterization of the cross as the Tree of Life (theologically speaking, because of its role in the crucifixion – a causal relationship spelled out in both Arundel images).[2] In this context, to choose an equivalent colour for the cross and the tree tops is to underscore the idea of the continuity between cross and tree within an intellectual tradition made up of diverse sources. One could make a related argument about the formal links between the head and veil of Mary and those of Luna in the first Crucifixion: the visual correspondence in this case engages aspects of crucifixion iconography and theology that turn on the balance of male and female vested in the figures of Sun and Moon and Mary and John. While we can think of the colour blue itself as a factor in the arguments built up in the representation of the second cross and its relationship to the trees, in the absence of further evidence there is no basis on which to bring the choice of green for Mary and Luna's veils into play. Here, we can work with the enhanced echo between the two female figures created by a common colour paired with a clear mirroring of shapes and lines, but the choice of the colour itself seems to have more to do with establishing rhythm and balance within a limited palette than it does with deploying a specific pigment for its intellectual connotations. The use of green for Sol's shoulder outlines, and in the corner roundels of the second Crucifixion, falls into the same category.

The evangelist symbols in the frame of the second Crucifixion represent a particularly interesting move on the part of the person who drafted this composition, because they stage another kind of contextualization for the figure at the centre: that of different image type altogether. The evangelist symbols clustered around the figure of Christ are visual elements most often associated with a depiction of Christ enthroned in heaven: they derive from the scriptural visions of Ezekiel and John including the 'four living creatures' gathered around a heavenly throne, and belong to an image type called a 'Majesty'. By framing the crucifixion with the evangelist symbols – especially a crucifixion depicting Christ as dead and bleeding – the image is designed to represent this event in a way that encapsulates the paradoxes pivotal for Christian salvation theology. The crucifixion is cast as Christ's human death and divine triumph; in an image like this he reigns from the cross (an argument that also involves the heavenly blue of the cross). Like the idea of the cross as the Tree of Life, these arguments are elemental to representations of the Crucifixion in multiple historical settings and in multiple media.

By viewing an image as part of a constellation of contexts in which ideas were worked out, it becomes possible to identify the strains of thinking that went into constructing a particular composition. The second Arundel Crucifixion brings out the point that contextualization is not only a priority in scholarship that helps to 'decode' an image, but also constitutes a strategy used in the eleventh-century design of the page. Using different components of the visual field, the central area and its frame, the designer blended two image types while simultaneously holding them separate in a way that mirrors the multivalent nature of contemporary thinking about the picture's central subject.

Manuscript context

The previous readings derive from methods of understanding images as both reflective and constitutive of the expansive intellectual contexts in which they were made. One could productively view the two Arundel Crucifixions primarily as emissaries of their image type, as it is transmitted in multiple media, and the variations within it that communicate nuances of interpretation and representational priorities of any one case's time and place. Similarly, one could productively contextualize the drawing style and handling of pigment in these cases within a broad history of drawing, painting, and the formation of figures. Further avenues in working with these compositions open when we view them in their immediate physical context – that is, specifically as *manuscript* images, bound (literally) to the type of book in which they appear and to their role within the particular instance of that genre represented by a unique codex.

The Arundel Psalter offers an exceptionally rich context in which to anatomize the kind of work one might do with images in manuscripts, because this book presents us with two compositions of the same type within the same book, rendered with the wealth of contrast in iconography, drawing style and painting technique mapped above. As discrete images, the two Arundel Crucifixions constitute a kind of master class in the kinds of visual distinction that can make a difference in reading a composition. But when we consider them as images that work within their own codicological context, and as part of the history of a certain type of book, a fuller understanding of their nature and importance to the manuscript emerges, alongside a greater picture of the manifold issues that bear on manuscript decoration at large.

In order further to gauge the interpretative possibilities presented by the doubled Crucifixions in the Arundel Psalter, we must establish the way these two images fit into the programme of decoration encompassing the entire manuscript. Describing the programme requires attention not only to subject matter, style, and technique, but also to codicology. The first Crucifixion appears on the last page of the first quire, which consists of twelve leaves (six bifolia). This gathering houses the psalter's calendar, along with further calendrical tables. The calendar is fitted with pen drawings of the zodiac. While not highlighted in coloured ink, these figures evince great formal and technical similarity to the first Crucifixion (Figure 4.3). Facing the first Crucifixion, the opening to Psalm 1 (*Beatus vir qui non abiit ...*) is framed like the second Crucifixion with a lush vegetal armature, painted in layered, opaque colour (Figure 4.4). The initial 'B' is enlarged and decorated with scrolling leaves like those in the frame, along with animal heads, interlace terminals for the spine of the letter, and two human figures in the bowls: a barefoot man in a cap clambering among the vines above; and King David seated, playing the harp below. The remaining letters on the page are rendered in capitals of alternating red, blue, and green ink. A comparably elaborate text page (although without any human figures) faces the second

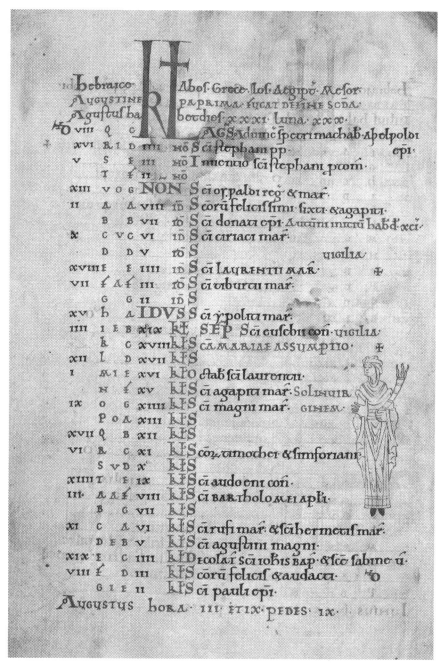

Figure 4.3 Calendar: month of August, Arundel Psalter. London, British Library, Arundel MS 60, fol. 5v. Photo: © British Library Board

Crucifixion, staging the opening of Psalm 51 (*Quid gloriaris . . .*) (Figure 4.5), and appears again at Psalm 101 (fol. 85r). Throughout the manuscript, alternating red and blue ink was used to enhance both the initials of psalm verses and the beginning of each new psalm, where the initials were drawn more than twice as large as the verse initials and sometimes elaborated with scrolls. The coloured initials were added after the main text (and an Old English gloss) had been written, which is evident, in part, from instances where the inks overlap.

The full decorative programme makes a difference to the ways one can conceive of the Crucifixion images themselves in a number of respects. Before we turn to these, please note that the way the decorative programme is represented in this chapter also makes a difference to the way a reader is asked to think about a manuscript. The first reproduction of folios 12v and 52v constructs a comparison between the Crucifixions that cuts them out of the book. This facilitates one way of looking at the images, and brackets away information that is essential to other ways of assessing them. The second reproduction provides the tight visual context of a single opening. If you turned to the digital facsimile on the website of the British Library for more information about colour and context, or a zoomed-in view of page details, consider also how this imaging technology affects the viewing of manuscript painting.

Returning to shifts in interpretation that are attendant on codicology: the programme as a whole presents a pressing historical question about the manuscript's design and manufacture. The fact that all the pen-drawn figures are concentrated in one quire while the rest of the major decoration is executed in a different style and technique raises a large flag: the manuscript was clearly illuminated in two separate phases, possibly by at least two people, differently trained or exercising markedly different technique and style. But were these phases completed in the same place and at or near the same time? In a situation like this, evaluating whether a programme should be understood as a composite or as integral, even if heterogeneous, requires that other types of evidence drawn from the manuscript be considered together with its artistic attributes. In the case of the Arundel Psalter, the question leads directly to discussion of how art history, book history, and political history intertwine, and I shall return to it at the end of this chapter.

Viewing the Crucifixions in the context of all the decorated pages underscores the choices that were made in rendering this motif as a full-page image, juxtaposed to the book's main text but not integrated with it directly. In the *Beatus* page (fol. 13r), the Arundel Psalter includes an alternate major mode of figural decoration, namely, the melding of letters and figures. As images, the depictions of King David and the capped man in the bowls of the 'B' are

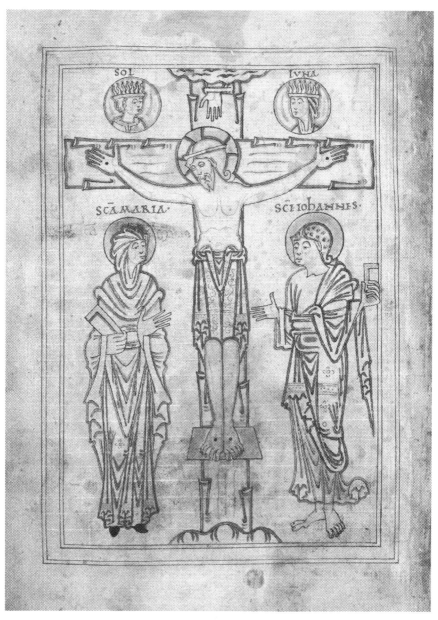

Figure 4.4 Crucifixion and Psalm 1, Arundel Psalter. London, British Library, Arundel MS 60, fols. 12v–13r. Photo: © British Library Board

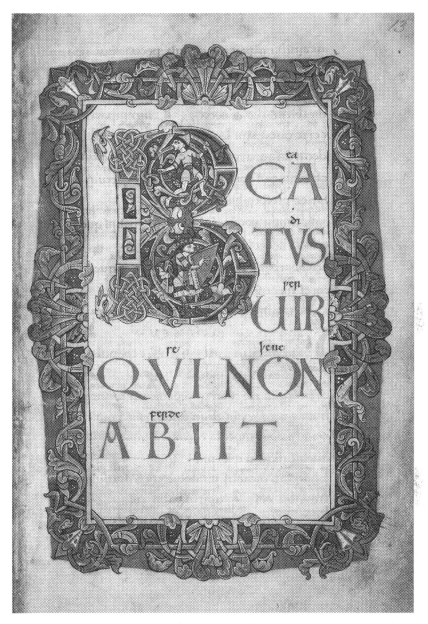

Figure 4.4 (cont.)

Figure 4.5 Crucifixion and Psalm 51, Arundel Psalter. London, British Library, Arundel MS 60, fols. 52v–53r. Photo: © British Library Board

Figure 4.5 (cont.)

subject to many of the same lines of analysis employed with the Crucifixions so far, but because they are set within the first letter of the psalm text these figures also raise some new considerations. Generally speaking, the figural illumination of initial letters proposes a particularly close connection between text and image. Simply by virtue of their occupying the same visual field, the conjunction of figure and letter stages a relationship of reciprocal definition – which is not to say that the image always directly 'illustrates' the text or that the text always has direct bearing on the subject of the image.

In this case, the choice to include David is readily derived from the text of the manuscript: the biblical king stood as the author of the psalms and the 'blessed man' of Psalm 1 was often explicitly identified with him. By placing David within the 'B', his gaze fixed in the direction of the words set down to the right and unfolding further through the rest of the manuscript, the king has been further identified with the very words he was thought to have composed. He is pictured playing the harp with his hands on the strings (rendered in minium on a pink ground; the strings have faded and may be hard to see in the photograph). In his representation as a musician, the figure of David also works as a reflection of the psalms' – and the psalter's – strong connection to performance and sound: the poems were sung as the backbone of the Christian liturgy, whether performed communally or as individualized prayer. The interlock of decorated letter and figure, enforced through the weaving of David's ankles through the scrollwork, comments on the genre of the manuscript as well as on the text at hand.

The man above David in the upper bowl of the 'B' is not identifiable as any scriptural or historical character. On the one hand, for us he may serve to represent the legions of medieval figures who do not readily fit into an established image type or scenic lexicon; the winged dragon-dog that forms the tail of 'Q' at Psalm 51 moves still further in this direction. On the other hand, it is possible to make a few conjectures about how to read this figure, based on his attributes, his pose, and his place within the letter. Psalm 1 contrasts the 'blessed man who hath not walked in the counsel of the ungodly' with the 'wicked' and 'sinners', who 'shall not rise again in judgement' (Douay-Rheims translation). The two figures in the 'B' are positioned as contrasts to one another, both spatially (on the same axis, in different segments of the letter) and in their dress (one rich and one poor). The man entangled in the vines – amplifying the letter's presence on the page by grasping it with his hands – wears a pointed yellow cap, a visual attribute often given to Jews in reflection of historic sumptuary laws. As such, it is reasonable to associate him with the 'sinner' juxtaposed to the *beatus vir* in Psalm 1, in the context of the negative position often assigned to Jews in medieval Christian exegesis and artwork.

Beyond his role as foil to David within the letter, the capped man plays another part within the decorative programme: with the turn of his head and the direction of his gaze, he binds the first page of the psalms together with the Crucifixion that faces them. At the second Crucifixion, the image on the verso and the psalm on the recto side of the codex opening are balanced pendants to one another thanks to their frames of equivalent size, shape and ornamentation, and the common colour palette that defines both pages. A comparable unity of style and page design does not reign at the Psalm 1 opening, but the capped man nevertheless was rendered in a pose that brings out the conceptual relationship between the two decorated pages, the visual continuity also implicating his figure in a possible meditation on the relationship of sinners to the crucifixion.

These observations lead to broader questions about how a manuscript's genre as well as its construction creates a context for images. The crucifixion is a composition frequently integrated into psalters for two principal reasons that have more to do with book-genre than with the favoured status of Crucifixions within personal books as an object of contemplation and prayer. First, Christ's ancestry includes David. Juxtaposing Christ and David provides a strong basis for meditation on themes such as kingship – a note emphasized in the first Arundel Crucifixion through Christ's completed coronation by the Hand of God. Second, depicting the crucifixion in a psalter proposes a prophetic relationship between Hebrew scripture and the gospels, bringing the psalms explicitly into a Christian framework. In this sense, pictures work similarly to the hymns and antiphons that contextualized the psalms in liturgical performance. The incorporation of images into a book creates a visual context for reading, and the combination of an image's subject and placement relative to text builds an interpretative characterization of the manuscript at hand.

Generic context

The immediate physical setting of the two Arundel Crucifixions within the psalter raises many context-orientated questions concerning an image type (Crucifixions) and its relationship to manuscript genre (psalters). One aspect of these questions has to do with trends and variations in image placement; for example, how do the Arundel Crucifixions compare in their position to Crucifixions in other psalters? Another has to do with the conceptual pairing of this iconography and genre: what does a Crucifixion do for a psalter?

A brief turn to the Tiberius Psalter (London, British Library, Cotton MS Tiberius C. vi), another eleventh-century Winchester production, offers useful perspective on these questions as they apply to the Arundel Psalter, as well as perspective on several categories of visual evidence treated above.[3] The Tiberius Psalter also includes a Crucifixion, which is different from both Arundel images in the subjects and details included in the scene, as well as the formal style in which the scene is rendered. It also has commonalities with each of the Arundel pictures (Figure 4.6). The technique of line drawing is similar to the first Arundel Crucifixion but not exactly the same, as more lines are rendered in discrete colours (rather than in pen with tinted outline). The formation of the figures contains more angled, curved, and shorter strokes, producing a looser effect of greater movement – especially in the spear- and sponge-bearers that flank the cross. Christ's position on the cross, his bleeding body, and the design of his loincloth are closer to the second Arundel Crucifixion. Most importantly at this juncture, the Crucifixion is again conceived as a full-page image but in the Tiberius Psalter it constitutes one within a complex set of drawings placed before the psalms (often called a 'prefatory cycle'). The cycle comprises scenes from the life of David, a long Christological series depicting gospel scenes prominent in the liturgical commemorations between Lent and Pentecost, an idiosyncratic image of the world's creation (fol. 7v), a cluster of images concerned with David's instruments that includes a depiction of the king as the psalmist, and a Christ in Majesty (fol. 18v). After a set of textual prefaces and prayers, a second depiction – fully painted – of David playing and singing faces the first psalm (fol. 30v).

Although differently structured, in terms of theological argument the visual programmes of the Tiberius and Arundel Psalters operate according to the same principle: the psalter as a genre is contextualized with reference both to its Hebrew origins and to its significance for Christian worship. The psalms were read and interpreted in close connection to the figure of Christ, and laced through Christian prayers and rites. The visual elements in both manuscripts characterize the psalter as a Christian book, composed by one of Christ's own ancestors. Within this essential framework, different compositional strategies are active in the two examples. An Arundel miniaturist incorporated David's image with the words of his psalm and Christ's image with the body of the psalter (twice). The Tiberius draftsperson presented David and Christ in continuous visual terms as part of the prefatory sequence, with David's image repeated as the pendant to Psalm 1. In different places, with different weights in the programme, the same image-type functions differently. In the Tiberius Psalter, the crucifixion becomes one stage in a multipart balance of Christ's story and David's (and note the inclusion of a Majesty as a separate image – the same type that was conflated with the crucifixion in the Arundel Psalter). In the Arundel Psalter, the image type is isolated from narrative, and multiplied as the book-defining visual theme.

Working with Images in Manuscripts

Figure 4.6 Crucifixion, psalter with additional texts (the 'Tiberius Psalter'). Winchester, third quarter of the eleventh century with twelfth-century additions. 345 × 250 mm (binding). London, British Library, Cotton MS Tiberius C. vi, fol. 13r. Photo: © British Library Board

The two Arundel Crucifixions appear at the first two major divisions of the psalter. The third (at Psalm 101, fol. 85r) is distinguished by an elaborate initial and frame, but no figuration. I will revisit the question of function for the Crucifixions in an interpretative and historical sense, but it is important to observe that illumination generally has a practical use within books otherwise not designed with navigational aids: decorated pages and large initials make stages within a text easier to identify. Psalter illumination follows a number of possible patterns that have to do with text division and function. Painting at the 'threefold division' of the psalter – like another compositional tradition that grants every psalm and even verses within the psalms individual vignettes – does not necessarily point to a particular function for the manuscript beyond the reading and representation of the psalms, as it follows a primarily exegetical tradition of thinking about the psalter (although it is difficult to generalize about use in this way: liturgical employment of the threefold division is also attested). Another 'scholarly' pattern divides the psalms into five 'books', mirroring the Pentateuch. However, psalters were also divided according to liturgical use, with the junctures between the seven psalms required for Matins in the daily office and one for Sunday Vespers all marked off with ornamentation. The Tiberius Psalter was designed with two division systems mapped out through decoration: framed initial pages and full-page images mark Psalms 1, 51, and 101, while coloured initials (one bordered) also chart an additional seven liturgical units. In a case like this, the distribution of illumination can indicate how the design of a manuscript intersects with its possible functions. The texts and charts added to a psalter to shape its function have bearing here as well, especially since they may be illuminated themselves (like fols. 2v–7r in the Tiberius Psalter).

Images on covers

I would like to touch on one more topic under the rubric of context, and that is the global contextualization for manuscripts provided by their covers. Most medieval books (including the Arundel Psalter) do not survive with their original bindings or casings, so it can be difficult to appreciate that thinking about the decoration of manuscripts does not only involve looking at the painting and drawing that appears inside them. Many manuscripts were bound or boxed in leather that might be stamped, tooled, or inlaid with patterns and pictures. The most luxurious books were fitted with 'treasure bindings' in gold, silver, ivory, gemstones, or silks worked in a range of techniques. Having begun this discussion with issues of material and technique, it is worth observing that the skills and materials required for such covers are different from those required to produce the written quires of a manuscript. The presence of elaborate covers therefore might signal the participation of more people – sometimes from different places and at different times – and more facets to the whole picture of material supply and production for a book at various stages of its journey.

Several examples of precious psalter bindings have come down to us, and these provide a good standpoint to consider how to work with images as part of manuscripts when different media and external/internal locations in the book are involved. The Dagulf Psalter represents one of the earliest surviving pairs of an illuminated book and its original binding in the medieval West. The manuscript is associated with the court of Charlemagne in the late eighth century and was made as a gift to Pope Hadrian in Rome (the manuscript is Vienna, Österreichische Nationalbibliothek, Cod. 1861; the covers are in Paris at the Louvre[4]). The cover plaques are made of carved ivory. One depicts two views of David as the psalmist, framed by small images of the four evangelists' symbols, angels, and the Lamb of God. The other shows two scenes of Jerome as the editor and translator of the psalms, framed by apostles, seraphim, and the Hand of God. The tradition of fitting manuscripts with precious bindings holds throughout the medieval period: the covers of the Felbrigge Psalter survive from the fourteenth century (London, British Library, MS Sloane 2400, named for the English nun who owned the book in the fifteenth century and added the death dates of her parents to the calendar).[5] This manuscript was written and decorated in France in the thirteenth century. When it came to England, the calendar was altered to replace several French saints with English ones, and to include the dedication date of Norwich Cathedral. In the early fourteenth century, the book was given a luxury textile binding of the type called *Opus anglicanum* ('English work'): technically spectacular embroidery in coloured silk and gold thread. The front cover depicts the Annunciation to the Virgin and the back cover depicts the Crucifixion.

In both these cases, the valuable nature of the manuscript was amplified and articulated by the addition of precious covers. The covers testify to the manuscripts' economic value as an investment of materials, and to their conceptual value as written scripture with functions ranging through the religious, the personal, and the diplomatic. Figural covers create an interpretative context for the whole book within. The eighth-century choices primarily frame the contents of the psalter as the product of two different processes of textual transmission: David's composition of the psalms and Jerome's translation. The David cover specifies the psalms' origin in Hebrew scripture; the Jerome cover depicts their incorporation into the Latin Church. The remaining image elements define these processes – composition, translation, transcription – along with the contents of the volume distinctly as

Christian, in a similar spirit to our previous discussion of Crucifixion images. The fourteenth-century example is designed for Christian contextualization of the psalter on a different compositional model also related to our eleventh-century examples. Two main events in the New Testament narrative frame the book: God's incarnation and death. The images work as a pair, and the fact that they cover a psalter means that we have an extra element to consider in reading these scenes, which are not unequivocally associated with the psalms in their subjects. The Annunciation and Crucifixion are not coupled only because they represent two major parts of the Christian story: early exegetes proposed that they occurred on the same day of the year (March 25). With the Felbrigge covers, the body of the manuscript is used to argue that unity of discrete events portrayed on the front and back of the book. The manuscript as a whole becomes representative of an argument about Christian history, in which the psalms are implicated because the images serve as their outer frame. A man kneels at the foot of the cross, signalling attention to the functions of the book itself within the contemporary medieval context of prayer.

Turning to book covers has revisited a number of principles central to our treatment of interior decoration. Primary among these is the idea that both placement and content matter in assessing how images work, and how images may relate to the contents of books with which they are associated. *What* the components of images comprise is just as important to their argument as *how* those components are rendered and work together. *Where*, and in what lights, any given image is to be seen fills out the interpretative picture.

Art/History

The small selection of examples we have encountered already present a number of fronts on which one can investigate the relationship of art to various kinds of history. Medieval manuscript decoration was made possible through networks and movements of people, raw materials, and other artworks and vehicles of thought and culture. In turn, illuminated manuscripts testify to these networks and movements through a web of interconnected types of evidence and research questions that involve asking how and where images were made, what they were made of, who made them, who wanted them, who changed them, what influenced their composition and how they were used. These questions lead directly to the kinds of circumstances that help to define the subject of this volume: medieval British manuscripts. The addition of the covers to the Felbrigge Psalter, for example, marks a juncture in the manuscript's history contingent upon a particular way someone desired the book to be visually staged, when they also had the resources to do it. This staging is part of a multivalent process by which a book made in France also became a manuscript constituted by an owner in England through a luxury technique particularly identified with the island. Did the Felbrigge Psalter become a 'British' manuscript then? Did it become so when it entered the British Library?

The Tiberius Psalter happens to be the earliest surviving example in the Latin tradition for a prefatory cycle of images worked into a psalter. As such, the book stands at the head of a design tradition in psalter composition that would grow ever stronger through the twelfth and thirteenth centuries. Conversely, the Tiberius Creation image represents a rare iconography particular to eleventh-century English monastic production. The book thus also stands as a potent reminder of the way in which the illumination of any particular manuscript is grounded in its own time and place. The prefatory cycle gives the Tiberius Psalter – and, through it, English illuminated psalters at large – a prominent place in the material history of the genre. Its illumination also imbricates the manuscript in other possible histories, such as that of typological theology coordinating the stories of David and Christ, the logic of scene selection in a sequence of pictures composed for a specific kind of book, or the appearance of radical new ways to imagine pictorial subjects. Any of these topics may take on a geographically inflected dimension. The line drawings that comprise most of the Tiberius decoration have their own place in a history of technique and style in book illumination. The first Crucifixion in the Arundel Psalter is often described as a 'hardening' or 'abstraction' of the kind of drawing seen in Tiberius – which in turn derives from an English tradition of drafting whose origins lie in the arrival of an enormously influential Carolingian psalter in Canterbury by the turn of the eleventh century (Utrecht, Universiteitsbibliotheek, MS Bibl. Rhenotraiectinae I Nr 32).[6] Remarkably, three surviving complete – and creative – copies were made of this same Carolingian Psalter in eleventh- and twelfth-century England. The last one – the Anglo-Catalan Psalter – was finished only in the fourteenth century, by a Catalan painter. Conversely, English illumination was profoundly influential on the practice of continental book painters throughout the Middle Ages. These two-way exchanges across the Channel existed thanks to the movement of manuscripts and people through trade, migration, diplomacy, pilgrimage, and warfare, among other impulses.

Speaking of war, to attempt to account for the design decisions in the Arundel Psalter that resulted in a manuscript visually defined by two Crucifixions made so differently from one another is to dive into the intersection of book history and socio-political history around the pivotal event of the Norman conquest. In a related vein, the Arundel Psalter prompts recognition of the ways artistic evidence may relate to other types of evidence drawn from a manuscript – their coordination taking scholars farther than any one strand of evidence alone. Nevertheless, the book also prompts acknowledgement of the knotty problems even an oft-studied manuscript can pose.

In its historiography, the study of Arundel MS 60 demonstrates how the coordination of evidence may affect understanding of a visual programme. The clear disparities in the style and technique of the images in the first quire and the remainder of the book long fostered consensus around the proposition that the line drawings (illumination of 'Anglo-Saxon type') were executed before 1066 and the painted pages (illumination of 'Norman' or 'Anglo-Norman type') were added only after Norman presence in England was established. This line of argument posited that differences in style and technique correlate to differences in date. In an article published in 2000, however, Peter Kidd combined palaeographic, artistic, and textual evidence to make a strong argument for the complete manuscript's date at c. 1073. If no great chronological gap may explain the heterogeneity of the decoration, what changes in the way we might think about the manuscript and history?

A conspicuous disparity in visual programme often heralds the involvement of people with different priorities on the patronage front; it also can denote a division of labour in manuscript production, by choice or by necessity, and a concurrent comfort with varied style in the completed book. Kidd identified two possible original owners of the Arundel Psalter, both of whom assumed powerful posts at Winchester around 1073 as Norman-affiliated replacements following the Conquest. Either man would have been in a position to adapt a manuscript-in-progress according to his own priorities. The ownership of the Arundel Psalter has not been fixed, however, and other circumstances factoring into the manuscript's diverse decoration are plausible. Alongside a possible change of owner, we also might imagine an illuminator leaving Winchester before completing the manuscript, or, indeed, arriving in time to contribute. Local artists learning alternate techniques in conversation with imported books creates another possible scenario for the visual shift. In the absence of further evidence, for the time being the question of exactly why the programme looks as it does in the light of political history remains open.

The manuscript was completed, though, and we have the character of the programme itself – as it was made and as it survives – as evidence to help define how its visual aspect works, including the rather surprising inclusion of two full-page Crucifixions. These images complement one another in their renderings of the scene: both emphasize the idea of the cross as the Tree of

Life and the combined divine and human natures of the Crucified, but the miniaturist or miniaturists used different pictorial strategies to achieve this complementarity. The Arundel Crucifixions, in other words, are not redundant. They offer varying terms by which to understand their common subject, especially regarding its relevance to the book where the images appear. At the beginning of the psalms, the first Crucifixion works in concert with the David in the initial to set a typological theme, and also reflects back on the calendrical material in the first quire as the key to Christian history. At Psalm 51, the Crucifixion furthers exegesis relating the psalm text to the figure of Christ (and the prominent trees may additionally relate to the 'fruitful olive' of verse 10). Both represent participation in established traditions for how a crucifixion image relates to a psalter, as well as traditions in how the subject itself is imagined and rendered in visual terms. At the same time, each image represents a unique imagination of the subject and works as party to the realization of the unique instance of the psalter genre that is Arundel MS 60. In this project, the visual programme enriches our understanding of the book as much as the book defines our understanding of its illumination.

Notes

1. A full colour digital facsimile is available at: http://www.bl.uk/manuscripts/Viewer.aspx?ref=arundel_ms_60_fs001ar.
2. See, for example, the gilded silver plaques dated to the sixth century now held at the Dumbarton Oaks Museum in Washington, DC (Inv. No. BZ.1963.36.9), image available at http://museum.doaks.org/Obj27472?sid=2193&x=4431&sort=76.
3. The Tiberius Psalter is available at: http://www.bl.uk/manuscripts/Viewer.aspx?ref=cotton_ms_tiberius_c_vi_fs001r.
4. Inv. Nos. MR 370, 371. For images, see www.louvre.fr/oeuvre-notices/plaques-de-reliure-du-psautier-de-dagulf-david-saint-jerome.
5. Images available through www.bl.uk/catalogues/illuminatedmanuscripts.
6. A digital facsimile with commentary is available at: https://bc.library.uu.nl/utrecht-psalter.html.

5

R YAN PERRY

The Sum of the Book: Structural Codicology and Medieval Manuscript Culture

Look at the image in Figure 5.1. Here is a medieval book in a wonderful state of decomposition. This codex, Manchester, John Rylands Library, MS Eng. 895, a fifteenth-century religious anthology, has somehow eluded the benign attentions of conservators over the centuries that have passed since its production, and like a cadaver subjected to a slow forensic dissection, now reveals its structuring mechanisms to us. The delicate and damaged alum-tawed leather cover is visible at the spine, and although the supports (or thongs) no longer traverse the spine from one board to the other (other than one limp, bifurcated vestige), we can see their imprints. We can even tell that each of the supports were split, 'which allowed the binder's needle and thread to pass through the middle ... around its back, and again through the middle'.[1] The quires, no longer tethered to the thongs by long undone stitches, are splayed, revealing both the manuscript's discrete gatherings and the darker shade of parchment in the first quire's outer folio (not the original outer folio, which has been lost), exposed for a considerable time not only to the smoke and wear of medieval life, but also for many years to the inner side of the oak board. The imprint of the text on the board demonstrates that the book has lacked its pastedowns for some time; that is, the glued inner cover for the boards that were usually originally made of membrane, and often from membrane recycled from other books. The missing pastedown means that we can see the v-shaped channels through which the six bifurcated thongs emerged from the outside of the board, before being pegged into place; the v-shape allows two thongs to be pegged at a single point, and this manner of attaching the boards to the supports, which gradually changed through the Middle Ages, gives us an approximate date for the binding (c. 1350–1459).[2]

Rylands 895, in its deconstructed state, lays bare at least some of the concerns inherent in what this chapter is calling 'structural codicology'. This chapter will discuss some of the material structures we perceive within the medieval books that we now find in libraries, private collections, and

106

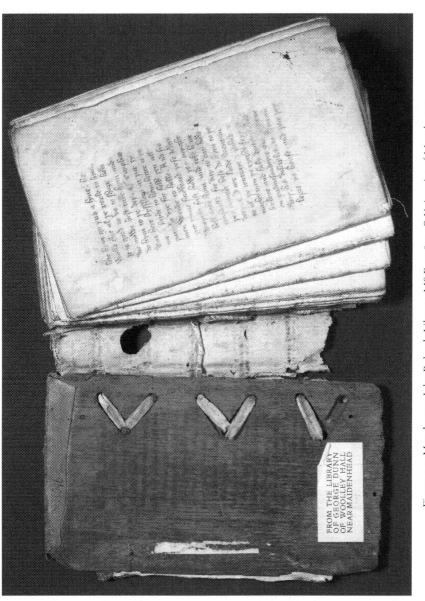

Figure 5.1 Manchester, John Rylands Library, MS Eng. 895. © University of Manchester

archives, and query what these physical remains tell us about the varied cultures of manuscript production in the Middle Ages, and furthermore, of the subsequent histories of those materials. Central to this chapter will be a discussion of the units of production that combine to make up the medieval manuscript. From the fundamental constituents of medieval book production – leaves, bifolia, and quires – this chapter will be especially interested in the things they combine to form – booklets (or fascicles), and clumps of texts copied together within books and booklets, namely, 'nodes' or 'clusters', to use Ralph Hanna's designations. This chapter will review the processes through which manuscript books came to be made in the Middle Ages, and the role that these subparts have to play in the story of the medieval codex.[3] Structural codicology requires that the chapter surveys some other vestiges of the manuscript record such as medieval bindings, and explores the value of such materials to the manuscript scholar, and to the student of medieval material culture more generally.

The chapter will also discuss the afterlives of medieval manuscript materials, and how they take on new forms. Some, we find as loose leaves, cut or torn at some intervening stage from the medieval codex to become a 'fragment' – such may have been the fate of the leaves lost from the opening (and elsewhere within) Rylands 895.[4] These fragments are often now housed in archives, encased in boxes of similarly disembodied scraps of text. Sometimes we instead discover fragments within other books, when they were recycled as pastedowns or as other parts of bindings to strengthen new (medieval) books; what can such remnants tell us, and how should we approach them?

In complete contrast to these atomized slivers from the medieval codex the afterlives of some medieval manuscript materials involved them being reformed into new 'composite' manuscripts.[5] This chapter will thus focus on fifteenth-century vernacular productions such as the Prose *Brut* and religious miscellanies in particular, and it will also attempt to chart the codicological issues at stake in books made in different eras, and in languages other than Middle English.

Structured Indeterminacy and the Medieval Codex

The most significant difference between the medieval codex and the modern book is the inherent structural-indeterminacy of the medieval manuscript. Whereas we think of a modern book as a complete object, the medieval codex was regularly viewed as a repository for text that had the potential to develop. Although copies of single texts might be completed and subsequently bound as a single-text book (and such books will be discussed

Structural Codicology and Medieval Manuscript Culture

later), the medieval book always had the potential to be expanded, to receive continuations – for the book to be added to and altered – for its relevance to be re-established and for it to continue to evolve. An anecdote from Asser's *Life of King Alfred* perfectly illustrates some of the key issues at stake within 'structural codicology':

> One day ... I (Asser) was reading aloud some passage to him (Alfred) from a certain book ... he suddenly showed me a little book which he constantly carried upon his person, and in which were written the day-time offices and some psalms and certain prayers ... He told me to copy the passage in question into the little book. But, when I could find no empty space in the little book in which I might copy the passage ... I said to him: 'Would it meet with your approval if I were to copy out the passage separately on another piece of parchment? For we don't know whether we might at some point find one or more similar passages which you would like; and if this were to happen unexpectedly, we would be glad to have kept it separate.' ... I quickly prepared a quire[6] and copied the passage near the quire's beginning ... while searching to this end, as we found equally pleasing passages the quire grew full ... the king ... took it upon himself ... to study these flowers collected here and there and from various masters and to assemble them within the body of one little book (even though they were all mixed up) as the occasion demanded. He expanded it so much that it nearly approached the size of a psalter. He wished it to be called his enchiridion (that is to say, 'handbook'), because he conscientiously kept it to hand by day and night. As he then used to say, he derived no small comfort from it.[7]

The account, purportedly by Asser, is the perfect starting point for considering 'the sum of the book' and the importance of 'structural codicology', if we begin to think of the processes that he describes in material terms. First, the author confirms the essentially protean nature of medieval textual production in which textual units might be added, altered, removed, and repositioned as part of the process of compiling a medieval book. The passage, penned by someone with an easy familiarity with manuscript culture, provides a window into the attitudes towards textual production in the Early English period, and arguably, throughout the Middle Ages. The quire made for Alfred comprises eight folios (it is described in Latin as a 'quaternion' – so, four bifolia), the standard unit of textual production in England from the earliest period to the late Middle Ages. These fourfolded leaves became, he tells us, the basis for a much more substantial accretion of texts, to the extent that the booklet ballooned in mass to resemble a psalter. How would this process have been manifested materially? Initially, bifolia may have been added to the quire made by Asser to produce a larger gathering, with leaves perhaps added to the centre of the *quaternion*, or instead as outer leaves

109

(after being sewn from the middle of the initial quire, the outer leaves on the recto side might be folded back to the rear of the quire). This was something that happened in non-institutional and non-professional production scenarios regularly, in which unwieldy quires of twenty and more leaves might be formed, such as in the hands of Robert Thornton, the patron-scribe of some books to be discussed later. Whether or not such a voluminous quire was formed in the case described in the *Life of Alfred*, at some stage new quires would need to have been added to the king's gathering while unbound, perhaps within some temporary cover. The quires would perhaps have been 'tacketed' (sewn) together by the scribe without the more permanent structures of supports, boards and cover.[8] In fact, Asser's text hints at the necessity of a temporary cover for this new textual unit. According to the Keynes and Lapidge translation of Asser's chronicle, the author informs us that he writes '*near* the quire's beginning'.[9] If Keynes and Lapidge have translated correctly, why 'near' the quire's beginning and not at the very beginning, on the recto side on the outside of this embryonic textual unit? The obvious answer is that it reveals the practical knowledge of someone who understands that the text would be vulnerable to wear if written there, in a book that is designed to evolve rather than to be immediately bound into a more permanent structure. Instead the blank recto side might act as a temporary cover, and filled with a filler-text perhaps, only soon once the quire, or booklet, was bound into Alfred's book.

Such a pattern of production and use can be seen, for instance, in a book from much later in the Middle Ages, Cambridge University Library, MS Ff. 6. 31 (John Colop's 'Common Profit Book'). The opening item in the book is the text 'Propur Wille' on the verso side of the first folio within an odd, nine-folio quire (that was probably constructed as a quire of ten leaves with the final leaf trimmed). The recto side of the first folio is very dark and grubby, suggesting that this text, and the gathering it was part of, spent time unbound before being included in the codex. A 'filler' text, that is, a text that takes advantage of a blank space in a gathering and that may or may not have been added by the original producer of the book, was subsequently penned into the empty recto side.

Other strategies to protect a growing assembly of texts might be employed to create temporary (and sometimes not so temporary) covers for such gatherings of materials, including having a 'limp' parchment binding, in which a parchment folder with a flap was formed to protect quires, and where new gatherings might be easily added.[10] The mid-fifteenth-century copy of the Middle English Prose *Brut* in Dartmouth College, New Hampshire (Dartmouth College, Rauner Special Collections Library, MS 003183), formerly part of the Foyle, Beeleigh Abbey collection, was contained in what the Dartmouth conservators describe as a 'stationery binding ... a tacketed or account book binding'.[11] This kind of binding has typically been associated with 'account books' and administrative documentation more generally. The limp leather binding of the *Brut* has been dated to the sixteenth century, but is certainly appropriate to the text and plausibly replaced a parallel fifteenth-century binding. The English *Brut* (as will be discussed further below) was one of the first vernacular texts that was being effectively mass-produced by metropolitan scribes for gentry and mercantile audiences – an audience who might have a particular familiarity with account books, and thus, with this kind of binding technology.

The Booklet

It is through such production strategies that the textual unit first tagged by P. R. Robinson as the 'booklet' (or fascicle) came to be formed.[12] The booklet is a codicological structure that can be discerned in so-called 'composite' manuscripts, a kind of volume described by Giovanna Murano as one 'formed by codicological units ... that come from different backgrounds and sometimes of different periods, which are assembled under a single covering'.[13] Robinson's seminal work on the idea of the booklet demonstrated that composite manuscripts containing early English texts were often brought together into a bound codex through a process of conjoining booklets at periods much later than those of their production – sometimes within a few centuries and in proximity to the ecclesiastical centres in which they had initially been produced, and sometimes much later, under the agency of bibliophilic early modern collectors such as Archbishop Whitgift.

Robinson argued that collections of booklets in limp bindings may initially have been constructed as being deliberately partible, and thus portable. She discusses booklets within manuscripts containing materials from the pre-Conquest period such as Oxford, Bodleian Library, MS Hatton 115 (as Scragg has discussed in Chapter 2 of this volume) and Cambridge, Corpus Christi College, MS 198. It is possible these now bulky codices may have been bound (in every sense) for a sedentary existence within institutional libraries, but as booklets, and probably in limp bindings, the homiletic material they contained could be transportable to sites for preaching and instruction. Indeed, there is a clear fold in the leaves of folios 140–7 of the Hatton manuscript, suggesting plausibly to Robinson that this quire containing a 'vernacular homily on hell became pocket sized when folded down the middle ... [or] fitted into a satchel or a sleeve'.[14]

In fact – adding nuance to Murano's definition of the booklet – the fascicles we find in medieval miscellanies (or anthologies) do not always originate from 'different backgrounds', and may even have been produced by a single scribe, and within the same production context. In the vast corpus of religious miscellanies produced in the late Middle Ages, for example, it is possible to discern long anthologizing productions that were compiled in discrete phases, even though the same scribe may have penned all the texts in the finally completed volume. There is strong evidence that such booklets may have had, much like the selected pre-Conquest materials discussed above, a dissemination history that predated their instantiation within a bound codex. Robert Thornton, the fifteenth-century Yorkshire gentleman and scribe of two large vernacular compilations – the Lincoln Thornton manuscript (Lincoln Cathedral Library, MS 91) and the London Thornton manuscript (London, British Library, MS Additional 31042) – appears to have circulated at least one section of his productions independently. A copy of a letter written into Cambridge University Library, MS Dd. 11. 45 records the loaning of the *Morte d'Arthure* from the scribe and owner of the 'buke' to an affiliate living in Norfolk:

> praying ʒow þat ʒe will resayfe and kepe ... ane Inglische buke es cald Mort Arthur, as ʒe may se wrytten of my hand in þe last end of þe buke ... I wold pray ʒow to send me þe forsaid Inglische buke ... als sone as ʒe myght.[15]

Recently published findings by Patrick J. Murphy and Fred Porcheddu have revisited this letter, and suggested that its author was no other than Robert Thornton.[16] If accepted, Murphy and Porcheddu's argument suggests that what is now booklet B of the Lincoln manuscript, a booklet focused on Romance literature and with the Alliterative *Morte* as its flagship text, once circulated independently.[17] We may note that what scholarship now understands as a booklet is described in the letter as a 'buke'. The letter may reveal that a booklet was understood as a discrete production in its own right, rather than as a constituent of something else. Indeed, it is interesting to speculate from both the early and late medieval evidence whether it is true that some 'booklets' performed their most dynamic cultural work before they became bound into the large codices which are stationed in library collections.

Clearly, recognizing booklets as codicological structures within miscellaneous or anthologizing compilations is crucial to understanding the utilities of premodern literatures. In these kinds of books, such methods for gathering and utilizing texts were a commonplace of socio-literary culture. The booklet allowed producers of text a freedom that is alien to modern conceptions of the book, in which texts are furnished complete and as part of an inflexible structure. The booklet, as Ralph Hanna records, offered some other distinct

Structural Codicology and Medieval Manuscript Culture

advantages to medieval bibliophiles exactly because of the creative latitude offered by this mode of compilation:

> the use of the booklet forestalls or delays quite indefinitely any very absolute decisions about the form of the final product ... the booklet creates an infinitely flexible situation in which the codicological form of the book may never be fixed during production.[18]

Returning to Alfred's increasingly thick 'enchiridion', described as growing to the size of a psalter, we gain a sense of the liberty afforded to medieval book compilers, with the fluid potential of the book coupled with and checked only by that nexus between the desires of the patron and the availability of exemplars to copy.

Cultures of Scribal Production and the Structure of the Book

When examining a particular book, attention to structural codicology means we are not only concerned with the codex itself; with handwritten books we are always mindful that books are progenies of other books. Manuscript books are usually formed from copies of exemplars that we might consider as parent texts. In the case of a book containing multiple texts, there might also be many parents, revealing a tangle of lines of descent. This section of the chapter is concerned with some of the methods through which books were constructed, and particularly in respect of the systems that scribes devised to enable the efficient circulation of exemplars, the parents of the texts in the books that we study.

One kind of book that most readily reveals the systems of exemplar circulation that existed in the Middle Ages is the so-called *pecia* manuscript. The *pecia* system, particularly associated with the universities where there was a predictable demand for certain texts, was a culture of production that permitted a single exemplar, parted into numbered pieces (*peciae*), usually of between four and twelve leaves, to be separately hired out by a stationer for copying.[19] In such a manner, a large number of copies might simultaneously be made from the same exemplar *peciae*. As Graham Pollard has written, there are signs that might allow one to distinguish a *pecia* book, and moreover, whether the book represents the now conjoined *peciae* 'the separate quires which the... stationers hired out piece by piece', or a '*pecia* copy', a book copied from the stationers' exemplars.[20] The stationers' *pecia*, the gathering that was rented for copying, will normally have a number (if it has not been trimmed) in the upper margin of the first folio, as well as often having signs of wear from regular use by copyists. It is likely to have spaces with guide-letters, rather than completed initials. 'Corrigitur', the term that signals the text has been read closely and corrected, is often found on the first or last side of the *pecia*.[21] In terms of the *pecia* copies, the key identifying feature is that the numbers that correspond to the *peciae* will be located in the side margins.

It appears that comparable systems were developed by 'professional' scribes in the fifteenth century, who collaborated to speed the production of lengthy texts commissioned by well-to-do patrons. I put 'professional' in quotation marks not because the people who produced such books and developed such copying systems did not earn recompense by writing books, but that this was often not their only, or even their primary occupation. Thomas Hoccleve, not only an author, but also, as a following case will demonstrate, a scribal collaborator in manuscript production, was a clerk in the office of the Privy Seal. Research by Linne Mooney and Estelle Stubbs has suggested that a number of administrators in London's Guildhall were also involved in book production, and usually at the upper end of the manuscript market, including Trinity College manuscript as in the following discussion. In such cases, described by A. I. Doyle and M. B. Parkes in the case of manuscripts of *The Canterbury Tales* and *Confessio Amantis*, and by Matheson, Mooney, and Mosser in the case of manuscripts of the Middle English Prose *Brut*, exemplars were parted and distributed among scribal teams, with this innovatory production method leaving material evidence within the books they produced.[22]

- Doyle and Parkes identified five scribes in Cambridge, Trinity College, MS R. 3. 2 (581):
- Scribe A: copied four complete quires: 1, 7, 10, 13, and sections of 11 and 14
- Scribe B:[23] copied three complete quires: 2, 3, and 4
- Scribe C: copied four complete quires: 5, 6, 8, and 12 (and 'supplemented the work of scribe B on a leaf added to quire 4')[24]
- Scribe D (John Marchaunt): copied six complete quires: 9, 15, 16, 17, 18, 19 ('and completed one quire (14) begun by scribe A')[25]
- Scribe E (Thomas Hoccleve): copied 'only the first two leaves and the first column of the third leaf of quire 11. Scribe A commenced on the verso side of this leaf and completed the quire'.

This scribal collaboration, with exemplars being parted among bureau-crats and writers of documents keen to engage in literary moonlighting, perhaps represents one 'solution to the problem of producing copies of the increasing number of vernacular texts which ... were being written at the time and of catering for the demands of a growing market for such copies'.[26] As mentioned above, towards the mid-fifteenth century there appears to be an especially voracious public demand for the Middle English Prose *Brut*, a text that now survives in over 180 copies (including fragments). Lister Matheson and Linne Mooney (supplemented by further research by Daniel Mosser) discovered a group of scribes, centring on the so-called 'Beryn scribe' (because he wrote the only copy of the *Canterbury Tales* containing the 'Tale of Beryn'), who were apparently collaborating as part of 'commercial multiple-copy production of vernacular texts'. These scribes were repeatedly producing the *Brut*, and most probably, given the functional rather than deluxe scripts and material features of the manuscripts, for aspirational middling consumers. It is in such production situations that we begin to see scribes servicing a level of demand that would make viable the risky venture of setting up the first print presses, something that happened in England perhaps within a decade or two of the Beryn scribe's endeavours.

Accretions and Continuations

Most medieval books, however, were constructed in ways that were profoundly different from the kind of scenario above; instead of the multiplication of copies, and even the production potentially occurring as part of the kind of speculative copying that reminds us of print culture, the medieval book was often a considerably more ad hoc affair. Books of history have, throughout the Middle Ages, been a genre of manuscript particularly prone, for obvious reasons, to receiving new materials that might continue the chronicle, or contribute something of relevance to the history. Cambridge, Corpus Christi College, MS 173, the 'Parker manuscript', containing, principally, the A-version of the *Anglo-Saxon Chronicle*, is exemplary in this regard.[27] The oldest extant copy of the 'common stock' of the *Anglo-Saxon Chronicle*, the writing of the materials that now form the Parker manuscript probably commenced around *c.* 900. The book appears to have been initiated in Winchester, the seat of the royal line of Wessex, before migrating to Christ Church, Canterbury at some point in the eleventh century, as Treharne and Da Rold also discuss in their chapter. This chapter is too short to attempt a detailed survey of the complex contents of the manuscript, which now encompasses five booklets in a number of different hands, with materials added and appended to the volume over hundreds of years; instead, a more general sense of the book's history will suffice. According to Malcolm Parkes, the foundational Winchester compilation, itself comprising several accretions, originally contained the following items:

1. The genealogy of the West Saxon royal house to Alfred (fol. 1r).
2. Annals to the year 891 (fols. 1v–16r).

3. Chronicle of Alfred's war with the Danes between 892 and 897 (16v–19v).
4. Annals for 898–918 (fols. 19v–22v).
5. Annals for 919–24 providing a uniquely surviving chronicle of the final campaigns of Edward the Elder (fols. 22v–25v).
6. The laws of Alfred and Ine (fols. 33–52).

Item 6 begins on a new gathering, but because quire signature 'c' is visible on fol. 25v (which was a singleton added to the third quire) and a further signature, 'e', is visible on fol. 42r, it is clear that item 6 was penned on a booklet of three quires that originally followed the three quires housing items 1–5. At this stage in its existence, the book of six quires 'consisted of a record of the achievements of the West Saxons royal house in war – down to the last campaign of Edward the Elder, and in peace – down to the legislation of Alfred'.[28] Once in Canterbury, the structure was changed. A quire of eight leaves (the eighth, probably blank leaf, has since been lost) was added between items 5 and 6, to provide a continuation to the Winchester chronicle. The Canterbury continuation provides annals from 925 to 1070 on fols. 26–32r in a variety of hands, providing a new regional historiographical perspective with a Canterbury inflection. A further local stamp is given via a late eleventh-century hand that adds the Latin *Acts of Lanfranc* on folio 32r–v. It should be noted that the Canterbury scribes did not limit themselves to writing only in the new sections of the growing volume, but as members of a bookish culture habituated in textual glossing, provided notes and additions to the Winchester sections of the book too. In due course the book would accrue more gatherings and materials – lists of popes, and of English bishops and Archbishops of Canterbury; texts by Sedulius, including the *Carmen Paschale*; and excerpts from Augustine, *De ciuitate Dei* – with the additions probably occurring within Christ Church before the volume ended up in the sixteenth century, like so many medieval books, in the collection of the reforming Archbishop of Canterbury, Matthew Parker. The Parker manuscript illustrates how books could become repositories for texts over hundreds of years of textual accretion, particularly in institutional settings, and how texts within that were accrued even centuries before might be revisited by continuators, glossators, and annotators.

As chronicles and annals gradually became the sort of book that might not only be owned by ecclesiastical institutions but increasingly by private secular consumers, there was also the same impulse to update one's work of history. The Middle English Prose *Brut*, a vast textual corpus masterfully surveyed by Lister M. Matheson, was a text that demonstrated the pervasiveness of the same instinct to provide continuations onto chronicles.[29] The original English

Structural Codicology and Medieval Manuscript Culture

Brut was closely translated from the Anglo-Norman version of the same text. The Anglo-Norman *Brut* was itself a text that had received instalments, with an original version to 1307, ending in the year of the death of Edward I, and with a later version to 1333, ending with the Battle of Halidon Hill, with Edward III's crushing defeat of the Scots. When this work of historiography, which in its Anglo-Norman iterations encompassed a heavy Lancastrian bias, was translated into English in the late fourteenth or early fifteenth century, a number of continuations quickly became appended to the text in its numerous manuscript copies. A version to 1377 (the end of the reign of Edward III) was followed by a particularly common continuation which brought the history to 1419, with Henry V's conquest of Rouen and English military domination of Normandy. The text would receive continuations up to and beyond its first printing by Caxton in 1480. Although some manuscripts would be copied in the first instance from the most recent version of the *Brut* then available to the patron, a number of manuscript witnesses allow us to see the way in which book producers went about appending new material to update the chronicle. Dublin, Trinity College, MS 490, a manuscript which may be one of the very earliest extant manuscripts of the *Brut*, was recorded by Matheson as a common version to 1419. Although the text ends in 1419 on fol. 177, it is in fact a new hand that has continued the chronicle following the Battle of Halidon Hill, taking over at the end of the common version of the *Brut* to 1333. Scribe B, who writes the continuation from 1333 to 1419 may have been writing two or three decades after the original production of the book, at the bequest of the book's patron who had become aware of the availability of a sequel to his or her book. However, the scribe has endeavoured to make the change appear fairly seamless, adopting a similar *anglicana formata* script to the first scribe, and penning the same number of lines per side as the first scribe. Indeed, the scribe's success was such that Matheson did not notice a changeover had occurred in his survey of the *Brut* manuscripts. Clues such as a change in quire signatures which begin again at 'a' on the first new quire following the change of scribal hands (the stint actually begins on leaves that had been left blank in the final quire used by the first scribe) are signs that the text represents a later continuation. Such cases demonstrate that even a potentially 'complete' book, perhaps bound and filled with one long text, as TCD 490 almost certainly was, had the potential to be unbound and augmented.

Textual Structuring: 'Nodes' and Themes?

Some of the books previously discussed have already provided a sense of the impulse among medieval book producers, whether in the case of institutionally produced books, or books owned privately, of attempts to structure textual contents. As already discussed, the Parker manuscript's foundational kernel was an assemblage of texts that grew around a focus on the achievements of the royal house of Wessex, and at least initially, there was an attempt to continue the historiographical theme in this book when it came to Christ Church in Canterbury, even if that focus became redirected to a history that pertained more closely to its new home. The issue of textual structuring in the medieval book is one that is somewhat fraught in codicological studies, particularly in respect of non-institutional books. There are tensions over terminology, and particularly the appropriateness of potentially loaded terms such as 'miscellany' or 'anthology' when describing a particular book. Derek Pearsall's warning about looking too deeply for guiding principles as part of the process of medieval book compilation is worth repeating here:

> [I]t is possible, and all too possible, to overestimate the activity of the controlling or guiding intelligence of the scribe-compiler in the making of late medieval English secular miscellanies. The necessities of production, the pressures of circumstance, the paucity of exemplars, as well as other factors, combined to make the work of compilation more random and inconsistent than many modern interpreters are happy to allow.[30]

And yet while we must be careful not to impose structuring rationales that are born of our own ingenuity, it is in human nature to discern patterns in the things that we study; thus, it would be counter-productive not to acknowledge the structures that we see. For, if it is in human nature to see structures in things, it is surely part of a related inclination to impose structures upon the things that we produce.

While there are undoubtedly inherently miscellaneous books, such as 'commonplace books' in which all kinds of ephemera might be gathered and written down with little discernible sense of order (my own Dropbox files bespeak such a lack of method), it might also be the case that certain kinds of books were understood by their compiler-patrons, either to require order, or to be constructed against some sort of imperative. One of Pearsall's caveats against recognizing structure is born from another pervasive, and undoubtedly useful trope in medieval codicological studies, the idea of 'exemplar poverty'.[31] This idea comes from Ralph Hanna who has indicated the sometimes arbitrary nature of later medieval book culture, the relative paucity of vernacular texts (compared to modern print culture) leading to, 'that inherently miscellaneous, often catch-as-catch-can, appearance that typifies late medieval books in English'.[32]

In his analysis, Hanna has provided a compelling idiom for the later medieval manner of locating vernacular texts for production, labelling such

Structural Codicology and Medieval Manuscript Culture

textual networking as 'gossip', a term which emphasizes the elusiveness and, perhaps, fleeting temporality of the conduits of textual dissemination, and explains an instinct among scribes to eagerly copy all the texts they found in their exemplars.[33] Hanna's model means that something might be arbitrarily copied as an 'interesting text' found in a miscellaneous exemplar but not, in fact, 'the one initially sought'.[34] Hanna has also added the term 'node' to the codicologist's lexicon, to indicate a cluster of texts that are repeatedly copied together within miscellanies, textual units that are regularly redeployed by diverse compilers.[35] One such a 'node', first recognized by A. I. Doyle as a 'little book of meditations on death', contains in the fullest version, five separate texts:

1. 'The gathered counsels of St. Isidore'.
2. St Augustine, *De contemptu mundi*.
3. Verse translation of 'Cursor Mundi'.
4. 'The sayings of St. Bernard'.
5. The B version of 'Earth upon earth'.

Hanna explains that this clump of texts 'is attested in some form in twenty-one different books', with some compilers copying all the bundled texts, and others partial versions of the textual unit (which in turn were copied).[36] Many similar nodes can be found within religious 'miscellanies', and particularly in the fifteenth century, when there appears to have been an extraordinarily dynamic culture of compiling these sorts of books. Of course, such nodes have potential to manifest 'organizing principles' in that they very often, like this example, have a clear thematic focus. The way in which they are deployed by compilers further suggests that the books to which they contributed were governed by culturally shared organizational principles. The most important classificatory aspect of this type of book (Robert Raymo classified these books as 'miscellaneous manuals') is that it will contain catechetical material in English that relates to central Christian formulae and prayers: the ten commandments, the seven deadly sins, the Creed, *Pater Noster* and *Ave Maria*, among others.[37] Such texts in these miscellaneous manuals range from basic English translations of fundamental religious lore to more lengthy commentaries that regularly deal with polemical doctrinal issues. These 'miscellaneous manuals' were most often structured in a way in which the basic pastoralia is written at the beginning of the books (or at the beginning of self-contained booklets within the volumes). Such catechetic material generally precedes more complex devotional materials in the middle sections of the books – meditative and contemplative works, or more complex and sometimes polemical tracts on pastoral issues. At the ends of these books we regularly find end things: treatises on visiting the sick and dying;

119

treatises on a good death; or on doomsday. The 'node' contemplating death discussed above is thus almost always placed near the end of the volumes in which it is contained (or if not at the end of the volume, at the end of a booklet within the volume). In Oxford, Bodleian Library, MS Laud Misc. 23, for example, the unit of texts occurs in the third and final booklet, comprising the 25th to 27th items in a collection of twenty-seven texts:[38]

Laud Misc. 23, Booklet III:
24. Middle English *Meditaciones de Passione Christi*, fols. 76r–102v[39]
25. *Counsels of Isidore*, fols. 102v–110 v[40]
26. Augustine, *De contemptu mundi*, fol. 111r[41]
27. 'Erthe upon Erthe', *IMEV* 3985, fols. 111r–114r[42]

Compilers, therefore knew what structure a devotional manual should have; the general shape of these books was understood, and the schemas within these books may have been imitated from widely circulated authored compilations, particularly *Pore Caitiff*, a text thought to have been composed in the 1380s and which provides a ladder from basic Christian lore to more complex modes of piety. What is fascinating is that while there seemed to have been a common understanding as to the shape of a devotional manual, it is the case that no one ever appears to have copied another such book in its entirety. These compilations are endlessly variable and book compilers blend texts in new ways, and according to subtle schema of their own devising.

One of the most interesting insights into the production circumstances of these books is provided by a collection of six closely related London anthologies that has been discussed in print by Margaret Connolly. At the core of each of the six anthologies is a group of texts to which each compiler adds materials that have been sourced individually. Each of the compilers must have had access to a shared booklet (or a genetic relation of that booklet) containing the same cluster of texts. In Connolly's case study, it is clear that some of the compilers of these volumes chose to omit and replace materials in the booklets that they sourced. She writes:

> not all compilers chose to include all of the texts in the booklet exemplar; when all texts were included their order was often rearranged. This may have been in response to the demands of a patron or the volume's perceived audience, with an individual compiler adapting the given material in order to meet particular needs.[43]

Indeed, the compilers often selected texts in a manner that suggests their books represented quite particular interests. Often, what can be only described as an idiosyncratic theme emerges within these books, and when this happens, it is tempting to think of the codicological boundaries and

Structural Codicology and Medieval Manuscript Culture

fissures – textual items, nodes, booklets – that we discover as book historians, as dissolving against the evident plan and will of the commissioner-compiler. Oxford, Bodleian Library, MS Bodley 938, for example, incorporates a large number of items that argue for, or assume the importance of, lay access to the scriptures; throughout the book, biblical references are clearly marked in the margins, with the textual discussion bolstered by biblical authority.[44] Bodley 938 also opens and closes with texts perhaps attributable to the compiler, and that again reinforce the efficacy of scriptural teaching. The opening text is in two parts, the first enjoining the reader to keep the law of the Old Testament, and the second to forgive one's neighbours their trespasses, as taught by Christ in the Gospels; the text contains side-notes and internal references to Exodus 13, Deuteronomy 26, John 14, Matthew 6, and Mark 11. The book closes with a reference from 2 Timothy, chapter 3:

> Euery scripture of god enspirid is profitable to techen & undur-nymen to chastisen & to leren in riȝtwisnes : þᵗ þe man of god be perfit enfourmed to euery good werk 2 . thimo . 3°[45]

Godly inspired scriptures, the volume's final text reveals, are the basis for our moral education, and make us aware of our faults. The texts collected in this long book of some 280 folios and around 55 items, and the manner in which it opens and closes with texts announcing the value of biblical learning reveal that study of the scriptures, and, perhaps, the idea of biblical translation, were values that were to key to the compiler, and that profoundly influenced the content of his or her book. All those nodes, those separable codicological units (of which there are many in MS Bodley 938), it may be argued, were subsumed within a greater religious and ideological manifesto.

Bits and Pieces: the Afterlives of Medieval Books

Although much of this chapter has been concerned with the capacity of the medieval codex to retain meaning and utility over long periods of time, it is obviously the case that manuscript books evolved in terms of their meaning and utilities over their often-protracted existences and sometimes radically so. Books might no longer be esteemed for their textual content at all, becoming mere useful stuff, used to protect other texts. Manuscripts were frequently cannibalized to form pastedowns, flyleaves, and material to strengthen bindings, and to act as sewing supports. This fate was particularly that of liturgical books, which existed in relatively vast numbers throughout the Middle Ages to facilitate not only the ministrations of the secular church, but also the various divine offices within monastic houses. Such books might need to be replaced because of becoming outmoded, whether that was because of changes to fashions in script or changes in the liturgy itself, or at least, changes in the kinds of books utilized in performing liturgical offices. The first fragment in a collection of such 'bits and pieces' titled *Fragmenta Manuscripta*, now held in the Rare Books department of the Ellis Library, University of Missouri, was once part of a liturgical manuscript of the tenth century.[46] The pre-Conquest liturgical fragment had been removed from the binding of another book of the same period, now London, British Library, MS Additional 24193, 'a continental codex containing the poems of Venantius Fortunatus', that had received new quires in tenth-century England.[47] Twelfth-century pen-trials on the Missouri fragment suggested to Linda Voigts that it was at this point, some two hundred years after its initial production, that it became repurposed as binding material, as fly-leaves, or perhaps as a pastedown, covering the boards in a new host manuscript. The fragment, now difficult to identify precisely in terms of its liturgical function, was plausibly part of a '"primitive" breviary', but by the twelfth century, was clearly no longer of continued usefulness (unlike, evidently, the equally venerable collection of Latin poetry it was used to protect).[48]

Liturgical material might even have its text scraped from the parchment to become a palimpsest, where at least two sets of writing have been penned onto the same piece of parchment. M. C. Seymour recognized six repurposed leaves within a copy of Chaucer's *Treatise on the Astrolabe* (Cambridge, St John's College, MS E. 2).[49] The leaves, perhaps 'from an abandoned or rejected antiphonal', were large enough to be turned ninety degrees and folded to form bifolia, so that three liturgical leaves became three bifolia in the Chaucer manuscript. The ghostly signs of musical notation running along a vertical axis on the leaves can still just be discerned.

The usefulness of liturgical manuscripts meant that they might also be donated to religious houses as part of bequests from donors, hoping to exchange the books for the prayers of the institution. The late fifteenth-century will of Cecily Neville records her gifting of a wide array of liturgical books to the colleges of Fotheringhay and Stoke by Clare.[50] Her will accounts for thirteen processionals, five antiphonaries, three breviaries, two Psalters, seven graduals, three Mass books, one book of collects, one book of gospels with epistles, and one book of legends. These were books that in her magnate household would have been accrued in the service of both personal piety and the ministrations within the chapel, a centre for religion that catered for a significant amount of people in such great houses. Interestingly, the books with the most elaborate and expensive bindings such as the 'prymour with claspes silver and gilt covered with blewe velvett', volumes that Cecily may have used herself in public contexts, are not

Structural Codicology and Medieval Manuscript Culture

destined to be used by the college canons, but are instead gifted to fellow members of the lay nobility.[51] It is interesting to speculate what changes in codicological fortune the glut of service books gifted by Cecily would have brought about. Perhaps tired service books already held by the canons of Fotheringhay and Stoke by Clare may have ended up being recycled and repurposed in manners similar to the book that once held the Missouri fragment.

Not all the sheaves of fragmentary material from manuscripts within archives emanates from bindings. Medieval books that avoided being broken up and utilized by bookbinders, nevertheless might also suffer damage, resulting in the creation of lone leaves and bifolia, and other kinds of fragments. If we consider the book that this chapter began with – the fifteenth-century copy of the Middle English 'Liber Aureus and Gospel of Nichodemus' – it lacks four leaves, the two outer bifolia from the unwieldy opening quire of eighteen leaves (folios 1, 2, 17, and 18 are now missing). We simply do not know where these leaves are. They might easily be in a box of manuscript scraps in some institutional collection, or, given the usefulness of parchment, and the probable early loss of the leaves from the book, may have been appropriated to a new purpose. The potential for such discoveries continues to exist, such as the leaf from the Middle English Prose Brut I discovered myself in the Special Collections Department of Queen's University, Belfast. The fragment was unknown to scholarship, and was found to be part of the book now catalogued as London, British Library, MS Harley 266.[52] In this case the fragment (Brett MS 3/12B) allowed a new understanding of the codex from which it was parted to emerge. MS Harley 266 had been understood as a chronicle beginning with the reign of Edward I, a misunderstanding that had been encouraged by its seventeenth-century antiquarian owner, Sir Simond D'Ewes. D'Ewes had penned a new heading on folio 1r and scraped away the original chapter numbers (which should have begun at chapter 161 and replaced them with a new run of chapter numbers beginning at 1). The Belfast fragment, which had been the leaf occurring immediately before the first leaf of MS Harley 266, provided the account of the end of the reign of Henry III, and the prophecy of Merlin relating to that king. The chapter number is, as it should be, provided in the fragment as capitulo 160, and thus demonstrated that MS Harley 266 was once a full copy of the Brut beginning with Britain's mythical prehistory. It was a case that demonstrated that those codicological scraps, often neglected by book historians entranced by the lure of the complete codex, may have much to tell us still about the books from which they came.

It is similarly the case, that appreciating the 'sum of the book' – that intersection between the material features of each manuscript book with its

123

unique functionalities and its history of evolving functionalities – is often neglected by textual scholars. This chapter has been intended to suggest the importance of these methods in helping us to excavate the varied material circumstances of medieval codices and how these circumstances relate to production, reception, and the endlessly varying utilities of medieval books.

Notes

1. R. Clemens and T. Graham, *Introduction to Manuscript Studies* (Ithaca and London: Cornell University Press, 2007), 52, figs. 4–9.
2. See G. Pollard, 'Describing Medieval Bookbindings', in J. J. G. Alexander and M. T. Gibson, eds., *Medieval Learning and Literature: Essays Presented to Richard William Hunt* (Oxford: Clarendon Press, 1976), 50–65, at 57.
3. See R. Hanna, 'Middle English Books and Middle English Literary History', *Modern Philology*, 102 (2004), 157–78.
4. See 'Geographies of Orthodoxy', www.qub.ac.uk/geographies-of-orthodoxy/.
5. G. Murano, 'Zibaldoni (Commonplace Books)', *Scriptorium*, 67 (2013), 394–406, at 394.
6. Translated as, 'a booklet of four folds', in A. P. Smyth, *The Medieval Life of King Alfred the Great: A Translation and Commentary on the Text Attributed to Asser* (Basingstoke: Palgrave, 2002), 42.
7. S. Keynes and M. Lapidge, *Alfred the Great: Asser's Life of King Alfred and Other Contemporary Sources* (London: Penguin Books, 1983), 99–100.
8. M. P. Brown, *Understanding Illuminated Manuscripts: A Guide to Technical Terms* (London: British Library, 1994).
9. Keynes and Lapidge, *Alfred the Great*, 99 (emphasis mine); Smyth provides an alternate translation, 'at the beginning of which I wrote down the quotation', *The Medieval Life*, 42.
10. See Special Collections Conservation Unit of the Preservation Department of Yale University Library, 'Medieval Manuscripts: Bookbinding Terms, Materials, Methods and Models', https://travelingscriptorium.files.wordpress.com/2013/07/bookbinding-booklet.pdf; J. A. Szirmai, 'Limp Bindings', in *The Archaeology of Medieval Bookbinding* (Aldershot: Ashgate, 1999), 285–319.
11. D. Howe and M. R. Warren, 'The Dartmouth Brut: Conservation, Authenticity, Dissemination', *Digital Philology: A Journal of Medieval Cultures* (2014), 178–95, at 182.
12. P. R. Robinson, 'Self-contained Units in Composite Manuscripts of the Anglo-Saxon Period', *Anglo-Saxon England*, 7 (1978), 231–8 and 'The "Booklet": A Self-contained Unit in Composite Manuscripts', *Codicologica*, 3 (1980), 46–69.
13. Murano, 'Zibladoni', 394.
14. Robinson, 'Anglo-Saxon Period', 238; Ch. 3 in this volume.
15. Letter printed in P. J. Murphy and F. Porcheddu, 'Robert Thornton, the Alliterative *Morte Arthure*, and Cambridge University Library MS Dd.11.45', *Modern Philology*, 114 (August 2016), 130–47, at 132. D. Pearson, *English Bookbinding Styles, 1450–1800: A Handbook* (London: British Library, 2005).
16. Porcheddu, 'Robert Thornton', 140.

Structural Codicology and Medieval Manuscript Culture

17. J. J. Thompson, '"The Compiler in Action: Robert Thornton and the Thornton Romances" in Lincoln Cathedral MS 91', in D. Pearsall, ed., *Manuscripts and Readers in Fifteenth-Century England* (Cambridge: D. S. Brewer, 1983), 113–24.

18. R. Hanna, 'Booklets in Medieval Manuscripts: Further Considerations', *Studies in Bibliography*, 39 (1986), 100–11, at 102–3.

19. See G. Pollard, 'The *Pecia* System in the Medieval Universities', in M. B. Parkes and A. G. Watson, eds., *Medieval Scribes, Manuscripts and Libraries: Essays Presented to N.R. Ker* (London: Scolar Press, 1978), 145–61, at 148; and *La Pecia Dans les Manuscrits Universitaires du XIIIe et du XIVe siècle* (Paris: J. Vautrain, 1935); A. J. Piper and M. R. Foster, 'Evidence of the Oxford Booktrade, about 1300', *Viator*, 20 (1989), 155–60.

20. Pollard, '*Pecia* System', 152.

21. See D. Wakelin, *Scribal Correction and Literary Craft: English Manuscripts 1375–1510* (Cambridge: Cambridge University Press, 2014), 125.

22. A. I. Doyle and M. B. Parkes, 'The Production of Copies of the *Canterbury Tales* and the *Confessio Amantis* in the Early Fifteenth Century', in Parkes and Watson, eds., *Medieval Scribes*, 163–210; L. R. Mooney and L. M. Matheson, 'The Beryn Scribe and his Texts: Evidence for Multiple-Copy Production of Manuscripts in Fifteenth-Century England', *Library*, 7th ser., 4 (2003), 347–70; D. M. Mosser and L. R. Mooney, 'More Manuscripts by the Beryn Scribe and His Cohort', *Chaucer Review*, 49 (2014), 39–76.

23. Scribe B is identified as London scrivener Adam Pinkhurst and scribe D as Guildhall clerk John Marchaunt in L. R. Mooney and E. Stubbs, *Scribes and the City: London Guildhall Clerks and the Dissemination of Middle English Literature, 1375–1425* (York: Boydell and Brewer, 2013); however, it should be noted that a number of reviewers have questioned the methodologies underpinning these identifications.

24. Doyle and Parkes, 'The Production', 164.

25. Ibid.

26. Ibid., 199.

27. N. R. Ker, *Catalogue of Manuscripts Containing Anglo-Saxon* (Oxford: Clarendon Press, 1957, repr., 1990), item 39; C. Plummer, ed., *Two of the Saxon Chronicles Parallel*, 2 vols. (1892–9; Oxford: Oxford University Press, 1952); S. Keynes, 'Manuscripts of the Anglo-Saxon Chronicle', in R. Gameson, ed., *The Cambridge History of the Book in Britain, vol. I: c.400–1100* (Cambridge: Cambridge University Press, 2012), 537–52; M. B. Parkes, 'The Palaeography of the Parker Manuscript of the *Chronicle*, Laws and Sedulius, and Historiography and Laws at Winchester in the Late Ninth and Tenth Centuries', *Anglo-Saxon England*, 5 (1976), 149–71.

28. Parkes, 'The Parker Manuscript', 167.

29. L. M. Matheson, *The Prose Brut: The Development of a Middle English Chronicle* (Tempe: Medieval and Renaissance Texts and Studies, 1998); the descriptions of the Middle English Prose *Brut* used here also depend upon those in 'The imagining History Project', www.qub.ac.uk/imagining-history/wordpress/index.php.

30. D. Pearsall, 'The Whole Book: Late Medieval English Manuscript Miscellanies and Their Modern Interpreters', in S. Kelly and J. J. Thompson, eds., *Imagining the Book* (Turnhout: Brepols, 2005), 17–29, at 29.

31. R. Hanna, 'Miscellaneity and Vernacularity: Conditions of Literary Production in Late Medieval England', in S. G. Nichols and S. Wenzel, eds., *The Whole*

Book: Cultural Perspectives of the Medieval Miscellany (Ann Arbor: University of Michigan Press, 1996), 37–5, at 47.
32. R. Hanna, Pursuing History: Middle English Manuscripts and Their Texts (Stanford: Stanford University Press, 1996), 9–10.
33. Hanna, Pursuing History, 8.
34. Ibid., 9.
35. Hanna, 'Middle English Books', 167.
36. Ibid.
37. R. Raymo, 'Works of Religious and Philosophical Instruction', in A. E. Hartung, ed., A Manual of the Writings in Middle English, 1050–1500, vol. 7 (New Haven: Connecticut Academy of Arts and Sciences, 1984), 2159–595, no. 24.
38. S. Kelly and R. Perry, '"Citizens of Saints": Creating Christian Community in Oxford, Bodleian Library, MS Laud Misc. 23', in N. Rice, ed., Middle English Religious Writing in Practice: Texts, Readers, and Transformations (Turnhout: Brepols, 2013), 215–37.
39. See Hartung, ed., Manual of Writings, vol. 9, no. 62.
40. P. S. Jolliffe, A Check-List of Middle English Prose Writings of Spiritual Guidance (Toronto: Pontifical Institute of Medieval Studies, 1974), I, 22 (a).
41. Ibid., I, 32.
42. See C. Brown and R. H. Robbins, Index of Middle English Verse (New York: Printed for the Index Society by Columbia University Press, 1943), no. 3895.
43. M. Connolly, 'Books for the "helpe of euery persoone þat þenkip to be saued": Six Devotional Anthologies from Fifteenth-Century London', Yearbook of English Studies, 33 (2003), 170–81, at 172.
44. R. Hanna, The English Manuscripts of Richard Rolle (Exeter: University of Exeter Press, 2011), 142–5.
45. Oxford, Bodleian Library, MS Bodley 938, fol. 278v.
46. L. E. Voigts, 'A Fragment of an Anglo-Saxon Liturgical Manuscript at the University of Missouri', Anglo-Saxon England, 17 (1988), 83–92.
47. Ibid., 83.
48. Ibid., 87.
49. M. C. Seymour, Catalogue of Chaucer Manuscripts: Works before the Canterbury Tales, vol. I (Aldershot:Scolar Press, 1995), 118; H. Ryley, 'Waste Not, Want Not: The Sustainability of Medieval Manuscripts', Green Letters, 19 (2015), 63–74.
50. A. J. Spedding, '"At the King's Pleasure": The Testament of Cecily Neville', Midland History, 35 (2010), 256–72.
51. R. Perry and L. Tuck, '"Wheþyr þu redist er herist redyng, I wil be plesyd wyth þe": Margery Kempe and the Locations for Middle English Devotional Reading and Hearing', in Spaces for Reading in Late Medieval England, ed. C. Griffin and M. Flannery (New York: Palgrave, 2016), 133–48.
52. R. Perry, 'Making Histories: Locating the Belfast Fragment of the Prose Brut', Digital Philology: A Journal of Medieval Cultures (2014, fall edition), 240–56; 'A Fragment of the Middle English Prose Brut in the Special Collections Department, Queen's University of Belfast', Notes and Queries (June, 2009), 189–90.

PART II

Why Do We Study the Manuscript?

6

ELAINE TREHARNE AND
ORIETTA DA ROLD

Networks of Writers and Readers

Producing and Disseminating Manuscripts

Unlike the rapid proliferation of books and documents that results from mechanized or electronic printing processes, manuscript production is a one-at-a-time effort that results in a uniquely individual object. From a detailed examination of the scribes' painstaking efforts in writing their texts, and from the form or genre of the texts themselves, it is often possible to reconstruct communities of authors, compilers, directors, and scribes all involved in the process of textual transmission. Here, we shall examine the physical circulation of a text, the adaptations of histories and chronicles that are fundamental within contemporary scholarship, and the networks of producers and users of manuscripts. Focusing on a small number of case studies, we shall show the ways in which medieval texts were adapted, individualized, and differently designed according to the tastes and desires of the scribe-compilers.

Writing, however, goes beyond the copying of books per se, and often the closely intertwined relationships between writing and the community of people who would be interested in reading, communicating, and archiving texts can be found in other types of writings, across religious and secular institutions. For example, at the death of Aphelisa (1208–21), Prioress of Lillechurch in Kent, a roll was carried around 378 religious houses in England reaching as far as Scotland.[1] The purpose of this document, also known as a mortuary roll, was to inform the religious communities of the death of the prioress, and to seek their prayers. The roll is 11 metres long and contains the contribution of 370 different scribes.[2] It starts with an encyclical letter, a circular communication about the death of the head of house, to which a title would be added, a dedication to the departed, and a prayer for this soul. This is quite a common practice, but not very many rolls have survived. In 2011, Lynda Rollason published a fascinating paper on the rolls that survive in Durham,[3] some of which are late fifteenth century; and

129

a French project has previously published an edition of the *tituli* and rolls across Europe in chronological order.[4] This sort of record demonstrates the potential range of textual mobility and the broad geographical extent of the religious network in medieval Britain. The variety of hands, as well as the type of knowledge, that can be derived from studying this type of record for book production is really very considerable, but such textual objects are rarely studied in detail.[5] More common in early manuscript research are the investigations into literary or historical textual production and dissemination, and this chapter will focus principally on the genre of historical writing to demonstrate the multiple forms of networks of texts and writers that one can encounter in the medieval period.

One of the most significant issues that scholars encounter in their work on medieval manuscripts is that of known authorship versus anonymity in the production and dissemination of works in Latin, English, French, Welsh, and the other languages in Britain. It may have been the case from *c.* 600 to 1500, as it is now, that there is a privilege pertaining to known authorship; that is, ascribing origin to a named person provided greater prestige to a text, especially when the writer was an *authority* as highly regarded as Bede, a monk and mass-priest of Monkwearmouth-Jarrow, who, in the first third of the eighth century, was responsible for some of the most famous Latin compositions in British literary history.

In the earlier Middle Ages, it was the monastery or nunnery which provided the most fundamental training in reading, interpretation, and writing. Bede, an exemplary product of this intellectual environment, wrote not only tracts that explained the scriptures, the world about him, and the reckoning of time, but also authored the most famous of histories – *Historia ecclesiastica gentis Anglorum*.[6] From his monastery of Monkwearmouth-Jarrow in northeast England, Bede's exceptional and broad erudition spread far and wide across Christian Europe, and drew extensively on the work of writers who preceded him, such as Gildas,[7] creating within his *Historia* a complex network of connections and textual relationships. He also, though, included in his historical account of the foundation of the English, eyewitness or verifiable accounts of events crucial to his construction of the Christian story. One of the most famous of these narratives is the story of the seventh-century Whitby Abbey cowherd Cædmon, who was given the gift of poetic composition through the miracle-working of God. As a recipient of such miraculous grace, Cædmon's verse about the Creation is the first recorded extensive poem in English combining the Germanic alliterative form with Christian content.[8] Bede transformed the poetic utterance of Cædmon into Latin in the production of his *Ecclesiastical History*, but in the transmission of the work, the scribes of two of the earliest manuscripts written around the time of Bede's death in 735CE incorporated not only the Latin poem as included by Bede, but also the Old English *utterance* of the poem. In terms of the manuscripts' layouts, however, the vernacular verse could not appear more differently, and just this one example provides an excellent illustration of the distinctions in layout involved in the dissemination of medieval works through the process of copying. Thus, in the 'Leningrad (or "St Petersburg") Bede' version at folio 107r,[9] the English poem is added in the bottom margin in long lines, making it stand out from the two-column Latin quite noticeably; while in the contemporary 'Moore Bede'[10] at folio 128v, the English poem is integrated into the main copying effort at lines 1–3 of the folio, though in long lines in a smaller manifestation of the main scribe's Insular minuscule script, again making the poem more visible, rather than less, but suggesting that the poem might have been thought of as a gloss to its Latin counterpart. Further down the same folio, a later hand added other texts in Caroline minuscule that demonstrates the manuscript had made its way to the European continent before the end of the eighth century. There, Bede's *Historia* was carefully scrutinized, and certainly used for the production of multiple continental versions of the text that provide excellent evidence for the tracing of intellectual exchange between monastic networks.

Intertextual Connections

Throughout the Middle Ages, the dissemination of Bede's works continued unabated. Well over 150 manuscripts survive of his *Historia ecclesiastica* alone,[11] and within a decade or so of his death, Bede was seen as a beacon of the church. In the eighth century, St Boniface, enquiring about the works of Bede, called him *candela ecclesiae*, 'candle of the church', for his contribution to religious and historical scholarship.[12] The twelfth-century Benedictine monk and prolific author William of Malmesbury summed up the historical achievement of Bede with understated admiration in the *Prologue* to his monumental twelfth-century *Historia Regum Anglorum*, completed in *c.* 1125:

> Res Anglorum gestas Beda, vir maxime doctus et minime superbus, ad adventu eorum in Britanniam usque ad suos dies plano et suavi sermone absolvit; post eum non facile, ut arbitror, reperies qui historiis illius gentis Latina oration texendis animum dederit.

> The history of the English, from their arrival in Britain to his own time, has been told with straightforward charm by Bede, most learned and least proud of men. After Bede you will not easily, I think, find anyone who has devoted himself to writing English history in Latin.[13]

Bede's learning, his lack of ego, his devotion to his craft, and his 'suavi sermone'[14] (his 'straightforward charm', or, more directly 'sweet words', 'charming conversation') are admirable qualities for Malmesbury, who employed Bede as a direct source for much of his recounting of the earliest centuries of pre-Conquest England. As Malmesbury himself relates, Bede dedicated his *Ecclesiastical History*, not, as one might expect, to his fellow monks or to a prelate, but to King Ceolwulf of Northumbria. This secular dedicatee shows that Bede intended a wide audience for his work, including the most highly educated nobility, with his *History* providing many episodes to illustrate what constituted exemplary kingship and its antithesis.

Malmesbury, along with many others, admired Bede as a historian greatly. In terms of the constituents of good historical writing, Malmesbury highlights Bede's familiarity with his sources and his regional focus ('Bede was particularly concerned with the Northumbrians, his own neighbours, who were familiar because they were so near'[15]). He emphasizes Bede's objectivity (Bede is 'incapable of flattery'[16]), his intelligent use of others' potential input into his narrative (as when Bede asked the Northumbrian king, Ceolwulf, to validate and emend his *Ecclesiastical History*), and his truth being sufficient to authenticate others' truth, like Malmesbury's own.[17] Malmesbury also prioritizes that which Bede chose to record, to make familiar through his own words, his own testimony ('And because Bede himself has briefly put this on record, when summarizing his whole life in a sort of epilogue, the reader will be able to recognize the familiar words, and I shall not, in the need to rewrite what he says, run the risk of adding or omitting something'[18]). Finally, Malmesbury praises Bede's 'great number of writings [and] modesty of style', his oratorical skill, his approval by the papacy, his learning, and his faith – unassailable testimony to his divinely inspired abilities to write with his eyes fixed heavenward.[19]

It would be difficult to counter the evidence of Bede, given the testimony provided here by Malmesbury, and, in turn, it would be difficult to counter the evidence mustered by Malmesbury himself in his *Gesta Regum Anglorum*. By the twelfth century, Malmesbury is careful to say that not *all* that Bede documented might still be verifiable. Thus, for example, in discussing whether the relics of the seventh-century Oswald, king of Northumbria – martyred in battle against the Mercian king, Penda – really were still at Bamburgh where Bede had declared them to be, Malmesbury muses:

> Whether they are kept in that place to this day, I am far from certain, and therefore do not venture a definite opinion; if other historians have committed themselves, I leave that to them, hoping that I shall always put a lower value on

Networks of Writers and Readers

mere rumour, and set down nothing except what deserves complete acceptance.[20]

Malmesbury's defence of his methods – declaring accuracy only where it is certainly merited – self-constructs a trustworthy historian, unlike those unnamed others who repeat rumour or legend. Through this nuanced, sophisticated rhetoric, Malmesbury makes his own case unassailable and effects a standard for historical writing that became widely disseminated: nothing is recorded in his history, except that which is unequivocally acceptable. It is this self-authentication and self-awareness, together with the comprehensiveness, critical scrutiny, and use of his large network of historical sources, that leads to the acceptance of Malmesbury's pre-eminent place in post-Conquest historical writing by modern historians, just as Malmesbury lauded Bede as the founder of best practice in historiography.

The Historical Writer's Work

The twelfth century is widely acknowledged as witnessing the most productive turn in the medieval period for historical texts. In remarks disparaging his earlier English predecessors, William of Malmesbury comments:

> With Bede was buried almost all historical record down to our own day; so true is it that there was no English competitor in his field of study; no would-be rival of his fame to follow up the broken thread. A few, whom favouring Jesus loved, achieved a not discreditable level of learning, but spent all their lived in ungrateful silence; while others, who had scarcely sipped the cup of letters, remained in idleness and sloth.[21]

The pre-Conquest English did not all produce historical texts in the precise way that Bede did, so Malmesbury dismisses the literati's wilful silence and the semi-literates' laziness. Yet this is to suggest that there is only one kind of narrative meriting praise. History, as Malmesbury understands it, is what Bede composed in his *Ecclesiastical History*; it is, among other things, 'original' work from recorded or eyewitness sources, and in his authoritative comments it is possible to trace then-contemporary knowledge of, and responses to, earlier medieval manuscript culture and monastic textual communities.

In the *Prologue* at the beginning of the *Gesta regum*, Malmesbury could stake his own claim and increase his significance accordingly, by commenting on the paucity of *Latin* sources after Bede and dismissing the *Anglo-Saxon Chronicle* – the name scholars have given to a collection of English manuscripts and fragments that narrate the history of England during the first millennium, up to 1154:

There are, it is true, some records in the form of annals in the mother tongue, arranged in order of date; and thanks to those the period since Bede has contrived to escape the dotage of oblivion. As for Æthelweard, a distinguished figure, who essayed an edition of these Chronicles in Latin, the less of him the better; I would approve his intention, did I not find his language distasteful.[22]

But the early English did, in fact, create a lively and extensive historical record: not only did a significant number of writers – many connected through the relationships between their monastic institutions – produce multiple vernacular histories (which Malmesbury, and other post-Conquest historians, knew and used), but also, perhaps as a result of Alfred's programme to educate noblemen in the late ninth century, a learned person (probably an Anglian scholar from the east of England) also adapted Bede's *Ecclesiastical History* into Old English, transforming this major text for audiences who could only access texts through their own language.[23]

The Old English *Ecclesiastical History* survives in six manuscript versions, three dating from the tenth century and three from the eleventh; numerous other instantiations, some listed in medieval repository catalogues, are now lost. Of the survivors, one is a single leaf (London, British Library, Cotton MS Domitian ix, folio 11r), which contains three extracts from the *Old English Bede*, along with runic characters and sixteenth-century annotations on the verso of the leaf. Other extant witnesses to what appears to have been a prolific manuscript tradition include some damaged codices (the tenth-century Oxford, Bodleian Library, MS Tanner 10 and London, British Library, Cotton MS Otho B. xi and the eleventh-century Oxford, Corpus Christi College, MS 279B) and two complete, but quite distinctive eleventh-century versions, Cambridge Corpus Christi College, MS 41 and Cambridge University Library, MS Kk. 3. 18.

These *Old English Bede* manuscripts, together with what can be reasonably surmised about other versions that circulated in early England, demonstrate networks of audiences interested in historical writing, just as they were in legal, or medical, or religious texts. Bede's agenda to create a Christian history of an English nation (or grouping of peoples, who could be called 'English') united under God and the Roman church still resonated very strongly in the tenth and eleventh centuries. The exempla that he used to show models of good and pious living were important to, and used by, successive generations of readers, and the reformist writer Ælfric (d. 1010), abbot of Eynsham, chose to continue Bede's moral and didactic impulse when Ælfric wrote about saints such as Cuthbert, and the seventh-century queen, abbess of Ely, and virgin saint Æthelthryth, whose lives he adapted from the *Ecclesiastical History* when he wrote his vernacular work, *Lives of*

134

Saints, in the 990s.[24] Indeed, that a known author need not remain precisely true to his authoritative sources is shown by Ælfric's adaptation of Bede's life of Æthelthryth, to which, among other various changes, he adds a sequence of lines at the end. This addition, explains that, according to Bede, Æthelthryth remained a virgin despite being married to two Northumbrian kings. Lest this should seem unlikely, Ælfric is at pains to reassure a, perhaps cynical, contemporary late tenth-century audience that such celibacy within marriage is actually attested by a married couple about whom he has heard. The husband, Ælfric reveals, was rewarded by celestial assumption after his death in a monastery; the wife, on the other hand, does not merit Ælfric's attention.

The ability of the medieval writer – whether they were composer of a text, or an editor, translator, or scribe – to change their source is one of the most significant characteristics of literate culture in the pre-print period. It means that no text is ever the same as its exemplar: even a handwritten text made with the effort of absolute fidelity would look different, because of the change in scribal hand, or *mise-en-page*, or the introduction of minor variation in spelling or punctuation. Larger, substantive alteration was common. Thus, in the *Old English Bede*, for example, the editor-translator, following the source, places considerable emphasis on providing role models for the multiple audiences of the text to emulate and yet he or she felt free to adapt other elements of Bede's text. The editor-translator excises dates and other parts of the original Latin work that could be regarded as too detailed for the newly repurposed vernacular; administrative materials included in Bede's original *Historia* are not included in the English version. Thus, traditionally 'historical' components providing chronological precision, as well as external and ostensibly objective validation of events and institutional relationships, are omitted, indicating that the editor anticipated different functions and constructed audiences for the *Old English Bede*: the broadest possible appeal and use for the work.

Narratives of History

The earlier medieval interest in history, despite William of Malmesbury's derision, is evinced by the multiple manuscripts of Bede's *Ecclesiastical History* in Latin and in Old English, and by the adaptation of Paulus Orosius's *Historiarum adversum Paganos libri septem* (*History against the Pagans in Seven Books*), completed in the early fifth century.[25] At this time, or shortly afterwards in the earlier tenth century, an Old English adaptation of the Orosius was made at Winchester (London, British Library, MS Additional 47967, fols. 2–87 (the *Tollemache Orosius*)).[26] A second surviving manuscript, London, British Library, Cotton MS Tiberius B. i, fols. 3r–111v, possibly from Abingdon, contains an eleventh-century incomplete version. Like manuscripts of Bede's *Ecclesiastical History*, the Orosius manuscripts compose history as a sequence of episodes linked in a narrative that falls into sections marked by large initials and Roman numerals. The years are described by the number of 'winters' that have passed since the foundation of Rome. Slipped into this account of universal history at fol. 11v of Cotton MS Tiberius B. i is a much more local event, contemporary with the Alfredian period in which the initial Old English *Orosius* was composed: the text known now as *Journeys of Ohthere and Wulfstan*.[27] The accounts of the travels of the Norwegian merchant Ohthere and the explorer Wulfstan are interpolated into the first chapter of the *Orosius* text. These travellers, who visited the court of King Alfred, told of their experiences so vividly that the stories were clearly felt to add significantly to the geographical and historical information provided in the *Orosius*. The interpolation, though, is added to the *Orosius* with a subtle visual marker indicating the opening of the text.[28] At line 8 of folio 11v a space equivalent to some two graphs precedes a red capitalized 'O', the beginning of the name 'Ohthere', which is given only the weight of a new section, not a new textual item or obvious insertion. The received historical text of *Orosius* is expanded and made local to the English context of production, illustrating the connections made between historical and travel narratives and highlighting the fluidity of textual boundaries, form, and genre.

The tenth-century Winchester scribe of the earlier manuscript of the *Old English Orosius* in Additional 47967 was someone working within a community of scholarly writers, translators, and scribes who had a marked interest in the composition of history. This scribe was responsible for compiling parts of the earlier tenth-century *Parker Chronicle* in Cambridge, Corpus Christi College, MS 173 (the earliest surviving manuscript of the related texts, known collectively as *The Anglo-Saxon Chronicle*),[29] and a colleague in the manuscript production team provided zoomorphic initials of interlaced dragons and knots in both the *Orosius* manuscripts and one of the books containing the *Old English Bede* (Oxford, Bodleian Library, MS Tanner 10).

Such a concerted effort in the late ninth and earlier tenth century to manufacture historical manuscripts, especially those in the vernacular with their emphasis on exemplarily clear teaching and learning intent, suggests 'a tradition of West Saxon historiography based on a revived scriptorium at Winchester'[30] that focused on the practical application of historical scholarship. The applications could include record-keeping in the manner in which

Networks of Writers and Readers

archival repositories seek to maintain texts from the past as testimony, as evidence, as collective recall to ensure a connection with future members of the monastic community and to provide institutional continuity.

Constructing Chronicles

That William of Malmesbury was overly negative about the lack of historical writing in England between Bede and Malmesbury's own work is undoubted. *The Anglo-Saxon Chronicle,* misleadingly *singular* in its modern editorial incarnation, represents multiple surviving independent, but interconnected, versions of history. The manuscripts that are extant represent others now lost, and indicate a broad effort, both in terms of geographical spread of institution and temporal extent of production, to record history in annalistic (and thus *chronicle*) form.[31]

The manuscripts of the *Chronicle* with their sigla are A, Cambridge, Corpus Christi College, MS 173, fols. 1r–32r, begun in the late ninth century at Alfred's capital, Winchester, continued through the tenth century sporadically, and then transferred in the eleventh century to Christ Church, Canterbury, where the last entry in English is dated to the period around the Norman Conquest. Manuscript B is London, British Library, Cotton MS Tiberius A. vi, fols. 1r–35v, produced principally in the late tenth century perhaps at Christ Church, Canterbury, and now incomplete, with annals extending up to 977CE.[32] The third manuscript (C), London, British Library, Cotton MS Tiberius B. i, fols. 115v–164r, is known as 'The Abingdon Chronicle', though it may have been written elsewhere by the seven or so mid-eleventh-century scribes, who trace the history of England up to 1066 from 60BCE.[33] Manuscript D, the 'Worcester Chronicle', is London, British Library, Cotton MS Tiberius B. iv, fols. 3r–9v, 19r–86v, which was copied by perhaps more than a dozen scribes at Worcester or York. It shows distinctive regional emphasis, with a focus on the North and Mercian events and was copied around 1060 or so, with some later additions.

One of the most famous of the manuscripts containing the Old English chronicles is Oxford, Bodleian Library, MS Laud Misc. 636, fols. 1r–91v, known as Manuscript E. Copied by two scribes who worked from 1121 to 1154 in Peterborough Abbey, it contains by far the latest annals in the set of *Chronicle* manuscripts, and is related to the Northern Recension, represented by Manuscript D. The Latin and Old English Manuscript F, London, British Library, Cotton MS Domitian A. viii, fols. 30r–70v, was written at Christ Church, Canterbury in around 1100CE, and its scribe-compiler also worked to revise Manuscript A. It is related to the source of Manuscript E, and, not surprisingly, also shows a close relationship to

137

A. Like E, it contains charters and materials that show a broader kind of remit than simply the annalistic. Manuscript G, London, British Library, Cotton MS Otho B. xi, was based on A, and copied at Winchester at the beginning of the eleventh century, before A made its way to Canterbury. G also contains a copy of the *Old English Bede*, evidencing a coherent historiographical focus. Finally, the fragmentary London, British Library, Cotton MS Domitian A. ix, fol. 9rv is known as Manuscript H, and contains only the annals for the years 1113–14.

Scholars have tended to work with these manuscripts as a set, representing one cogent work, *The Anglo-Saxon Chronicle*. In fact, though, each manuscript instantiation of the chronicles is an individual work, related by content or by context or by intertextual relationship to one or more of the other manuscripts, but unique, distinctive in its entirety, and telling its own national, regional, and institutional history. As a group of texts, it is the annal form (year date in Roman numerals, often in the left margin, followed by an account of one or more events from that year) that creates the chronicle format. Gervase of Canterbury, writing in the later twelfth century draws a distinction between the chronicler and the historian:

> They differ in form and style, for a historian goes along diffusely and eloquently, while the chronicler goes along simply and briefly . . . It is characteristic of the history to persuade those who listen or those who read with gentle and elegant words, and to inform them about the deeds, customs and lives of whomever it truthfully describes; it is in essence a rational study. A chronicle, meanwhile, reckons the years, months and calends of the Incarnation of the Lord, telling briefly the deeds of kings and princes that happened at those times, as well as recording events, portents and miracles.[34]

Many annals in the English manuscripts A–H do contain the barest detail, and for the earliest centuries, all witnesses to the English historical tradition derive from shared annals – the Common Stock.[35] Thus, for example, MS A, while retrospectively writing the year-by-year account, maintains an abbreviated style for numerous entries in the early centuries, from 'Here Ceol ruled for five years' (591 CE) to 'Here Cenwalh was baptized' (646 CE). But many annals are much more expansive in their description of major events, detailing major participants in battles, or ecclesiastical relationships, focusing on principal figures in the history of early English and, sometimes, continental European royal, political, diplomatic, religious, and governmental affairs. Differences between the manuscript accounts, which are many, permit a more nuanced reconstruction of the sequences of events, and an estimation of the relative importance of particular people and occurrences within the framework of individual institutions' foci. The 'Peterborough Chronicle',

Manuscript E, is determinedly centred on the locality at which it was written, even while it relates the history of Christianity and England pre-1150. It contains diplomatic material – grants and administrative documents – specifically made for (or forged in favour of) Peterborough through the centuries, seeking to secure the landholdings and privileges of the abbey; it is explicitly hostile to abbots appointed to the abbey in the post-Conquest period who are not respectful of the institution's history and property; and it is scathing about the social and cultural damage caused by the civil war between Stephen and Mathilda in the mid-twelfth century.[36] These entries in the period 1121–54 are roughly contemporary with the two scribes writing them, and here the prose is detailed, presenting a complex narrative with a determinable English and Benedictine perspective. It is more the work of the historian than the chronicler (in Gervase of Canterbury's definition), belying the simplicity that one might expect from the annalistic mode. This manuscript E, Laud Misc. 636, might fruitfully been seen in the context of major twelfth-century Latin histories, by authors as well known as Henry of Huntingdon, John of Worcester, Hugh Candidus (of Peterborough), the Anglo-Norman Gaimar, and Gervase of Canterbury, all of whom knew and used manuscripts of *The Anglo-Saxon Chronicle* in the detailed constructions of their own histories, and who thus owed a debt to their pre-Conquest historiographical predecessors.[37]

Immortality and Time

In his *Lestorie des Engleis*, Geoffrey Gaimar, writing between 1135 and 1147, recorded that,

> Il [Alfred] fist escrivere un livre Engleis,
> E des aventures, e des leis,
> E de batailles de la terre,
> E es reis ki firent la guere.[38]

The Anglo-Saxon Chronicle's fame as the work of King Alfred rendered his intellectual, as well as his martial, prowess immortal, even if misattributed in this case. At the pen of Gaimar, Alfred's *Chronicle*, the history instigated by his court's attention to recording knowledge of people and events, becomes a narrative that sounds more akin to a post-Conquest Romance, than to the dull-sounding annalistic enterprise mentioned by William of Malmesbury. As Simon Keynes points out, though, in the best introduction to the *Chronicle* manuscripts to date,[39] within this seemingly definable mode of writing 'The fact is that there were no rules, not even any conventions.'[40] Shorter annals are juxtaposed with longer prose annals –

such as the famously detailed account of a skirmish between two related noblemen, known as *Cynewulf and Cyneheard*, that took place in 755. Embedded among these are also poems providing retellings of the deeds of kings, just as Gaimar comments. The poems illustrate clearly that the *Chronicle* is to be regarded as a multigeneric, flexible form of storytelling and memorialization; of reckoning of notable events and persons and their contributions nationally and regionally.

The *Battle of Brunanburh*, so-called because it describes Æthelstan's battle to control the whole of England by defeating the Norse kings and lords in the north of the country, took place in 937 and forms the long entry for that annal in four of the surviving *Chronicle* manuscripts. Part of its effectiveness is the surprise of the piece in the restrained prose surroundings of the reign of Æthelstan (924–39), where numerous annals are left empty (or 'barren'), rendering the poem more notable and glorious by contrast.[41] Far from providing us with abbreviated or terse who-did-what, this poem captures the heroic ethos with effective drama and grandeur. The poet reveals that Æthelstan and his brother

> left behind them to enjoy the corpses
> the dark-coated one, the black raven,
> the horny-beaked one, and the dun-coated one,
> the eagle, white from behind, to enjoy the carrion,
> the greedy bird of war, and the grey animal,
> the wolf in the wood. Never was there a greater slaughter
> of people killed on this island
> by the sword's edge, even up until now
> or before this, of which the books of ancient scholars
> tell us;

> Letan him behindan hræw bryttian
> saluwigpadan, þone sweartan hræfn,
> hyrnednebban, ond þane hasewanpadan,
> earn æftan hwit, æses brucan,
> grædigne guðhafoc, ond þæt græge deor,
> wulf on wealde. Ne wearð wæl mare
> on þis eiglande æfer gieta
> folces gefylled beforan þissum
> sweordes ecgum, þæs þe us secgað bec,
> ealde uðwitan;[42]

The beasts of battle, eager for the carrion of the dead, are clearly to be sated by the innumerable corpses of Æthelstan's enemies. The individuation of the birds of prey and carnivorous wolves emphasize the feast of meat for every ravenous creature. And the poet places this historic victory within the context of not just the whole history of early England, but the long history of Britain itself, reinforcing Æthelstan's claim to be *Bretwalda* – ruler of the whole island.[43] The importance of 'books of ancient scholars' is made most evident, reminding every audience member – literate or not – of the significance of record, of recorded history. As the poet demonstrates his own sense of Æthelstan's achievements, he reminds the reader-listener of the function of each individual within time and the broader political, national, and geographical contexts in which they live.

For Æthelstan's reign in the Parker Chronicle (A), the earliest of the surviving witnesses, there are annal entries for years 924, 931–4, 937, and 941. In the Peterborough Chronicle (E), annals for 924, 925, 927, 928, 933, 934, 937, and 940 make up a very short account of the reign (937 succinctly stating 'Here Athelstan led an army to Brunanburh'). Manuscript D, from Worcester, omits the battle at Brunanburh, and – with its northern interests – emphasizes the submission of all the British kings to Æthelstan in 926 and his raid on Scotland in 934. The D-manuscript also does not include A and F's reference to the accession of the bishop of Winchester, Frithustan, to his see in 931, and it is possible through comparative study of the manuscripts to determine that the chroniclers often leave out information that is not pertinent to their specific interests at any given point during the text's transmission. Both through what is incorporated and what is omitted, it is possible to discern particular emphases and regional or institutional biases, challenging any notion that the chronicles are objective or static or 'the same' – an observation that is equally true for the longer narrative histories of post-Conquest Latin authors.

In the Parker Chronicle (A), as in the Peterborough Chronicle (E), annal numbers are written into the manuscript line-by-line. In the latter, these annal numbers are written in red, sometimes in two columns (as on the opening folios of E). It is striking to see the single entry in Manuscript E on fol. 5r, where fifty-five annal entries in two columns are written out (two columns clearly saving space and physical resource), with only one entry filled for the year 311. This annal contains the very retrospective and somewhat vague observation that this was the era of 'St Silvester, the 23rd pope, in whose time the Council of Nicaea was held, also the first council at Arles attended by Avitianus, archbishop of Rouen.' In this one entry is demonstrated the clear interest of the Peterborough Chronicler in Roman ecclesiastical and conciliar history and the place of northern Europe within it. But this entry sits surrounded by empty years, entered into the manuscript in a way that suggests the Chronicler thought completeness (filled with the space of absent entry) was essential; there is a sense that the Chronicler anticipates someone else might be knowledgeable enough to fill the gap, such is the potential of narrating history.

Fascinatingly, Cotton MS Tiberius A. vi (B), written retrospectively in the latter decades of the tenth century, also includes all the early annal numbers, and retains their complete lack of content, but in a disguised form; that is, parts of or whole folios consist of annal numbers written in linear sequence, as if they were prose. Rather than listing the annals, line-below-line, and leaving the rest of the line empty where there is nothing known for the entry, or nothing deemed worth recording, the Tiberius A. vi compiler-scribe, among other *Chronicle* scribes, compresses the information, but still insists on incorporating the barren entries in full. Time is telescoped, though the most recent edition has chosen misleadingly to display a line-below-line layout for these empty annals.[44] This telescopic layout makes the chronicle seem complete to all but the attentive reader. On closer examination, it reveals – perhaps shockingly to its audience – the rapid passage of time and the significance of years between recorded events. It forcefully reminds all those who encounter it, and other chronicles, of every individual's slightness in the scheme of universal time and of our momentary presence in this temporal life.

Other Networks of Knowledge

If recording history was embedded into early medieval institutional interests and the scholarly understanding of the passage of time, other networks of knowledge contributed to the circulation of ideas and texts which transcend genres, genders, and connect institutional domains from royal courts to monastic institutions, clerics, and queens. Tyler has discussed the powerful connections that 'emerged between the English royal women of the Anglo-Saxon, Anglo-Danish, and Anglo-Norman dynasties, from Emma to Edith/ Matilda, and the literary cultures whose patronage they made an essential part of the exercise of queenship'.[45] Her investigation demonstrates the boundary-less borders of eleventh-century European medieval learning, and the aristocratic interest in actively forging and influencing the writing of history and biography in Latin. The *Encomium Emmae reginae* was written to account for the Danish Conquest of England probably by a monk from Saint-Bertin in Saint-Omer, France, and shows the wide-ranging implications of writing history pertaining to England, but with a continental library full of classic texts, including Cicero, Macrobius, and Isidore.[46]

Many other examples could demonstrate the ways in which networks of learning and knowledge developed in Britain, and how texts that circulated widely were altered by respective institutions or copyists. It has often been observed that the circulation of texts and ideas were influenced by, and in collaboration with, a community of individuals geographically residing in distant countries or regions as well as local circles. Richard de Bury, born Aungerville (1287–1345), was an avid bibliophile. In his *Philobiblon*, he writes of his passion for seeking books and creating spaces for building his library. He writes of his keen interest in making books: 'we had always in our different manors no small multitude of copyists and scribes, of binders, correctors, illuminators, and generally of all who could usefully labour in the service of books'.[47] Having studied in Oxford in the Faculty of Arts, he entered the household of the young prince Edward, Prince of Wales, in 1316 and concluded his life as Bishop of Durham.[48] Bury travelled to continental Europe on several occasions, on diplomatic missions and, during a visit to Avignon in 1333, he met Petrarch.[49] Not much is known about the scholarly conversations that might have happened between the two scholars. Collette has, however, noted the close connections between Bury's intellectual life and the influence he exercised on the bookish culture of the early fourteenth-century royal court.[50] She also observed that Bury entertained a sizable network of scholars in his household, and by so doing she reminds us of the very fertile and learned background within which Chaucer's works developed.[51] Edward III, it is argued, for example, had a rather large library made up of 160 books.[52]

The investigation of aristocratic learning and the creation of book collections at this early point in time still requires much investigation.[53] It is certainly true that some texts became widely available during the latter part of the medieval period. This accessibility of texts has offered scholars an opportunity to study further the social and cultural implications of the circulation of manuscripts. The Prose *Brut* provides a good example. It narrates the history of Britain from the arrival of Brut, through King Arthur and through the Anglo-Saxon Kingdom to Henry III, with continuations and additions, which are often interesting vignettes of local and cultural practices.[54] A continuation of the *Brut* from 1430 to 1446, now Cambridge, Trinity College, MS O. 9. 1, tells of a woman from Kent who spoke too boldly to the king in London and was arrested and brought to court. When asked to recant she refused and was condemned to stand in a cart taken through London with 'a paupire about hir hede, of hir proude and lewed langage þat she had spoke and shewed to þe Kyng', for all the people to see.[55] The paper hat as a symbol of shame, which recounts the reason for such condemnation, is just one of the local and individual ways in which this popular text was appropriated in the many histories of late medieval Britain.

143

Matheson perusing the vast manuscript tradition of *The Brut* demonstrated that it survives in hundreds of manuscripts written in Anglo-Norman, English, and Latin. He noted: 'It is no exaggeration to say that in the late Middle Ages in England the *Brut* was the standard historical account of British and English history.'[56] In this broad textual tradition, the *Brut* circulated in royal circles (Edward III inherited a French *Brut* from his mother Isabella), and in baronial households. It was considered a suitable gift by the Earl of Warwick to Bordesley Abbey, Worcestershire, for example. Books of this text were owed by rectors and religious houses, and landowners. Men and women had the *Brut* among their books and it appears in the possession of merchants and clerks.[57] The social networking opportunities of owning this book, as well as a genuine curiosity in the past, made this text highly desirable among a wide range of people.[58]

If the Chronicles and the *Brut* can be offered as examples of networked readers and book owners, Chaucer's *Canterbury Tales* has similar potential. Much has now been written about the copying environment which may have facilitated the transmission of Middle English texts in London.[59] Other social interactions around the circulation of books can also be discovered by closely reading household accounts, in which illuminated gospel books, psalters, primers, psalters, cookery, and etiquette books were purchased across aristocratic households, such as the ones of Sir William Mountford of Kingshurst, Warwickshire (1433–4) and Thomas of Lancaster, Duke of Clarence (1418–21). Networks of knowledge, however, go beyond the idea of centres and peripheries. The connectivity and mobility of medieval people, and the adaptability of literary and historical works, demand a more nuanced understanding of the way in which we talk about how texts circulated and the possibilities that may arise from this mobility and flexibility. In this sense, every node in a network is a potential centre of production, connected by the many occasions that may facilitate opportunities for copying and obtaining texts.

The picture that emerges from piecing together how texts were sought out, copied, and then circulated does not have one predominant trajectory. It is rather a lively picture, with much potential for further research on the varied and variable writing environments in which texts were copied anew, but also repackaged and adapted for new audiences. More research on those who participated within these medieval networks of knowledge, and how such networks operated geographically and in practice, will significantly enhance our understanding of manuscript transmission, of the appreciation by writers and audiences of their inherited learning, and of the ways in which knowledge exchange took place across medieval Britain.

Notes

1. Cambridge, St John's College, MS N. 31. See: www.joh.cam.ac.uk/library/spe cial_collections/manuscripts/medieval_manuscripts/medman/N_31.htm

2. C. E. Sayle, 'The Mortuary Roll of the Abbess of Lillechurch, Kent', *Proceedings of the Cambridge Antiquarian Society*, 10.4 (1904), 383–409.

3. L. Rollason, 'Medieval Mortuary Rolls: Prayers for the Dead and Travel in Medieval England', *Northern History*, 48 (2013), 187–223.

4. J. Favier and J. Dufour, *Recueil des rouleaux des morts (VIIIe siècle-vers 1536)* (Paris: Diffusion de Boccard, 2005–8).

5. See, for example, R. Beadle, 'Dated and Datable Manuscripts in Cambridge Libraries', *English Manuscript Studies 1100–1700*, 3 (1992), 238–45, at 243.

6. B. Colgrave and R. A. B. Mynors, ed. and trans., *Bede's Ecclesiastical History of the English People*, Oxford Medieval Texts (Oxford: Clarendon Press, 1969).

7. K. George, *Gildas's De Excidio Britonum and the Early British Church*, Studies in Celtic History 26 (Woodbridge: Boydell Press, 2009).

8. D. P. O'Donell, ed., *Cædmon's Hymn: A Multimedia Study, Edition and Archive*, SEENET 8 (Cambridge: D. S. Brewer, 1999).

9. St Petersburg, National Library of Russia, MS lat.Q.v. I. 18, known as 'P'.

10. The Moore Bede, Cambridge University Library, MS Kk.5.16, known as 'M', is digitized at https://cudl.lib.cam.ac.uk/view/MS-KK-00005–00016/1 (accessed 10 January 2018).

11. See T. Webber, 'Bede's *Historia Ecclesiastica* as a Source of Lections in Pre- and Post-Conquest England', in M. Brett and D. Woodman, eds., *The Long Twelfth-Century View of the Anglo-Saxon Past* (Aldershot: Ashgate, 2015), 47–74.

12. Cited by P. Darby, *Bede and the End of Time*, Studies in Early Medieval Britain (London: Routledge, 2012), 215.

13. William of Malmesbury, *Gesta Regum Anglorum (The History of the English Kings)*, ed. and trans. R. A. B. Mynors with R. M. Thomson and M. Winterbottom, Oxford Medieval Texts, 2 vols. (Oxford: Clarendon Press, 1998), I, Bk I, *Prologue*, 14–15 (hereafter *GRA*).

14. Words used by Paul the Deacon in the *Versus in Laude Sancti Benedicti* from the *Historia Langobardorum*, Monumenta Germaniae Historica (1881), I, 36.

15. *GRA* i.47.1, 64–5.

16. *adulari nescius*: *GRA* i.51.2, 80–81.

17. *GRA* i.53.1, 82–3.

18. *GRA* i.55.1, 84–5.

19. *GRA* i.56.1–i.60.2, 86–91, *passim*.

20. *GRA* i.49.7, 72–5.

21. *GRA*, i.62, 94–5.

22. *GRA*, *Prologue*, 14–15.

23. See T. Miller, ed., *The Old English Version of Bede's Ecclesiastical History of The English People*, EETS, os 95, 96, 110, 111 (1890–8; London: Oxford University Press, 1959–63); S. Rowley, *The Old English Version of Bede's Historia Ecclesiastica*, Anglo-Saxon Studies 16 (Cambridge: D. S. Brewer, 2011).

24. M. Gretsch, *Ælfric and the Cult of Saints in Late Anglo-Saxon England* (Cambridge: Cambridge University Press, 2006); G. Molyneaux, 'The *Old*

English Bede: English Ideology or Christian Instruction', *English Historical Review*, 124 (2009), 1289–323.

25. See J. Bately, ed., *The Old English Orosius*, EETS, ss 6 (Oxford: Oxford University Press, 1980); A. Campbell, ed., *The Tollemache Orosius (British Museum Additional MS 47967)*, Early English Manuscripts in Facsimile (Copenhagen: Rosenkilde and Bagger, 1953); J. Fernandez Cuesta and I. Senra Silva, 'Ohthere and Wulfstan: One or Two Voyagers at the Court of King Alfred?', *Studia Neophilologica*, 71 (2000), 18–23.

26. Digitized by the British Library: www.bl.uk/manuscripts/FullDisplay.aspx?ref=Add_MS_47967.

27. C. Fell, trans. *Two Voyagers at the Court of King Alfred* (York: William Sessions, 1984); M. Godden, 'The Old English *Orosius* and Its Context: Who Wrote It, for Whom, and Why', *Quaestio Insularis*, 12 (2012), 1–30. *Ohthere and Wulfstan* occurs in both manuscripts – MS Additional 47967 and Cotton MS Tiberius B. i – though it is incomplete in the former.

28. Digitized by the British Library: www.bl.uk/manuscripts/Viewer.aspx?ref=cotton_ms_tiberius_b_i_f112r (accessed 10 January 2018).

29. J. Bately, ed., *The Anglo-Saxon Chronicle: A Collaborative Edition* 3, MS. A (Cambridge: D. S. Brewer, 1986).

30. M. B. Parkes, 'The Palaeography of the Parker Manuscript of the Chronicle, Laws and Sedulius, and Historiography at Winchester in the Late Ninth and the Tenth Centuries', in *Scribes, Scripts and Readers: Studies in the Communication, Presentation and Dissemination of Medieval Texts* (London: Hambledon Press, 1991), 143–69, at 163.

31. The manuscripts are presented here with their common sigla in square brackets. See Bately, note 30; S. Taylor, ed., *The Anglo-Saxon Chronicle: A Collaborative Edition* 4, *MS B* (Cambridge: D. S. Brewer, 1983); K. O'Brien O'Keeffe, ed., *The Anglo-Saxon Chronicle: A Collaborative Edition* 5, *MS C* (Cambridge: D. S. Brewer, 1996); G. P. Cubbin, ed., *The Anglo-Saxon Chronicle: A Collaborative Edition* 6, *MS D* (Cambridge: D. S. Brewer, 1996); S. Irvine, ed., *The Anglo-Saxon Chronicle: A Collaborative Edition* 7, *MS E* (Cambridge: D. S. Brewer, 2004); P. S. Baker, ed., *The Anglo-Saxon Chronicle: A Collaborative Edition* 8, *MS F* (Cambridge: D. S. Brewer, 2000); J. Earle, and C. Plummer, eds., *Two of the Saxon Chronicles Parallel, with Supplementary Extracts from the Others: A Revised Text on the Basis of an Edition*, 2 vols. (Oxford, 1892–9; rev. imp., by D. Whitelock, 1952).

32. Digitized by the British Library: www.bl.uk/manuscripts/Viewer.aspx?ref=cotton_ms_tiberius_a_vi_f001r.

33. See S. Baxter, 'MS C of the *Anglo-Saxon Chronicle* and the Politics of Mid-Eleventh-Century England', *English Historical Review*, 122 (2007), 1189–227.

34. See Gervase of Canterbury, *Chronica*, ed. W. Stubbs, in *The Historical Works of Gervase of Canterbury*, Rolls Series 73, 2 vols. (London: Longmans, 1879–80), II, 84–594, at II, 87; P. A. Hayward, ed., *The Winchcombe and Coventry Chronicles: Hitherto Unnoticed Witnesses to the Work of John of Worcester* (Tempe, AZ: ACMRS, 2010), 57, fn 184; C. Clark, 'The Narrative Mode of the *Anglo-Saxon Chronicle* before the Conquest', in P. Jackson, ed., *Words, Names and History: Selected Writings of Cecily Clark* (Cambridge: D. S. Brewer, 1998), 3–19, at 6–8.

Networks of Writers and Readers

35. See T. A. Bredehoft, *Textual Histories: Readings in the Anglo-Saxon Chronicle* (Toronto: Toronto University Press, 2001); A. Jorgensen, 'Introduction', in A. Jorgensen, ed., *Reading the Anglo-Saxon Chronicle: Language, Literature, History* (Turnhout: Brepols, 2010), 11–17.

36. See M. Home, *The Peterborough Chronicle: Rewriting Post-Conquest History* (Woodbridge: Boydell Press, 2015).

37. P. Baker, ed., *Anglo-Saxon Chronicle: MS F*, ix–x.

38. T. D. Hardy and C. T. Martin, eds., *Lestorie des Engleis: La Translacion Maistre Geffrei Gaimar*, RS 91, 2 vols. (London, 1888–9) I, 144, ll. 3451–4. My translation: 'He [Alfred] wrote a book about the English and their adventures and their lineage and about battles about the land and about kings who waged war.'

39. S. Keynes, 'Manuscripts of the Anglo-Saxon Chronicle', in R. Gameson, ed., *The Cambridge History of the Book in Britain, vol. I: c.400–1100* (Cambridge: Cambridge University Press, 2012), 537–52.

40. Keynes, 'Manuscripts of the *Anglo-Saxon Chronicle*', 541.

41. A. Campbell, ed., *The Battle of Brunanburh* (London: Heinemann, 1938). William of Malmesbury translated the Old English poem into Latin in his *Gesta Regum Anglorum*.

42. E. Treharne, ed., *Old and Middle English: An Anthology, 890–1450*, 3rd edn (Oxford: Wiley-Blackwell, 2009), 32–3.

43. S. Walker, 'A Context for *Brunanburh*', in T. Reuter, ed., *Warriors and Churchmen in the High Middle Ages: Essays Presented to Karl Leyser* (London: Hambledon Press, 1992), 21–39.

44. Taylor, *Anglo-Saxon Collaborative Edition MS C*.

45. E. M. Tyler, *England in Europe: English Royal Women and Literary Patronage, c. 1000–c. 1150* (Toronto: University of Toronto Press, 2017), 4.

46. Ibid., 51–100.

47. R. de Bury, *The Love of Books, the Philobiblon, of Richard de Bury*, trans. E. C. Thomas (London: Chatto and Windus, 1907).

48. W. J. Courtenay, 'Bury [Aungerville], Richard (1287–1345)', *Dictionary of National Biography*, https://doi.org/10.1093/ref:odnb/4153.

49. Courtenay, 'Bury'.

50. Petrarch comments on this encounter in his letters to Tommaso da Messina. See C. P. Collette, *Rethinking Chaucer's Legend of Good Women* (Woodbridge: York Medieval Press, 2014), 15, n. 12.

51. Collette, *Rethinking*, 14.

52. J. Vale, *Edward III and Chivalry: Chivalric Society and Its Context 1270–1350* (Woodbridge: Boydell Press, 1982), 50; W. M. Ormrod, *Edward III* (New Haven, CN: Yale University Press, 2011), 13–15.

53. See Webber's chapter in this book, p. 214–233; and on later learning, see D. Wakelin, *Humanism, Reading, and English Literature, 1430–1530* (Oxford: Oxford University Press, 2007).

54. F. Brie, ed., *The Brut*, EETS, os. 131,136 (London: Pub. for the Early English text society, by K. Paul, Trench, Trübner & Co., 1906).

55. Brie, *The Brut*, 484.

56. L. M. Matheson, *The Prose Brut: The Development of a Middle English Chronicle* (Tempe, AZ: ACMRS, 1998), 8–9, at 9.

57. Matheson, *The Prose Brut*, 8–16.
58. See Chapter 5 in this volume, p. 123.
59. See L. R. Mooney and E. Stubbs, *Scribes and the City: London Guildhall Clerks and the Dissemination of Middle English Literature, 1375–1425* (York: York Medieval Press, 2013); L. Warner, *Chaucer's Scribes: London Textual Production 1384–1432* (Cambridge: Cambridge University Press, 2018); Chapter 3 in this volume, p. 49.

7

JANE GILBERT AND
SARA HARRIS

The Written Word: Literacy across Languages

To modern readers, the primary fact about a medieval manuscript page is often the language in which it is written. However, medieval written words were situated not only within but also often across languages. Medieval British literacy was essentially comparative, evolving as it did against a background of at least two languages: most commonly, the formal Latin of the liturgy and the schools, and a vernacular mother-tongue. There were almost certainly no literate monoglots during the period covered by this volume. Interlingual relations were more evident, or more exploited, in some contexts more than in others, as we shall show, but they were always at least latent. This chapter therefore favours a relatively flat and broad approach to 'medieval multilingualism'. On the one hand, we treat language choice as one among a range of elements that convey cultural context and meaningfulness, and which include the choice of text copied, as well as codicological features such as format, script size and style, *mise-en-page* and *mise-en-texte*, practices of abbreviation or of commentary, and decoration. On the other hand, we foreground how linguistic variations run within and across distinct languages, communicated through style and register, local or supra-local usage, and orthography, as well as through code-switching, borrowing, quotation, and hybridization. Drawing on the resources of more than one language was a pleasure and an art of medieval literacy, we argue, in many more cases than is commonly recognized.

The variety of languages written and spoken in medieval Britain offered scribes subtle opportunities to shape new readings of their texts. Throughout the medieval period, they would have learned to read and write first in Latin: the language of the Church, of diplomacy, of most legal documents, and of international scholarship. The vast majority of surviving manuscripts are written wholly in Latin. But to write in medieval Britain was to write within a multilingual nexus: although English was the most widely spoken vernacular, significant communities speaking French,

Welsh, Cornish, Gaelic and Norse were supplemented at different times by smaller numbers speaking Flemish, Hebrew, Italian, Breton, and other languages. Language knowledge was influenced by a person's region of origin or habitation. Social factors were also important, particularly where knowledge of elite languages was concerned. French offered access to the higher social echelons in England and to trade, landholding, diplomacy, law, and travel on the Continent and beyond, into the eastern Mediterranean and Adriatic. Latin was essential for access to Christian circles whose self-definition relied on learning, literacy, or ritual, its role paralleled by Hebrew for the significant number of Jews living in England between the Conquest and their expulsion in 1290. As this last point highlights, knowledge and practice of different languages in Britain varied significantly over the medieval period, affected by historical events and by micro- or macro-cultural shifts. The influence of events such as the Viking invasions or the Norman Conquest appear easy to track, but complicated cultural strands and religious and ethnic politics might affect even a single milieu in a particular place over a few short generations. The varying status of French in England, for instance, defies generalization. Moreover, manuscript survival rates have been uneven: catastrophic for Scotland and relatively bad for Wales, hence our focus here on England.

Medieval England's multilingual breadth ensures that its manuscripts are situated amidst and across different linguistic traditions. Medieval written language emerges as a nuanced series of negotiations between convention and innovation, where each element of the page carries its own cultural weight. To differing extents, the process of copying a text, whatever its language or languages, was shaped both by deliberate scribal decisions and by less consciously considered responses to existing cultural pressures: how far to adhere to existing paradigms of written language and how far to experiment with reflecting the rhythms of everyday speech; whether to use an international language variety or a very local one; whether to employ the script and *mise-en-page* of the exemplar, to follow the existing conventions for the written form and type of text and its language, or to draw upon another tradition. Further questions were created by varying degrees of linguistic expertise and perception across audiences, times, and places: how far to include translations or glosses to aid, display, or (sometimes) problematize comprehension; how far to modernize, and how far to accentuate antiquity. Medieval English authors and scribes often evoked more than one set of conventions, relating their work to different genres and audiences and thus raising the question of the boundaries between them. Such overlapping associations imparted to words in many manuscripts a certain liminality – the sense of opening

150

The Written Word: Literacy across Languages

onto other languages and therefore contexts – which we aim to explore here through a number of case studies.

The potential for multiple linguistic interpretations on the part of scribe or reader is exemplified by a few lines jotted on the endleaf of Oxford, Bodleian Library, MS Bodley 340 (Figure 7.1). Endleaves are unusually receptive to scribal practices which depart from formal norms, and in this respect are atypical; however, the idiosyncratic jottings they preserve throw light on how language and languages worked for the communities producing or receiving the manuscript. MS Bodley 340 was part of a two-volume set designed to provide a comprehensive collection of the highly popular and widely disseminated Old English sermons by Ælfric, homilist, grammarian, and abbot of Eynsham (c. 950–c. 1010). Writing in the first quarter of the eleventh century, one main hand copied the full sermon series. Contemporary additions by this scribe and others indicate that he probably worked at Rochester Cathedral Priory, where the volumes apparently remained after the Norman Conquest. Annotations and glosses suggest that they continued to be read throughout the twelfth century; although Old English posed greater difficulties after this period, some readers into the sixteenth century still tackled the text.[1] But MS Bodley 340 is most famous for a brief pen-trial made c. 1075–c. 1100 on its closing flyleaf (fol. 169v). This seems to be part of a vernacular love song, but who was the singer?

Hebban olla uogala nestas hagunnan hinase hi[c e]nda thu – uu[at] unbidda[t] [uu]e nu?

All the birds have begun their nests, except for me and you. What are we waiting for now?

These lines have attracted wide attention as one of the earliest surviving traces of Old Dutch literature, but recent work has raised a more complicated set of linguistic possibilities. The poem's word-forms are also compatible with the Old English local to Rochester, so we may have here not a Dutch, but a Kentish song.[2] Whatever its original affinity, monks familiar with either side of the Channel could have shared its pleasures. Other details locate the text amidst an even wider audience. The scribe subsequently added a Latin passage above 'hebban olla vogala' (it is clear that the Latin came second because the scribe ran out of space for the final clause and had to insert it above the rest of the text). This closely translates the vernacular:

Abent omnes uolucres nidos inceptos nisi ego et tu – quid expectamus nu[nc]?

All the birds have begun their nests, except for me and you. What are we waiting for now?

151

Figure 7.1 Oxford, Bodleian Library, MS Bodley 340, fol. 169v. Photo: © Bodleian Libraries

The Written Word: Literacy across Languages

Was this Latin addition intended as a scholarly gloss for those who did not understand a catchy local (or/and imported) song, or does it form the second verse of a multilingual lyric?[3] Writing in the decades after the Norman Conquest, the scribe would certainly have known of the French-speaking monks recently arrived in Rochester from Benedictine houses in Normandy, and also of the Flemish churchmen whose migrations straddled the Conquest. Palaeographical evidence suggests that he may have been one of them himself: he wrote in a compact type of Caroline minuscule unmistakably derived from the Continent.[4] Did he originally come from the Flemish- or Dutch-speaking Low Countries, was he perhaps a Norman in England, or even a local man? And would his knowledge of Dutch or English have sufficed to read the Old English sermons in the volume, or did he pick the book up simply to try out his pen? Finally, we might ask how he would have understood the gender of the lyric's implied speaker, who could be construed as a man or a woman, an 'insider' or an 'outsider' to the monastery. 'Hebban olla vogala' invites us to read across and between Kent, Normandy, and the Low Countries; pre- and post-Conquest readers of Old English; scholarly glossing, popular poetry, and scribble; and English and continental literary communities under the early Normans. At the juncture of these differing linguistic and interpretative traditions, the juxtaposition in this manuscript of a range of cultural resonances creates a new setting for a poem concerned with what it means to be 'at home'.

The example of MS Bodley 340 shows how we may miss important meanings if we approach medieval manuscripts with assumptions about language use that depend on nineteenth- and twentieth-century developments in nationalism and state formation. Recent literature has interrogated how medieval notions of the relationships between language and social group compare with modern ones.[5] Broadly speaking, some medieval pronouncements seem to invite nationalist treatment. Associations between language, law, and *gens* may be found throughout the period, and the issue of a 'national' vernacular arises especially in the fourteenth and fifteenth centuries.[6] However, such notions differ from the modern versions underpinned by later ideas about states, ethnicity, and language. Conversely, we should not assimilate medieval multilingualism to modern multiculturalism. The several languages of medieval manuscripts represent only a few, elite cultures (clerical, legal, mercantile, noble, etc.), most of which considered themselves to be transnational.[7] In efforts to understand the varying, unfamiliar ways in which medieval language-scapes organized linguistic difference, not only historical scholarship but also modern linguistics, literacy studies, and translation studies have much to offer our sense of variances within particular languages and of continuities across them.

153

Historical linguists suggest that in many contexts, translating from Latin into the vernacular, or vice versa, may have appeared to medieval writers and readers primarily as a transfer between registers or discourses: usages stylistically appropriate to varying communicative situations and activities. Affectively and conceptually, transposition between a 'langue de culture' ('language of high culture') and a 'langue de diffusion' ('language of wide circulation') would be akin to what today is called intralingual translation, rather than to modern interlingual translation.[8] In a different mode, scholars working in several medieval areas have recently argued that what were once thought to be incompetent mixtures of different languages in many cases represent conscious deployments of specifically written language varieties which gained prestige from their variegated character.[9] Such insights enrich our ability to grasp the fine detail of some of the cultural negotiations that language choice always involves.

This chapter, therefore, focuses on the linguistically liminal and bridging practices of scribes and authors in medieval English manuscripts and on the multiple, complex literacies inscribed therein. In our next section, we look at some of the ways in which manuscripts create different effects by presenting 'book languages' alongside 'non-book languages'. We turn thereafter to discuss the centrality of translation to medieval reading and writing, stressing the connections between the transmission, acquisition, and display of knowledge on the one hand, and movement across and between languages on the other. Our final remarks return to question our starting point, as we draw together these liminal, bridging practices to ask: what counts as an 'English' manuscript?

'Book Languages' and Others

Building on Charles Ferguson's classic essay on diglossia – a situation in which a community uses two languages but perceives and feels them to carry quite different valences, 'high' or 'low' – we observe that in the Middle Ages, certain languages are presented as 'book languages', while others are not.[10] Book languages define what literacy means in particular cultural contexts. They are deemed the proper vehicles of record, of administration and government, of literary heritage and cultural excellence, and of ritual and the sacred. They promise access to truths of various kinds: religious, scientific, historical, ethical, poetic, legal, and so on. They make things happen and shed lustre on what they express. Book languages are considered to possess stable grammatical structure and to be, if not universal and perpetual, at least resistant to changes of time and place. Their special functions and qualities supposedly make book languages markedly different from other linguistic

The Written Word: Literacy across Languages

codes in use, whether oral or written. Contrastingly, linguistic varieties perceived as 'non-book languages' display reduced prestige, agency, and efficacy; are less standardized, grammatical, and beautiful; are more responsive to space and time; and carry weaker truth-values. Later we shall argue that medieval English manuscripts' use of non-book languages suggests the existence of creative ambiguity between the poles that Ferguson distinguishes. But first, we show how his characterization of the 'high' illuminates medieval book languages.

Medieval perceptions of languages were often strongly hierarchical, and religious significance heavily shaped views of linguistic prestige. All the Abrahamic religions considered divine truth to be revealed not merely through the written word, but also through particular forms of written language: Hebrew for the Torah, Arabic for the Quran. Although only a tiny minority of Christians in England could read biblical texts in their original languages, many knew that the Old Testament was first written in Hebrew (which some thought to be the ancestor of all other languages, given by God to Adam in Eden) and the New Testament in Greek. If Hebrew, Greek, and Latin were for English Christians the *tres linguae sacrae*, nevertheless Latin dominated.[11] In practice most believers approached the Bible – the archetypal book – via St Jerome's fourth-century Latin translation, known later as the Vulgate, which provided the basis for worship throughout Western Christianity.[12]

The authority inherent in Latin as the principal language of scripture was further, and variously, fortified, complicated, and sometimes destabilized by its historical inheritance and geographical context. Latin was the language both of the ancient Roman Empire and its successor kingdoms and of the major Western religious institutions, many of which also looked to Rome; when used in other contexts, Latin carried some of this associated cultural, technological, and political prestige. For many Westerners, indeed, Latin was profoundly entangled in ideas of what books and writing meant per se. *Litteratus* meant Latin-literate, and Latin scribal conventions shaped presentations of other languages by providing ready-made models where writing was a fresh innovation, or by influencing existing conventions when people or texts moved into new cultural areas. Practices first developed in association with Latin endured in pages written from Ireland to Sweden, Poland, and Spain. Many western European vernaculars were encoded in Latin's writing system: a repertoire of letters that represented the phonology of the Roman alphabet. As we shall see later, scribes sometimes struggled to fit this writing system to the particular phonology of the language in which they wrote, evidently reflecting on the challenge of vernacular orthography. True vernacular versions of the Roman alphabet took some time to emerge.

155

Vernacular words were both dignified and overshadowed by inevitable comparisons with Latin and its cultural associations with the literature and learning of pagan antiquity and with Christian sacrality. Our following case studies explore some of the ways in which their raising to book-language status generally meant emphasizing resemblances with Latin manuscripts. For the distinction is not purely linguistic: the high and specific status of a book language is also created by association with particular writing systems, materials, formats, layouts, and paratext, as well as by the kind of text copied. Such features bestow and reflect prestige, and are susceptible to wide imitation and adaptation. This enables considerable variety and fluidity in English manuscripts' presentation of book languages.

Moreover, not all the languages found in medieval English books claim the dignity proper to book languages. Many manuscripts include non-book languages in supporting roles; for instance, in interlinear glosses, as pen-trials or owner's marks, or via quotation. If Latin (or an equivalent) primarily underpinned depictions of authoritative written language, scribes and authors also recognized that other factors could influence a text's credibility and utility. Non-scriptural languages could be endowed with intellectual prestige, not only when successfully evoking the paradigms of sacred texts, but also when demonstrating their links to specific royal, scholarly, social, professional, or regional circles. Temporal power did not only aspire to perpetuity, but also was significantly anchored in the here and now. Linguistic authority in manuscripts was constructed through complex layers of references and, although many scribal choices and conventions recall the technologies and theologies associated with the writing of sacred or other institutionally sponsored languages, others are more deeply rooted in linguistic, grammatical, and visual details which advance the local, the oral, or the experimental. Although underrated today, this is a significant strand in the aesthetics and philosophies of medieval manuscripts: the effect of the vernacular line on MS Bodley 340's endleaf, for example, depends on it. At different moments and for different purposes, language in manuscripts can suggest either the eternal or the transient, while pages may play with distributing book and non-book status in order to draw out varied, often subtle effects.

The glossed Hebrew psalter, Paris, BnF, MS hébreu 113 (first half of the thirteenth century) illustrates both how complex and how culturally specific such effects may be (Figure 7.2). A small number of bilingual manuscripts apparently produced for Christian Hebraists interested in the biblical language and text survive from medieval England.[13] Most lay out the different texts in separate columns, a common pattern in contemporary Christian bilingual Latin-vernacular psalters (see the Eadwine Psalter in Figure 7.5).

156

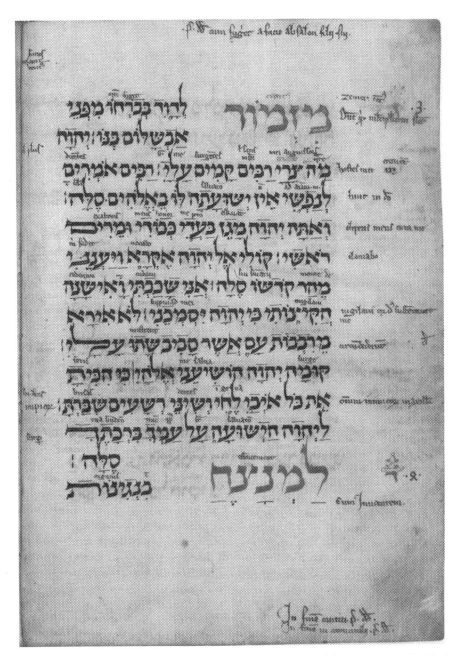

Figure 7.2 Paris, Bibliothèque nationale de France, MS hébreu 113, fol. 2v. Reproduced by kind permission of the Bibliothèque nationale de France

Our example is unusual in having been ruled only for the Hebrew text, and in having been copied from right to left (thus the page shown here is a verso side: fol. 2v).[14] Such features highlight the manuscript's Jewish associations and credentials, to which we shall turn in a moment. The example also shows how medieval Hebrew manuscripts were influenced by the practices of dominant, non-Jewish cultures.[15] The alternate red and blue colouring of the initial word of each psalm (here Psalms 3 and 4) follows a fashion popularized by Parisian book production and widely found in Christian manuscripts, as well as throughout the large Ashkenazi Jewish area of (at this period) England, northern France, the Rhineland, and northern Italy. Manuscripts in Hebrew script produced within this area during the twelfth and thirteenth centuries are so similar in appearance that modern scholars turn to other features to establish their date and place of origin. This similarity reflects the notable strength of Jewish networks and the mobility of Jewish individuals, but practitioners also made pronounced efforts to preserve traditional paradigms. This conservatism may have helped written Hebrew to approximate the ideal status of the book language in Christian as well as non-Christian eyes. And indeed, in the manuscript MS hébreu 113, Hebrew is presented as the primary book language: the square Ashkenazi script is large, clear, formal, and beautiful, and occupies the page's central, ruled area. Latin is present but has seemingly lesser status, being marginal and interlinear. Nevertheless, the Latin writing in the margin, consisting of short quotations from St Jerome's Latin translation, the *Hebraicum* or *Psalterium iuxta Hebraeos*, refers the reader to a prestigious Latin book, whose presence at hand it implies. By virtue of being manifest on the page, even in fragmentary, marginal form, Latin also claims the status of book language.

Still more culturally composite are the interlinear glosses, mainly in Latin but sporadically in insular French; spellings such as 'curuz' (l. 5) and 'purpris' (l. 9) on fol. 2r are strongly indicative of an insular origin for the scribe. In the middle of line 3 on fol. 2v, for example, appears Latin *surge[ren]t*, whereas on the right-hand side (thus at the beginning of the line) we find the French *mei anguissces* (contrast the Latin *hostes mei* 'my enemies' next to it in the margin, whose function is not a gloss but a finding aid relative to Jerome's Latin text). The presence of these French words seems odd: surely a Christian reader sufficiently educated to tackle Hebrew had no need of a vernacular crib? But it is likely that the Christian copyist accessed the Hebrew initially via French: specifically, via translations of and commentaries (*le'azim*) on Hebrew sacred writings, written in French, the everyday tongue of Ashkenazi Jews at this time (although they wrote French using Hebrew script instead of the Latin alphabet, with its Christian associations). The Latin interlinear

158

The Written Word: Literacy across Languages

glosses in MS hébreu 113 are either translated from or modelled on original vernacular glosses. That French should be the primary vehicle of sacred learning upsets the traditional Christian hierarchy of languages, which the language practice of this manuscript restores by relegating French to the occasional term. The end product may resemble the strictly hierarchical pages of the Eadwine Psalter (see Figure 7.5), where the interlinear, insular French translation of the *Hebraicum* gives local colour and affect to the 'universal' text represented by the three complementary Latin translations of the psalms. However, MS hébreu 113 is witness to cultural contacts and practices that took place in English monasteries and universities and that imply different models of intellectual learning and exchange for Christians.

Status as book language could fluctuate with larger cultural attitudes as well as across individual texts and manuscripts. In northern and western Europe, vernacular languages achieved 'book' status unevenly: at different times and rates, in different places, and in different contexts. An early eleventh-century manuscript written in Standard Old English would have carried a particular linguistic weight for contemporaries, since this regularized form of late West Saxon was also associated with the royal court.[16] But after 1070, royal writs largely abandoned this form of English: the (now Norman) king's court and administration placed new weight on French and Latin.[17] A late eleventh- or early twelfth-century reader of a pre-Conquest English manuscript might or might not have preferred to make a copy which reflected the speech patterns of his or her own era more closely. Moreover, the boundaries between book and non-book language were profoundly permeable, both within the manuscript and outside it: at different times, readers could interpret the same language in different lights. This could spark unexpected developments. As Standard Old English gradually declined in cultural prestige, some scribes moved away from early English norms: they were now reading their exemplars with an eye to experimentation. Crucially, their re-shapings of book language took place both in English and beyond it. Many of the earliest surviving manuscripts containing French texts were produced in post-Conquest England:[18] it seems that the sophistication of Old English intensified interest in the potential of Old French to function as a book language. Thus, the conceptual parameters of individual languages often overlapped, informing, disrupting, and enriching written conventions.

These shifting views of book language emerge from habitually multilingual environments: scribes, authors, and audiences constructed and negotiated texts by drawing on multiple frames of linguistic expertise. Such frames could be pointedly juxtaposed or could coexist harmoniously, sometimes within the same document. Oxford, Bodleian Library, MS Ashmole 328 was written in the mid-eleventh century by a single scribe (Figure 7.3). This

159

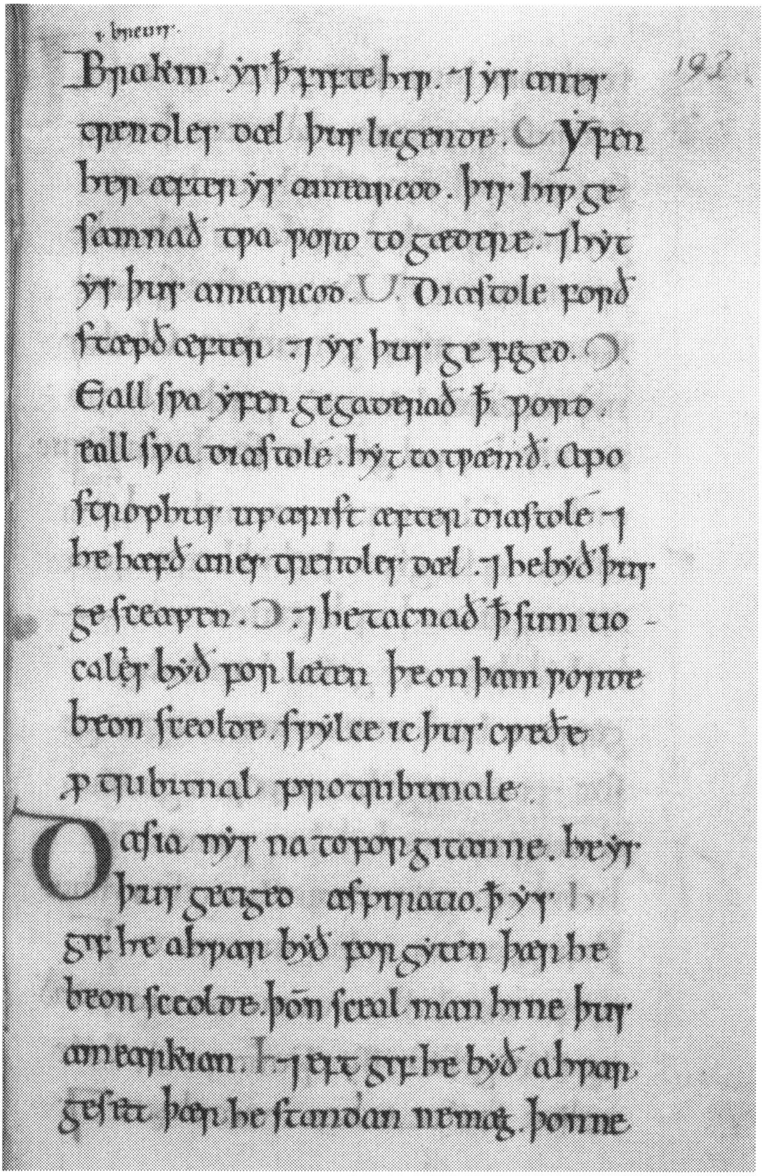

Figure 7.3 Oxford, Bodleian Library, MS Ashmole 328, fol. 195r. Photo: © Bodleian Libraries

manuscript is a copy of the *Enchiridion*, a text composed in 1010–12 by Byrhtferth, a monk at the Benedictine Abbey of Ramsey. It offers miscellaneous material loosely pertinent to the computus, the methods used to

The Written Word: Literacy across Languages

calculate various astronomical phenomena and moveable feasts. Byrhtferth envisages a wide-ranging audience across monks, priests, and minor clerics, from 'scholars and learned men' to 'clerks and rustic priests'.[19] Although fascinated by numerical esoterica, he was also eager to teach the basics of the calendar: computus calculations were an essential practical skill for the clergy. These twin considerations of the scholarly and the necessary may have influenced Byrhtferth's initial plan to compose the *Enchiridion* in Latin and the vernacular. He depicts English as a pedagogical support for the revelation of divine truth in Latin, stating that it is included so that 'young men would therefore understand the Latin more easily' (120–1). But, in practice, Byrhtferth almost immediately lost interest in alternating Latin computus explanations with English translations. The task was 'to langsum' ('too tedious', 20). Instead, he adopted a far more fluid structure: complicated and often *recherché* material is presented across both Latin and the vernacular. We might see these complementary idioms as forming a single, cohesive, and highly wrought writing style, which reflects Byrhtferth's enjoyment of arcane vocabulary in both languages. The linguistic contrasts and coherences facilitated by this structure are explored further in the different scripts of Ashmole 328. The scribe, following contemporary norms, visually marked out the text's two languages by employing a late style of Anglo-Caroline minuscule for the Latin, and English Vernacular minuscule for the Old English. However, a few details blur these distinctions: some Insular letterforms were used for copying not only English, but also Latin (**a**, horned **e**, **f**, **g**, **r**); conversely, some Caroline minuscule letterforms were used for copying not only Latin, but also English (**h**).[20] While Byrhtferth occasionally differentiates the functions of Latin and English, at other moments he implicitly depicts them as book languages of equal stature; indeed, he almost creates a composite, hybrid book language.

As literacy was a specialized skill, medieval texts were often performed to a group in a classroom, religious, or domestic setting; even where literacy was more widespread, performance continued to be a common means of consumption. Book languages were not limited to the page. In some cases, these contacts with the spoken word prompted profound re-imaginings of how written language might appear. In the twelfth century, the gradual shift away from the written norms of Standard Old English offered exciting opportunities to explore new ways of depicting the sounds of the vernacular. Oxford, Bodleian Library, MS Junius 1 preserves the only copy of the *Orrmulum*, a collection of English Gospel homilies written by one main hand.[21] This scribe's lack of expertise caused him difficulties, resulting in a highly idiosyncratic manuscript. He used poor quality quills, ink, and parchment. His work seems so painstaking that it is presumed he can only be the text's author, who names himself as Orrm. An Augustinian canon, perhaps working at Bourne in Lincolnshire, he wrote and revised the manuscript until the early 1180s.[22] Using Old English and Latin sources, Orrm aimed to produce a text which would communicate the message of the Gospels to the laity as clearly as possible.

For Orrm, an important part of this clarity was phonological. He was unusually sensitive to the potential of written English to give guidance to the spoken voice, producing one of the most sophisticated depictions of Middle English sounds ever attempted. Orrm had a uniquely systematic concern with *mise-en-texte*, particularly where it could aid pronunciation: he distinguishes the similar sounds normally included under a single English letter through diacritical accent marks (e.g., <a> vs <á>) and using different scribal forms (e.g., three varieties of <g>). He was particularly anxious that later scribes should imitate his gemination of consonants (e.g., <t> vs <tt>):

> 7 whase wilenn shall þiss boc
> Efft oþerr siþe writenn,
> Himm bidde ice þatt het write rihht...
> 7 tatt he loke wel þatt he
> An bocstaff write twiȝȝess,
> Eȝȝwhær þær itt uppo þiss boc
> Iss writenn o þatt wise.

And he who shall afterwards wish to copy this book another time, I ask him that he copy it correctly... and that he take care that he write each letter twice, everywhere that it has been written that way in this book.

These scribal practices single out the manuscript as a distinctive aesthetic object. They give the pages of MS Junius 1 such an eye-catching appearance that Orrm's text superficially seems unprecedented, both in its written form and in its interpretation of Middle English. But closer examination reveals the presence of England's other languages to varying degrees of visibility. Most evidently, a second, contemporary hand wrote Latin finding aids into the manuscript. More obliquely, the regularized orthographies of Latin and Standard Old English form an obvious point of comparison with Orrm's spelling system. Finally, some scholars have detected the potential influence of French in Orrm's attention to cultivating a convincing English accent: in multilingual Lincolnshire, his careful spellings may have been intended to ensure that francophone canons preached the homilies with correct pronunciation.[23] In some ways, Orrm's English seems hyper-written in its strictly regulated yet idiosyncratic scribal conventions. But other motivations may underpin this insistence on textuality: the *Orrmulum*'s orthographical

The Written Word: Literacy across Languages

fixedness may also respond to the profound fluidity of twelfth-century oral practices.

The notion of the book language, therefore, is not a simple one. Not all instances of a book language are equal: the perceived status of writing in any language depends on its time, place, and audience. Latin remained preeminent as a liturgical, academic, and administrative book language in medieval Britain, and much of its popularity rested on its international scope and unbroken classical legacy. When other linguistic codes aspired to book language status, they might mimic these qualities. But scribes and authors could also choose to ground their texts in geographically and temporally specific contexts, and the presentation of French, English, Welsh, Irish, and more, often indicates a wish to exploit the powers of what were used as book languages in particular contexts. In the same spirit, writers of Latin might elect to use either self-conscious archaisms or more modern lexis and syntax. The ambitious classicism of John of Salisbury is a long way from the Latin administrative documents whose idioms creatively reflect the vernacular paradigms of oral business practice. Far from being static or monolithic, practical instances of book languages were always subject to significant internal variation, prompted by the circumstances of composition of individual texts and manuscripts.

The scribes of other manuscripts also construct book languages by exploring the relationship between clarity and convention, transience and permanence, sometimes with priorities very different from those of Orrm. Vatican, Vatican Library, MS Ottobonianus Latinus 1474 (Figure 7.4) considers a new problem: how to translate the mysterious, vernacular language of Merlin's prophecies for the consumption of an international, Latinate, scholarly audience. In the 1130s, the appearance of Geoffrey of Monmouth's *History of the Kings of Britain* had caused astonishment across Western Europe. Controversially, Geoffrey claimed to have found new material absent from standard sources such as Bede: he depicted the ancient British kings as descendants of the Trojans, and greatly amplified the deeds of figures such as Arthur.[24] Contemporaries were quickly captivated by his work on the prophecies of Merlin: like the rest of the history, it purported to be a Latin translation from a very old manuscript written in ancient British.[25] Merlin's obscure, allegorical language seemed to offer veiled references to contemporary events and future developments, temptingly inviting further elucidation. During the subsequent international craze for decoding the prophecies, one text stands out. While all other twelfth-century interpretations of Merlin's prophecies are based on Geoffrey's text, John of Cornwall wrote a new Latin translation and commentary which seem to be based on independent Brittonic sources.[26]

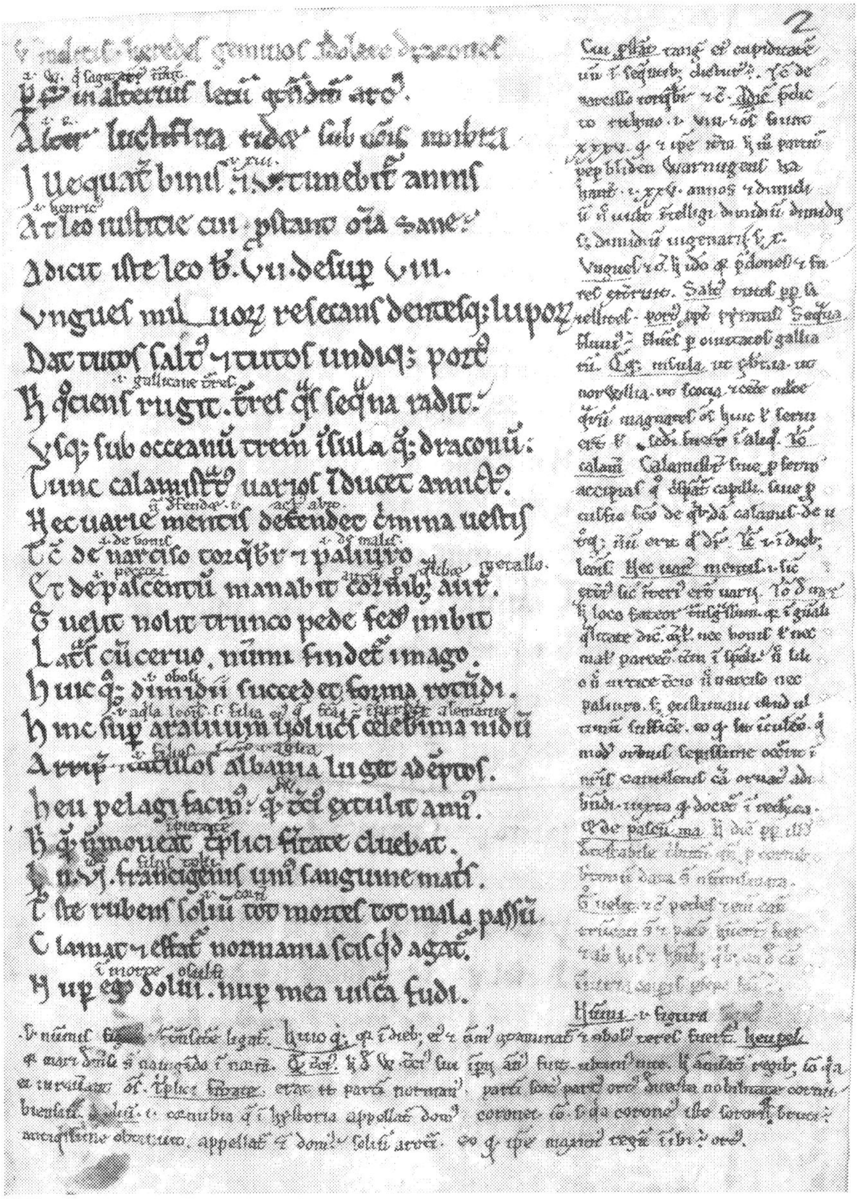

Figure 7.4 Rome, Vatican Library, MS Ottobonianus Latins 1474, fol. 2r. © 2018 Biblioteca Apostolica Vaticana

MS Ottobonianus Latinus 1474 now offers our only witness to John's work. Folios 1–4 form a booklet written by a single scribe sometime between 1166 and 1225, subsequently bound together with a late medieval cartulary.

164

The Written Word: Literacy across Languages

Writing in or just before 1154, John was attempting to reshape the local, oral, vernacular, and ephemeral into a book language shared by scholars across Latin Europe. The scribe has supported this academic presentation, carefully differentiating the scripts used for Merlin's verse and John's commentary. By wrapping this commentary around the main text to create an L-shaped layout, he creates a *mise-en-page* reminiscent of glossed Latin manuscripts for the academic study of the Bible and the Liberal Arts.

This Latinate setting for the vernacular conceals subtle linguistic elisions even as it displays the translator's mastery of his subject matter. John's text contains six Brittonic vernacular glosses: some are definitely Cornish, some definitely Welsh; others could be located across Wales, Brittany, or Cornwall. In contrast to the Latin translation, which is presented as a single, unified text, the glosses suggest work assembled from a variety of written, and perhaps oral sources. The scribe was not familiar with Brittonic languages, and has copied them without comprehension. He may not have been very careful because he did not anticipate that his readers would understand the vernacular glosses either. Rather than encouraging his audience to explore Merlin's language, the scribe may have included these vernacular fragments as a visual authentication of John's credentials as translator. Instead of deepening understanding, the glosses heighten our sense of this prophetic text's complications and obscurity, and thus its authority.

The individual cases discussed above represent only some of the varied effects which medieval scribes and writers created by presenting written words in many combinations of formats, styles, and languages. These effects could be employed to explore perpetuity and eternity, the sacred, the official, the universal, or the learned, but equally, they could emphasize the fragility, confinement, and immediacy of earthly life. These cases show, moreover, how the writing of Latin and vernacular tongues often advanced together – unsurprisingly, given the many crossovers between these languages which our case studies manifest. Written languages of all sorts were intimately connected to living voices.

Knowledge and Translation

MS Ottobonianus Latinus 1474 introduces our next section, which examines how medieval ideas and practices relating to 'knowledge' – its nature, presentation, and dissemination – involved, or even implied, the use of different languages. For medieval people, knowledge was typically found in translation. Important works were translated into Latin from other book languages or vernaculars to facilitate the transnational communication of learning, while translations from Latin into vernacular languages expanded the scope and flexibility of the target language, and in some cases also increased the number and social range of the educated. The typical presentation of an erudite manuscript – authoritative text supported by explanatory commentary – foregrounds translation, since the gloss which re-articulates and contextualizes the primary textual material may be thought of as a free translation, intra- or interlingual. Indeed, the world history of translation sponsored by today's professional body for translators and interpreters, the Fédération Internationale des Traducteurs, regards the Middle Ages wistfully as a Golden Age when translators could 'omit passages and insert commentaries to an extent never again equalled in the history of translation in the West'.[27] Whereas in modern publishing, translation is generally defined narrowly and commentary relegated to footnotes or appendices as mere accessories, medieval pages present both 'translation proper' (in the modern sense) and gloss as prestigious and significant components of *translatio studii* (the transfer of learning between cultures, often associated with that of political hegemony: *translatio studii et imperii*).[28]

Translation owed its high status largely to its foundational role in biblical interpretation: later Christian translators could consider themselves the divinely inspired heirs of St Jerome. Medieval institutions with the necessary economic and cultural assets often responded to this prestigious exegetical legacy with thoughtfulness and flair. The Eadwine Psalter (Cambridge, Trinity College, MS R. 17. 1) (Figure 7.5) was created in Christ Church Cathedral, Canterbury, *c.* 1155–*c.* 1160.[29] This luxury volume offers a meditation on what translation can capture. Its superb penmanship, large dimensions, and expensive membrane are matched only by its unusually comprehensive contents, which display the exceptional scholarly and artistic resources of the Christ Church scriptorium.

The Psalter situates itself in a complex network of insular, continental, and historical connections. A typical page features three columns for St Jerome's three different Latin translations of the Hebrew Psalms (known as the *Gallicanum*, *Romanum*, and *Hebraicum*). Each version appears alongside an accompanying study aid. The *Gallicanum* has been glossed with a Latin explanatory text (the *Parva Glosatura* of Anselm of Laon); the *Romanum*, with an English translation; and the *Hebraicum*, with a French translation. These respectively direct us to theological study at the University of Paris, to the long history of English translation at Christ Church, and to the fusion of these traditions with a new, socially prestigious vernacular following the Norman Conquest. In the light of our previous remarks about MS hébreu 113, we propose that this juxtaposition of French with the *Hebraicum* is equally important because it draws attention to the compilers' Hebraist

The Written Word: Literacy across Languages

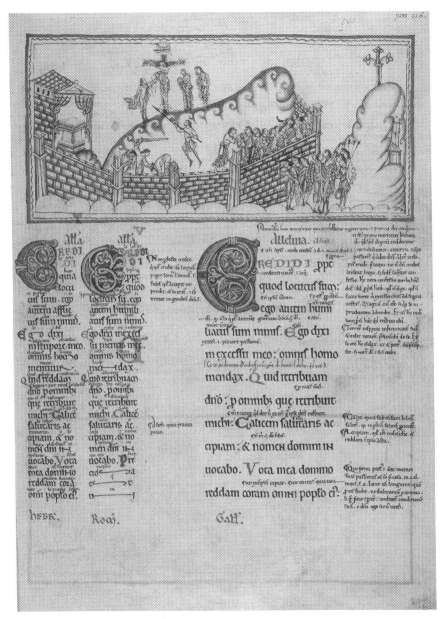

Figure 7.5 Cambridge, Trinity College, MS R. 17. 1, fol. 207r. Reproduced by kind permission of the Master and Fellows of Trinity College Cambridge

credentials. The presentation of Latin, French, and English as mutually reinforcing, complementary book languages is further supported by bibliocentric aspects in the visual programme. The manuscript's lavish paratextual materials include a famous portrait of Eadwine, after whom the volume is known by modern scholars, and who may be the main, skilful scribe. This stress on cutting-edge institutional expertise is combined with an awareness of wider continental legacies: the Psalter's finely poised illustrations and *mise-en-page* recall the ninth-century Carolingian Utrecht Psalter, also at Christ Church. This not only signals the manuscript's authoritative nature, but also flatteringly reminds those able to recognize the references to the Utrecht Psalter that they are members of an exclusive international network of *cognoscenti*.

In some ways, the Eadwine Psalter makes clear distinctions between languages: its script and *mise-en-page* distinguish between Latin, English, and French. Given that the manuscript was designed to encapsulate the best of Christ Church talent and traditions, this suggests the community saw its multilingualism as a valuable aspect of its inheritance. These careful linguistic distinctions also coalesce to form a larger page where the Latin, English, and French glosses, and the further languages they imply (Greek, Hebrew) are read in dialogue with one another.

Despite this emphasis on language and interpretation, both vernacular versions are awkward to use in their current form. The first English gloss was created through seemingly ad hoc recourse to a wide range of sources with varying levels of accuracy. The earliest French gloss was similarly problematic, featuring many *lacunae*. Both were later subjected to thoroughgoing programmes of correction to rectify difficulties with the initial choice of exemplar, but neither was fully revised. This may reflect hasty production for a high-status patron, but it also elucidates the compilers' criteria for 'finished enough'. The fine detail of explication was apparently less important than the project's conceptual ambition: its trilingual *mise-en-page* carried more weight than its practical potential as a scholarly reference work. As the volume stands, it encourages us to explore translation as a large-scale form of hermeneutics. Knowledge here is generated and performed through simultaneous linguistic comparisons across Latin, French, and English, rather than being embodied in any single language.

The Eadwine Psalter's translations demonstrate the geographically and historically far-reaching transfers of knowledge enabled by life in a multilingual monastic community in twelfth-century Canterbury. Our next two examples of the connections between knowledge and translation take us to the late medieval explosion in manuscript culture, and to lay contexts. A familiar modern narrative relates how a nationalistic attachment to written English emerges over the fourteenth and fifteenth centuries out of the twin contexts of the Hundred Years' War with France and of England's conflicts with Scotland, Wales, and Ireland. However, as will be seen,

168

The Written Word: Literacy across Languages

vernacular pride was characteristically more inclusive than exclusive of other languages and cultures.

Surviving in thirty-two copies or fragments, among them Cambridge, University Library, MS Dd. 3. 53 (first half of the fifteenth century) (Figure 7.6), Chaucer's *Treatise on the Astrolabe* (*c.* 1391) was the writer's most commonly copied work after *The Canterbury Tales*.[30] It purports to initiate the author's ten-year-old son into the mysteries of that exotic and 'noble ... instrument' (fol. 1r), and exhorts the boy to master the object practically so as to open the way to further geographical and cosmological knowledge.[31] The vogue for vernacular translations of learned works into French and English from the second half of the fourteenth century not only disseminated knowledge from specialist contexts to new audiences, but also expanded the resources, functions, and prestige of the target language by appropriating those of the source language – or rather languages, since English translations, for example, often drew upon earlier compositions in or translations into French, Latin, Greek, and Arabic (often with admixtures of Spanish or Hebrew). Chaucer opens his *Treatise* by requesting that the 'trewe conclusiouns' he imparts 'suffise' to his son in 'naked wordes in englissh' as well as they do to Greek clerks in Greek, to Arabians in Arabic, to Jews in Hebrew, and 'to the latyn folk in latyn' – these last having first translated them into 'hir owne tunge', just as Chaucer himself has done (fol. 1r). Chaucer's justification echoes Nicole Oresme's prologue to his French translation of Aristotle's *Ethics* and *Politics* for Charles V of France (1370).[32] Copied in lavish presentation volumes and self-consciously grandiose, Oresme's learned texts introduced such beautiful and useful words as *aristocratie*, *democratie*, and *architectonique*, ornamenting with distinction and charisma both the French language and the king who presided over its ornamentation. Oresme's work forms part of a large cultural movement which in the late Middle Ages transformed French into a new 'ancient' tongue, at once innovative and antique, most obviously via the massive introduction of Latin- and Greek-derived lexis and the (re-)Latinization of existing wordforms and meanings.[33]

Chaucer, in contrast, only glancingly refers his English compilation to the king as 'lord of this langage' (fol. 1v). Instead he places it in a domestic, private sphere and emphasizes its modesty and diminutiveness, addressing it to 'Litel Lowys my sone' (fol. 1r). Unfamiliar technical lexis is carefully related where possible to the boy's 'latyn ... smal' (fol. 1r): 'than ben the daies and thes nyht illike of lenghthe in al the world ¶ [and] ther fore ben thise two signes called the equinoxiis' (fol. 6v). The glosses for more outlandish, Arabic-derived terms are supported by reference to a familiar, concrete,

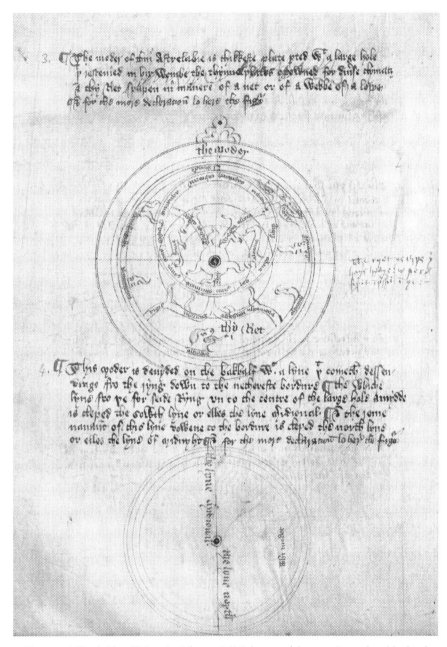

Figure 7.6 Cambridge, University Library, MS Dd. 3. 53, fol. 213v. Reproduced by kind permission of the Syndics of Cambridge University Library

The Written Word: Literacy across Languages

domestic world. Thus 'this forseide cenyth is ymagened to ben the v[er]rey point ov[er] the crowne of thyn heued' (fol. 7r: 'this aforementioned "zenith" is taken to be the point directly above the crown of your head'), while the azimuths are 'lik to the clawes of a loppe or elles like to the werk of a womanes calle' (fol. 7r: 'like the legs of a spider or like the design of a woman's hairnet').

In their different ways, both Oresme and Chaucer occupy intermediate places on the notional spectrum stretching from what Lawrence Venuti calls 'domesticating' translation practice, 'an ethnocentric reduction of the foreign text to receiving cultural values, bringing the author back home', to the opposite pole of 'foreignizing practice, an ethnodeviant pressure on those values to register the linguistic and cultural differences of the foreign text, sending the reader abroad'. Both lay claim to the riches of the classical world and of the Orient. The ideological situations they sketch are nevertheless quite different. Oresme, a noted Aristotelian scholar and philosopher of place, space, time, and motion, of cosmology and astronomy, of mathematics and economics, brings the resources of the university to dignify the royal court and ideas of kingship and of government.[34] Chaucer's *Treatise* 'send[s] its reader abroad' into a world of exotic terminology and knowledge, but it does so under parental rather than royal guidance.[35] His text appears comfortably removed from centres of public life and, despite its Oxford setting, it asserts no more than an amateur's engagement with advanced learning. Imputing the need for instruction to children, he tactfully portrays the adult layman as knowledge's purveyor as well as its consumer.

Chaucer's book is, nevertheless, an ambitious one. The diagrams that punctuate the text in this manuscript emphasize how the first section of the *Treatise* is organized by assembling an astrolabe in imagination, piece by piece. This stress on practical utility suggests that the technical language being elaborated in the vernacular is similarly instrumental, thus drawing our attention to its specialist vocabulary and methods of argumentation, and to the distinctive use of prose.[36] The mystique underpinning Chaucer's declared effort to encourage boyish curiosity is represented by the Arabizing names that the stars bear on the astrolabe's rete in the diagram shown in the manuscript (the first image of the astrolabe proper in MS Dd. 3. 53, and well before the rete's description). 'Arabic' names lie alongside Latin ones but resist assimilation. The equivalence between 'Alhabor' and the dog-star (known today by its antique name, Sirius) is mutely conveyed by the dog's head, in a visual parallel to the text's glossing of Arabic terms by domestic objects. The vernacular acquires dignity by association with the highest branches of human knowledge; used correctly, an astrolabe can situate the user and everything else accurately in relation to the globe, the cosmos, and time. The exotic *rete* thus communicates the vast ambition of the translational project that seeks to build a bridge between contemporary everyday life and the highest, most inaccessible human knowledge. Chaucer, characteristically, miniaturizes and domesticates his own contribution to this international project.

Oxford, Bodleian Library, MS Bodley 264 offers us a different viewpoint on the English engagement with imported traditions and artefacts in the late medieval period, 'domesticating' an entire existing manuscript (Figure 7.7). The manuscript's first scribes created a comprehensive biography of Alexander the Great by incorporating into Alexandre de Paris's twelfth-century verse *Roman d'Alexandre* (fols. 3r–208r) several independent French Alexander texts, such as the early fourteenth-century *Les Vœux du paon* (fols. 110r–163v) and *Le Voyage au paradis terrestre*, of *c.* 1260 (fols. 185r–188r). Evidently made in the Low Countries in 1338–44, this beautiful manuscript travelled to England – it was, literally, 'translated' – since, on fol. 67r, an early fifteenth-century hand has added a note in English:[37]

> Here fayleth a prossesse of þis rommauce of alixaud' þe wheche prossesse þat fayleth ʒe schulle fynde at þe ende of þis bok ywrete in engelyche ryme and whan ʒe han radde it to þe ende torneþ hedur aʒen and turneþ ouyr þys lef and bygynneþ at þys reson Che fu el mois de may que li tans renouele and so rede forþ þe rommauce to þe ende whylis þe frenche lasteþ

> Here an episode of this romance of Alexander is missing, which missing episode you shall find at the end of this book, written in English verse; and when you have read it to the end, turn back to this point, and turn over this page, and begin where it says: '[in French] It was in the month of May, when the spring returns', and so read on to the end of the romance, as long as the French continues.

Turning obediently to the end of the fourteenth-century text (fol. 209r), we find that the fifteenth-century annotator has added the story of Alexander's encounter with the king of the Brahmins, in Middle English alliterative verse. Variously entitled *Alexander and Dindimus* or *Alexander Fragment B*, the additional poem is often considered to be a fragment of a lost, longer English Alexander romance. Whether or not that is so, it is treated here as an interpolation into the frame text, of exactly the same sort as the other French poems. When he 'inserts' an independent Alexander text into the frame narrative at the appropriate chronological point in Alexander's biography, the fifteenth-century English scribe embraces the project of the book's first compilers to create 'a kind of verbal and visual *summa Alexandriana*', showing a high degree of cultural competence.[38]

The short passage on fol. 67r is not shy about interrupting the frame text or about marking its linguistic difference: it identifies that frame as 'frenche',

The Written Word: Literacy across Languages

Figure 7.7 Oxford, Bodleian Library, MS Bodley 264, fol. 67r. Photo: © Bodleian Libraries

and quotes verbatim the beginning of the next folio. It differentiates itself visually not only by hand and by ink (fading may have made this more obvious), but by the distinctive thorn (þ) and yogh (ȝ) characters, in common insular use for English but not for French. However, once again distinguishing features also work to bridge cultures and languages and to extend horizons. The early fifteenth-century insular reader here installed in the manuscript is evidently comfortable reading verse both in the linguistically demanding Middle English alliterative style and in French alexandrine laisses dating from the late twelfth to the mid-fourteenth centuries. Thorn and yogh appear here in the late forms which underline their similarity to the y and z of Romance alphabets; moreover, the English hand also added French-language rubrics missing from other *Alexandre* texts in the manuscript. The English scribe builds into the manuscript both divergences and continuities, exhibiting insular practices as legitimate variations on the International Gothic style. The reworking of MS Bodley 264, therefore, introduced specifically insular elements into a valuable manuscript in such a way as to underline connections with the prestigious global and local traditions that it conveys. It is worth noting that these connections do not centre on Paris, often considered today to be the core of francophone cultural and political activity. The fifteenth-century scribe uses insular French when supplying rubrics, and carefully copies the 'Che fu el mois de may que li tans renouele' that begins fol. 68r (fol. 67v presents one of several full-page miniatures). 'Che' identifies the language variety as Picard, the French used in the wealthy, politically and culturally distinct area that extended across the north of modern France and the southern Low Countries. Shared in the late medieval period between the French kingdom, the Holy Roman Empire, and Valois Burgundy, this area nevertheless maintained close economic and political links with England, and was always a significant point of entry for English activity on the Continent. Through the successful grafting of *Alexander and Dindimus* into MS Bodley 264, the wealth and expertise of the exotic East, as well as those of the Low Countries, accrue to an England which is also Continental.

We have moved from Eadwine's parallel texts and multiple glosses, through the lexical enrichment of MS Dd. 3. 53, to MS Bodley 264's repurposing of a prestigious imported manuscript. In each case, translation and multilingualism offer the opportunity to display impressive linguistic and cultural resources, wealth, and power. Their central and ambiguous position within any narrative of 'the rise of English' shows how the ambitions carried by domestic linguistic developments might be far from merely 'insular'.

Given the fundamental equivocations created by the bridging and liminal practices that we have outlined in this chapter, we may ask whether medieval readers knew what language a manuscript was employing at any particular

The Written Word: Literacy across Languages

moment, and, if so, how? In one sense, the answer is obvious: language choice was communicated not only through strictly linguistic means but also through a variety of cues, ranging variously and in different periods from features of letterforms and lexis to page layout and genre. But in other ways, the multivalent resonances of all these elements ensured that anchoring the text within a single, specific language remained deeply ambiguous. Juxtaposing, translating, and evoking different languages in manuscripts encouraged cultural porousness, both as comparison and as contrast. We turn, therefore, to our final manuscript, to ask: could it also be considered 'English'?

Conclusion: an 'English' Manuscript?

One of a group of around thirty courtly prose manuscripts made in late thirteenth-century Genoa by Pisan prisoners of war, Paris, BnF, MS français 1463 is witness to the northern Italian vogue for Arthurian materials. Rustichello da Pisa (or Rusticiaus de Pise) begins his Arthurian compilation by claiming that 'cestui Romainz fu treslaites dou liure monseingneu Odoard li Roi dengleterre a celui tenz qu'il passe houtre la mer en s[er]uise nostre Sire damedeu pour c[on]quister le Saint Sepoucre' ('this romance was drawn from the book of my lord Edward, king of England, at that time when he crossed overseas in the service of our Lord God to conquer the Holy Sepulchre'; that is, 1270–4).[39] There is a venerable medieval tradition of citing non-existent sources, and many modern scholars think that Rustichello was inventing his. Nevertheless, there is ample evidence that manuscripts belonging to owners from the various parts of Britain reached Italy and the eastern Mediterranean, just as others made the journey westwards. The cultural contact situations in which manuscripts were produced in Britain formed part of the networks of a much larger world.

BnF MS fr. 1463 not only directs us towards British manuscripts lost today, but also raises more complicated questions about cultural identity. The letterforms, decoration, and illustrations are characteristically Italian, and the language is Franco-Italian (a literary *koinè* combining Italian with Old French features). Nevertheless, Edward's putative book (in what language?) underwrites that of Rustichello, which is privileged to relate 'plusor chouses [et] plusor battailles que furent entraus que ne trueueres escrit en trestous les autres livres pource que li maistre le trueve escrit eu livre dou Roi dengleterre' (fol. 1r, a37–b1: 'many things and many battles which befell between [the heroes] that you will not find written in all the other books, because the master found it written in the book of the king of England'). It is clearly important for the reception of this manuscript and its contents that its

175

written words be felt to be 'English'. 'Englishness' connects it to the fountainhead that guarantees its authority. Emerging from the very land where its heroes, Tristan and Lancelot, adventured, and pointing towards the East where Grail romance and real-life crusade meet, it travels in the entourage of a king of the line of Uther Pendragon and Arthur. All three kings are represented by the royal figure who presides over fol. 1r of the manuscript, endorsing text and book.[40] The transnational networks to which BnF fr. 1463 bears witness and the complexity of its construction of identity have parallels in many of the manuscripts that we have discussed earlier, and prompt our concluding question: how then, in this complex cultural period, do we decide whether or not a manuscript is 'English', or even 'British'?

Notes

We thank Anne Cobby, Simon Gaunt, Nicola Morato, Máire ni Mhaonaigh, Thomas O'Donnell, Judith Olszowy-Schlanger, Israel Sandman, Dirk Schoenaers, and, especially, Teresa Webber. Any remaining mistakes, of course, are our own.

1. See E. Treharne, *Living through Conquest: The Politics of Early English, 1020–1220* (Oxford: Oxford University Press, 2012).
2. L. de Grauwe, 'Zijn *olla vogala* Vlaams, of zit de Nederlandse filologie met een koekoesei in (haar) nest(en)?', *Tijdschrift voor Nederlandse taal- en letterkunde*, 120 (2004), 44–56.
3. P. Dronke, 'Latin and Vernacular Love-Lyrics: Rochester and St Augustine's, Canterbury', *Revue bénédictine*, 115 (2005), 400–10.
4. E. Kwakkel, '*Hebban olla vogala* in historisch perspectief', *Tijdschrift voor Nederlandse tall- en letterkunde*, 121 (2005), 1–24, at 6.
5. See, for example, *Interfaces*, 1 (2015), http://riviste.unimi.it/index.php/inter faces/issue/view/1/showToc; D. Wallace, ed., *Europe: A Literary History, 1348–1418* (Oxford: Oxford University Press, 2016).
6. J. Wogan-Browne et al., eds., *The Idea of the Vernacular: An Anthology of Middle English Literary Theory, 1280–1520* (Exeter: University of Exeter Press, 1999).
7. E. M. Tyler, 'Introduction: England and Multilingualism: Medieval and Modern', in E. M. Tyler, ed., *Conceptualizing Multilingualism in Medieval England, c.800–c.1250* (Turnhout: Brepols, 2011), 1–13.
8. C. Buridant, '*Translatio medievalis*: Théorie et pratique de la traduction médiévale', *Travaux de linguistique et de littérature*, 21 (1983), 81–136, at 119.
9. J. Bisagni, 'Prolegomena to the Study of Code-Switching in Old Irish Glosses', *Peritia*, 24–5 (2014), 1–58; L. Wright, *Sources of London English: Medieval Thames Vocabulary* (Oxford: Clarendon Press, 1996).
10. C. A. Ferguson, 'Diglossia', *Word*, 15 (1959), 325–40. See also R. A. Lodge, *French: From Dialect to Standard* (London: Routledge, 1993); A. Putter, 'Code-Switching in Langland, Chaucer and the *Gawain*-Poet: Diglossia and Footing', in H. Schendl and L. Wright, eds., *Code-Switching in Early English* (Berlin: de Gruyter, 2011), 281–302.

The Written Word: Literacy across Languages

11. I. M. Resnick, '*Lingua Dei, lingua hominis*: Sacred Language and Medieval Texts', *Viator*, 21 (1990), 51–74.
12. *New Catholic Encyclopedia*, 2nd edn, 15 vols. (Detroit: Thomson/Gale; Washington, DC: Catholic University of America, 2003): 'Latin (in the Church)', VIII, 360–6; 'Vulgate', XIV, 591–600.
13. J. Olszowy-Schlanger, *Les Manuscrits hébreux dans l'Angleterre médiévale: Étude historique et paléographique* (Paris: Peeters, 2003). For héb. 113, see especially 19–22, 140, 181–7.
14. http://gallica.bnf.fr/ark:/12148/btv1b60004143/f16.item.zoom.
15. M. Beit-Arié, *Hebrew Manuscripts of East and West: Towards a Comparative Codicology* (London: British Library, 1992).
16. See H. Gneuss, 'The Origin of Standard Old English and Æthelwold's School at Winchester', *Anglo-Saxon England*, 1 (1972), 63–83.
17. D. Bates, ed., *Regesta Regum Anglo-Normannorum: The Acta of William I (1066–1087)* (Oxford: Clarendon, 1998), 48–50.
18. M. Careri, C. Ruby, and I. Short, *Livres et écritures en français et en occitan au XIIᵉ siècle: Catalogue illustré* (Rome: Viella, 2011).
19. P. S. Baker and M. Lapidge, eds., *Byrhtferth's Enchiridion*, EETS s.s. 15 (Oxford: Oxford University Press, 1995), 120–1.
20. Baker and Lapidge, eds., *Byrhtferth's Enchiridion*, cxv–cxvi.
21. M. Parkes, 'On the Presumed Date and Possible Origins of the *Ormulum*', in E. G. Stanley and D. Gray, eds., *Five Hundred Years of Words and Sounds: A Festschrift for Eric Dobson* (Cambridge: D. S. Brewer, 1983), 115–27.
22. Parkes, 'Presumed Date', 120, 122, 126–7.
23. M. Worley, 'Using the *Ormulum* to Redefine Vernacularity', in F. Somerset and N. Watson, eds., *The Vulgar Tongue: Medieval and Postmedieval Vernacularity* (University Park, PA: Pennsylvania State University Press, 2003), 19–42.
24. See Geoffrey of Monmouth, *The History of the Kings of Britain*, ed. M. Reeve, trans. N. Wright (Woodbridge: Boydell, 2007).
25. See J. Crick, 'Geoffrey of Monmouth, Prophecy and History', *Journal of Medieval History*, 18 (1992), 357–71.
26. M. J. Curley, 'A New Edition of John of Cornwall's *Prophetia Merlini*', *Speculum*, 37 (1982), 217–49.
27. J. Delisle and J. Wordsworth, eds., *Translators through History*, rev. edn (Amsterdam and Philadelphia: John Benjamins, 2012), 133.
28. M. Shuttleworth and M. Cowie, *Dictionary of Translation Studies* (Manchester: St Jerome, 1997; London: Routledge, 2014); R. Copeland, *Rhetoric, Hermeneutics, and Translation in the Middle Ages* (Cambridge: Cambridge University Press, 1995).
29. See M. Gibson et al., eds., *The Eadwine Psalter: Text, Image, and Monastic Culture in Twelfth-Century Canterbury* (London: MHRA, 1992); Treharne, *Living through Conquest*, 167–87.
30. E. Talbot Donaldson, quoted in S. Eisner, ed., *A Variorum Edition of the Works of Geoffrey Chaucer. Vol. VI: The Prose Treatises. Part One: A Treatise on the Astrolabe* (Norman, OK: University of Oklahoma Press, 2002), 28.
31. K. A. Rand Schmidt, *The Authorship of 'The Equatorie of the Planetis'* (Cambridge: D. S. Brewer, 1993), 150–85. See also, for context, C. Burnett,

177

The Introduction of Arabic Learning into England (London: British Library, 1997).

32. N. Oresme, *Le Livre de Ethiques d'Aristote*, ed. A. D. Menut (New York: Stechert, 1940), 101; Oresme ascribes to Cicero's *Academica* the idea that 'things that are difficult and very authoritative are delectable and very agreeable to people in the language of their land' and further points out that in Rome, 'the vernacular and maternal tongue was Latin'. The idea was an old one.

33. See G. Zink, *Le Moyen Français (XIVe et XVe siècles)* (Paris: Presses Universitaires de France, 1990), especially 82–121. See also the *Dictionnaire du Moyen Français (1330–1500)*, www.atilf.fr/dmf/.

34. S. Kirschner, 'Nicole Oresme', *The Stanford Encyclopedia of Philosophy*, ed. Edward N. Zalta (Fall 2013), https://plato.stanford.edu/archives/fall2013/entries/nicole-oresme/.

35. L. Venuti, *The Translator's Invisibility: A History of Translation*, 2nd edn (London: Routledge, 2008), 15. See also M. Inghilleri (and C. Baker), 'Ethics', in M. Baker and G. Saldanha, eds., *Routledge Encyclopedia of Translation Studies*, 2nd edn (Abingdon: Routledge, 2009), 100–4.

36. S. Lehmann, 'La Mise en scène du texte scientifique à la fin du moyen âge: propriétés macro- et microstructurelles', in O. Bertrand, ed., *Sciences et savoirs sous Charles V* (Paris: Champion, 2014), 87–112.

37. M. Cruse, *Illuminating the 'Roman d'Alexandre': Oxford, Bodleian Library, MS Bodley 264: The Manuscript as Monument* (Cambridge: D. S. Brewer, 2011). See also C. W. Dutschke, 'The Truth in the Book: The Marco Polo Texts in Royal 19. D.1 and Bodley 264', *Scriptorium*, 52 (1998), 278–99.

38. Quotation from K. Busby, *Codex and Context: Reading Old French Verse Narrative in Manuscript*, 2 vols. (Amsterdam: Rodopi, 2002), I, 308.

39. Paris, BnF, fr. 1463, fol. 1r, a18–23. Digitized at http://gallica.bnf.fr/ark:/12148/btv1b60005205. See F. Cigni, ed. and Italian trans., *Il romanzo arturiano di Rustichello da Pisa* (Pisa: Pacini, 1994).

40. Perhaps alternatively or also Rustichello himself. See R. Trachsler, 'Le Visage et la voix: L'Auteur, le narrateur et l'enlumineur dans la littérature narrative médiévale', *Bibliographical Bulletin of the International Arthurian Society*, 57 (2005), 349–71, at 370–1.

8

ELIZABETH SOLOPOVA

The Wycliffite Bible

The Wycliffite Bible (WB), the first complete translation of the Vulgate in English, is the most widely disseminated medieval English text; it survives in over 250 manuscripts. The authorship and date of the translation are uncertain, but it was almost certainly produced in Oxford in the last quarter of the fourteenth century by the followers of the reformist theologian John Wyclif. It must have been a collaborative undertaking of a group of academics, probably including Nicholas Hereford, a fellow of Queen's College, Oxford, and a colleague of Wyclif, and perhaps John Trevisa, known as a translator of several major historical and encyclopaedic works.[1] Nicholas Hereford is referred to as a translator in a contemporary colophon at the end of Oxford, Bodleian Library, MS Douce 369, an important early fifteenth-century copy of WB.

The Bible survives in two redactions: a highly literal Earlier Version (EV) and its revision, a more idiomatic Later Version (LV). EV was probably intended as a translation for scholarly purposes; it is used as the biblical text in the *Glossed Gospels*, a late fourteenth-century Wycliffite commentary on the gospels,[2] whereas LV, surviving in a much larger number of manuscripts, may have been designed for a wider circulation. Though accurate and entirely unbiased, the translation was banned by the English Church within twenty-five years of its appearance. In a series of measures at the end of the fourteenth and the beginning of the fifteenth centuries, the authorities attempted to impose control over the teaching of theology, preaching, and biblical translation in order to arrest the dissemination of Wyclif's ideas. Ecclesiastical Constitutions, sponsored by Archbishop of Canterbury Thomas Arundel, drafted in 1407 and promulgated in 1409, prohibited the making of new translations and the use of any existing translations of the Bible produced at the time of Wyclif or after, without episcopal approval of both the version and the owner.

It seems, however, that initially at least censorship entirely failed to stop the copying of WB. Moreover, its manuscripts were produced to a high standard by the mainstream book trade. Contrary to what one may expect, a great majority of copies of WB do not look like those of a prohibited text and are professionally and sometimes luxuriously produced, almost always written on parchment. A number are in very large format, presumably made for use on a lectern, though there is no evidence that the translation was ever used in a formal liturgical setting. About 40 per cent of the manuscripts are illuminated, some by established artists whose work has been identified in other books made for the nobility.[3] The decoration is rarely figural, but typically consists of foliate borders and initials in penwork, pigment, and gold. The script used in the majority of copies is an approximation of *textura*, easily legible, but not approaching the formality of the script of high-end Latin liturgical books.[4]

Like other medieval manuscripts, WBs rarely contain indications of medieval ownership, but the owners whose identity is known comprise tradesmen, women, priests, and members of religious orders, as well as members of the nobility, including several kings. Among aristocratic owners of WBs are kings Henry IV, Henry VI, and Henry VII, Thomas of Lancaster, son of Henry IV, and Thomas of Woodstock, youngest son of Edward III.[5] Apparently the translation circulated not only among Lollards, but also much more widely in society – a great majority of its owners were probably entirely orthodox. Such evidence suggests that censorship operated selectively and that in spite of prohibitions it was possible to own WB legitimately: members of the nobility, clergy, and generally those wealthy, educated, and perceived as orthodox could use their books without challenge from authorities.[6] The ownership of the Bible in English is occasionally mentioned in trial records as evidence against suspects of heresy, but it is never the main or the only evidence.

Several factors seem to have contributed to this unusual situation. At the end of the fourteenth and early in the fifteenth century, Lollards had some limited support among the nobility. The patronage of Wyclif and other prominent Lollards by John of Gaunt is well attested, and contemporary chroniclers identify a group of 'Lollard knights', the supporters of Wyclif's views at the royal court.[7] Attitudes to Lollards hardened later in the fifteenth century, but it seems that earlier in the century it was possible to own texts with explicitly declared Lollard opinions without supporting or appearing to support more extreme views associated with Wyclif. Works that are, unlike WB, openly Lollard also survive in manuscripts from this period known to have been made for aristocratic patrons.[8]

These observations agree with what is known about the chronology and patterns of the production of the manuscripts of WB. The earliest datable copy is London, British Library, MS Egerton 617/618, originally a three-volume

The Wycliffite Bible

complete Bible in EV made for Thomas of Woodstock, Duke of Gloucester, whose arms appear at the beginning of what is now the first volume. It was almost certainly the Bible in English, listed among his possessions in 1397 following his imprisonment and murder. The production of the manuscripts of WB peaked in the first quarter of the fifteenth century, but slowed down towards the middle of the century and almost entirely stopped by its end, presumably because eventually the effects of persecutions started to be felt, and support for Wyclif's ideas among the nobility and in academia was undermined. The latest known medieval copy of WB is Oxford, New College, MS 320, dated to c. 1500. A great majority of illuminated WBs, some with lavish decoration, were also made from the 1390s and until c. 1420, but after that their production declined sharply, with hardly any Wycliffite texts with illuminated decoration surviving from the middle of the fifteenth century.[9]

Lollard communities, threatened by persecutions and in most cases poor, would not have been able to support the making of illuminated and professionally written copies on the scale evident in the surviving corpus. Moreover, the extant manuscripts are probably only a part of what originally existed: though there is no evidence that WBs were ever subject to ritual burning, they are known to have been confiscated, rarely returned even if found orthodox, and presumably in some cases destroyed.[10] Their large-scale production would have been impossible without the support of the nobility, but also without another, even more important category of patrons: the clergy, who seem to have used the English Bible professionally.

Earlier scholarship overwhelmingly assumed that WB, as a vernacular translation, was used primarily by laity. My research on the manuscripts of WB, however, suggests that many owners were priests and members of religious orders, and that manuscripts were made for clerical patrons. WB is an exceptionally learned translation requiring a well-educated reader. This is evident in its highly literal nature, reliance on a corrected Latin original, and extensive effort that apparently went into the English text, including the development of an adequate translation technique, of an appropriate biblical vocabulary and new methods of scholarly presentation of the biblical text.[11] Uniquely for this period, there is evidence that the translators not only studied the Vulgate, but also attempted to produce a corrected source text for their work. They were aware that Latin biblical text, most commonly circulated at the time in the form known as the 'Paris Bible', was variable and corrupt. They seem to have undertaken a comparison of different biblical manuscripts and used various philological and textual-critical aids, such as commentaries and the *correctoria*, lists of variant readings that were circulated with Latin bibles, to produce an accurate basis for their translation.[12]

181

This is evident in the description of their work in the so-called General Prologue that accompanies the translation in a small number of manuscripts, as well as in the divergences between the two versions and texts attested in individual manuscripts that sometimes result from differences in underlying Latin readings.

In the manuscripts, the biblical text is accompanied by a complex and extensive liturgical and scholarly apparatus, suggesting learned, and professional use. Only about twenty of the surviving manuscripts of WB, mostly large-format copies, contain a complete biblical text. The most common textual type among the manuscripts of WB is complete or partial New Testament. In many manuscripts, the New Testament is accompanied by an Old Testament lectionary, a collection of liturgically organized readings for the Mass, instead of a complete text of Old Testament books. Manuscripts contain other liturgical aids as well, including Latin and English calendars, tables of Mass lections, and calendar-lectionaries. The tables of lections contain biblical references for readings, presented in a highly disciplined tabular form. Entries for different feasts include abbreviated titles and chapter numbers of biblical books, as well as indexing letters and the opening and closing words of each reading in the Wycliffite translation. The indexing letters are a device that was first used in the thirteenth century by the Dominicans at St Jacques in Paris for a widely disseminated biblical concordance.[13] Chapters of the biblical text were subdivided into sevenths, usually mentally rather than physically in manuscripts, each designated by the first seven letters of the alphabet, A–G. The letters were then used as part of biblical references, in addition to the title of a book and a chapter number, to make references more precise. In the manuscripts of WB, probably for the first time in a vernacular work, the same system is employed to key references in the tables of lections to the biblical text. Some copies attest to the original seven-letter sequence, A–G, but in most a twelve-letter sequence, A–L, is used, presumably a modification of the A–G system to make references in longer chapters even more accurate. Indexing letters appear not only in the tables of lections, but also at the start of readings in the margins of biblical text. The use of the tables of lections and indexing letters seems to have replaced various earlier ways of marking Mass readings in WBs: some manuscripts, mostly of EV, contain liturgical rubrics at the start of readings in the biblical text, as well as other devices to indicate their beginnings and ends. The ubiquity of liturgical aids, most in the original hands, but occasionally added – the tables of lections occur in about 40 per cent of surviving manuscripts of WB – indicates patronage and professional use by the clergy, and so does the scholarly apparatus that is found in most copies of the translation.[14]

The Wycliffite Bible

Several manuscripts of LV include extensive commentary in the margins. The material provided is fairly diverse, but what is particularly noticeable is that it is, first, almost entirely orthodox and, second, that its concerns are primarily scholarly, rather than polemical: a topic that repeatedly comes up is the difference between the Latin and Hebrew versions of the Bible. The same interest in authority, accuracy, and correct presentation of the biblical text is evident in the practice of marking non-biblical additions found in many carefully produced manuscripts. Intertextual glosses (short explanations of words and concepts) and 'alternative translations' (multiple English terms rendering a single Latin word in order to cover its semantic range more fully) are typically underlined in red, or sometimes in black. Such underlinings alert the reader to the status of additions as part of the apparatus, rather than biblical text. Both the translation itself and its manuscripts seem to have been designed with a scholarly user in mind: many of their aspects would have been redundant, impractical or confusing for anyone without the knowledge of Latin, liturgy, the Bible, and academic techniques structuring and retrieving information.

The manuscripts were believed by earlier scholars to have been made primarily in London because of the scale and professionalism of their production that must have required the resources of a major centre of book trade. Recently new evidence has emerged that puts attribution of many manuscripts to London on a much firmer ground. An art historical investigation has demonstrated that most of the decorated copies surviving from the period 1390–1420 were London productions.[15] The border styles and decorative motifs attested in these manuscripts developed in London and are stylistically affiliated to decoration in books with secure London provenances and sometimes firm dating evidence. My analysis of liturgical texts that were circulated with WB supports the same conclusion: several liturgical calendars have London features, including the presence of St Erkenwald, a characteristically London saint.[16]

The copying of WB has been described as commercial and mass production, suggesting a possibility of speculative trade, without commission, and of the making of multiple similar or identical copies for sale. Though the London book trade was highly organized and involved specialization and cooperation between different craftsmen, the existence of speculative book production in the late fourteenth and fifteenth centuries remains uncertain. There is no evidence that WBs, or any other books that were produced in large numbers, such as Latin pocket bibles in the thirteenth century, were supplied simultaneously in quantity to booksellers in London or elsewhere.[17] The question of commercial or mass production is most relevant for complete and partial New Testaments in LV that survive in particularly large

183

numbers and constitute more than two-thirds of all manuscripts of WB. There is considerable evidence of standardization in such New Testaments, including consistent use of parchment; of very similar, difficult to date or distinguish *textura* hands in contrast to Anglicana hands of some EV copies; of identical rubrics, chapter headings, and running titles; of similar programmes of decoration; and of standardized liturgical aids, such as tabular tables of lections and indexing letters in the margins of the biblical text discussed above.[18]

On the other hand, and as pointed out by Ian Doyle,[19] no two manuscripts of WB are particularly similar. Even LV copies differ in size considerably and have different orders and variable selections of biblical books and other materials. This is true even of manuscripts believed to have been made by the same team of artists and scribes, such as Oxford, Bodleian Library, MSS Bod. 183 and Fairfax 11, which have very different contents and programmes of decoration.[20] Other evidence also suggests that copies were bespoke rather than produced to the same pattern for speculative trade. Bibles are often accompanied by selections of liturgical texts that are adapted and cross-referenced in the original workshop to facilitate their use within a particular volume. The tables of lections were often painstakingly edited to reflect the contents of an individual copy: references to biblical books not included in a manuscript were typically edited out.[21]

WB shares many of its features with other Wycliffite texts. Such features include the use of the vernacular, collaborative authorship, scholarly orientation, and a large scale of textual and editorial projects, as well as generally a high standard of production in spite of censorship, even if modest, probably amateur copies, also survive. Manuscripts of major Wycliffite texts, including the *Glossed Gospels*, the *Revised Psalter Commentary*, *English Wycliffite Sermons*, *Floretum* and *Rosarium*, as well as the translation of the Bible, attest to an interest in accuracy and appropriate presentation of theological and academic content. Scholarly origin is evident even in modestly produced, inexpensive manuscripts. They are typically provided with detailed rubrics, chapter numbers and running titles, and are meticulously and systematically corrected. Corrections in widely circulated texts, such as WB and the *English Wycliffite Sermons*, are numerous and often concerned with minute linguistic detail, such as the omission or inclusion of the definite article. They are also highly visible, often executed in red as if their presence is evidence of quality, which contrasts with a more usual practice in medieval manuscripts of making corrections discrete to avoid ruining the appearance of a page.[22] Major Lollard productions also display a concern with accessibility and an interest in the provision of scholarly and interpretative aids. Both Wyclif's works and the works of his disciples survive with summaries and indexes that

184

The Wycliffite Bible

were presumably intended to make lengthy texts more accessible for preachers.[23] Sophisticated liturgical and scholarly apparatus attested in the manuscripts of WB, described earlier, fits in with this more general tendency, and is probably informed by the translators' involvement in the work on other Lollard texts, such as the *Glossed Gospels* and the *Revised Psalter Commentary*. The features that WB shares with other Lollard texts identify it as part of a network of ambitious academic projects that existed in England in the late fourteenth and early fifteenth centuries.

Notes

1. A. Hudson, 'The Origin and Textual Tradition of the Wycliffite Bible', in E. Solopova, ed., *The Wycliffite Bible: Origin, History and Interpretation* (Leiden: Brill, 2017), 133–61.
2. A. Hudson, *Doctors in English: A Study of the English Wycliffite Gospel Commentaries* (Liverpool: Liverpool University Press, 2015), xlviii–lii, at cxl–cxli.
3. L. Dennison and N. Morgan, 'The Decoration of Wycliffite Bibles', in Solopova, ed., *The Wycliffite Bible*, 259–341.
4. R. Hanna, 'The Palaeography of the Wycliffite Bibles', in Solopova, ed., *The Wycliffite Bible*, 246–65.
5. M. Dove, *The First English Bible: The Text and Context of the Wycliffite Versions* (Cambridge: Cambridge University Press, 2007), 44.
6. M. Jurkowski, 'The Selective Censorship of the Wycliffite Bible', in Solopova, ed., *The Wycliffite Bible*, 360–81.
7. K. B. McFarlane, *Lancastrian Kings and Lollard Knight* (Oxford: Clarendon Press, 1972), 139–232.
8. E. Solopova, 'The Manuscript Tradition', in Solopova, ed., *The Wycliffite Bible*, 228–9.
9. Dennison and Morgan, 'The Decoration of Wycliffite Bibles'.
10. Jurkowski, 'The Selective Censorship'.
11. E. Solopova, 'The Wycliffite Psalms', in F. Leneghan and T. Atkin, eds., *The Psalms and Medieval English Literature* (Cambridge: D. S. Brewer, 2017), 128–48.
12. A. Hudson and E. Solopova, 'The Latin Text' in Solopova, ed., *The Wycliffite Bible*, 107–32.
13. R. H. Rouse and M. A. Rouse, 'The Verbal Concordance to the Scriptures', *Archivum Fratrum Praedicatorum*, 44 (1974), 5–30.
14. M. Peikola, 'Tables of Lections in Manuscripts of the Wycliffite Bible' in E. Poleg and L. Light, eds., *Form and Function in the Late Medieval Bible* (Leiden: Brill, 2013), 351–78, at 351.
15. Dennison and Morgan, 'The Decoration of Wycliffite Bibles'.
16. E. Solopova, *Manuscripts of the Wycliffite Bible in the Bodleian and Oxford College Libraries* (Liverpool: University of Liverpool Press, 2016), 25–6; E. Solopova, 'A Wycliffite Bible Made for a Nun of Barking', *Medium Ævum*, 85 (2016), 77–96.
17. A. I. Doyle, 'The English Provincial Book Trade before Printing', in P. Isaac, ed., *Six Centuries of the Provincial Book Trade in Britain* (Winchester: St Paul's Bibliographies, 1990), 13–29, at 24.

18. Solopova, *Manuscripts of the Wycliffite Bible*, 17–25.
19. Doyle, 'The English Provincial Book Trade before Printing', 24.
20. Solopova, *Manuscripts of the Wycliffite Bible*, 41–9, 147–51.
21. E. Solopova, 'Manuscript Evidence', in E. Poleg and L. Light, eds., *Form and Function in the Late Medieval Bible* (Leiden: Brill, 2013), 338–40.
22. Solopova, *Manuscripts of the Wycliffite Bible*, 19.
23. A. Hudson, *The Premature Reformation: Wycliffite Texts and Lollard History* (Oxford: Oxford University Press, 1988), 128.

9

HELEN FULTON

Editing Medieval Manuscripts for Modern Audiences

For most readers, their first encounter with a medieval text in the original language is through the medium of a modern edition. Transcribed from one or more manuscripts, collated, emended, sometimes modernized in its orthography and punctuation, and annotated with useful information about date, language, and variants, the medieval text is given new life as a normalized and accessible modern book or as a digital edition.

Beneath this apparently simple process lies a rich layer of skilled decision-making on the part of the editor. Which manuscripts of a text should be transcribed if there are multiple copies? How should one decide on the 'correct' version when there are different copies available? What level of intervention is justified when emending apparent scribal errors? How does one deal with multimedia manuscripts, containing images, or layers of text? And not least, how should the edition be presented to readers in terms of format, layout, and medium, whether print or digital or both?

The aim of this chapter is to provide a new look at some of these problematic aspects of the process by which a medieval text copied into a manuscript codex becomes a modern edition, available in a printed book and/or as a digital version. Starting with an evaluation of current methodologies, many of them with their own lengthy histories, the chapter will consider some of the practical and theoretical challenges faced by many editors of medieval texts. It will then show how these challenges have been met by modern editorial projects with clear protocols for their editorial practice, and how these protocols are to some extent determined by, and determine, the intended readership and use of the editions. The chapter will end with an example of how editors work, using a medieval Welsh poem surviving in multiple manuscript copies.

In what follows I refer particularly to two examples of major ongoing editorial projects, the Early English Text Society (EETS), and *Cyfres Beirdd yr Uchelwyr* ('The Poets of the Nobility Series') and its associated digital editions. The EETS series, founded in 1864 by F. J. Furnivall, is the earliest and most comprehensive series of editions of Old and Middle English texts, whose methodologies, while not without change and innovation over time, have been extremely influential on Anglo-American editorial practice.[1] Other series of edited texts in Middle English, particularly the Middle English Texts series produced by Winter, the university press of Heidelberg, and the TEAMS Middle English Texts series produced by the Medieval Institute at Western Michigan University, can usefully be compared with EETS editions in terms of their methodologies.

My second example comprises the published volumes and two digital editions of medieval Welsh poetry produced by Canolfan Uwchefrydiau Cymreig a Cheltaidd (Centre for Advanced Welsh and Celtic Studies), a research institute of the University of Wales located in Aberystwyth, Wales. Each volume and digital edition presents the work of one or more named poets of the fourteenth to sixteenth centuries and conforms to a set of editorial protocols established in the 1980s with an earlier series of the works of the Poets of the Princes (eleventh to fourteenth centuries). Regarding the digital editions, *Dafydd ap Gwilym.net* was produced during the first decade of the twenty-first century under the leadership of Professor Dafydd Johnston, then professor of Welsh at Swansea University. It presents a large corpus of poetry (totalling 170 poems) confidently attributed to the fourteenth-century court poet Dafydd ap Gwilym, in Welsh with facing English translations accompanied by a bilingual apparatus. A hard-copy edition of the poems, in Welsh only (the Middle Welsh texts with facing-page translations into modern Welsh), was published in 2010.[2] A second digital project by an expanded team based in the Canolfan in Aberystwyth produced an edition of the works of Guto'r Glyn, a fifteenth-century poet, edited in Welsh with facing English translations and extensive notes, many of them bilingual.[3] These two digital editions, along with similar and often larger projects such as the *Canterbury Tales Project* (1993–) raise significant questions about the practice of digital editing, its strengths and weaknesses, and the future of digital editing as a viable method of presenting medieval texts to modern readers.[4]

Editorial Methodologies

Before considering some of the practices adopted by modern editors of medieval texts, we need to think about the theory that lies behind these practices. What do editors think they are doing when they set about transcribing and emending a set of medieval manuscripts and turning them into a readable text? Up until the 1980s, this was a fairly uncontroversial issue. The role of the editor was to retrieve, as accurately as possible, what the

Editing Medieval Manuscripts for Modern Audiences

author had written, even if this meant peeling back layers of textual variation accrued through scribal transmission over time.[5]

A classic example of an edition which proceeds on this basis, and indeed which takes for granted that retrieving an 'original' text is the editor's driving purpose, is the Manly–Rickert edition of Chaucer which appeared in eight volumes in 1940.[6] The two editors, plus a team of assistants, collected and collated all known manuscripts containing any of Chaucer's work, using linguistic and material evidence, to rank the quality and status of the manuscripts as copies of what Chaucer himself wrote. In other words, the Manly–Rickert edition aimed to reconstruct the original text on the basis of the surviving witnesses, a laborious process which drew admiration as well as critique, but the fundamental aim was never questioned. Thus F. N. Robinson, himself the editor of one of the most authoritative texts of Chaucer's works, said: 'Manly's rigorous procedure of printing his reconstructed archetype even when he rejects a reading as unlikely to have been Chaucer's – a method wholly correct for his edition – would have been unsuited to my purpose.'[7] Editorial differences aside, the fact that Manly believed he could, and should, replicate what Chaucer actually wrote was taken for granted by Robinson and other Chaucer scholars.

This aim of retrieving the 'original' work is supported by the methodology of stemmatics, or recension, in which a family tree of manuscripts is constructed in order to find the earliest recoverable form of the text, before later generations of copyists made changes to it. Editors compare different manuscript versions of the same text, looking for shared scribal forms or errors that might link certain manuscripts together, with the assumption that one or more of these manuscripts were derived from another in the same group. The goal, as Douglas Moffat has said, 'is to discover the archetype, the copy from which all other copies derive, or at least the surviving witnesses that are closest to the lost archetype'.[8] The role of the editor, as it has traditionally been perceived, is to honour the work of the author who had written the original text which, in the case of many medieval texts, did not survive in the author's own handwriting or even in a manuscript written during the author's lifetime. There are, however, theoretical problems attached to two of these terms, namely 'author' and 'original'.

The emergence of French cultural theory into the world of English-language scholarship began in the 1970s, but its full impact was felt during the 1980s when texts such as Roland Barthes's 'The Death of the Author' and Michel Foucault's 'What is an Author?' began to penetrate literary studies in Britain.[9] Both these theorists presented a serious challenge to the liberal-humanist assumption that the 'author' of a work is a knowable, coherent, and retrievable individual who has full control over the production and meaning of his (almost always 'his') text. Figures such as Chaucer and Langland are assumed to be just such 'authors', and this assumption normalizes the editorial aim of retrieving the 'original' work of the author. Barthes summarized the emergence of the modern liberal-humanist author as a function of 'English empiricism, French rationalism and the personal faith of the Reformation', resulting in a positivist view of the author as a prestige individual:

> The image of literature to be found in ordinary culture is tyrannically centred on the author, his person, his life, his tastes, his passions, while criticism still consists for the most part in saying that Baudelaire's work is the failure of Baudelaire the man, Van Gogh's is his madness, Tchaikovsky's his vice. The *explanation* of a work is always sought in the man or woman who produced it, as if it were always in the end, through the more or less transparent allegory of the fiction, the voice of a single person, the *author* 'confiding' in us.[10]

Working from a philosophical viewpoint, Foucault was similarly engaged with dismantling the strategies of traditional textual criticism which attempted to construct a unified reading by reference to the supposedly unified subjectivity of the originating author. For modern critics, the person of the author, including their historical location and specific biographical events, is used to explain and interpret the text:

> The author explains the presence of certain events within a text, as well as their transformations, distortions, and their various modifications (and this through an author's biography or by reference to his particular point of view, in the analysis of his social preferences and his position within a class or by delineating his fundamental objectives). The author also constitutes a principle of unity in writing where any unevenness of production is ascribed to changes caused by evolution, maturation, or outside influence.[11]

Foucault redefines the 'author' as a function of discourse, a means of classifying texts into a particular group marked as material property (subject to laws of ownership, copyright, libel, and so on), marked as 'truthful' (because they can be attributed to a single person), and marked as the work of an 'individual' (in the sense of someone who pre-exists the text).

This radical rethinking of the concept of the 'author' scarcely percolated into the world of scholarly editing of medieval texts, where texts by named authors – Ælfric, Gaimar, Chaucer, Langland, Hoccleve, Lydgate, Gower, Julian of Norwich, Margery Kempe, Dafydd ap Gwilym, Iolo Goch – are consistently privileged over anonymous works as the prestige focus of scholarly attention. Anonymous texts regarded as having particular aesthetic merit are conventionally provided with a place-holding author – for example, 'the Gawain-poet', also known as 'the Pearl-poet' – or have become the subject of intense detective work and speculation designed to reveal the 'true' (i.e., singular, identifiable, biographicalized, and no doubt male) intelligence which produced the 'original' text. The convention in Welsh editorial practice of naming every edition of poetry by means of the formulaic title *Gwaith...*, 'The Work[s] of [a named poet]', constructs a legion of individual poets about whom very little is actually known, apart from their names and a corpus of work by which each is identified, despite the fact that many poems in the manuscripts are attributed to several different poets or to none, rendering authoritative 'authored' canons almost impossible to achieve.

This leads on to the second theoretical issue which editors must address, which is how we might identify, or whether it is in fact possible to identify, the 'original' text. Medieval texts, even more so than modern texts, are subject to change and revision, including at the point of composition, as other chapters in this volume demonstrate. Each manuscript version may have been the product of several written (or oral) versions by one or more authors and/or compilers. The evidence of Hoccleve's holograph manuscripts, surely examples of authored texts, shows a continuous process of self-emendation and changes to words and phrases which makes the concept of an 'original' problematic.[12]

In response to theories of meaning developed by writers such as Barthes and Foucault, challenges to the goal of retrieving the original 'authorized' text or its most likely form (the 'best text' that preserves the author's intentions) through the editorial process have been issued by, among others, Jerome J. McGann and Tim William Machan. McGann has argued that texts emerge in a social context and are produced and reproduced numerous times, to the point where any concept of a text that represents the author's 'final intentions' has to be abandoned.[13] Machan theorizes language as a social semiotic, generating texts whose meanings are constantly in negotiation.[14] This essentially post-structuralist theory of language and meaning is incompatible with the liberal-humanist view of the individual gifted author producing an original work of genius, the view which lies behind traditional editorial practice. Such practice includes vigorous attempts to distinguish between what the 'author' actually wrote and what subsequent scribes and copyists made of it, using techniques of linguistic comparison, studies of scribal habits, and an informed sense of what a particular author is most likely to have written. Even these techniques are far from infallible: distinguishing between author and scribe on the basis of language and style can easily become a circular argument where the modern editor becomes the author of a reconstructed 'best text'.[15] Though the challenges of post-structural theory have caused editors to become more aware of the theories underlying their own editorial practice, the traditional methods still prevail in major series such as EETS and *Cyfres Beirdd yr Uchelwyr*.

Editorial Practice: Difficulties and Approaches

However an editor approaches the task of remediating the contents of a medieval manuscript into a modern text, there are a number of inescapable challenges which have to be met. In each case, various options have been adopted, though the underlying purpose of reconstructing an authorial or 'best' text (i.e., the one most likely to resemble what the author actually wrote) continues to be the driving force behind the production of a scholarly edition of a medieval text, containing a full apparatus of information including a description of the manuscripts, an assessment of their likely provenance and reliability, an introduction to the text covering points such as date, language, transmission, and so on, the reconstructed text with variants noted, and a glossary and/or index.

Sorting the Manuscripts

Though a few Middle English and Middle Welsh texts survive in a single manuscript copy, the majority survive in multiple copies, some of them dating from as late as the eighteenth and nineteenth centuries when handwritten copies of earlier texts continued to circulate. Editing a text from a single surviving manuscript has pros and cons: it is fairly straightforward to produce a transcription and then an edited version of what is written in one manuscript, but there is no help to be found for difficult or corrupt readings. Single-manuscript texts bring home the essential truth that an editor is, in most cases, editing the work of a scribe rather than an author.

Where there are several or many manuscript copies of a text, the editor has to decide how many to read and/or transcribe to produce the edited version. Do all manuscripts have the same value as a witness to the authorial text? This is where the practices of recension and collation come in. Where the relative dating of the manuscripts is known and they can be arranged in chronological order, it is likely that the oldest manuscripts will be closer to an originating text, but this cannot always be taken for granted. A manuscript of the sixteenth century might have been copied directly from a now-lost fourteenth-century text, whereas a fifteenth-century manuscript might be a copy of another copy from the same period. Some editors therefore try to create stemmata to show how later manuscripts were derived from earlier ones, either by direct copying or by sharing a common (possibly lost) exemplar. Careful comparison of all the manuscripts, noting similarities and differences in language, orthography, glossing and other markers (the process known as collation), can enable editors to group several manuscripts together as a single strand in the transmission of the text, thereby saving some time when it comes to the work of noting all the variants appearing in the different manuscripts. Walter W. Skeat's edition of *Piers Plowman*, first published in 1886, adopted this approach to make sense of the numerous manuscript copies of each of the three main versions of the poem, the A, B, and C-texts. Each group of manuscripts representing the three main versions was divided into subgroups of closely related copies which were then treated as a single witness.[16]

Volumes in the EETS series typically devote considerable space to descriptions of the manuscripts and their likely relationship to each other. As an example, the 2003 edition of *The Siege of Jerusalem*, edited by Ralph Hanna and David Lawton, provides a full codicological description of the nine surviving manuscripts followed by a detailed transmission history showing that all the surviving copies descended from a single (lost) archetype.[17] The TEAMS edition of *The Siege of Jerusalem*, edited by Michael Livingston in 2004, gives a much simpler list of the manuscripts and wisely refers the reader to the Hanna and Lawton edition for the full details.[18]

Choosing a Base Text

A common approach to editing is to select one manuscript as the 'base text', or copy-text, and then use variants (alternative readings) from the other manuscripts to fix problems such as corrupt readings, gaps in the text, obvious scribal errors, or problematic readings which the editor considers to be somehow wrong or a mistake. The production of the 'best text' of a work therefore has to start with what is regarded as the best surviving manuscript to use as the basis for the edition. Choosing the base text is a matter of editorial judgement about which of the manuscripts is the most authoritative and authentic as a representative of the author's work. Douglas Moffat, apparently not a fan of best-text editing, asks how the best manuscript can be chosen and replies:

> Presumably this is achieved through an examination of codicological, linguistic, and literary evidence in all the extant copies, from which one copy will emerge as the most worthy of being edited, because of its relative fidelity to the imagined original.[19]

This sums up the methodology for choosing the base text, though as Moffat and others have argued the intervention of the editor in privileging one text over another and then replacing words and phrases taken from other manuscripts somewhat undermines the goal of producing an 'authentic' text. Different editors, of course, do not always agree over which manuscript is the most appropriate base text, as in the case of Chaucer's *Canterbury Tales* where some major and influential editions have been based on the Ellesmere manuscript while others, equally admired, have been based on the Hengwrt manuscript.[20] In the case of the Welsh series, *Cyfres Beirdd yr Uchelwyr*, a base text is sometimes identified using a chronological approach in which all the variant copies are shown to be derived, directly or indirectly, from older texts.[21]

The Hanna and Lawton edition of *The Siege of Jerusalem*, like an increasing number of modern editions, at least acknowledges the difficulties of selecting a base text, saying that their choice of manuscript L (Oxford, Bodleian Library, MS Laud Misc. 656) 'involves certain irritations'.[22] They have also chosen to edit L more or less as it is, with variants listed below the text, accepting that 'the manuscript cannot function as a conventional "copy-text", in the sense that it does not approximate authorial forms, either in spelling or orthography ... After considering the prospect for some time, we have resisted any normalization and simply follow the manuscript'.[23] This method comes close to that of the single-manuscript edition, with a very small number of instances where the reading of L is replaced with a reading from another manuscript (see, for example, lines 927, 936, 1089, and 1337).

Other approaches can be more eclectic, in that the edited text is a composite, weaving together readings from several manuscripts identified as authoritative (due to their dating, scribe, transmission route, or similar information) without privileging a single base text. This is the case with the Welsh edition of the work of the fifteenth-century poet Ieuan ap Llywelyn Fychan, where the editor explains that: 'Gan na ellid yn aml ganfod "prif destun" o blith y gwahanol gopïau, lluniwyd testunau cyfansawdd o'r cerddi gan ddangos y darlleniadau amrywiol' ('Since it is often not possible to establish a "chief text" from among the different copies, composite texts of the poems have been constructed with variant readings shown').[24] At the other extreme, some editions provide the text of a single manuscript with a minimum of editorial interventions and few or no emendations or corrections, simply to make accessible a complete scribal text and thereby bypass the theoretical difficulties of trying to retrieve an authorial text. One example of this approach is Judith Perryman's edition of the Middle English romance *The King of Tars* in which she makes a case for editing the Auchinleck version of the text with minimal intervention.[25] A different approach altogether is that of the parallel text, where two or more manuscripts are edited in parallel and printed on facing pages to draw attention to significant differences of form and content.[26] This approach signifies the equal importance of two or more redactions from which a single authoritative archetype cannot be retrieved. Mary Elizabeth Barnicle's EETS edition of *The Seege or Batayle of Troye* prints all four of the surviving manuscript versions of the poem, three in parallel on each page and the fourth included in an appendix.[27] This is justified on the basis that 'despite the fact that the four texts are following the [lost] original faithfully ... individual differences plainly prove that one text cannot be a copy of another; rather do they show each to be an independent copy of the common original'.[28] This method, though relatively cumbersome for both publisher and reader, has a number of advantages. With access to all four versions of the text in one volume, the reader can see for themselves the various changes and choices made by each of the four scribes, while the editor can take a step back and let the texts speak for themselves.

Variants

When editing a text that survives in more than one manuscript copy, the editor has to collate the manuscript witnesses noting any differences, or variants, in the text. These can range from simple orthographical differences – *iwis* (ME 'indeed') compared to *iwisse*, for example – to dialectal differences (*hi*, 'she', in southeastern Middle English compared to *heo* in Southwest Midland dialect) to a full replacement of words or phrases. Even the first two types can be significant, enabling an editor to identify a particular scribe or a place of production, while the third type requires the editor to make an informed choice among two or more options. The choice that is made invariably depends on what kind of text the editor is aiming to produce: an 'authorial' text that is as near as possible to what the author actually wrote, a 'best text' that approximates most closely to the oldest and most authoritative copy, or an edition of a single manuscript. A scholarly edition with a full editorial apparatus will include all the variants deemed significant by the editor for each line of the text, so that the reader can see the choices that have been made.

In the case of poetry, the line order of the poems can provide another type of variant, since different recensions may put the lines in a different order, or add or omit lines. This is a particular issue with medieval Welsh poetry, where early written versions were (it is assumed) based on oral performances in which different reciters might deliver slightly different versions of the same poem. The practice of *Cyfres Beirdd yr Uchelwyr* is to provide in the apparatus at the end of each poem the alternative line orders found in different manuscripts where they occur. There is also the issue of

195

lines – usually couplets – which appear in some manuscripts but are omitted in other versions, and an editorial decision must be made about whether to include such lines or to record them as variants in the apparatus. In some cases, this leads to the problem of 'editor as author' – the desire to include in the edited poem as many lines as survive in the various manuscripts can lead to a finished poem which does not exactly correspond to any of the manuscript witnesses. The supposedly 'original' medieval poem has in fact been written by the modern editor.

Emendations

At various points in the text, the editor may feel obliged to provide a reading which is not actually attested in any of the surviving manuscript copies. This may be because of an obvious scribal error such as word-skip or line-skip,[29] which subsequent scribes have simply copied, leaving a gap in the sense unit, or because a particular form does not correspond to known versions of the word and must therefore be regarded as corrupt and in need of emendation to a standard form. Since, as A. S. G. Edwards has said, 'any editorial activity constitutes a form of interpretation', the practice of emendation, however conservative, comes closest to a kind of subjective interpretation (of the author's intention, of the nature of the original text) that compromises the supposedly evidence-based task of editing the text.[30] We are left with questions about how much intervention an editor should make, how the editor can identify a 'correct' reading without making assumptions about authorial intention, and at what point does the editor become the author.

Punctuation

In general, the system of written marks that we know as punctuation is the product of early print culture. While medieval scribes used abbreviations and various other markers, such as line breaks or rubrication, the systematic use of commas, full stops, semicolons, quotation marks, and so on is a post-medieval phenomenon.[31] The editorial practice of adding punctuation to largely unpunctuated medieval texts therefore provides editors with another arena for subjective interpretation, since the judicious addition of a semicolon or a question mark can significantly direct the way in which a reader makes sense of the text. Different editions of the same text often use punctuation in slightly different ways, according to the editor's own interpretation of what the text means and their own experience of what a 'literary' text looks like on the page.[32]

The addition of modern titles to poems or prose texts which are untitled in the manuscript sources is another way in which the editor takes control of the text and directs the reader towards a preferred understanding of the text. There are some suggestive differences in the titles given to poems by Dafydd ap Gwilym by the respective editors of the first and second standard editions of the corpus, Thomas Parry and Dafydd Johnston.[33] A poem about unrequited love is titled 'Difrawder' ('Indifference') by Parry (no. 110) but is called 'Y Ffŵl a'i Gysgod' ('A Fool and his Shadow') by Johnston (no. 80), which nicely echoes a simile used twice in the poem and shifts the balance away from the indifferent beloved, presented as a remote and unsatisfactory object, to the lively perspective of the lover, all too aware that his persistence in a hopeless cause makes him foolish. Another poem on the same theme uses the metaphors of magic and enchantment (W. *hud, hudoliaeth*) to describe the falseness of the beloved, giving Parry his title of 'Hudoliaeth Merch' (no. 84, 'A Girl's Enchantment'). Johnston calls the poem 'Telynores Twyll' (no. 135, 'The [female] Harpist of Deceit'), a phrase picked up from the poem itself where an extended image of the harp played by the beloved, perhaps to accompany the poet's recitation, is elaborated as a symbol of her deviousness. Again, the change of title shifts the focus from the object of the beloved, whose 'magic' is a quality assigned to her by others, to the voice of the unlucky poet whose subject position we are invited to take up.

Apparatus

In preparing the edition for publication, the editor must decide what supporting material to include along with the actual text. It is not unusual in older editions for the scholarly apparatus to occupy a vastly greater number of pages than the text itself. While editors have a certain amount of discretion over what should be included in the apparatus – such as introduction, variants, notes, glossary, index – series editors often have their own guidelines which text editors are asked to follow. The EETS series currently sets out its Guidelines for Editors on its webpage, and these include not only a style guide but also the preferred model of the scholarly apparatus, comprising an introduction, abbreviations and bibliography, the text itself with substantive variants, explanatory notes, and a glossary.

While all aspects of the editorial process signal to some extent the intended audience for the publication (or rather each edition constructs an audience type through its methods and choices), this is particularly true of the apparatus included with an edition. Scholarly editions, with a maximum of apparatus, construct a scholarly audience of readers who are sufficiently informed to be able to make judgements about the editorial choices that have been made, including variant readings, possible datings, emendations, and speculations about the 'original' form of the text. An undergraduate student readership, on the other hand, is more likely to want a 'clean' text with little clutter from variants and additional support in the form of glosses and notes. The difference in purpose is very evident when comparing the two editions of *The Siege of Jerusalem* in the EETS series and the TEAMS series. In the latter, the emphasis is on explaining the historical and literary context of the text and providing glosses, making it comprehensible to a relatively inexperienced reader of Middle English texts.

The Welsh series *Cyfres Beirdd yr Uchelwyr* strikes something of a balance by providing, for the most complex poems, not only the edited text of the Middle Welsh poem but also, immediately following it, a translation into modern Welsh. While translations of Middle English texts into modern English are generally not regarded as appropriate inclusions in a scholarly edition, the Welsh series pragmatically recognizes that Welsh readers, even those with competence in the modern language, need some support in reading the highly arcane verse of the early court poets. The modern Welsh versions also preclude the need for a glossary, not routinely provided in this particular series.

The Digital Edition

Anyone familiar with *The Canterbury Tales* project or the *Piers Plowman Electronic Archive* will acknowledge the ambition, not yet fully realized, of such projects to provide digital texts of all the manuscript copies of major works of Middle English literature. The main objective of these two projects is to make all the manuscript texts available online, in diplomatic or edited forms, enabling 'instructors, students, and researchers to explore late medieval literary and manuscript culture'.[34] Based on these single-manuscript transcriptions, best-text or composite text editions are also being produced in digital format alongside the manuscript copies, thus providing 'the evidence on which the edition is based in a form much fuller and more comprehensible than a list of variants'.[35] The advantages of searchable electronic editions, where the amount of material that can be digitized is limited only by economics and the logistics of human endeavour, seem obvious.

The online editions produced by the TEAMS Middle English Texts series are basically sophisticated uploads of the hard-copy volumes adapted to webpage reading. They are therefore digitized editions, rather than 'born digital' editions constructed in accordance with what Patrick Sahle calls a 'digital paradigm'.[36] Nonetheless, they are useful and successful examples of online editions that are sufficiently accessible, and include enough apparatus, to be valuable resources for both teachers and students. Most of the editions include manuscript variants, and the text and footnotes can be read together on the same screen via split-screen technology. Though the individual texts are not searchable, the whole series site can be searched for individual words or phrases occurring in any of the published texts. Apart from this searchability function, however, the online editions offer little more than their hard-copy equivalents, though their free online availability is a boon for students and encourages teachers to set these texts for study in their classrooms.

The recent digital editions of the works of two major medieval Welsh poets by teams of scholars in Wales are outstanding examples of what can be achieved in a born-digital scholarly edition. *Dafydd ap Gwilym.net* (launched in 2007) and *Guto'r Glyn.net* (launched in 2013) provide edited texts and translations of the works of these two poets, including manuscript transcriptions, images of some of the manuscripts, variants, line orders, stemmata, notes, and contextual essays. In the case of *Dafydd ap Gwilym. net* there are digital recordings of each of the poems being read aloud. *Guto'r Glyn.net* includes an essay by the project's director, Professor Ann Parry Owen, outlining the computer technologies which made the edition possible.[37] She notes the milestone emergence of TEI (Text Encoding Initiative) in 1987 as the first standardized system of coding, and the development of Unicode in the early 1990s which made it possible for an accented language like Welsh to be digitized, along with a number of orthographical forms found in early Welsh manuscripts. These technologies have resulted in digital editions which are so comprehensive in their information that readers can either use the editions and translations immediately for their own research or spend time exploring the different manuscript versions with considerably more ease than if they were sitting in the National Library of Wales in Aberystwyth. The reader can become, if they wish, the actual editor, selecting their own version of the text from the manuscript readings laid out for them on the screen.

These Welsh digital editions are light years away from earlier digital editions. They are user-friendly, flexible, beautifully designed and presented, and completely functional, with split screens to compare text and translation or text and variants. Their value can be appreciated by comparing *Dafydd ap Gwilym.net* with its hard-copy equivalent, *Cerddi Dafydd ap Gwilym*, which contains the same edited texts and some of the apparatus but no English translations or detailed manuscript variants or images (though it does contain translations into modern Welsh). It is unlikely that any print publisher would have the resources to include all the same information as the website, and even if it were economically possible, such a book would be huge and unwieldy compared to the easily navigable website where text, translation, and notes can be viewed simultaneously.

Why, then, do we not move all our medieval editing projects onto the web? The answer, primarily, is to do with the cost of digital editing. Both the Welsh projects were financed by substantial grants from, first, the Arts and Humanities Research Board (AHRB) and, subsequently, the Arts and Humanities Research Council (AHRC). Each edition employed a team of academics and technical assistants, some of them working full time on the project for a number of years. Compare this with the way in which a standard print edition is produced, usually by a single editor. One of the most recent publications in the 'Poets of the Nobility' series, *Gwaith Hywel Dafi*, is a two-volume edition containing over 100 poems, edited with a full scholarly apparatus by one person, Dr Cynfael Lake, then a full-time academic at Swansea University.[38] Though the project took several years, and was supported by some research-leave funding from the British Academy, its published output was significantly quicker and cheaper than the digital editions which contain a comparable number of poems. If digital editing has a future – and the looming advent of mandatory open-access publishing in UK Higher Education suggests it must look to such a future – then funding will have to be found to pay for it, perhaps along the lines of the less labour-intensive TEAMS model. At the very least, the Welsh projects have provided an impressive and successful model of best practice for the digital editions of the future.

Editing a Text: a Middle Welsh Case Study

The corpus of poetry attributed to Guto'r Glyn – more than 120 poems in total – contains a broad range of the genres or types of poetry characteristic of the late medieval poets who travelled around the gentry houses, monasteries, and priories of Wales entertaining the occupants and, indirectly, enhancing their status as the elite class of Wales and the borders. Guto's poetry includes political verse, satires, poems of request and thanks for gifts, and above all praise poetry addressed to the patrons who supported him, ecclesiastical and lay.[39] Among these poems is a *cywydd* addressed to Sir Hywel ap Dai of Northop (fl. *c.* 1476–84) in northeast Wales, in the modern county of Flintshire.[40] Sir Hywel is representative of the Welsh gentry in that area, a canon at St Asaph cathedral in 1476 and a parson in the parish of Whitford in 1484. This is Guto's only poem to Sir Hywel and it is likely to have been commissioned by Sir Hywel or a member of his family as a celebration of his career in the church.

Editing Medieval Manuscripts for Modern Audiences

'In Praise of Hywel', the title given to it in *Guto'r Glyn.net* by its modern editor and translator, survives in five manuscripts, a relatively small number compared to many of Guto's poems which typically survive in upwards of twenty, thirty, or even seventy manuscripts, and this smaller number makes the editor's task of collation considerably easier. The basic information required by the editor is the location and shelfmark of each manuscript, the folio or page numbers on which the text appears, and the (approximate) date of each manuscript. For our poem, the list looks like this:

- Aberystwyth, National Library of Wales, MS 3021F, 585–6, 1684x1686
- Aberystwyth, National Library of Wales, MS 3049D, 194–5, 1560x1580
- Aberystwyth, National Library of Wales, MS 8497B, 43v–44v, 1570s
- Aberystwyth, National Library of Wales, MS 21248D, 108v–109r, *c.* 1630
- Bangor, Bangor University Library, MS Gwyneddon 4, 238–40, *c.* 1575.

The editor is now faced with the task of deciding how to prioritize the manuscripts: whether to select one as a base text and edit it with variants from the others, to edit a single manuscript, to present two or more in parallel, or to construct a composite text using all of them. The editor of this poem in *Guto'r Glyn.net*, Eurig Salisbury, has, in line with the editorial policy of the project, constructed a stemma for the manuscripts, concluding that all five derive from the same lost source, a manuscript collection of Guto's verse (Figure 9.1).[41]

Salisbury has based his edition of the poem on the three oldest manuscripts, with the editorial aim of retrieving a 'best text' which is as close as possible to what was in the lost source. The edition is therefore a composite based on three out of the five manuscripts; readings from the later two manuscripts, which derive directly from the earlier ones, are not included in the variants.

Even before looking at the text, then, a number of editorial decisions have already been made, of necessity, and these will shape what happens when we start looking at the poem itself. Figures 9.2, 9.3, 9.4 show the first eight lines of the poem in the three oldest manuscripts.

Of these, two are by known scribes. Gwyneddon 4 was written by William Salesbury (*c.* 1520–*c.* 1584), the great Renaissance scholar who was, among other things, largely responsible for the first translation of the New Testament into Welsh. NLW 8497B was written by Thomas Wiliems of Trefriw (*c.* 1545–*c.* 1622), a cleric and scholar who was a prolific collector and copyist of early Welsh manuscripts.[42] Both manuscripts are therefore reliable and either could be used as a base text against which to compare variants, but for the purposes of this case study I will use Gwyneddon 4 as the base text. In Table 9.1, I have transcribed the first few lines of the poem as they appear in Gwyneddon 4, showing the variants from the other two manuscripts.[43]

201

HELEN FULTON

TABLE 9.1: Transcriptions of first eight lines of Gwyneddon 4

Line	Gwyneddon 4	NLW 8479B	NLW 3049D
1	Pwy'r map llen per ympop llys	mab; ymob	mab; ym hob
2	Piau bonedd pop ynys	pob	piav; pob
3	Person o Von i Vynyw	o von i vynyw	o von i vynyw
4	Pren ir o bob barwn yw		obob
5	Prif enw o Wepra i vyny	(6) prifenw	(6)
6	Pren ai vric ympop bron vry	(5) vrig; ymhob	(5) ymhob
7	Syr Howel yn Llan Elwy		elwey
8	Saint Ass ei personiaid hwy	i	i

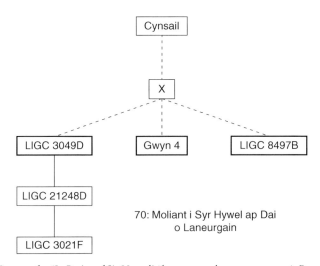

Figure 9.1 Stemma for 'In Praise of Sir Hywel' (from gutorglyn.net, poem 70). Reproduced with permission of the University of Wales Centre for Advanced Welsh and Celtic Studies, Aberystwyth

The variants are not particularly significant, representing orthographical differences for the most part (e.g., *map*, 'son', as opposed to *mab*, both forms being relatively common in Middle Welsh, with *map* the older of the two). The couplet in lines 5–6 has been reversed in NLW 8479B and NLW 3049D and this requires editorial intervention: should one keep strictly to the readings of Gwyneddon 4 or follow the reversed couplet of the other two manuscripts? Eurig Salisbury, on the *Guto'r Glyn.net* website, has chosen the latter course, but we could perhaps decide to edit Gwyneddon 4 as it is and simply note the variants where they occur. We also need to decide on a policy regarding orthography and punctuation. How much should we modernize

Editing Medieval Manuscripts for Modern Audiences

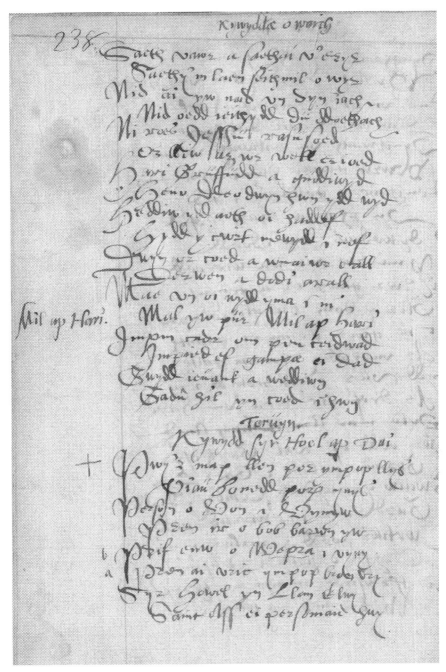

Figure 9.2 Archives and Special Collections, Bangor University, Gwyneddon MS 4, p. 238. Reproduced by permission of Archives and Special Collections, Bangor University

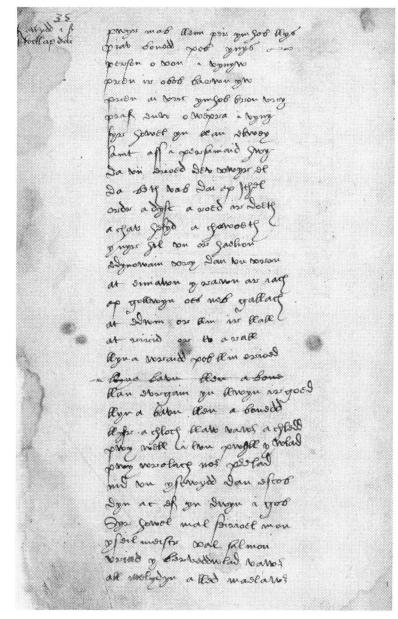

Figure 9.3 Aberystwyth, National Library of Wales, MS 3049D, p. 194. Reproduced by permission of Llyfrgell Genedlaethol Cymru/The National Library of Wales

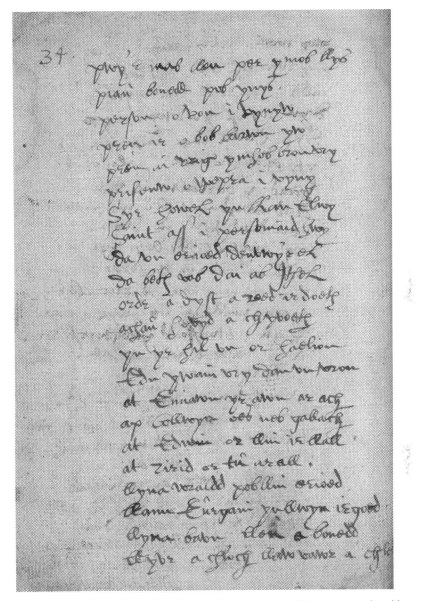

Figure 9.4 Aberystwyth, National Library of Wales, MS 8497B, fol. 43v. Reproduced by permission of Llyfrgell Genedlaethol Cymru/The National Library of Wales

these early modern texts, presumably copied from older examplars? To make them accessible to a wide readership, we can modify the orthography to something close to Modern Welsh, including diacritics, while preserving the

Middle Welsh grammatical features, and add some modern punctuation to help readers understand the sense of the lines. My edited text of Gwyneddon 4 thus looks like this:

1 Pwy'r mab llên pêr ym mhob llys,
2 Piau bonedd pob ynys?
3 Person o Fôn i Fynyw,
4 Pren ir o bob barwn yw.
5 Prif enw o Wepra i fyny,
6 Pren a'i frig ym mhob bron fry.
7 Syr Hywel yn Llanelwy,
8 Saint As eu personiaid hwy.

The manuscript sources, conventionally listed by alphabet letter to save space and to enable a group of manuscripts to be considered as one witness, together with the variants are normally shown at the end of each poem. In my apparatus below, every time the letter A appears it means that my text has diverged from Gwyneddon 4, my base text. Every time all three letters appear in the variants, it means that my reading is not found in any of the manuscripts (representing the highest level of editorial intervention).

Manuscripts
A: Bangor MS Gwyneddon 4
B: NLW MS 8479B
C: NLW MS 3049D

Variants
1. map; ympop A; ymob B; ym hob C. 2. pop A; piav C. 4. obob C. 5. prifenw B. 6. vric; ympop A; vrig; ymhob B; vric; ymhob C. 7. elwey C. 8. Ass ABC; ei A; i BC.

Line order
BC: 1–4, 6, 5, 7–8

Despite the care I have taken to follow the text of Gwyneddon 4, the orthographical changes have introduced some forms which do not appear in any of the manuscripts. In the case of *ym mhob*, for example, in lines 1 and 6, meaning 'in every', this is the correct Modern Welsh form showing the regular nasalization caused by the preposition *yn*, 'in'. None of the manuscripts, however, uses this form but rather a variety of other spellings, indicating the instability with which initial mutation (a phonological phenomenon) was represented in written texts before the introduction of a standardized spelling system. The inclusion of the line order is necessary

Editing Medieval Manuscripts for Modern Audiences

to show that the manuscripts vary in their line order and that an editorial choice (and hence an interpretation) has been imposed.

Finally, the edited text requires some notes, normally located towards the end of an edition, after all the text or texts have been presented. Even these few lines throw up some points that need explicating for readers unfamiliar with medieval Wales (thereby constructing a particular kind of audience):

NOTES

3. *o Fôn i Fynwy*, 'from Anglesey to St David's'. This is a common alliterative phrase in medieval Welsh poetry, metrically useful, and signifying the length of the country, since Anglesey is in the far northwest of Wales and St David's is the most westerly point of the Welsh coastline in the south.

5. *Wepra*, 'Wepre'. A Saxon place name in northeast Wales near Sir Hywel's home in Northop. The name is first attested in 1086.

7. *Llanelwy*. The Welsh name of the town and parish of St Asaph in the county of Flintshire, located on the river Elwy. St Asaph is the smallest cathedral in the UK.

8. *Saint As*, 'Saint Asaph'. The form *Ass* appearing in the manuscripts is an abbreviated form of *Assa*, an alternative name for this sixth-century British saint. The precise meaning of this line is difficult to elucidate; Williams and Williams in *Gwaith Guto'r Glyn* (p. 223) emend the line to: 'saint ar eu personiaid hwy' ('a saint for their parsons').

In my mini-edition of the first eight lines, I have included a sample of as many parts of the normal scholarly apparatus as possible, including the brief introduction describing the subject of the poem, Sir Hywel ap Dai. In addition, a glossary would normally be provided at the end of the edition, and more could have been said about the *cywydd* metre, as the metrical pattern of a poetic text is often a key feature in helping the editor to decide between variant readings. The apparatus indicates this is a scholarly edition, and I have provided sufficient information for readers to check my editorial choices. My theoretical position as an editor has perhaps been left a little opaque, but my decision to edit one of the manuscripts as faithfully as possible, rather than weave together a composite text, indicates my sense of the integrity of a manuscript text and my reluctance to impose editorial interpretations beyond the remit of producing an accessible and readable text for those interested in the content rather than the manuscripts.

Before leaving the case study, we might want to think about the kind of audience that my edition has constructed. On the one hand, it is a readership which is familiar with Middle Welsh, since I have provided very little in the way of translation or linguistic explanation. On the other hand, as I have edited the text through the medium of English, rather than

Welsh, I am expecting at least a bilingual if not a monolingual English readership, and one which is not completely familiar with the geography of Wales or the literary conventions of medieval Welsh poetry. Though I did not consciously set out to do so, I realize I have constructed an audience of students of Middle Welsh poetry working outside Wales.

Looking Forward

At the moment, the practice of editing medieval texts seems to be balanced between the traditional methods of best-text and composite editing on the one hand and more modern digital approaches on the other hand. One might ask, though, what other trends are on the horizon, and is there any possibility of producing a 'post-structuralist' edition which takes account of the problems of authorial intention and the 'original' text? Michael G. Sargent has recently proposed a model of the 'rhizomorphic' edition which he calls a 'post-modern' challenge to the methodology of recension and the contruction of stemmata.[44] Sargent shows that the complex manuscript history of Walter Hilton's *Scale of Perfection* (*c.* 1375x1385) is not conducive to establishing a stemma or stemmata as a genetic line of descent. Instead he advocates 'a historical edition representing a strategically important stage in the development of a text *mouvant*' – using Paul Zumthor's notion of *mouvance* as a description of an unstable text hovering between orality and literacy.[45] The metaphor of the rhizome, a category of plant that grows horizontally as well as vertically, replaces the family-tree metaphor of recension and suggests that the connections between manuscripts are not simply those of descent but can be due to horizontal associations and influences from one to another.

Sargent therefore refuses to privilege any one manuscript as being more authoritative than another, which means that he rejects the concept of a single definitive edition of a text. Instead, readers would ideally have access to all the manuscripts and would be able to produce different readings of the same text by choosing a different base text each time: 'A truly "rhizomorphic" edition would require the intertextual capabilities of electronic media, by which every reading of every manuscript would be available to the reader, who would be able to read any form of the text, using any manuscript representing that particular form as his base-text.'[46] This methodology, 'non-genetic, non-evolutionary, non-authoritative, non-positivist, post-modern', thus preserves the *mouvance* of the inevitably unstable text.[47] On the other hand, leaving it to the reader to find their way through all the manuscript versions might be seen as an abrogation of the role of the editor, whose very familiarity with the manuscripts and expertise in relation to the language and context of the text equips them to make at least some choices on behalf of the reader.[48]

The potential to produce multiple readings, without claiming one as being the 'best' or 'original' text, already exists in digital editions such as the Welsh poetry examples. Similarly, the practice of editing one manuscript at a time, as a complete text in its own right, retains the integrity of what a scribe (or scribes) wrote and what was read by a reader (or readers) at the time of its production. Single manuscripts therefore have an authenticity quite unlike the traditional composite text based on multiple manuscripts where the editor has produced a 'medieval' text that is not actually found in any medieval manuscript; rather, it is a synthetic construct which showcases the editor's skill in reproducing what a medieval text is supposed (by modern editors) to look like.

A focus on the manuscript itself as a material artefact is another way in which the process of editing can be re-theorized. If texts are seen in relation not to other versions of the same text, but to other texts in the same manuscript, new understandings of each text can emerge in illuminating ways. Such a method involves transcription, together with some orthographical standardization, much as an editor does when editing a text that occurs only in a single manuscript. But when the whole manuscript is transcribed and made available to modern readers as a readable text, new worlds of literary transmission and scribal networks can be opened up. One recent example of such a project is the TEAMS edition and translation, in three volumes, of Harley 2253 (London, British Library, MS Harley 2253), which contains some famous and much-edited Middle English texts including the Harley Lyrics, the prophecy of Thomas of Erceldoune, and the romance of *King Horn*.[49] While these texts have previously been edited as separate works, their presence together in a continuous sequence preserves the authenticity of the manuscript and of the reading experience.

The assimilation of manuscript studies, once the preserve of palaeographers, codicologists, and archivists, into the broader field of History of the Book has facilitated this closer study of manuscripts as complete works in themselves, which are often in meaningful dialogue synchronically and diachronically (to paraphrase Sargent's 'rhizome' metaphor). Comparative examinations of bindings, collations, writing surfaces, ink, watermarks, and the paratextual material provided by marginalia and illustrations can help to identify scribes, provenance, and modes of transmission and thus add to our understanding of the texts contained within each manuscript. The traditional editorial method of picking bits of text out of several manuscripts closes off the possibility of reading any text as it was most likely to have been read by a medieval audience, while getting us no closer to anything that might be considered an 'original' text. Rather than fixating on 'the author', we can learn just as much by focusing on the scribe (or scribes) whose idiosyncrasies of orthography, style, and *mise-en-page* enrich our reading of the texts that they have copied, compiled, or even, like Hoccleve, composed. Linne Mooney's work on Chaucer's scribe, Adam Pinkhurst, and on the scribes of the Guildhall in medieval London, has been particularly influential in establishing methodologies for reading texts through the lens of their scribes.[50] Though there is a risk in trying to personalize and biographicalize the scribe as if this was another author, at least the scribe 'owns' the text he or she has written. It is their original work.

Finally, it is vital to remember the importance of the reader or user of edited texts, whose needs will determine the nature of the edition they are likely to prefer. Different kinds of editions serve different purposes, whether a glossed text for students, a scholarly edition for researchers, or a heavily annotated facsimile or digital edition for palaeographers. This means that there is no single 'right' way to edit a text, or to answer the questions I set out at the beginning; rather, there are multiple ways of answering those questions, just as there are multiple ways of making meaning from any kind of text.

There are two important provisos. First, we need to acknowledge that editorial practice is limited by economic factors, including the amount of resource (including labour that is often so undervalued in the hierarchy of what does and does not constitute praiseworthy scholarship, especially in the United States) that can be directed to editing at any given time and the readiness of publishers to produce, normally at a loss, compendious scholarly editions for a tiny audience. The TEAMS series has cornered the market in student-facing editions, without sacrificing too much scholarship, while the subscription model of EETS and *Cyfres Beirdd yr Uchelwyr* (supplemented by uncosted time provided by academics and professional staff) can work for non-profit academic publishers. Second, whatever their methodologies, editors must be transparent about what they are doing, the choices they are making, and the assumptions that lie behind their editorial practice.

Editors have a free hand to create their text as part of the social semiotic of editing, whose primary meaning is to produce a readable and comprehensible text for a modern (digitally aware, media literate) audience. But whatever the methods used, none of these will succeed in retrieving the 'original' text written by a coherent and singularly gifted individual called 'the author'. It is time for editors to set different goals and to look for new ways of achieving them.

Editing Medieval Manuscripts for Modern Audiences

Notes

1. See D. Matthews, *The Making of Middle English, 1765–1910* (Minneapolis and London: University of Minnesota Press, 1999); A. Singleton, 'The Early English Text Society in the Nineteenth Century: An Organizational History', *Review of English Studies*, 56 (2005), 90–118; H. L. Spencer, 'The Early English Text Society 1930 to 1950: Wartime and Reconstruction', in V. Gillespie and A. Hudson, eds., *Probable Truth: Editing Medieval Texts from Britain in the Twenty-First Century* (Turnhout: Brepols, 2013), 15–35; Y. Cowan, 'Reading Material Bibliography and Digital Editions: The Case of the Early English Text Society', in D. Cullen, ed., *Editors, Scholars and the Social Text* (Toronto: University of Toronto Press, 2012), 279–99.
2. D. Johnston et al., eds., *Cerddi Dafydd ap Gwilym* (Caerdydd: Gwasg Prifysgol Cymru, 2010).
3. *Guto'r Glyn.net* (2013), www.gutorglyn.net/gutorglyn/index/ (accessed 30 September 2018).
4. See B. Millett, 'Whatever Happened to Electronic Editing?', in Gillespie and Hudson, eds., *Probable Truth*, 39–54.
5. R. M. Liuzza, 'Scribal Habit: The Evidence of the Old English Gospels', in M. Swan and E. Treharne, eds., *Rewriting Old English in the Twelfth Century* (Cambridge: Cambridge University Press, 2000), 143–65.
6. J. M. Manly and E. Rickert, eds., *The Text of the Canterbury Tales: Studied on the Basis of All Known Manuscripts*, 8 vols. (Chicago: University of Chicago Press, 1940). For critiques of their methods, see G. Kane, 'John M. Manly and Edith Rickert', in P. C. Ruggiers, ed., *Editing Chaucer: The Great Tradition* (Norman, OK: Pilgrim Books, 1984), 207–29; N. F. Blake, 'Editorial Assumptions in the Manly-Rickert Edition of *The Canterbury Tales*', *English Studies* 64 (1983), 385–400.
7. F. N. Robinson, 'Preface to the Second Edition', in *The Works of Geoffrey Chaucer*, ed. F. N. Robinson, 2nd edn (Oxford: Oxford University Press, 1978), vii–x, at vii.
8. D. Moffat with V. P. McCarren, 'A Bibliographical Essay on Editing Methods and Authorial and Scribal Intention', in V. P. McCarren and D. Moffat, eds., *A Guide to Editing Middle English* (Ann Arbor: University of Michigan Press, 1998), 25–57, at 28.
9. R. Barthes, 'The Death of the Author', in *Image, Music, Text*, trans. S. Heath (London: Fontana/Collins, 1977), 142–8; M. Foucault, 'What Is an Author?', in *Language, Counter-Memory, Practice: Selected Essays and Interviews*, ed. D. F. Bourchard, trans. D. F. Bourchard and S. Simon (Oxford: Blackwell, 1977), 113–38.
10. Barthes, 'The Death of the Author', 143.
11. Foucault, 'What Is an Author?', 128.
12. See M. Fisher, 'When Variants Aren't: Authors as Scribes in Some English Manuscripts', in Gillespie and Hudson, eds., *Probable Truth*, 207–22.
13. J. J. McGann, *A Critique of Modern Textual Criticism* (Chicago and London: University of Chicago Press, 1983), especially at 75.
14. T. W. Machan, *Textual Criticism and Middle English Texts* (Charlottesville, VA: University Press of Virginia, 1994).

15. See H. Fulton, 'The Editor as Author: Re-producing the Text. A Case Study of Parry's *Gwaith Dafydd ap Gwilym*', *Bulletin of the Bibliographical Society of Australia and New Zealand* 19.2 (1995), 67–78.

16. W. Langland, *The Vision of William Concerning Piers the Plowman in Three Parallel Texts*, ed. W. W. Skeat, 2 vols. (Oxford: Oxford University Press, 1886; repr. 2001). Skeat's description of the classification of the manuscripts is in vol. II, lxv–lxxii.

17. R. Hanna and D. Lawton, eds., *The Siege of Jerusalem*, EETS o.s. 320 (Oxford: Oxford University Press, 2003), lvii.

18. M. Livingston, ed., *The Siege of Jerusalem*, TEAMS Medieval Texts Series (Kalamazoo, MI: Medieval Institute Publications, 2004); online edition (2004), http://d.lib.rochester.edu/teams/publication/livingston-siege-of-jerusalem (accessed 30 September 2018).

19. Moffat, 'A Bibliographical Essay', 32.

20. See C. Moorman, 'One Hundred Years of Editing *The Canterbury Tales*', *Chaucer Review* 24 (1989), 99–114; R. Hanna, 'Problems of "Best-Text" Editing and the Hengwrt Manuscript of *The Canterbury Tales*', in D. Pearsall, ed., *Manuscripts and Texts: Editorial Problems in Later Middle English Literature* (Cambridge: D. S. Brewer, 1987), 87–94.

21. See, for example, B. J. Lewis, ed., *Gwaith Gruffudd ap Maredudd 1: Canu i Deulu Penmynydd* (Aberystwyth: Canolfan Uwchefrydiau Cymreig a Cheltaidd Prifysgol Cymru, 2003).

22. Hanna and Lawton, eds. *The Siege of Jerusalem*, lxxxvi.

23. Ibid.

24. M. P. Bryant-Quinn, ed., 'Dull y Golygu', in *Gwaith Ieuan ap Llywelyn Fychan, Ieuan Llwyd Brydydd a Lewys Aled* (Aberystwyth: Canolfan Uwchefrydiau Cymreig a Cheltaidd Prifysgol Cymru, 2003), v.

25. J. Perryman, ed., *The King of Tars*, Middle English Texts 12 (Heidelberg: Winter, 1986). Perryman provides a list of variants from the other manuscripts.

26. See J. Fellows, 'Author, Author, Author . . . : An Apology for Parallel Texts', in McCarren and Moffat, eds., *A Guide to Editing Middle English*, 15–24.

27. M. E. Barnicle, ed., *The Seege or Batayle of Troye*, EETS o.s. 172 (London: Oxford University Press, 1927).

28. Ibid., xxxviii.

29. Such scribal errors are called 'haplography', where scribes accidentally anticipate a part of text they are coming to later; or 'dittography', where scribes re-write a word or phrase they have already written.

30. See A. S. G. Edwards, 'Editing and the Teaching of Alliterative Verse', in McCarren and Moffat, eds., *A Guide to Editing Middle English*, 95–106, at 98.

31. For a full account of the history of English punctuation, see M. B. Parkes, *Pause and Effect: An Introduction to the History of Punctuation in the West* (Berkeley and Los Angeles: University of California Press, 1993).

32. See H. Fulton, 'Punctuation as a Semiotic Code: The Case of the Medieval Welsh *Cywydd*', *Parergon*, n.s. 13.2 (1996), 2–17.

33. T. Parry, ed., *Gwaith Dafydd ap Gwilym* (Caerdydd: Gwasg Prifysgol Cymru, 1952); Johnston, ed., *Cerddi Dafydd ap Gwilym*.

34. *Piers Plowman Electronic Archive* (2014), http://piers.chass.ncsu.edu (accessed 30 September 2018).

35. T. Turville-Petre, 'Editing Electronic Texts', in Gillespie and Hudson, eds., *Probable Truth*, 55–70, at 56.

36. P. Sahle, 'What Is a Scholarly Digital Edition?', in M. J. Driscoll and E. Pierazzo, eds., *Digital Scholarly Editing: Theories and Practices* (Cambridge: Open Book Publishers, 2016), http://dx.doi.org/10.11647/OBP .0095.02 (accessed 30 September 2018).

37. A. Parry Owen, 'Golygu Digidol: Profiad Prosiect Guto'r Glyn', *Guto'r Glyn.net*, www.gutorglyn.net/gutorglyn/tuchwith/ (accessed 30 September 2018).

38. A. Cynfael Lake, ed., *Gwaith Hywel Dafi*, 2 vols. (Aberystwyth: Canolfan Uwchefrydiau Cymreig a Cheltaidd Prifysgol Cymru, 2015).

39. See *Guto'r Glyn.net*; J. E. Caerwyn Williams, 'Guto'r Glyn', in A. O. H. Jarman and G. R Hughes, eds., *A Guide to Welsh Literature vol. 2: 1282–c.1550*, rev. 2nd edn D. Johnston (Cardiff: University of Wales Press, 1997), 197–221; D. F. Evans et al., eds., *Gwalch Cywyddau Gwŷr: Essays on Guto'r Glyn and Fifteenth-Century Wales* (Aberystwyth: Centre for Advanced Welsh and Celtic Studies, 2013).

40. Poem no. 70 in *Guto'r Glyn.net* ; *Gwaith Guto'r Glyn*, ed. J. Llywelyn Williams and I. Williams (Caerdydd: Gwasg Prifysgol Cymru, 1939), no. LXXXV, at 223.

41. In this Stemma, 'Cynsail' ('Base') refers to the assumed original as composed or written by Guto himself, while 'X' is the common symbol used to indicate a lost source. The stemma uses the abbreviation LlGC (Llyfrgell Genedlaethol Cymru) in the shelfmarks rather than the English abbreviation, NLW (National Library of Wales), which I have used. The title is given in Welsh, meaning 'Praise [poem] to Sir Hywel ap Dai of Llaneurgain'.

42. There are useful entries for both William Salesbury (by R. Brinley Jones) and Thomas Wiliems (by J. E. Caerwyn Williams) in the *Oxford Dictionary of National Biography* (online edition, 2004).

43. My translation of these lines is as follows: 'Who is the fine man of letters in every court, / Whose is the lineage of every region? / A parson from Anglesey to St David's, / he's a green tree from every baron. / A major name from Wepre upwards, / a tree and its sprig on every high hill. / Sir Hywel in Llanelwy, / the St Asaph of their parsons.'

44. M. G. Sargent, 'Editing Walter Hilton's *Scale of Perfection*: The Case for a Rhizomorphic Historical Edition', in Gillespie and Hudson, eds., *Probable Truth*, 509–34, at 509.

45. Ibid., 531.

46. Ibid.

47. Ibid., 529–30.

48. N. Jacobs, 'Kindly Light or Foxfire? The Authorial Text Reconsidered', in Gillespie and Hudson, eds., *Probable Truth*, 3–24, at 22.

49. S. Fein with D. Raybin and J. Ziolkowski, eds., *The Complete Harley 2253 Manuscript*, 3 vols., TEAMS Middle English Texts (Kalamazoo, MI: Medieval Institute Publications, 2014–15); http://d.lib.rochester.edu/teams (accessed 30 September 2018).

50. See L. R. Mooney and E. Stubbs, *Scribes and the City: London Guildhall Clerks and Their Dissemination of Middle English Literature, 1375–1425* (Woodbridge: Boydell and Brewer, 2014).

10

TERESA WEBBER

Where Were Books Made and Kept?

It was never the norm for the makers of Western medieval books to record in them information about their circumstances of production, or for owners, whether institutions or individuals, to enter an inscription of ownership. Likewise, the making of other forms of record of the manufacture or ownership of books, even within religious and academic institutions, never appears to have become routine. Such information as was recorded may be ambiguous or an incomplete representation of the circumstances in which a book was made and kept. The problems surrounding the direct evidence for placing medieval books within their precise historical contexts are compounded by those presented by the uneven survival of books from medieval Britain. The purpose of this chapter is to highlight some of the many challenges involved in evaluating and interpreting the various forms of evidence for localizing the place of origin and subsequent locations of manuscript books in medieval Britain, despite the various difficulties, and with reference to the principal published scholarship that has already assembled and assessed the evidence. It is unwise to extrapolate directly from the evidence that may survive about a book or books from one context in order to establish the history of those from another for which such evidence is lacking; yet, the richer survivals from particular periods or places, or of particular kinds of book, may be helpful in drawing attention to issues of interpretation or kinds of analysis and approach that might not otherwise have been considered.

Mapping the Field

The surveys of book production, ownership, book collections, and libraries presented in the relevant volumes of the *Cambridge History of the Book in Britain*, the *Cambridge History of Libraries in Britain and Ireland*, and a number of other volumes and individual articles are an essential starting point for investigating the place of origin and ownership of medieval manuscripts from Britain, since they outline the contours of what is knowable in the present state of research from the currently available evidence about the settings and circumstances involved.[1] These broad contours provide a framework of possibilities constructed from specific examples and, where sufficient evidence exists, an indication of what was widespread practice as well as the range of variations from it (including divergence from prescriptive norms), with references to the published scholarship where the complexities are discussed in greater detail.

The difficulties confronted when interpreting and extrapolating from the more exiguous survivals of the earlier Middle Ages have long been recognized, the discipline of palaeography from its beginnings being especially focused upon early medieval manuscripts, as is evident from the disproportionate space devoted to the period before the twelfth century by Bernhard Bischoff in his palaeographical textbook.[2] The problems of methodology and underlying assumptions involved in the appraisal of the more plentiful materials of the later Middle Ages, however, are not always laid out so transparently. M. A. Michael and A. I. Doyle's surveys of late medieval book production in urban and monastic settings are therefore especially valuable for their discussion of such issues.[3]

Origin and Provenance

When one turns from the wider landscape to the task of placing specific medieval manuscript books within it, it is essential to distinguish between the evidence for establishing place of origin (where a book was produced) and that for establishing provenance (the subsequent history of place of ownership or possession and use). Evidence of the one cannot on its own be assumed to constitute evidence for the other. A second *caveat* is that any explicit statement about the manufacture or the circumstances of acquisition of a book, if recorded at a later date, must be acknowledged as noncontemporary and, therefore, not constituting direct evidence for what is being asserted. Third, since medieval books were liable to change hands, through gift, loan, purchase, or theft, any piece of evidence of provenance on its own can only be confidently applied to the period from which that evidence itself dates. For example, a late medieval institutional *ex libris* inscription entered into a book of earlier manufacture cannot be assumed to provide evidence of earlier ownership there. Finally, the analysis of surviving books and records of individual books must take into account the potential flexibility of the manuscript book as an artefact, whose quire structure and forms of binding made it amenable to being supplemented, reconfigured, or to having elements removed. Any explicit or other form of evidence of place of production or subsequent location in any kind of composite manuscript must therefore only be applied to those elements of the manuscript that were structurally united at the time from which that evidence itself dates, as may be illustrated by the following example.[4]

Cambridge, Trinity College, MS B. 1. 37 is a manuscript whose medieval history had, until recently, been wholly unknown, but which had attracted attention as a unique witness to certain letters of St Anselm. It is a rather small book, now comprising 116 parchment leaves measuring *c.* 205 × 150 mm, arranged in eleven quires. Truncated medieval annotations at the upper, lower, and outer edges of several of the leaves indicate post-medieval trimming in the course of rebinding. The book is now in a binding which is substantially that manufactured for John Whitgift, archbishop of Canterbury from 1583 until his death in 1604, and through whose bequest the manuscript came to Trinity. The binding, however, was temporarily removed on at least one occasion, since a late seventeenth-century note on fol. 105v records the removal of one item (a quire of at least thirteen leaves), and its incorporation as part of another manuscript (Cambridge, Trinity College, MS R. 15. 18). It was perhaps when the manuscript was rebound that another quire, whose contents correspond with missing text between fols. 27 and 28, became misbound as fols. 98–105.

Palaeographical and codicological analysis indicates that the manuscript bound for Whitgift was not originally produced as a single codex but represents six different production units. Two of these (the quire that was removed and fols. 106–16) are datable from their handwriting to the fifteenth century; the remainder of the manuscript is in handwriting of the late eleventh and earlier twelfth centuries. These earlier quires comprise four originally separate units, to judge from the way in which the texts are distributed between the quires, the lack of any common scribes as well as differences in written space, quire structure, and number of ruled lines. They are as follows:

1. Anselm, *Cur deus homo* (fols. 1–37 + 98–105, with the opening leaf of the first quire now missing and the final leaf of that quire misbound at the front, and with the fourth quire misbound later in the manuscript).
2. Anselm, *Epistola de incarnatione Verbi* and *Epistola 65* (fols. 38–45, a single quire, with the text of Epistola 65 ending incomplete at the end of the quire, with the loss of at least one leaf).
3. Anselm, *Proslogion, Sumptum ex eodem libello*, 'Cur Deus magis assumpserit', fifteen letters, plus another six letters on subsequently inserted leaves, Prosper of Aquitaine, *Responsiones ad capitulum obiectionum Vincentianarum* (fols. 46–66, 69–73; fols. 67 and 68 subsequently inserted singletons).

Where Were Books Made and Kept?

4. Anselm, *Monologion* (fols. 74–97, the text ends incomplete at the end of the quire reflecting the loss of at least one quire).

The verso of the last leaf of the final quire of unit 3 is heavily stained, indicating that it had originally circulated as an independent booklet. However, it was certainly accompanying units 1 and 4, and probably also 2 by the thirteenth century, when a note in an informal somewhat cursive hand was written in the lower margin of the recto of what was originally the final leaf of the first quire of booklet 1 (now bound as fol. 1), which records the titles of the principal contents of units 1, 3, and 4. Units 1 and 2 were already in the same place by this date, since they contain marginalia in the same late twelfth- or early thirteenth-century hand, and it therefore seems likely that unit 2 was also bound with units 3 and 4 at the same time. No evidence survives to indicate when the two fifteenth-century units first became associated with the earlier ones.

None of the units contains any direct evidence of origin or medieval provenance. Scribal evidence, however, places both the origin and early twelfth-century ownership history of unit 3 at Salisbury Cathedral. The hand of the principal scribe of the original part of the booklet is identifiable as that of one of the most prolific scribes active at Salisbury at the turn of the eleventh/twelfth centuries.[5] Since this scribe may also have worked elsewhere, the identification of his hand alone is insufficient to demonstrate a Salisbury origin for the booklet. The identification, however, of the hands of the two scribes who supplied the six additional letters of Anselm on the inserted fols. 67 and 68 as those of two scribes also active at Salisbury a generation or so later[6] places its early history of ownership at Salisbury, and, together with the known activity of the original scribe, strengthens the likelihood of a Salisbury place of origin. The contents of the added letters supply further (albeit circumstantial) evidence, comprising the only known surviving copies of letters sent by Anselm to Osmund, bishop of Salisbury (1078–99) (*Epp.* 177, 190, 195 and a further letter not included in the edition of Anselm's letters), and to Eulalia, abbess of Shaftesbury (*Ep.* 183) and Matilda, abbess of Wilton (*Ep.* 185).[7]

These contents do not demonstrate a Salisbury origin or provenance, although it is reasonable to hypothesize that unique copies of letters to heads of religious houses all within the Salisbury diocese are likely to have been made within that diocese. It is, instead, the combination of scribal evidence, from two different generations of scribes active at Salisbury, that confirms the Salisbury origin and early history of the booklet. But it is impossible to demonstrate that it remained at Salisbury, or that the other early booklets were also written and kept there. No substantial listing of books survives from Salisbury from before the time that Whitgift acquired the manuscript; no manuscript corresponding to this one is recorded in any of the records that do survive. It would be tempting to combine the evidence provided by booklet 3 with the circumstantial evidence of impressive levels of intellectual interest among the early canons of Salisbury, and the physical correspondence between the four booklets and the characteristics of books demonstrably produced at Salisbury, to speculate that all four, important witnesses to the works of Anselm, formed part of the book collections of the cathedral community. This, however, must remain no more than hypothesis. An equally plausible alternative is that, since the Salisbury canons were permitted to own personal property which they could dispose of as they wished, booklet 3 could have left Salisbury before becoming combined with units 1, 2, and 4, and that all four were or became part of a personal book collection, passing from hand to hand (including that of the person who annotated units 1 and 2 – not yet identified in any of the surviving Salisbury manuscripts). The Salisbury manuscripts are unusual when compared with those from other institutions in post-Conquest England for the generally informal characteristics of their handwriting and manufacture, but such characteristics are not unique to books from Salisbury.

Where Were Books Made?

There has yet been no attempt to assemble all the explicit evidence for book production in medieval Britain, whether inscriptions recording the circumstances of production in surviving manuscripts or narrative and documentary records of the production, materials and/or makers of manuscripts. Nevertheless, three projects with different objectives have each assembled significant amounts of such evidence.

Medieval Libraries of Great Britain began as a collaborative project to assemble lists of surviving manuscripts containing evidence of medieval institutional ownership. In the second edition, N. R. Ker provided a list of individuals named in inscriptions that comprise some of this evidence, and who had been involved in some way with the books concerned, including those named as scribes.[8] Ker included in the list any relevant wording that described the nature of the activity or involvement, and, in his introduction and glossary, provided guidance regarding its ambiguities and other difficulties of interpretation.[9]

Another source of explicit evidence are inscriptions in books assembled in the catalogues of dated and datable manuscripts.[10] The objective of this project, an international initiative of the Comité Internationale de Paléographie Latine ('Latine' here denoting the Roman alphabet not a restriction to the Latin language), is to identify and reproduce specimens of handwriting in books datable within certain limits on the basis of explicit evidence or reliably inferred from other evidence, as a palaeographical resource to assist in dating other books. The scope of the British volumes is not restricted to manuscripts written or owned in medieval Britain but encompasses all relevant manuscripts currently in British institutional collections. They do not follow the French practice of including undated and undatable manuscripts written by named scribes or of known medieval institutional provenance, but they do assemble a great deal of information about the circumstances of book production, albeit disproportionately weighted towards the fifteenth century. It is a body of evidence that is still comparatively under-exploited, but episodic browsing pays dividends. The introductions to each volume explain the criteria for inclusion; additional guidance for the handling of evidence that can be ambiguous and sometimes misleading is provided in the Cambridge introduction.[11]

A third collaborative project, the Corpus of British Medieval Library Catalogues, was envisaged as a counterpart to *Medieval Libraries of Great Britain*, to edit all surviving medieval records of books in institutional own-ership. Such lists sometimes comprise records of books produced for an institution, and may state where that production took place and by whom. The introductory notes provided for each institution for which such evidence survives also include brief mention of the available evidence for the acquisi-tion as well as the ownership of books by that institution, including in-house production. Much of the evidence assembled for the monastic houses, and for Oxford and (to a lesser extent) Cambridge, has already received repeated attention, but the unusually rich survivals of inventories from late medieval collegiate churches and from non-academic secular institutions has thus far been subjected to less scrutiny, but are especially worth mining for such information.[12]

Two unpublished individual initiatives to assemble evidence concerning the production of books in later medieval England, albeit of more restricted scope, have provided important foundations for subsequent published work. The materials gathered by Graham Pollard for his Lyell Lectures delivered in 1961 on the medieval book trade in Oxford were drawn upon first by N. R. Ker and then M. B. Parkes for a detailed survey of book provision at Oxford, one of the earliest urban centres in Britain for which evidence survives of a commercial trade in books.[13] A. I. Doyle's unpublished Lyell Lectures, 'Some English Scribes and Scriptoria of the Later Middle Ages', delivered in 1967, formed the basis of a number of articles on individual scribes and, in combination with other available published evidence, two important more wide-ranging surveys on the book trade outside London and on monastic book production in later medieval England.[14]

Explicit evidence of book production in secular contexts, other than inscriptions found in the surviving books, is especially limited. Little documentary evidence survives from medieval Britain of the kinds drawn upon by Richard and Mary Rouse to reconstruct the topography of book production in late medieval Paris.[15] The accounts kept by the wardens of Old London Bridge (extant from 1381), which include a record of rents from (among others) numerous craftsmen involved in making books, are a rare exception in the quantity of information they preserve.[16] Nevertheless, enough examples can be cited from more scattered evidence to demonstrate the presence from the mid-thirteenth century onwards of individuals with scribal expertise and other craftsmen involved in book production in numerous urban centres, and associated with institutions and private households in more rural settings, as well as a wide diversity of ways in which their skills were remunerated and materials (including exemplars) supplied.[17]

Surviving books themselves constitute a major source of evidence for their production. Two concepts have dominated the inferences about the location and other circumstances of their manufacture drawn from the analysis and interpretation of their script, decoration, and physical characteristics: 'scriptorium' (especially for the period before *c.* 1200) and 'workshop' (for the period after).

'Scriptorium' is a term that has been used to refer both to the physical space in which copying took place and to the organization of copying.[18] Neither phenomenon was uniform or unchanging during the Middle Ages, making it necessary to define more precisely the sense in which the term is used in any given context. Evidence for the physical space within which books were copied within institutional or private settings is highly exiguous; the requirements for such activity were limited and even within religious institutions a designated room may not have been employed.[19] When used to refer to the process of copying, the term has encompassed any form of organized, non-commercial, collaborative book production undertaken within an institutional setting. Before the thirteenth century, the available evidence indicates that most book production was of this kind, taking place within monastic and other ecclesiastical institutions. The duration of such activity in any one place, the degree of organization, the status and training of the individuals involved, however, were more diverse than is sometimes assumed, with important implications for how the script and other visual and material evidence of the surviving books is analysed and interpreted.

The starting point for manuscript-based studies of book production within British religious or ecclesiastical settings, given the lack of direct evidence, has been the relatively richer evidence of groups of manuscripts of a given date with the same provenance. Evidence of ownership does not constitute evidence of origin, but, as Ker observed: 'The handwriting and illumination of the manuscripts ... acquire new significance when a sufficient number from the same institution are brought together.'[20] Very few such groups of manuscripts survive from before the Norman Conquest.[21] Evidence accumulates only from the late eleventh century onwards, forming the basis for Ker's Lyell lectures of 1953, the published version of which has provided the inspiration and methodological template for several detailed studies of book collections and manuscript production in post-Conquest England.[22] The pioneering palaeographical work of scholars on early medieval, and especially pre-Carolingian, continental scriptoria, demonstrated that, in such settings, certain aspects of book production, including handwriting and other scribal conventions, could be closely similar in the work of one or more generations of collaborating individuals, and might be distinctive of a single institution, locality, or region.[23] Ker and subsequent scholars have shown that this was no longer necessarily the outcome in England by the late eleventh century. The presence of one or more scribes trained elsewhere, or the coexistence of different generations of scribes trained in different traditions, could produce diversity in the handwriting of books produced at the same time in the same place.[24] Conversely, historical circumstances from the tenth century onwards contributed to the emergence of more widely shared practices within and beyond England, developed through different channels and under various stimuli, making the products of individual scriptoria less identifiable from the characteristics of their handwriting, display script, scribal conventions, and decoration. When assessing what may be judged locally distinctive, it is necessary to take into account not only surviving material from elsewhere but also potential distortions introduced by what has been lost: the survivals from one institution may only appear distinctive because of the loss of books from neighbouring or related houses. Even where the available evidence indicates that a distinctive element of style was cultivated at a particular institution, it cannot be assumed to be unique to that particular place of production. Such factors call into question the widely used concept of 'house-style', as Rodney Thomson acknowledges, with reference to twelfth-century books from Bury St Edmunds: 'The decoration is sufficiently characteristic to be termed a "house-style", but it is hard to differentiate clearly from that of some other centres.'[25]

The limitations of stylistic similarity as a basis for localizing the products of scriptoria can be addressed by the identification of the hands of individual scribes and their patterns of collaboration. Beneficiary-produced charters, which in the twelfth and earlier thirteenth century were often written in formal handwriting, expand the pool of localizable specimens of scribal hands, some of which have been identified in surviving books.[26] Their dating, however, must be treated with caution, since 'original' charters were sometimes manufactured decades after their purported date. Scribal identification on its own may not always provide straightforward evidence of place of production. The recurrence of one or more scribes in a group of manuscripts with the same later medieval provenance might, conceivably, be the result of those books having been produced for export by scribes from another institution. Complex patterns of collaboration between scribes and artists in manuscripts owned by the communities of Exeter and Durham Cathedrals and St Albans Abbey have also demonstrated the existence of scribes and artists who must have been itinerant professionals from at least the earlier twelfth century.[27]

A. I. Doyle's assessment of evidence for book production within English religious houses in the later Middle Ages has demonstrated the continued importance of such settings.[28] In the absence of explicit evidence, however, the criteria for attributing individual books to particular institutions becomes more difficult because the circumstances of production were even less conducive to the emergence of locally distinctive habits. Not only was increasing recourse being made to more or less temporarily resident secular professionals, but also, as Doyle observes,

> In the fourteenth and fifteenth centuries, most members of the religious orders must have learned to write (a matter about which we know little) primarily in the cursive utilitarian scripts with similar models and often in the same schools as their secular and lay contemporaries. The forms and styles of their writing and decoration, when they are identifiable in books, do not readily reveal features special to them and their nearest colleagues.

Carthusian scribes in the fifteenth century were unusual in the extent to which they identified themselves in their work, but this evidence only serves to show that, in England, even the Carthusians, an order that encouraged uniformity in many of its liturgical and other customs, did not cultivate similarity of appearance in handwriting or shared practices in matters such as punctuation.[29]

The localization of secular book production on the basis of palaeographical, codicological, and art-historical analysis is equally challenging. It is clear from the extant later medieval evidence that manuscript books could be produced anywhere, without formal organization, by those with the relevant skills.[30] As with manuscripts from the earlier Middle Ages, the methodology employed by scholars has involved the observation of similarities of stylistic conventions, materials, and practices of production as well as the

Where Were Books Made and Kept?

identification of individual hands, likewise taking as a starting point books whose early provenance can be established from other evidence. Analysis has concentrated most heavily upon the palaeographical and art-historical evidence, but the materials and physical construction of the books are now attracting sustained attention.[31]

The concept of 'workshop' has played an important role in localizing collaborative book production.[32] The term should not imply a discrete physical space. For scribes, at least, it is recognized that collaboration upon a single book, even when organized on a commercial basis by an entrepreneur such as a stationer, did not require scribes to be working alongside one another; the absence of such close proximity has been demonstrated in the case of certain early copies of the works of John Gower and Geoffrey Chaucer.[33] Nevertheless, the localization of late medieval illuminated manuscripts has sometimes depended upon the assumption that closely similar styles of decoration and other elements of art may reflect local practice, arising variously from shared training, repeated collaboration, and familiarity facilitated by working within the same neighbourhood if not under the same roof. Such evidence has been combined with evidence of ownership (especially that derived from liturgical information) and other information from which particular places may be inferred in order to localize the place of production to certain major urban centres, such as Oxford and London, and regions (especially East Anglia). Yet this methodology has its limitations: cumulatively such evidence (when all the attendant potentially reductive dangers have been allowed for) may point to the sustained activity of certain artists and those they trained or influenced in a particular locality or region, but in any individual case, production in that place or region cannot be taken for granted, given the potential for artists to be itinerant.[34]

The sheer number of later medieval manuscripts containing less-elaborate forms of decoration presents a challenge to attempts to identify distinctive local or regional styles. The discovery of recurring elements of style in script or minor decoration, or of other scribal habits, in a body of material from one locality or region must remain only provisionally diagnostic of place of production until it becomes evident that such elements are not found in material produced elsewhere.[35]

By no means can all handwriting be easily assigned to individual scribes, either because the degree of variation within the stint of a single scribe precludes identification elsewhere, or because of an absence of sufficient idiosyncratic characteristics.[36] From the thirteenth century onwards, the task becomes especially difficult. The extraordinary diversification in handwriting greatly increases the range and combinations of different scripts and resources of style that could be drawn upon, and the increasing importance of easily replicable elements of style, and the reduction of the most formal handwriting to repeated sequences of identical elements, further impedes the recognition of the hand of the same scribe writing different types, varieties, and grade of script, or the hands of individual scribes from closely similar handwriting or easily imitable embellishments. In recent years, the efforts of a number of scholars to identify the products of the scribe originally identified by Parkes and Doyle in their study of early copies of Chaucer and Gower ('Scribe B') have highlighted the degree to which such identifications rest upon personal judgement, and the need to set out fully the evidence and methods of analysis upon which such judgements are based.[37] Differences of opinion concerning scribal identification should not be a deterrent to further endeavour. Rather, the growing attention paid by scholars to 'the material text' should stimulate constructive debate of the methodological issues of analysis and interpretation raised by the use of handwriting as evidence to place written artefacts within their correct historical contexts of production and use.

The place of origin of surviving manuscripts has sometimes been localized on the basis of their contents, but this can be treacherous. First, it risks the so-called fallacy of the anticipated audience: the assumption that the readers of a text can be assumed from its contents. Second, contents (such as liturgical information) might be customized for use in one locality but the book itself manufactured elsewhere. Examples include the quantities of fifteenth-century Books of Hours produced in the southern Netherlands but customized for an English market (where they might be further customized over time by their owners).[38] Third, a copy might be loaned elsewhere as an exemplar, and information originally of local relevance replicated there.

In copies of texts written in the vernacular, linguistic evidence of dialect may reflect where a scribe was from or received his formative training, but not necessarily where the copying itself took place. Such evidence presents its own complex combination of issues of interpretation, requiring specialist expertise.[39]

Where Were Books Kept?

The contours of book ownership in medieval Britain can be delineated, for institutional ownership at least, in rather more detail since the available evidence is more abundant, and it has been more extensively collated and assessed. Nevertheless, the vagaries of survival have resulted in some significant gaps (evidence for the north Midlands, Wales, and Scotland is especially exiguous). The limited extent to which owners marked their books also impedes their localization, especially before the twelfth century.[40] The task of establishing ownership of books by individual clerics and lay people is even more difficult.[41] It is only with the accumulation of numbers of wills in the fifteenth century that more significant evidence of personal book ownership exists. Even so, testamentary evidence provides an incomplete and misleading record of the books in an individual's possession.[42]

The term 'library' is as ubiquitous in discussions of the ownership of books as 'scriptorium' and 'workshop' in the study of their production. It likewise requires careful definition. Already in the Middle Ages it was used to refer to a specific physical space as well as being invested with a range of more abstract meanings. Before the later Middle Ages, however, references to 'a library' ('biblioteca') usually refer to all or part of the holdings of an institution conceived collectively but not necessarily housed in the same space.[43] The phenomenon of a library room as a place in which books were not only stored but also consulted *in situ* and thus to which all or particular categories of members of an institution might have direct access was only introduced to England in the fourteenth century, and more specifically within the university context, imitating the arrangements introduced in the late thirteenth century at the Sorbonne.[44] These practices were adopted by the larger religious and ecclesiastical institutions in the fifteenth century, where they existed alongside earlier arrangements by which books were variously stored according to convenience and use, in book-storage rooms (usually located in the cloister at or near the junction of the east range of the cloister and the transept of the church), wall-recesses, and perhaps also free-standing cupboards and chests.[45] Within religious houses, with the exception of personal collections and the books used by officiants in the performance of the liturgy (as well as others regarded as part of the treasury or sacristy), the communal book collections were in the custody of a designated officer. It was this individual (or a deputy) whose duty it was 'to know' the books, and who supplied books to members of the community on a daily basis and, in Benedictine communities, at the annual ritual of distribution of books at the beginning of Lent.[46] The term 'librarian' risks evoking anachronistic misconceptions. Active 'library management' was limited and fitful, and the ways in which the custodian discharged his (or her) duties varied from institution to institution as well as changing over time, in ways that have had a direct bearing upon the extent and forms of written evidence for the locations in which books were kept.

The Corpus of British Medieval Catalogues is an essential tool that assembles documentary and other textual evidence of books in institutional ownership. Here, 'catalogue' is shorthand for any kind of list of books (with the exception of lists recording exclusively liturgical books). The purpose, scope, and date of each list must first be assessed before its contents can be used as evidence for the character or specific contents of the holdings of an institution. Only a relatively small proportion of the total survivors was compiled as a bibliographical finding aid.[47] Many lists treat books primarily as items of property, recorded in some instances as part of larger inventories; some combined this function with that of recording the donation of books (and other goods) as benefactions to be commemorated. Lists were not necessarily made with direct reference to the books, but might replicate an earlier record; information about contents might be taken from a list of contents (not necessarily complete) from an endleaf, or be restricted to the first or main item. Booklists were entered on blank leaves in books, on rolls and in various kinds of more administrative compendia in book-form, such as cartularies. Some of the lists included in the Corpus, however, are not administrative records but extracts from narrative texts such as local chronicles, in which the acquisition or donation of books might be recorded among other good deeds. The purpose of each list conditioned the choice and level of detail supplied in the description of each item, but it is sometimes impossible to infer the precise purpose for which a list had been compiled. In the absence of a descriptive heading, the physical context in which the list is found and any associated contents may provide some clue. Any use of booklists as a source must therefore take account of the codicological and textual context in which each is found (details provided in the document headnotes). Some of the lists were not made in-house and must be assessed in the light of the purpose, scope, and methods of the particular initiative. For a significant number of Cistercian houses and houses of the regular canons, for example, the only record of books to survive are the early fourteenth-century 'union-catalogue' of primarily patristic authors and texts compiled by the Oxford Franciscans and the brief notes recorded by John Leland and by one other individual shortly before the Dissolution.[48] In such cases it is obvious that the surviving record cannot be regarded as representative of the holdings of each institution. But this reservation also applies to records made in-house, very few of which demonstrably encompass the entire holdings.

The essential resource for localizing the institutional ownership history of the surviving books is the second edition and Supplement of *Medieval Libraries of Great Britain* (*MLGB*). Books owned by the medieval Oxford and Cambridge colleges that remain *in situ* were not included but are being incorporated in the online digital resource, *MLGB3*.[49] In the printed version, the categories of evidence upon which a book has been localized are indicated by *sigla* (denotational numbers or letters), without recording the date at which that piece of evidence was made or the form of words comprising an inscription. This information is among enhancements supplied in *MLGB3* from the details originally recorded on cards from which the printed entries were distilled, together, in some instances, with digitized images of the inscriptions and medieval location and identification marks.

Each of the different categories of evidence presents its own issues of interpretation, to which valuable guidance is provided in the introduction to the second edition.[50] For example, *ex libris* inscriptions referring to an institution are usually straightforward in their meaning, but where they survive in only truncated form, or where reference is just to the patron saint, the particular formula, its position on the page or location within the book can be of significance. The baggier category of *ex dono* inscriptions can be rather more ambiguous with regard to the circumstances in which a book was acquired or the role of any individual mentioned. The same form of wording can have different meanings in different institutions at different times: 'liber' plus a name in the genitive may record a donor, but in the later Middle Ages could denote a book in the temporary keeping of an individual monk. In religious institutions, temporary possession (as opposed to permanent ownership) was permitted in various circumstances,[51] and might be indicated by the verbs 'constat' or 'possidet'. 'Per' plus a name should not be assumed to denote prior ownership but some unspecified role in the acquisition of the volume for an institution. Even apparently explicit inscriptions may be misleading or incomplete. Among the books at Salisbury Cathedral containing a record of the chancellor, Ralph II, as their donor, is Salisbury Cathedral Library, MS 11, an early twelfth-century book whose handwriting identifies it as one of the collaboratively produced books made for the early cathedral community. Had the book ceased to be regarded as communal property some time before, or had Ralph's temporary possession become confused as personal ownership, or did the inscription record some other kind of involvement?[52]

Marks comprising combinations of Roman or Arabic numerals, letters of the alphabet and other symbols, were entered into books for various purposes in different houses: as means simply of identifying individual volumes, or as accession, location and/or classification marks.[53] By no means all such marks are locally distinctive, but those that are not may sometimes be found to correspond with entries in certain late medieval institutional booklists in which it was the practice to record a location mark.

A book's contents require the same careful handling as evidence for provenance as when used as evidence for place of production. Subsequent additions or adaptations that relate very specifically to a particular institution or locality may be more indicative of local initiative than a strongly local emphasis in the text originally copied (which might simply reflect the contents of the exemplar). Additions and annotations may also provide palaeographical evidence if the hand is also identified in one or more books that can be localized on the basis of other evidence. But not all annotators were the owners of the books they annotated; in such cases the annotation is evidence of use not provenance. A well-known example is the fifteenth-century scholar Thomas Gascoigne, a prolific annotator of manuscripts in the various libraries he visited.[54]

From the thirteenth century onwards, a significant proportion of institutional accessions were books donated by former owners to their own institution (as was required of monks, regular canons and friars) or several different institutions. The inclusion of such evidence in the Corpus and *MLGB* makes them important resources for the study of personal as well as institutional book ownership. Several booklists take the form of donation lists, or record the names of donors,[55] information that can combined with that found in inscriptions in surviving books, as has been done to rich effect in the case of St Augustine's, Canterbury.[56] Evidence from wills has usually not been edited in the Corpus, unless it can be demonstrated that the books mentioned reached their destination, but, exceptionally, such evidence has been collated under the name of each donor in a separate listing in the volumes on the universities and colleges of Cambridge and Oxford.[57]

Systematic collation of the documentary and physical evidence of individual book ownership has otherwise been limited. The largest-scale initiative remains the thesis of Susan Cavanaugh.[58] A significant amount of evidence of ownership by members of Oxford, from wills and other sources (including inscriptions in books), was also collated by A. B. Emden.[59] The potential and the limitations of wills as a source for personal book ownership across a wider social spectrum has been assessed by a number of scholars.[60]

Assessment of the evidence of inscriptions mentioning individuals is subject to the same caution as that noted earlier concerning such evidence in books that made their way into (or out of) institutional ownership. Informal notes of names on endleaves or in the margins provide evidence of provenance but require the kind of careful handling deployed, for example, in Kate Harris's meticulous analysis of the names found in the so-called 'Findern Anthology'.[61] One category of named inscription that should be discounted as anything other than a pen-trial or scribble are notes comprising the open words of the protocol of a royal or episcopal charter, such as 'Iohannes dei gratia rex …'. Such formulae, sometimes extended to include part of the address clause, can be found on endleaves or in the margins of a number of books. Any temptation to read anything substantive into them, including hypothetical ownership or readership, should be resisted.

By the late fifteenth century, book ownership had become widely diffused within society, facilitated by the circulation of books second-hand as well as by the use of cheaper materials and other economies. We know very little

Where Were Books Made and Kept?

about where books were kept within private households, and how they were conceived: as collections or as individual written artefacts; as goods to be kept within the family or disposed of as gifts and benefactions during lifetime or after death. One category of fifteenth-century book that came into the hands of private individuals was explicitly proscribed from being treated as personal property, and was intended to remain without a permanent fixed location. These are the so-called 'common-profit' books, assigned by a donor as a charitable act for use of others for the term of their life in return for prayers for the soul of the donor. Evidence assembled by Wendy Scase has shown how this particular practice forms part of a wider range of conventions whereby books were designated for circulation and use by those who might need them, demonstrating that the boundaries between communal and personal ownership, possession and use were more fluid than can easily be encompassed by a simple binary division between institutional libraries and personal book collections.[62]

If one browses the descriptions in catalogues of medieval manuscripts, the large proportion of manuscripts whose place of origin and medieval provenance remains uncertain becomes swiftly apparent. A catalogue description is confined to direct evidence, but elsewhere a scholar may hypothesize based upon inferences drawn from indirect evidence and contextual information. When doing so, the dangers lie in insufficient knowledge of the wider context and the alternative possibilities it might suggest, or inferring too much from too limited evidence. As one scholar has remarked: 'Le manuscrit isolé ne "parle" pas'.[63] Or, in the words of another: 'sensible hypothesis can be very useful. However, it is important to know when to step back and admit uncertainty.'[64]

Notes

1. R. Gameson, ed., *The Cambridge History of the Book, I*; Morgan and Thomson, eds., *The Cambridge History of the Book, II*; L. Hellinga and J. B. Trapp, eds., *The Cambridge History of the Book in Britain, Volume III, 1400–1557* (Cambridge: Cambridge University Press, 1999); E. Leedham-Green and T. Webber, eds., *The Cambridge History of Libraries in Britain and Ireland, Volume I, to 1640* (Cambridge: Cambridge University Press, 2006); J. Griffiths and D. Pearsall, eds., *Book Production and Publishing in Britain, 1375–1475* (Cambridge: Cambridge University Press, 1989); M. B. Parkes, *Their Hands before Our Eyes: A Closer Look at Scribes* (Aldershot: Ashgate, 2008), 1–53; A. I. Doyle, 'Book Production by the Monastic Orders in England (*c.*1375–1530): Assessing the Evidence', in L. L. Brownrigg, ed., *Medieval Book Production: Assessing the Evidence* (Los Altos Hills, CA: Anderson-Lovelace, 1990), 1–19; A. I. Doyle, 'The English Provincial Book Trade before Printing', in P. Isaac, ed., *Six Centuries of the Provincial Book Trade in Britain* (Winchester: St Paul's Bibliographies, 1990), 13–29.

2. B. Bischoff, *Latin Palaeography: Antiquity and the Middle Ages*, trans. D. Ó Cróinín and D. Ganz (Cambridge: Cambridge University Press, 1990); see M. B. Parkes, *Beiträge zur Geschichte der deutschen Sprache und Literatur* 105.2 (1983), 292–6.

3. M. A. Michael, 'Urban Production of Manuscript Books and the Role of the University Towns', in Morgan and Thomson, eds., *The Cambridge History of the Book*, 168–94; Doyle, 'Book Production'.

4. See Chapter 5 in this volume; R. Sharpe and T. Webber, 'Four Early Booklets of Anselm's Works from Salisbury Cathedral: MS. Cambridge, Trinity College, B.1.37', *Scriptorium*, 63 (2009), 58–72, pls 1–2.

5. Group I, Scribe 2: T. Webber, *Scribes and Scholars at Salisbury Cathedral, c.1075–c.1125* (Oxford: Oxford University Press, 1992), 11–13.

6. Group IIb, Scribes 14 and 17: Webber, *Scribes and Scholars*, 24–5.

7. F. Schmitt, ed., *S. Anselmi Cantuariensis archiepiscopi opera omnia*, 6 vols. (Edinburgh: Nelson and Sons, 1946–61), IV, 60–1, 67–71, 76, and 85–6; F. Schmitt, 'Zur Überlieferung der Korrespondenz Anselms von Canterbury: neue Briefe', *Revue Bénédictine*, 43 (1931), 224–238, at 238.

8. N. R. Ker, *Medieval Libraries of Great Britain*, 2nd edn (London: Offices of the Royal Historical Society, 1964), 225–332; A. G. Watson, *Supplement to the Second Edition* (London: Royal Historical Society, 1987), 75–113.

9. Ker, *Medieval Libraries*, xxvii, 326–31.

10. *DDBL, DDCL, DDLL, DDOL.*

11. *DDCL*, I, 1–12, 17–18.

12. N. Ramsay and J. M. W. Willoughby, eds., *Hospitals, Towns and the Professions*, CBMLC 14 (London: The British Library, 2009); J. M. W. Willoughby, ed., *The Libraries of Collegiate Churches*, 2 vols, CBMLC 15 (London: The British Library, 2013).

13. M. B. Parkes, 'The Provision of Books', in J. I. Catto and T. A. R. Evans, eds., *The History of the University of Oxford, Volume II: Late Medieval Oxford* (Oxford: Oxford University Press, 1992), 407–83.

14. Doyle, 'Book Production'; Doyle, 'English Provincial Book Trade'; E. Rainey, 'A Bibliography of the Published Writings of A. I. Doyle', in R. Beadle and A. J. Piper, eds., *New Science Out of Old Books: Studies in Manuscripts and Early Printed Books in Honour of A. I. Doyle* (Aldershot: Scolar Press 1995), 420–33, with additions to 2014 in A. S. G. Edwards, 'A. I. Doyle, a Tribute at 90', *The Book Collector* 64 (2015), 583–90.

15. R. H. Rouse and M. A. Rouse, *Manuscripts and Their Makers: Commercial Book Producers in Medieval Paris 1200–1500*, 2 vols. (Turnhout: Harvey Miller, 2000).

16. C. P. Christianson, *Memorials of the Book Trade in Medieval London: The Archives of Old London Bridge* (Woodbridge: Boydell and Brewer, 1987).

17. Doyle, 'English Provincial Book Trade'; Michael, 'Urban Production'; C. P. Christianson, 'Evidence for the Study of London's Late Medieval Manuscript-Book Trade', in Griffiths and Pearsall, eds., *Book Production and Publishing*, 87–108; M. A. Michael, 'English Illuminators c.1190–1450: A Survey from Documentary Sources', *English Manuscript Studies 1100–1700*, 4 (1993), 62–113.

Where Were Books Made and Kept?

18. D. Ganz, 'Can a Scriptorium Always Be Identified by Its Products?', in A. Nievergelt et al., eds., *Scriptorium: Wesen, Funktion, Eigenheiten* (Munich: Bayerische Akademie der Wissenschaften, 2015), 51–62, at 51–3.

19. Parkes, *Their Hands before Our Eyes*, 8, 24–5.

20. Ker, *Medieval Libraries*, vii.

21. D. Ganz, 'Anglo-Saxon England', in E. Leedham-Green and T. Webber, eds., *The Cambridge History of Libraries in Britain and Ireland to 1640, Volume I* (Cambridge: Cambridge University Press, 2006), 91–108.

22. N. R. Ker, *English Manuscripts in the Century after the Norman Conquest* (Oxford: Clarendon Press, 1960); T. Webber, 'English Manuscripts in the Century after the Norman Conquest: Continuity and Change in the Palaeography of Books and Book Collections', in E. Kwakkel, ed., *Writing in Context. Insular Manuscript Culture, 500–1200* (Leiden: Leiden University Press, 2013), 185–228.

23. Bischoff, *Latin Palaeography*, 104–118; Ganz, 'Scriptorium'.

24. T. Webber, 'Script and Manuscript Production at Christ Church, Canterbury, after the Norman Conquest', in R. Eales and R. Sharpe, eds., *Canterbury and the Norman Conquest: Churches, Saints and Scholars* (London: Hambledon Press, 1995), 145–58; M. Gullick, 'A Christ Church Scribe of the Late Eleventh Century', in J. H. Marrow et al., eds., *The Medieval Book: Glosses from Friends and Colleagues of Christopher de Hamel* (Houten: Hes & De Graaf, 2010), 2–10.

25. R. M. Thomson, 'Monastic and Cathedral Book Production', *Cambridge History of the Book, II*, 136–67, at 149–50.

26. For example, M. Gullick, 'Christ Church Scribe' and 'The Scribes of the Durham Cantor's Book (Durham, Dean and Chapter Library, MS B.IV.24) and the Durham Martyrology Scribe', in D. Rollason, M. Harvey, and M. Prestwich, eds., *Anglo-Norman Durham 1093–1193* (Woodbridge: Boydell, 1994), 93–109; 'The Hand of Symeon of Durham: Further Observations on the Durham Martyrology Scribe', in D. Rollason, ed., *Symeon of Durham: Historian of Durham and the North* (Stamford: Shaun Tyas, 1998), 14–31, 358–62.

27. M. Gullick, 'Professional Scribes in Eleventh- and Twelfth-Century England', *English Manuscript Studies 1100–1700*, 7 (1998), 1–24.

28. Doyle, 'Book Production'.

29. Ibid., 13–15; A. I. Doyle, 'William Darker: The Work of an English Carthusian Scribe', in C. Baswell, ed., *Medieval Manuscripts, Their Makers and Users: A Special Issue of Viator in Honour of Richard and Mary Rouse* (Turnhout: Brepols, 2011), 199–211.

30. Doyle, 'English Provincial Book Trade'; J.-P. Pouzet, 'Book Production Outside Commercial Contexts', in A. Gillespie and D. Wakelin, eds., *The Production of Books in England* (Cambridge: Cambridge University Press, 2011), 212–38.

31. O. Da Rold, 'Codicology, Localization, and Oxford, Bodleian Library, MS Laud Misc. 108', in C. M. Meale and D. Pearsall, eds., *Makers and Users of Medieval Books: Essays in Honour of A.S.G. Edwards* (Cambridge: D. S. Brewer, 2014), 48–59.

32. Michael, 'Urban Production', 174.

33. M. B. Parkes and A. I. Doyle, 'The Production of Copies of the *Canterbury Tales* and the *Confessio Amantis* in the Early Fifteenth Century', in M. B. Parkes and A. G. Watson, eds., *Medieval Scribes, Manuscripts and Libraries: Essays Presented to N. R. Ker* (London: Scolar Press, 1978), 163–210; M. B. Parkes, 'Patterns of Scribal Activity and Revisions of the Text in Early Copies of Works by John Gower', in Beadle and Piper, eds., *New Science Out of Old Books*, 81–121.

34. M. A. Michael, 'Oxford, Cambridge and London: Towards a Theory for "Grouping" Gothic Manuscripts', *Burlington Magazine* 130 (1988), 107–15; Michael, 'Urban Production', esp. 185–6.

35. See A. I. Doyle review of J. B. Friedman, *Northern English Books, Owners, and Makers in the Late Middle Ages* (Syracuse, NY, Syracuse University Press, 1995), *Modern Language Review*, 93 (1998), 171–2.

36. T. Davis, 'The Practice of Handwriting Identification', *The Library*, 7th series, 8 (2007), 251–76.

37. J. Roberts, 'On Giving Scribe B a Name and a Clutch of London Books from *c*.1400', *Medium Ævum*, 80 (2011), 247–70; L. Warner, *Chaucer's Scribes: London Textual Production 1384–1432* (Cambridge: Cambridge University Press, 2018).

38. K. M. Rudy, *Piety in Pieces: How Medieval Readers Customized Their Manuscripts* (Cambridge: Open Book Publishers, 2016).

39. S. Horobin, 'Mapping the Words', in Gillespie and Wakelin, eds., *The Production of Books in England*, 59–78; J. J. Thompson, 'Books beyond England', in Gillespie and Wakelin, eds., *The Production of Books in England*, 259–75.

40. P. P. Ó Néill, 'Celtic Britain and Ireland in the Early Middle Ages' and Ganz, 'Anglo-Saxon England', in Leedham-Green and Webber, eds., *Cambridge History of Libraries*, I, 69–90, 91–108.

41. J. Stratford and T. Webber, 'Bishops and Kings: Private Book Collections in Medieval England', in Leedham-Green and Webber, eds., *Cambridge History of Libraries*, 178–217, at 178–83.

42. K. Harris, 'Patrons, Buyers and Owners: The Evidence for Ownership and the Rôle of Book Owners in Book Production and the Book Trade', in Griffiths and Pearsall, eds., *Book Production and Publishing*, 163–99; P. J. P. Goldberg, 'Lay Book Ownership in Late Medieval York: The Evidence of Wills', *The Library*, 6th series, 16 (1994), 181–9.

43. T. Webber, 'The Libraries of Religious Houses', in E. Kwakkel and R. M. Thomson, eds., *The European Book in the Twelfth Century* (Cambridge: Cambridge University Press, 2018), 103–21, at 104–11.

44. R. Gameson, 'The Medieval Library (to c.1450)', in Leedham-Green and Webber, eds., *Cambridge History of Libraries*, 13–50.

45. A. J. Piper, 'The Libraries of the Monks of Durham', in Parkes and Watson, eds., *Medieval Scribes, Manuscripts and Libraries*, 213–49.

46. R. Sharpe, 'The Medieval Librarian', in Leedham-Green and Webber, eds., *Cambridge History of Libraries*, 218–41.

47. R. Sharpe, 'Library Catalogues and Indexes', in Morgan and Thomson, eds., *The Cambridge History of the Book*, 197–218.

48. R. H. Rouse and M. A. Rouse, eds., *Registrum Anglie de libris doctorum et auctorum veterum*, CBMLC 2 (London: The British Library, 1991); D. N. Bell, ed., *The Libraries of the Cistercians, Gilbertines and Premonstratensians*, CBMLC 3

Where Were Books Made and Kept?

(London: The British Library, 1992); T. Webber and A. G. Watson, eds., *The Libraries of the Augustinian Canons*, CBMLC 6 (London: The British Library, 1998).

49. http://mlgb3.bodleian.ox.ac.uk

50. Ker, *Medieval Libraries*, xv–xxiii, xxv–xxix.

51. B. F. Harvey, 'The Monks of Westminster and the *Peculium*', in G. H. Brown and L. E. Voigts, eds., *The Study of Medieval Manuscripts of England: Festschrift in Honour of Richard W. Pfaff* (Tempe, AZ: Arizona Centre for Medieval and Renaissance Studies, 2010), 325–48.

52. T. Webber, 'The Scriptorium and Library of Salisbury Cathedral', in F. Coulson, ed., *Oxford Handbook of Latin Palaeography* (Oxford: Oxford University Press, 2020).

53. Ker, *Medieval Libraries*, xviii–xx; Sharpe, 'Library Catalogues', 207–8; R. Sharpe, 'Accession, Classification, Location: Pressmarks in Medieval Libraries', *Scriptorium*, 50 (1996), 279–87.

54. R. M. Ball, *Thomas Gascoigne, Libraries and Scholarship* (Cambridge: Cambridge Bibliographical Society, 2006).

55. Sharpe, 'Library Catalogues', 204–5.

56. A. B. Emden, *Donors of Books to S. Augustine's Abbey Canterbury* (Oxford: Oxford Bibliographical Society, 1968); B. C. Barker-Benfield, ed., *St Augustine's Abbey Canterbury*, 3 vols, CBMLC 13 (London: The British Library, 2008), I, lxxxiii–lxxii; III, 1839–83.

57. P. D. Clarke, ed., *The University and College Libraries of Cambridge*, CBMLC 10 (London: The British Library, 2002), 655–752; R. M. Thomson, ed., *The University and College Libraries of Oxford*, 2 vols., CBMLC 16 (London: The British Library, 2015), II, 1250–389.

58. S. H. Cavanaugh, 'A Study of Books Privately Owned in England, 1300-1450' (unpublished PhD thesis, University of Pennsylvania, 1980).

59. A. B. Emden, *A Bibliographical Register of the University of Oxford to A.D. 1500*, 3 vols. (Oxford: Clarendon Press, 1957–9).

60. Harris, 'Patrons, Buyers and Owners'; Goldberg, 'Lay Book Ownership'; J. T. Rosenthal, 'Aristocratic Cultural Patronage and Book Bequests, 1350–1500', *Bulletin of the John Rylands Library*, 64 (1982), 522–48; A. F. Sutton, 'The Acquisition and Disposal of Books for Worship and Pleasure by Mercers of London in the Later Middle Ages', in E. Cayley and S. Powell, eds., *Manuscripts and Printed Books in Europe, 1350–1550* (Liverpool: Liverpool University Press, 2013), 95–114; K. L. Scott, 'Past Ownership: Evidence of Book Ownership by English Merchants in the Later Middle Ages', in Meale and Pearsall, eds., *Makers and Users of Medieval Books*, 150–77.

61. K. Harris, 'The Origins and Make-up of Cambridge University Library MS Ff.1.6', *Transactions of the Cambridge Bibliographical Society*, 8 (1983), 299–333.

62. W. Scase, 'Reginald Pecock, John Carpenter and John Colop's "Common-Profit" Books: Aspects of Book Ownership and Circulation in Fifteenth-Century London', *Medium Ævum*, 61 (1992), 261–74.

63. G. Ouy, 'Les bibliothèques', in C. Samaran, ed., *L'histoire et ses methodes* (Paris: Gallimard, 1961), 1061–108, at 1091.

64. J. M. Luxford, *The Art and Architecture of English Benedictine Monasteries, 1300–1540: A Patronage History* (Woodbridge: Boydell, 2005), xvii.

PART III

Where Do We Study the Manuscript?

11

SIÂN ECHARD AND
ANDREW PRESCOTT

Charming the Snake: Accessing and Disciplining the Medieval Manuscript

Prologue: at the Readers' Desk

Consider a typical scholarly encounter with a medieval manuscript book. I am sitting in the Manuscripts Reading Room at the British Library. To enter that room, I have passed the scrutiny of a guard who has checked my Reader Pass and ensured that I am not wearing a coat or carrying a bag (what type of coat I might be allowed to wear and what bags I may carry are carefully codified by the library). To secure the manuscripts on my list, I have also had to pass other levels of scrutiny, because some of my manuscripts are restricted, requiring a letter of introduction for access. This particular manuscript – London, British Library, Cotton MS Tiberius A. iv, a manuscript containing Latin poetry by John Gower – is not in that more rarefied category, and so I am able to photograph it myself for scholarly purposes. Were this manuscript to have been classified as 'Select', then I would be sitting at a row of desks more directly in view of the librarians, and amateur photography would be off limits. As it is, I arrange 'my' manuscript on the reading stand provided; pin its pages back with leaded book snakes; and prepare, not so much to read it, as to mine it and record it, for material to be digested later.

There is much to unpack from this specific instance about the larger questions of manuscript access with which this chapter is concerned. Even the manuscript number I have given earlier is contentious. To be consistent with the editorial conventions of this volume, it is given as Cotton Tiberius A. iv, but current British Library usage is 'Cotton MS. Tiberius A. IV'. The 'MS.' component is essential to distinguish the volume from the various charters and rolls that also form part of the Cotton collection. Correct spacing and capitalization can be essential to successfully ordering the manuscript. The delivery of Tiberius A. iv to the reading room is dependent on a number of institutional classification and control systems, such as cataloguing, numbering, stamping, foliation, and shelving. Many of these

237

processes are driven by the desire of institutions to bring order and consistency to the organization of manuscripts in their custody and to ensure that 'every manuscript is in its place'.[1] Manuscripts are routinely cleaned, repaired, refoliated, renumbered, and rearranged in ways that fundamentally affect the way in which they are presented to us: as a result of my use of Tiberius A. iv, a curator notices that the rear binding board is becoming loose and it is placed in a grey archive box to protect it. In this chapter, we shall examine these curatorial systems in order to explore the roles institutions have played, and continue to play, in delivering to us the objects of the medieval past. As Tiberius A. iv will show, no institutional framing is neutral.

Tiberius A. iv is quite a large manuscript. It needs to be supported by the book cradle because it is heavy and unwieldy, and it needs book snakes to hold its pages back. Bookstands are not the invention of a modern library: medieval manuscripts are full of images of books on stands. Sometimes these are tables for scribes at work. Sometimes these are lecterns to support magnificent Gospel books, books that are intended both to be read from and to be displayed. There are also manuscript depictions of studies that include reading stands, and scholarly accounts of reading in the Middle Ages often consider the interplay between public and private reading – the former often requiring a book stand, and the latter sometimes symbolized by small, portable books such as Books of Hours.

Many manuscripts of the works of John Gower are quite large and heavy, and might well, from the start, have demanded a reading support. But this manuscript's current state is the result of post-medieval moments. It was singed in the Ashburnham House fire in 1731 and, like many of the manuscripts damaged in that fire, it was eventually conserved, in this case in 1851, by being placed in stiff paper frames. The small triangular cuts that can be seen in the vellum leaves were made in the process of flattening them. A decorative pen rectangle has been drawn on the paper frame around the inlaid vellum leaf, and then the rest of the portfolio-style paper frame is blank space. Some of the vellum leaves contain British Museum stamps. The edges of the paper frames have been gilded, presumably when the heavy nineteenth-century leather and gold institutional binding was made.

This is, in short, a large, impressive, and ponderous book, but much of its current physical presence is the result of forces that have worked upon it long after the point of its original production. The effect of these interventions is one reason why we need to sit in front of the 'real thing', but the fact that we need to do so under the watchful scrutiny of manuscript custodians, using supports and aids, in a room with lighting dimmed for conservation reasons, reminds us that whatever we are doing when we access medieval manuscripts

Institutional Frameworks

in most situations today, we are not reading them in anything like the way they might once have been read.

In framing our engagement with Tiberius A. iv, the first point to consider is the type of institution in which it is kept. The most celebrated British medieval manuscripts are found, like Tiberius A. iv, in major libraries such as the British Library in London, the Bodleian Library in Oxford, and the Parker Library at Corpus Christi College, Cambridge. However, medieval manuscripts are also found in many other types of institution. The quantity of medieval documents held in the National Archives or local record offices vastly exceeds those held by the British Library. Many museums and art galleries hold important collections of medieval manuscripts.

There are major differences in the intellectual and curatorial assumptions shaping galleries, libraries, archives, and museums, and these affect the way different institutions treat medieval manuscripts. This is reflected in the terms used for the rooms in which researchers consult manuscripts. I am sitting with Tiberius A. iv in the Manuscripts Reading Room of the British Library's St Pancras building, but when the British Library was housed in the British Museum, this facility was known as the Manuscripts Students' Room. 'Students' Room' was the term used by British Museum departments for the room where reserve collections were consulted, and this terminology indicates the museum origins of this collection. On the other hand, record offices refer to 'search rooms', reflecting the origins of access to archives in searches for legal purposes.

Our assumptions about the dividing lines between different types of cultural institutions are of recent origin. When the British Museum was established in 1753, its chief concern was not with the material culture which dominates the museum today, but with enabling access to the major collections of manuscripts given to the nation by the Cotton family, the Earls of Oxford, and Sir Hans Sloane. As the British Museum grew, its foundation collections were distributed among many different institutions, including the Natural History Museum, the National Gallery and, in 1973, the British Library. As a result, such items from the Cotton Library as Sir Robert Cotton's coins of Anglo-Saxon kings or the wax disc with magical designs used by John Dee are now in the British Museum, separated from Cotton's other collections in the British Library.[2]

Nineteenth-century museums became preoccupied with classifications of objects according to different formats. In the British Museum, for example, impressions of medieval seals were held in the Department of Manuscripts, but the matrices used to make the impressions were kept in the Antiquities Department.[3] The concern with classification led to turf wars between different departments, with Sir Frederic Madden (1801–73), Keeper of Manuscripts at the British Museum from 1837 to 1866, engaging in a guerilla campaign to seize from the Department of Printed Books the manuscripts from the libraries of George III and Thomas Grenville. The unfortunate effects of this obsession with categorization are evident from London, British Library, MS Additional 23211, which consists of two ninth-century fragments containing lists of Anglo-Saxon kings.[4] These were originally pastedowns in a small printed book and were 'Received from the Dept of Printed Books, 31 March 1859'. It is impossible now to trace which book these fragments were taken from, thus depriving us of clues as to where further fragments might be found.

Another fundamental institutional distinction is that between libraries and archives. Archives chiefly comprise administrative documents, and the way in which officials filed and arranged these documents tell us a great deal about the way in which the administration functioned. The curatorial processing of archives focuses on preserving the administrative groupings of records, known as *fonds*, and cataloguing of archives concentrates on the administrative characteristics of the *fonds* rather than describing the physical format of individual records. Thus, the National Archives description of the Pipe Rolls, a core series of Exchequer records which begins in 1130, includes a lengthy essay on the development of the Exchequer's accounting system and the function of the Pipe Roll, but for each individual roll, the only details provided are the dates covered by the roll and brief publication details. Details that would normally be expected in descriptions of twelfth-century manuscripts, such as number of membranes or description of the hand, are not provided.

By contrast, library collections of manuscripts are selective and individual items may be catalogued in great detail. An illustration of this selectivity is the collection of Henry Yates Thompson (1838–1928) now in the British Library, which was restricted to one hundred manuscripts of the highest quality, excess manuscripts being sold off as necessary. The high cost of medieval manuscripts frequently means that such selectivity is unavoidable. For example, when the collector Charles Dyson Perrins (1864–1958) died, he bequeathed two of his most precious manuscripts, including the Gorleston Psalter (London, British Library, MS Additional 49622), to the British Museum, and his executors sold eight others, including the De Brailes Hours (London, British Library, MS Additional 49999) and Oscott Psalter (London, British Library, MS Additional 50000), to the Museum at a reduced price, but the huge value of the collection meant that over 140 other manuscripts had to be sold.[5] Curators of library collections have also often been selective in acquiring material because storage space was limited. As long ago as 1830, Sir Nicholas Harris Nicolas ridiculed the haphazard way in which Sir Henry Ellis of the British Museum selected charters from the muniments of Baron de Joursanvault relating to English incursions in France during the Hundred Years War.[6]

English archival theorist Sir Hilary Jenkinson was very critical of such selectivity and described collections of charters such as those in the British Library as 'formed out of the wreck of hundreds of earlier sets of muniments', and declared that no archivist 'could possibly allow full Archive value to documents which have been violently torn from the connexion in which they were originally preserved'.[7] Jenkinson's remarks nowadays seem overly rigid in their insistence on the significance of official custody. Moreover, Jenkinson underestimates the importance of the collection as an organizing unit of manuscript libraries. The great manuscript libraries have been built around the collections formed by such figures as Matthew Parker, Sir Robert Cotton, Richard Rawlinson, Robert Vaughan of Hengwrt, the Earls of Oxford, Sir Hans Sloane, and Francis Douce. The significance of the collector and the collection as an organizing unit is evident even when manuscripts are incorporated into larger series such as the Additional Manuscripts or Additional Charters at the British Library. While the archivist seeks to reconstitute old administrative structures and processes, the curator of the manuscript library seeks to reconstruct old libraries and collections and understand their relationship.

The use of the term 'curator' to describe the professional staff in museums and libraries is very recent. The more historic term is 'Keeper', which was used in many British institutions until the early 1980s and only abandoned as a result of civil service restructuring. 'Curator' conveys a more proactive and inclusive image than 'keeper', which sounds restrictive. Nevertheless, curators are often figures of cultural anxiety, criticized for promoting established cultural canons and 'increasingly bonded into the circuits of capital between entertainment, tourism, heritage, commercial sponsorship and investment'.[8] For many commentators, the curator is a gatekeeper who ensures that 'The archive is overdetermined by facts of class, race, gender, sexuality and above all power.'[9] From the perspective of the readers' desk it is easy to develop an over-simplistic view of the curator as the agent of a panopticon. It is important to remember that curatorial activities in administering manuscript collections are wide-ranging and complex, and staff working with the collections range from expert scholars to administrative support staff. Moreover, in large libraries such as the British Library, responsibility for the systems supporting cataloguing, storage, and reading room may be divided among several departments, none of which is exclusively concerned with manuscripts.

Above all, curators in large libraries are concerned not just with medieval manuscripts, but also with an enormous range of manuscript materials of different types and periods, from classical papyri to the papers of prime ministers. Curators juggle time and resources in order to cope with all these different types of material. It may be more urgent to process a large modern archive than revise a catalogue entry for a well-known medieval manuscript. The need to deal with a variety of materials can explain some baffling procedures. For example, the index of the British Library's *Catalogue of Additions to the Manuscripts* for many years retained the use of 'b' rather than 'v' in referring to versos. This was because modern papers were not books, and therefore did not strictly speaking have versos; the antiquated 'b' convention covered both medieval manuscripts and modern archives.

Searching

The process that allows us to sit in front of a manuscript usually begins with consulting a catalogue, in this case the British Library's online 'Explore Archives and Manuscripts' catalogue. This is separate from the British Library's main 'Explore' catalogue because the detailed descriptions required for manuscripts do not fit easily into the data structures used for printed books. For printed books, the online ordering process is integrated into the catalogue. To order Tiberius A. iv, it is necessary to select the confusingly labelled 'Request Other Items' and enter the manuscript number. The simple process of ordering conveys a sense that manuscripts are complex, non-standard, and awkward.

Tiberius A. iv is a late fourteenth or early fifteenth manuscript of John Gower's Latin poetry, containing the *Vox clamantis*, the *Chronica Tripertita*, and, as the online catalogue has it, 'Versus' on 167r–177r. I am reading it precisely for the material elided under that last, maddening entry. I am working on John Gower's shorter Latin poems. The conventional understanding of these poems – their length, their titles, even how many individual items there are – is based on how G. C. Macaulay decided to divide them up in his magisterial late nineteenth century edition of the works of Gower.[10] Some poems that Macaulay separates appear, in some manuscripts, as if they are intended to be read as a sequence; others, presented as a single poem by Macaulay, might, in some manuscript contexts, seem instead to be several separate pieces, by virtue of such features in their *ordinatio* as display capitals. It seems reasonable, then, to ask exactly how the short Latin poems are presented in the manuscripts in which they survive.[11]

Accessing and Disciplining the Medieval Manuscript

My experience with Tiberius A. iv illustrates the difficulties of answering this apparently simple question. I have already remarked on the frustratingly laconic contents description. The rest of the entry in 'Explore Archives and Manuscripts' is equally terse. It notes that the leaves were 'damaged by fire in 1731'. It gives the dimensions as approximately 320 × 230 mm (without noting how much of that size reflects fire damage and the 1851 restoration rather than the original size of the codex). And it tells me that, before coming into Cotton's hands, the manuscript belonged to John Lumley, first Baron Lumley (d. 1609). Because I am in London while reading this notice, the easy answer to my frustrations is simply to call up the manuscript in question, and indeed, I began this chapter seated in front of that manuscript. But what if I were not in London? As a manuscript scholar based on the west coast of Canada, this is a basic access problem I encounter all the time. It is the reason that catalogue entries matter, and why the frustratingly truncated contents list for Tiberius A. iv, which groups the short pieces under the title 'Versus', is a problem.

As it happens, even when I am not in London, I am sufficiently familiar with the vagaries of manuscript cataloguing to know that there is probably a fuller contents list, somewhere, and indeed, the catalogue of the Cotton manuscripts compiled by Joseph Planta (1744–1827) between 1793 and 1796 and published by the Record Commission in 1802 provides a complete list of all the short poems. 'Versus' turns out to indicate over a dozen items, with foliation such that I can be sure of the sequence of items.[12] So, while Planta's catalogue has not been translated in its entirety to the online access point, there is enough to point a knowledgeable user to appropriate sources of information.

But the pursuit of the manuscripts of Gower's shorter poems quickly reveals another quirk in the British Library's access framework. I know that some of these short poems also appear in two Harley manuscripts – MS Harley 3869 and MS Harley 6291. However, only about 800 of the Harley manuscripts are currently described in 'Explore Archives and Manuscripts. Like many users of the catalogue, I first discovered this limitations in 2013, when the then-new 'Explore Archives and Manuscripts' catalogue made its debut. I was perplexed that I could find some Harley manuscripts but not others. I knew that the Harley manuscripts had not been fully catalogued in the earlier online manuscript catalogue, but the new catalogue – and the apparent manipulation of metadata that must have been necessary to combine the originally separate archives and manuscripts interfaces – led me to expect new content as well as new form. A query secured the response that, indeed, the Harley manuscripts had not been migrated fully, and that 'The British Library publishes its electronic

243

catalogue records progressively rather than waiting for completion.'[13] More than five years later, one of the Gower manuscripts in which I am interested is still not available through this catalogue; indeed, it is only because I already know that the manuscripts exist at all, that I have any idea what to do next. The front page does not make clear the limitations of the catalogue; one wonders what the novice user is failing to find as a result.

It happens that the two particular Harley manuscripts I was seeking were featured in an older online access initiative, the 'Catalogue of Illuminated Manuscripts', a project that began in 1995, and has proceeded in fits and starts since then, in response to various infusions of funding.[14] The Harley manuscripts were added to the project thanks to funding from the Getty Foundation, between 2006 and 2009. 'My' Harley manuscripts both have entries in the 'Catalogue of Illuminated Manuscripts', though both entries emphasize provenance and physical description rather than detailed contents lists. The entry for MS Harley 6291, for example, gives the full contents as 'Vox Clamantis (beginning imperfectly) (ff. 1–134v), *Cronica Tripertita* (ff. 134v–49v), and shorter poems (ff. 149v–61)'. There is more detail about the decoration, pen-flourishing, and ink colour, than there is about the texts the manuscript contains, but then, this is the 'Catalogue of Illuminated Manuscripts'. That is to say, cataloguing is never a neutral function, but always operates within the parameters established by the catalogue's goals and chosen objects, in this case, illuminated manuscripts and their decoration. Once again, because I am an expert user, I know there is likely to be more information of the sort I need somewhere, and as in the case of Tiberius A. iv, that turns out to be in a nineteenth-century catalogue, the 1808 catalogue of Harleian manuscripts, which shows me the titles and order of those shorter poems.

Another layer of complexity was added to this situation as this chapter was being prepared for the press. In summer 2018, MS Harley 3869 was digitized and added to the British Library's digitized manuscripts website. A full description of the manuscript was prepared by the Library, differing from that in the Catalogue of Illuminated Manuscripts, and made available with the digital facsimile. Initially, there was no indication in 'Explore Archives and Manuscripts' that this description was available elsewhere on the library's webpages. Then, just as I did final revisions of this chapter in autumn 2018, I found that this description had been added to 'Explore Archives and Manuscripts'. One imagines that catalogues are systematic and consistent in their coverage, but the treatment of the Harley manuscripts shows how random, piecemeal, and ultimately opaque the structure of manuscript catalogues can be. Sometimes it seems as if online manuscript catalogues have made things more complex and difficult.

244

Accessing and Disciplining the Medieval Manuscript

Lest it seem that I am singling out the British Library here, I should note that I can replicate these sorts of experiences across many manuscript repositories. This fact reflects the way in which no consistent standards have been adopted for the online cataloguing of manuscripts. While the Anglo-American Cataloguing Rules (now superseded by the Resource Description and Access or RDA framework) and MARC (MAchine Readable Catalogue) records have ensured consistency in descriptions of printed books, and the International Standard of Archive Description (ISAD-G) and the Encoded Archival Description (EAD) have more recently enabled a more consistent approach to archives, no similar standardization has emerged for the manuscript book. One of the difficulties in using the 'Explore Archives and Manuscripts' catalogue at the British Library is that it yokes together archival and manuscript procedures, and the archive structure used for the catalogue does not cope well with the manuscript book.[15]

Some online experiences are better. At Cambridge, for example, I can access both a complete online facsimile of Cambridge, Trinity College, MS R. 3. 2, and M. R. James's catalogue description of it at the same site.[16] In some cases, while there are no 'official' online portals, the internet can nevertheless offer some help: I can access the nineteenth-century descriptive catalogue of All Souls Oxford through archive.org, for example. It is in fact much easier to be a manuscript scholar from the western edge of North America than it has ever been, and these musings are not meant to sound churlish. What they do show, however, is that the illusion of easy and instant access promised by technological innovation in the world of libraries remains an illusion. The same kind of esoteric, advanced training that used to be a necessary precondition of a visit to the British Library, or the Bodleian, or any other major repository, with their centuries of built-up catalogues, remains useful.

Numbering and Grading

When you collect Tiberius A. iv from the issue desk at the British Library, you are handed a utilitarian grey box made from archive-quality cardboard. The manuscript has been put in a box because one of the heavy boards of its Victorian binding is becoming loose, and the box slows the deterioration of the binding. In the nineteenth century, manuscripts were often rebound at the first sign of wear and tear, leading to the loss of many early bindings and the destruction of much codicological information. Institutional enthusiasm for rebinding was evident as late as the 1960s, but boxing is nowadays preferred as a less intrusive way of protecting the manuscript.

As you open the box, it reveals the imposing leather binding of Tiberius A. iv with the arms of Sir Robert Cotton in gilt tooling on the front cover. The practice of using armorial stamps on the bindings of collections such as the Harley, Lansdowne and Egerton manuscripts was another initiative of Madden's, who ordered the stamps in 1841.[17] The online catalogue has told us that the manuscript was rebound in 1851, but does not say where this information came from. Details of the rebinding can be found in a ledger kept by Madden which records that the manuscript was inlaid and bound in April 1851 by 'T', who was the Museum's binder, Charles Tuckett.[18]

On the spine of the manuscript is the following inscription in gilt tooling: 'Johannis Gower / Cronica, / Intitulata / Vox Clamanti / Ejusdem Cronica Tripartita / et Poemata'. The wording for the tooling on the spine would have been composed by Madden or one of the assistants working with him on the Cotton Manuscripts, such as Edward Maunde Thompson (1840–1929). In the third panel on the spine is an emphatic statement of national ownership in gilt letters: 'Mus. Brit. / Bibl. Cotton.' The fourth spine panel provides housekeeping information: 'Tiberius A. IV. / Plut. XVIII. F.' Here, 'Plut' stands for 'Pluteus' (shelf), and the fact that the placing of the manuscript was tooled in gold letters on the spine of Tiberius A. iv suggests great confidence as to where the manuscript would be placed in the British Museum and that it would be there for a long time.

When Sir Robert Cotton arranged his library, he distinguished the various book presses by placing a bust of a Roman emperor on each one. Tiberius A. iv was the fourth manuscript on the first shelf of the bookcase with the bust of the Emperor Tiberius on it.[19] During the eighteenth century, such quaint arrangements were regarded with disfavour. When the Sloane and Harley collections of manuscripts were transferred to the British Museum in 1756, they were at the insistence of the Museum's trustees renumbered and shelved according to a subject classification, reflecting the way in which manuscript libraries were, at that time, regarded still as working scholarly libraries. However, partly due to the fire damage in 1731, the Cotton and Royal manuscripts were not rearranged, and the 1808 Synopsis to the British Museum apologetically notes that the Cotton and Royal manuscripts 'are not classed in strict scientific order'.[20]

The miscellaneous contents of manuscripts make it difficult to arrange them by subject. As Josiah Forshall (1795–1863), Keeper of Manuscripts at the British Museum from 1827 to 1837, explained, 'It is scarcely possible, without unbinding and even cutting up manuscripts to make anything like a regular classification of them upon the shelves of a library, seeing that 10 or 12 manuscripts upon very different subjects are not infrequently bound in a single volume, and sometimes several written upon the same fasciculus of

Accessing and Disciplining the Medieval Manuscript

paper or vellum.'[21] In 1827, Forshall supervised the move of the manuscripts from the British Museum's old home in the seventeenth-century Montagu House to new accommodation in Robert Smirke's British Museum building. Forshall introduced a new system for shelving the manuscripts. While collections were broadly kept together, they were arranged according to size, with the smallest manuscripts on the highest shelves and the largest on the bottom. Each press was designated by a number, painted on the top, while the shelves were designated by letters. The shelfmark 18 E thus indicated that the manuscript was placed on the fifth shelf down in press 18. Manuscripts were placed in alphabetical order of collection and numerical order on the shelf. Tiberius A. iv has not moved much since 1851; printed labels on the spine show that its current shelfmark is 18 E.

Forshall's placing system was introduced across the collections, providing an adaptable and consistent pressmark system which could readily cope with new acquisitions. Forshall's system was sufficiently flexible to be retained in an adjusted form in the move to St Pancras. In order to locate on which press and shelf a manuscript would be found, it was necessary to compile a handlist. Its counterpart, the shelflist, was an inventory of the contents of each shelf. The handlist was the definitive statement of the contents of the collection, since, without an entry on the handlist, an item could not be located and effectively did not exist. In the case of older collections such as the Cotton manuscripts, many details were available in the handlist which were not in the old printed catalogues, such as which manuscripts were transferred to the care of the new Keeper of Oriental Manuscripts in 1867, or whether old bindings had been retained. Until recently, much of this information was not available to readers, but nowadays some of it can be accessed using the 'Browse this Collection' facility in the online catalogue. For the Cotton manuscripts, this listing can be used to identify items missed from earlier catalogues such as Cotton MS Otho E. xiv, a twelfth-century manuscript of Hugh of St Victor, added to the Cotton Library between 1695 and 1734 by David Casley (d. 1754), the Keeper of the Royal and Cotton Libraries, and not mentioned by Planta.

Grading

While the system devised by Forshall suited the needs of the British Museum, other libraries adopted different methods of shelving. In the Bodleian Library, for example, a complex form of subject placing was used.[22] Almost every manuscript library has its own system, but three consistent features should be noted. First, libraries are concerned to ensure that the identity of historic collections is retained, even if the collections are not

247

shelved together. Second, manuscripts are shelved separately from printed books, even where there is integrated catalogue access to manuscript, printed, and other formats. Third, there is provision within the housekeeping systems for the most valuable 'select' manuscripts to be shelved separately, with restrictions on access.

Tiberius A. iv is not included in the British Library's 'Select' manuscripts. Nevertheless, it is an important early manuscript of a major medieval author, with a striking illustration of Gower the Archer as a frontispiece for *Vox Clamantis* (fol. 9v). Why is this manuscript available for photography and without a letter of introduction, whereas MS Additional 59495, containing Gower's *Cinkante Balades* and *Traitié* is categorized as select? How are these decisions made?

In the British Library, manuscripts and printed books were initially read in the same reading room. Security precautions in the reading room were relaxed; readers were not required to show tickets until 1873. Exceptionally precious manuscripts were identified as select, to be consulted in the offices of the Department of Manuscripts. As the general reading room became larger and busier, Madden increased the number of such select manuscripts. The risks of using manuscripts in a large general reading room were demonstrated in 1879, when a thirteenth-century French manuscript, MS Royal 16 E. viii, disappeared after it had been returned by a reader, probably getting mixed up with printed books.[23]

The impetus for the identification of large numbers of select manuscripts was the need to prepare for evacuation when the Museum was threatened with air raids during the two world wars.[24] During the First World War, forty-seven cases of the 'best' manuscripts were sent for safekeeping to the National Library of Wales in Aberystwyth. Shortly before the Second World War, the three senior curators in the Department graded the manuscripts in four categories, A*, A, B, and C, in descending order of value. The first two classes represented the cream of the collection, about 100 manuscripts. A fifth category, D, was established by block selection, including, for example, manuscripts from the foundation collections not already in higher categories. Tiberius A. iv would have been graded 'D'. In August 1939, all the manuscripts graded A*, A, and B, together with most of those in the D category, were sent to Aberystwyth. When the manuscripts returned after the war, it was decided to place all the manuscripts in the A*, A, and B categories together, forming the basis of the present 'Select' category. This process took place very hurriedly under wartime conditions and involved many snap judgements, but nevertheless continues to have major ramifications for access today. A large Chubb safe was also installed (probably during the First World War) which was used to house the most precious items, such

Accessing and Disciplining the Medieval Manuscript

as the Lindisfarne Gospels or Luttrell Psalter. This was known as 'Safe Z', even though it was the only one, and this name has been transferred to a pen area at St Pancras, providing a designation for one of the highest levels of restriction. There were rumours in the 1970s that if a nuclear attack was imminent, a van would appear at the British Museum for the evacuation of Safe Z.

The complexities of these systems, not only in the British Library but also in all manuscript libraries, are almost endless, but it is important to try to understand them because they are the key to understanding how manuscripts have been rearranged and reordered over the years. Numerical conventions, and the fondness of curators for numbering additional parts with asterisks or letters, may be important bibliographical clues, as can be seen by the use of an asterisk (now replaced by the designation /1) to mark a transcript of London, British Library, Cotton MS Otho A. xii.[25] The names given to collections may be deceptive: many of the so-called Sloane Charters in the British Library have no connection with Sir Hans Sloane, while some of the Cotton Charters were only purchased in the late eighteenth century.[26] Almost every time the manuscript collections of a major institution such as the British Library are rearranged to separate out, for example, oriental or musical manuscripts, further anomalies are created.[27]

Even the manuscript number itself may be puzzling. Thomas Smith in 1696 uses the form Tiberius A. IV, as does Planta. This is how the number is given on the spine of the manuscript. However, by 1850, Madden was putting the Roman numeral in lower case in the *Catalogue of Additions*: Tiberius A. iv.[28] This became the conventional usage and was adopted by such authorities as Neil Ker. A few authors such as Derek Pearsall in his description of Gower manuscripts prefer to omit the space: Tiberius A.iv.[29] However, at some point after 1950, usage in the Department of Manuscripts reverted to that of Planta and Smith: Tiberius A. IV. The reasons for this change are unclear, but it was endorsed by the guides to the collections produced by Skeat and Nickson.[30] With the arrival of the present online catalogue, the 'reference code' has changed again, losing the full stop after the 'A': Tiberius A IV.

The formats of the different manuscript numbers express long-standing curatorial practice in shelving and organizing the manuscripts. One of the most fundamental divisions in many manuscript libraries is between manuscript volumes and single-sheet documents categorized as charters. The form of number frequently used by many scholars 'London, British Library, Additional 40542' is nonsensical, because there are two Additional series, Additional Manuscripts and Additional Charters, both numbered separately. Additional Charter 40542 is a deed said to have been written by

Adam Pynkhurst, who has been claimed as Chaucer's scribe; Additional MS 40542 is a volume of the correspondence of the nineteenth-century prime minister Sir Robert Peel. To make matters more complicated, there is a series of Additional Rolls whose numeration forms part of the charter sequence. Understanding these numbering sequences is essential to understanding the history of a collection. The numbers assigned to the Cotton Charters and Rolls or the Detached Seals in the British Library document the shelving history of the collections.

Does any of this have any practical significance? It can be essential in ensuring you get the manuscript you want. If you order Additional 40542 hoping to investigate the hand of Adam Pynkhurst, you will be disappointed when you receive Victorian political correspondence. In order to get access to our Gower manuscript, you must pay attention to these conventions. Fortunately, the British Library's ordering system is not case sensitive, so a lower case 'a' in Tiberius A. iv does not matter. But, on the other hand, the space is vital: following Pearsall and searching for Tiberius A.iv will produce no results.

The numeration of manuscripts may be about to become even more contentious, as librarians are currently discussing the introduction of an international system of unique identifiers for manuscripts. This is desirable to facilitate sharing and comparison of digital images, but may require manuscript scholars to abandon many old habits in referring to manuscripts.[31]

In the Manuscript Saloon

By 1859, the Cotton manuscripts had been placed in presses 17–27 which were on the ground floor of the northeast corner of the Manuscript Saloon of the British Museum, a large room abutting the southern end of Robert Smirke's great gallery for the King's Library. Pencil annotations on the flyleaf of Tiberius A. iv show how it stayed in press 18 in the Manuscript Saloon for most of its time in Smirke's building, with only one brief sojourn to press 29, probably due to building work. The Manuscript Saloon is now Room 2 of the British Museum. At St Pancras, the manuscripts are hidden from view, in air-conditioned enclosed storage areas, but in the British Museum, the collections were very much on display. Smirke covered every wall of the King's Library and Manuscript Saloon with book presses from floor to ceiling, with access to the upper presses via a narrow gallery. This arrangement created a strong visual impact, giving an exaggerated impression of the size of the collection. This visual effect was enhanced by the way in which doors were concealed with false bookshelves, complete with fake leather spines,

Accessing and Disciplining the Medieval Manuscript

elaborately tooled with titles and fictitious manuscript numbers, carefully composed in a convincing fashion by Madden.

The binding of Tiberius A. iv was expected to make its contribution to this imposing display, and this was one reason why ornate bindings were used and why Victorian curators had little patience with scruffier older bindings. The Manuscript Saloon was a public area. Until 1885, it was the main office area of the Department of Manuscripts, where the various assistants and attendants had their desks and even washstands. Readers consulted select manuscripts in the Saloon. In 1851, in honour of the Great Exhibition, displays of manuscripts and printed books were arranged in the Manuscript Saloon and King's Library and they were opened to the public. From 1885, when new office and reading room accommodation was built for the Department of Manuscripts, the Manuscript Saloon became one of the main exhibition areas for manuscripts. The imposing presses of manuscripts were part of the show, to the extent that in public areas a system of colour-coded boards was used for binding manuscripts for visual effect.

Photographs of the Manuscript Saloon in the 1920s show crowded displays of manuscripts, which sought to classify and illustrate all the major forms of handwritten textual artefacts. The display of manuscripts aimed 'to illustrate the progress of handwriting' by showing over 160 objects ranging in date from the third century BCE to the end of fifteenth century, crammed into just five display cases. Crowded and perilous to the manuscripts as these displays now seem, they nevertheless marked a major step forward in public access to the national collections. The accompanying guides, with their authoritative accounts of the development of handwriting and illumination, are testimony to Victorian educational zeal. Curators such as Edward Augustus Bond (1815–98) and Sir George Warner (1845–1936) also enthusiastically explored the potential of photography to enhance public access to these manuscripts, launching initiatives such as the New Palaeographical Society to produce and distribute photographic facsimiles of important manuscripts.

The success of these displays encouraged the arrangement of special temporary exhibitions, allowing manuscripts from a variety of collections to be seen together. A landmark in the evolution of such blockbuster temporary exhibitions was the exhibition of illuminated manuscripts arranged by Sydney Cockerell (1867–1962) at the Burlington Fine Arts Club in 1908, which included 269 items drawn from fifty-eight separate collections. The exhibition was documented in a major scholarly catalogue, which remains a useful source of information. The exhibition paved the way for such modern temporary exhibitions as the series of coordinated exhibitions in London since 1984 which offered an overview of medieval artistic achievement and placed manuscripts in their wider artistic context. In order to hold such exhibitions, manuscripts are frequently borrowed from across the world, despite the cost and difficulty of customs and security clearances and the need for the manuscript to travel business class to its destination, accompanied by a curator.

It does not seem that Tiberius A. iv has ever been exhibited, despite its striking illustration of Gower. In the late Victorian displays at the British Museum, medieval literature from England largely consisted of works in English, and Gower was represented by a manuscript of the *Confessio Amantis*, London, British Library, MS Additional 12043, with no indication given of his work in Latin and French. As the British Museum's permanent exhibitions were thinned out from the 1950s, prominence was given to superstar manuscripts, such as *Beowulf* and Chaucer, and Gower disappeared from sight. Tiberius A. iv was not included in the exhibition of Cotton manuscripts held in the British Museum in 1931 on the tercentenary of Sir Robert Cotton's death. The exhibition history of a manuscript is very important, since it helps shape canonical assumptions about the prestige of an author or their works. The selection of a manuscript for exhibition can influence scholarly views on its significance. Priority for digitization may be given to manuscripts or authors represented in exhibitions. In short, exhibitions can be as powerful a tool in creating canons as publication or digitization. And, of course, exhibition can be another barrier between the scholar and the manuscript. It is not unknown for scholars to arrive in London to find that the manuscript in which they are interested is on exhibition not far from their home.

Conservation, Foliation, and Stamping

The most striking feature of the modern history of Tiberius A. iv is of course the damage during the fire at Ashburnham House in 1731, which also destroyed and badly damaged many manuscripts in the Cotton Library. The process of recovering and restoring material from this catastrophe began immediately after the fire and has continued to the present day. A list of manuscripts damaged in the fire was compiled by David Casley in 1732. When the Cotton manuscripts were transferred to the British Museum in 1756, a further report on their condition was prepared by Matthew Maty and Henry Rimius, which found that some items stated by Casley to have survived the fire had disappeared, while others said to have been destroyed had now been found. Maty and Rimius reported that the condition of other items, such as one of the exemplars of Magna Carta, had deteriorated since the fire. They also found that a vast number of loose fragments had survived

Accessing and Disciplining the Medieval Manuscript

from the fire. These fragments were taken to the Museum and placed in a garret room with charters from the Harley collection.

In 1793, Joseph Planta was instructed by the Trustees to compile a new catalogue of the Cotton manuscripts. Planta proposed that the new catalogue should be 'in a classical order, which no doubt ought always to have the preference',[32] but luckily the Trustees were unwilling to pay for this, and Planta's catalogue followed the existing emperor number order. Under Planta's supervision, over forty burnt manuscripts were restored, but many important manuscripts were left as loose sheets in cases. Planta did not tackle the vast mass of burnt fragments stored with the Harley Charters. The main campaign of restoring these fragments began with the work of Josiah Forshall in the 1820s and was continued by Sir Frederic Madden until his retirement in 1866. Planta's catalogue was published in 1802, and remained the principal catalogue for the Cotton manuscripts until very recently. However, because much of the work on the restoration of the Cotton manuscripts took place after Planta's catalogue was published, it is a deceptive document, since most of the items reported by Planta as burnt or missing were recovered and made available during the nineteenth century.

Tiberius A. iv was one of the lucky ones in that it was not considered very badly damaged by the fire and was reported by Casley, Maty, and Rimius to have been preserved. It appears in Planta's catalogue and has been consistently available for consultation by readers since the eighteenth century. Nevertheless, on its transfer to the Museum, the manuscript was in a parlous condition with the singed edges of the vellum leaves being very fragile and prone to crumbling. The binding of the manuscript at the time of the fire had been irreparably damaged, and the manuscript may even for a time have been left as loose leaves or gatherings. Planta had some of the Cotton manuscripts rebound to protect them, and Tiberius A. iv may have been among these. As a result, when Forshall and Madden began their great work of restoring the Cotton manuscripts, Tiberius A. iv was not on the priority list, sadly singed though it appears to us today.

Under Forshall, burnt crusts and fragments from the Cotton manuscripts were soaked in a solution of zinc and water, and then cut open. This accounts for the resemblance of the leaves in some Cotton manuscripts to a tiger skin rug. Madden used an external bookbinder called Henry Gough, who was able to open up the crusts without so much damage. As Kevin Kiernan has described, Gough carefully traced round each of the fragments to make the paper frames that today protect them, and Gough's pencil tracings can still be seen on the frames.[33] The frames have protected the fragments well, but at the expense of concealing some of the manuscript fragment on the verso. Madden was initially hesitant about using the Museum's usual binder,

253

Charles Tuckett, on this delicate work, but the immensity of the task encouraged Madden to give Tuckett some of the simpler work. By 1851, Tuckett had become so adept at the restoration process that Madden was starting to think his skill was greater than Gough's. The inlaying and rebinding of Tiberius A. iv by Tuckett in April 1851 was part of Madden's final tidying-up of the Cotton collection. The way in which Madden considered the work on Tiberius A. iv is evident from the fact he does not mention the rebinding in his work diary, although he is careful to record all the other work going on with the Cotton collection at that time.

The more straightforward nature of the work is evident from the fact that Tuckett did not need to trace round the leaf to inlay it. The margins of the manuscript had survived, so on the whole the frames do not conceal text, although on a number of folios the frame obscures small erased annotations in the margin, as well as other codicological details such as pricking. The biggest problem is that the paper frames are made from acid paper. Eventually, the acidity of the paper will make it so fragile that it will start to come away from Tuckett's binding. Because the manuscript leaves cannot be detached from the frames without damaging them, it will probably be necessary for them before too long to be enclosed in archival polyester leaves similar to those which today protect another burnt manuscript, London, British Library, Cotton MS Otho A. xii. This is another access complication, since it is very difficult to use ultraviolet or other specialist light sources to examine damaged details when a leaf is enclosed in plastic. The order of the leaves would have been checked by a curator before Tuckett bound them up. In this case, it perhaps was not Madden, since he does not mention the manuscript in his diary, but one of those assisting him in the work on the Cotton manuscripts at this time, such as Thompson.

The most important function of the foliation of a manuscript is security. It enables curators to quickly establish whether the manuscript is intact and if leaves have been cut, for example. Foliation is also important in providing an unambiguous means of identifying particular leaves in the manuscript for such housekeeping purposes as cataloguing or photography. One of the first actions of Planta in working on the Cotton manuscripts in the 1790s was to have folio numbers written on them, and the ink folio numbers inserted under Planta's direction can still be seen on Tiberius A. iv, together with a statement 'Cons. fol. 176' for the benefit of curators checking the manuscript. However, as the Cotton manuscripts were restored, the foliations of manuscripts became confused.

In 1867, after it was found that two folios had been removed from a volume of sixteenth-century state papers, Lansdowne 5,[34] it was decided to introduce a more thorough and consistent foliation procedure, and most

Accessing and Disciplining the Medieval Manuscript

of the British Library's manuscripts were refoliated over the following years. In the case of Tiberius A. iv, the old Planta ink foliation was lightly struck through in pencil, and a new pencil foliation added which included the seventeenth-century list of contents omitted from Planta's foliation, so that the new foliation differs by one throughout, giving a new folio count for the manuscript of 177. A pencil note at the end states that this refoliation was undertaken in April 1884 by 'FM', who was Frederick Mackney and checked by 'GG' who was George Gatfield. Mackney and Gatfield were attendants in the Department of Manuscripts and refoliated many of the Cotton manuscripts. The way in which foliation is seen as concerned with security and access rather than a curatorial statement as to the structure of the manuscript is evident from the way in which entering folio numbers was (and still is) a clerical task.

The refoliations undertaken in the late nineteenth century by Mackney, Gatfield, and their colleagues have annoyed many scholars since. The manuscript containing *Beowulf*, London, British Library, Cotton MS Vitellius A. xv, was refoliated shortly after a facsimile had already been published by the Early English Text Society, so that many scholars continued to use the old Planta foliation, causing great confusion, and Kevin Kiernan has argued strongly for a reconsideration of Mackney's 'official' foliation.[35] Likewise, Peter Meredith and Richard Beadle criticize the 1882 foliation of the register containing the text of the York Play, London, British Library, MS Additional 35290, because of its failure to include blank leaves which were part of the original manuscript, and their facsimile uses a third foliation specially devised by them.[36] In Tiberius A. iv, a vellum leaf at the beginning is also excluded from the 1884 foliation, even though it contains the number of the manuscript in ink in a modern hand, probably from the time of Planta's catalogue, together with the Montagu House pressmark of the manuscript in brown ink, while on the verso of this unfoliated leaf is a seventeenth-century inscription recording the Cotton pressmark. The existence of this unfoliated leaf is noted in the online description, which gives the foliation of the manuscript as i + 177, even though the blank leaf does not have a Roman numeral on it. The online description then also gives an alternative count which takes account of the fact that the list of contents on fol. 1 was added in the seventeenth century: i + 1 (fols. i, 1: early modern endleaves) + 176 (fols. 2–177).

The British Museum rule that blank leaves should be omitted from the foliation, even if the leaf was part of the original manuscript, was reiterated by Theodore Skeat (1907–2003) as Keeper of Manuscripts in the 1960s, but has been recently relaxed in the case of medieval manuscripts. Differing foliation practices are an expression of the tension between, on the one hand, the curator's pragmatic requirements to ensure that valuable manuscripts can be safely and securely used in public reading rooms and, on the other, the scholarly anxiety to document and preserve the structure of the manuscript as artefact. This tension is also apparent in the use of ownership stamps on manuscripts. Under Planta, large square stamps in red ink reading 'MVSEVM BRITANNICVM' were used. These were placed very prominently on folios, frequently even within decorations and illuminations, in order to discourage the cutting out of decorations and to make it more difficult to scrub out the stamp. Madden introduced more discreet smaller stamps but it seems that no additional stamping was undertaken after the rebinding of the manuscript in 1851. In the 1930s, however, some additional stamps were inserted in the binding, using the 'Type 3' stamps, which were in use from 1929 to 1973.[37] Although these 'Type 3' stamps are more discreet, their use of the royal arms nevertheless conveys a strong message about the status and prestige of the manuscript.

Surrogates

As previously noted, one of us is located on the west coast of Canada, far from the repositories that hold the majority of the world's medieval manuscripts, and as a result, the availability of reproductions of those manuscripts is a central aspect to access. In a sense this is nothing new in the world of scholarship. Early modern antiquarians, for example, exchanged and copied manuscripts, and collectors such as Cotton or Parker who amassed large collections employed archivists and copyists on their own account, and also made their collections available to other scholars, even lending manuscripts. At the end of the seventeenth century, the palaeographer Humfrey Wanley (1672–1726) compiled a 'Book of Specimens', or 'Book of Hands', comprising representative facsimiles of Greek, Latin, and Anglo-Saxon script, selected from various ancient manuscripts. Wanley's magnificent collection is still preserved in Longleat House and includes facsimiles of leaves from a number of manuscripts badly damaged in the Cotton fire.[38] The Victorian antiquary Henry Shaw (1800–73) made exquisitely detailed hand copies of illuminations from items in the collection of the British Museum, so that they could be accessed by the students of the newly established South Kensington Museum (later renamed the Victoria and Albert Museum).

The potential of photography for the study of manuscripts was quickly realized. The inventor of the calotype method of photography, Henry Fox Talbot (1800–77), corresponded with the manuscript collector Sir Thomas Phillipps (1792–1872) about how photography could assist the manuscript scholar and contemplated a photographic facsimile of the 1225 Magna Carta

Accessing and Disciplining the Medieval Manuscript

in his home at Laycock abbey. Fox Talbot's famous book *The Pencil of Nature* includes a photographic facsimile of a fifteenth-century printed collection of statutes, and Fox Talbot declared that for antiquarians the preparation of photographic facsimiles 'seems destined to be of great advantage'. In 1852, Madden pasted a small photograph of a cartulary into his diary and wrote that

> If this wonderful art should be carried to a higher perfection it is easy to foresee that the time will come when accurate facsimiles of any number of pages of a manuscript as well as charters or letters may be taken without difficulty and at trifling expense. In this manner manuscripts that are unique may be copied and transmitted to other libraries.[39]

In 1856, the photographer Roger Fenton (1819–69), celebrated for his photographs of the Crimean War, produced a photographic facsimile of the so-called Epistles of Clement in the early biblical manuscript the *Codex Alexandrinus* (London, British Library, MS Royal MS 1 D. v–viii). The manuscript was disbound so that the leaves could be removed and flattened for photography. In order to obtain sufficient light for the photographs, the leaves were fixed to an external wall of the Museum.[40] In the 1870s, a dispute about the dating of the Athanasian Creed led to the loan to the British Museum of the ninth-century Utrecht Psalter (Utrecht, Universiteitsbibliotheek, MS 32). While this manuscript, formerly part of the Cotton Library, was in London, a facsimile was made using the autotype process, the first complete photographic facsimile of a medieval manuscript.[41] The success of the Utrecht Psalter facsimile led to the formation of the New Palaeographical Society. The autotype process also enabled private bodies such as the Roxburghe Club to produce photographic facsimiles of manuscripts.

Commercial microfilm became widespread in the 1930s and rapidly began to be used for preservation and access to library materials, which were expensive to store and conserve, such as newspapers. During the Second World War, a major microfilming project of manuscripts in England and Wales was undertaken by the American Council of Learned Societies and the Library of Congress. The 'British Manuscripts Project' was undertaken both as a precaution in case of war damage and as a means to facilitate access by American scholars to manuscripts in the British Isles. The project filmed over 10,000 manuscripts from a wide range of repositories producing over 2,600 reels of microfilm. Among the manuscripts microfilmed by this project was Tiberius A. iv. The description of the manuscript in the checklist of microfilms, prepared by the Library of Congress, differs again from those elsewhere, this time itemizing the shorter verses conflated under the term 'Versus' in the present online catalogue.[42]

At about this time, the British Museum was experimenting with new imaging technologies. In 1929, the Chaucerian scholar John Manley (1865–1940) presented to the British Museum an ultraviolet fluorescence cabinet that made erasures and faded text easier to read,[43] and at the same time, other institutions such as the National Library of Wales were also experimenting with ultraviolet photography.[44] As a result of the long history of imaging manuscripts, we can now sometimes see how manuscripts have changed over the past 150 years, even though they have been safely kept in a library or archive. For example, it has been pointed out how an important ownership inscription in the Hengwrt manuscript of the Canterbury Tales, Aberystwyth, National Library of Wales, Peniarth MS 392D, is visible in photostatic copies and microfilms dating from 1929, but had disappeared by the time a black and white facsimile was published in 1979.[45] A possible explanation is that the inscription was accidentally removed when the manuscript was conserved and rebound in 1956.

Today, many of us live in a world of comparatively easy access; from a desk in Vancouver, it is possible to leaf through Matthew Parker's entire collection, thanks to the Parker on the Web project; or to sample dozens of the manuscripts of Robert Cotton now found in the British Library, through that institution's various digitization initiatives; or to place Shaw's copies next to their originals on a virtual desktop, because images of both exist in the databases of the Victoria and Albert and the British Library.

We previously noted that reading a manuscript in a modern library is an exercise in distance, as the contemporary scholar cannot interact with a manuscript with anything like the freedom enjoyed by a medieval or early modern reader. Technological intermediaries often try to fill at least something of that gap. For example, annotation and manipulation can be possible when what we access is not the original, but a facsimile, and most commonly, these days, a digital facsimile. Even the simplest of image files can be magnified, rotated, cropped, and repurposed, and in addition, there is an increasing array of tools that allow more elaborate reading and annotation. Early digitization projects sometimes favoured skeuomorphic approaches, such as the British Library's *Turning the Pages* animations: these were often to be found in projects aimed at what was understood to be a more popular, casual readership. Other early experiments developed specialized software to allow for comparison and collation. A dizzying number of viewers, intended to allow users to flip and zoom in on pages online, developed, some requiring special browser plug-ins. Later waves of technology-driven access included images and descriptions embedded in iOS apps, sometimes created to accompany exhibitions or built around a particularly famous manuscript.

258

Accessing and Disciplining the Medieval Manuscript

What all these approaches share is the danger of obsolescence. Some projects have doggedly kept pace with technological change – Kevin Kiernan's *Electronic Beowulf*, which first appeared on CD in 1997, has now migrated to an online format in version 4.0. Zoomify, used in many older library-based exhibition projects, is a Flash-based online viewer that increasingly does not play well with all browsers, and Microsoft Silverlight is another popular online format whose use often results in would-be viewers needing to install plug-ins or updates, even as Microsoft itself is now urging content providers to move away from Silverlight altogether.[46] While Microsoft is addressing a community of commercial content providers who might have the nimbleness to abandon one model for another, many of the public digitization projects that have brought medieval manuscript access to new levels have come about as the result of one-time funding, and/or in cash-strapped institutions that are not necessarily able to migrate easily to new formats. Indeed, this explosion of access in a sense serves to highlight the many other factors, beyond the technological, that continue to manage access. The Parker on the Web project, for example, was available in its fullest form for its first decade only to institutions that purchased a subscription; since 2018, it has been Open Access. The digital repositories of such public institutions as the British Library and the Victoria and Albert Museum are open access, but they also represent only a sampling of the material they contain. And many manuscripts are of course dispersed within much smaller repositories, which often lack the resources to digitize even a small portion of their collections.

Parker 2.0 is a flagship for the International Image Interoperability Framework (IIIF) which many major libraries and cultural heritage institutions are now promoting as a means of more easily sharing and comparing digital images. The adoption of such IIIF-compatible browsers as Mirador and the Universal Viewer will perhaps reduce the problems of obsolescence by allowing development costs to be shared across institutions. However, the exciting possibilities offered by IIIF will be of little comfort to curators finding it difficult to raise the funding and resources required for large-scale digitization projects.

We can return to Gower to illustrate what variable access can look like in the digital age. The British Library, including Tiberius A. iv, has thirteen manuscripts of the works of Gower.[47] Four of these are Harley manuscripts and one of these, MS Harley 3869, has recently been fully digitized, with a complete description as part of that presentation. For the others, however, their catalogue descriptions are not currently available through the online Archives and Manuscripts catalogue. There are a few images of each of the remaining three in the Digital Catalogue of Illuminated Manuscripts; as one

259

might expect, the images selected privilege decoration, and so, although Gower manuscripts tend not to be lavishly illustrated (though they are often handsome), the impression gained from these few images could be misleading. There are complete catalogue descriptions for these manuscripts (as for other Harley manuscripts that happen to be decorated – searching the Illuminated Manuscripts catalogue is a common workaround for scholars looking for easily accessible descriptions for Harley manuscripts), but as the underlying entry template is not identical to that in the Archives and Manuscripts catalogue, one cannot tell from these entries if these manuscripts may be photographed by a user. Of the other Gower manuscripts in the Library's collection, three more are also represented by an image or two in the Illuminated Manuscripts catalogue, while five have, at present, no online images here at all. As for taking one's own photographs on a research trip in order to address that gap, four of the Gower manuscripts in the Library were not user-photographable on my last trip. In short, while the British Library is increasingly making complete digital facsimiles of its manuscripts available online, selections must always be made. Of the triumvirate of laureate Middle English poets – Chaucer, Gower, and Lydgate – Chaucer is, at the time of writing, represented by two complete digital facsimiles, of MS Harley 7334, a beautiful but textually idiosyncratic manuscript, and MS Harley 1758; and Lydgate, surprisingly perhaps, by six manuscripts.[48] The best way to ensure one has complete access to the British Library's Gower manuscripts, then, continues to be what it has been since the British Museum Library opened: one must go to London and sit in front of the manuscripts in person.

Oxford and Cambridge are also home to many Gower manuscripts, and again, variable policies regarding cataloguing, photography, and digitization inevitably control which manuscripts are likely to receive the most attention. The Bodleian allows photography, at the discretion of the Library staff. However, many college manuscripts reside in their college libraries, and it is rare for there to be any kind of online presence for these manuscripts. Cotton MS Tiberius A. iv is a significant manuscript of Gower's Latin poems, but the other important manuscript, used, along with Tiberius A. iv as the base text for G. C. Macaulay's standard edition of these poems, is All Souls College, MS 98, which is not digitized; at the time of writing, it does not seem that All Souls allows personal photography for research purposes. A student of the Latin poems, then, must plan to travel to Oxford. Students of scribal practice, on the other hand, can consult a Cambridge college-based manuscript, Trinity College, MS R. 3. 2, in its entirety from their desktops, thanks to a project at Trinity to scan manuscripts and link them to the M. R. James catalogue.[49] Given the centrality of this particular manuscript to Parkes and

260

Doyle's seminal discussion of fifteenth-century urban vernacular manuscript production,[50] the availability of MS R. 3. 2 is significant. Access to James's catalogue is also important, and indeed, remote access to manuscript catalogues that are often owned in hard copy only by the largest research libraries, is an important element of access. The Bodleian, for its part, has digitized such major resources as the Summary and New Catalogues, the Quarto Catalogues, and the Western Manuscripts Card Catalogues. While Digital Bodleian offers over 800,000 images from Oxford collections, with an ability to create your own albums and compare images across repositories using IIIF,[51] the coverage of individual manuscripts of Gower consists of select images of many manuscripts, designed for the casual user looking to sample the collection visually. The image scans of the individual cards in the old catalogue, on the other hand, are unapologetically aimed at a user who is not merely expert, but already thoroughly familiar with this particular repository and its collections.

Further afield, we find again a range of access affordances and restrictions for Gower manuscripts. Trinity College Dublin, for example, has an Archives and Manuscripts catalogue online, but thus far, the Middle English manuscripts are not included (nor are the Irish manuscripts, among other important material). Some Dublin manuscripts are available in their entirety online through the Irish Script on Screen initiative, but as the name suggests, these are the Irish-language manuscripts, with digitization efforts focused on such culturally and historically central books as The Book of Leinster (Dublin, Trinity College, MS 1339). The Gower manuscript (Dublin, Trinity College, MS D. 4. 6, containing some of Gower's Latin poems) is unlikely to be at the top of a digitization queue in this repository. There is a Gower manuscript in the Fondation Bodmer in Cologny, Switzerland (Bodmer MS 178), but while over 100 of the manuscripts from this important collection have been digitized in full through the e-Codices project, which seeks to create a Virtual Manuscript Library of Switzerland, the Gower manuscript is not among them. In the United States, Yale's Beinecke Library has an ambitious programme of digitization, so there is a full digital facsimile of MS Osborn fa.1, a copy of the *Confessio Amantis*. Other United States-based copies, such as Columbia University Library, MS Plimpton 265, or Pasadena, Huntington Library, MS EL 26 A 13, can be accessed through the cooperative Digital Scriptorium project. In this case, the manuscripts are represented by only a few images, but these images are available in very large formats, and full catalogue descriptions are also included.

In short, what is true for Gower is true for all medieval manuscripts. Access is controlled in ways that go beyond the restrictions of reading rooms with which we began this chapter. There are far more surrogates available now than was the case for scholars in the past, but availability is a matter of economic considerations as well as the goals of a given digitization project. These goals might be disciplinary, as in the predominance of image-based archives responding to the needs of art historians; they may be historical/cultural, as in the expectation that public national libraries will make culturally important objects accessible; and they may even derive from the expectations or needs of individual scholars who secured grant funding to underwrite the digitization. Access is a practical matter, but it is also an intellectual one. Macaulay drew on two manuscripts, Tiberius A. iv and All Souls 98, for most of the editing of Gower's Latin poems. He made the All Souls manuscript his base text, but if one were to re-edit Gower's Latin poems today, it would be far more convenient to use Tiberius A. iv as the base. In this particular case that would not necessarily be a bad decision, but it is not difficult to see how now, as always, the conditions under which we use medieval manuscripts can determine the use we decide to make of them.

Epilogue: 'The Bokes Duelle'

Like many medieval writers, John Gower was particularly interested in books and their fate. The opening English lines of his *Confessio Amantis* remind us that 'Of hem that writen ous tofore / The bokes duelle'. Books in lines like these can be shorthand for poetic posterity, but for the medieval poet and the modern manuscript scholar alike, they are also very tangible, material objects (it is worth noting that Gower designed his tomb so that his effigy's head would rest on a stack of three books, bearing the titles of his main works). Quite a few of Gower's books remain, including the copy of his Latin works with which we began this chapter. But the means by which we access medieval books today have inevitably changed the reading experience that their original producers might have imagined. Consider, for example, Gower's own tale of Aristotle and Xantippe. Aristotle, we are told, 'Was sett and loked on a bok / Nyh to the fyr, as he which tok / His ese for a man of age'.[52] Chaucer, too, gives us cosily domestic books, as in the case of the narrator of the *Book of the Duchess*, who uses books to combat insomnia: 'Upon my bed I sat upright / And bad oon reche me a book, / ... To rede and drive the night away'.[53] These are books read in private spaces, and, it seems, held in the hand.[54] Even Chaucer's Clerk keeps his 'twenty bookes clad in blak or reed' at his bed's head.[55] A large, elaborate decorated manuscript of stories – such as any copy of Gower's *Confessio Amantis* – might be too large for easy reading in bed, but these too were often social and domestic manuscripts, read aloud to

Accessing and Disciplining the Medieval Manuscript

groups,[56] as in the scene Pandarus stumbles upon when he finds Criseyde and her ladies listening to an account of the siege of Thebes.

To read a medieval book today, on the other hand, is a constrained exercise. If one has access to the 'original' manuscript, it must be read, not by the fire or in bed or aloud to a group of friends, but at a reading desk, on a bookstand, and in silence. Medieval scholars might well have read some of their books in a similar way, of course: visual and descriptive representations of scholars seated at desks poring over books abound in the medieval manuscript record. Nevertheless, while the book's pages may bear signs of generations of interactive reading – underlining, nota marks, manicules, annotations – the modern scholar cannot add to that conversation, which has now become fixed. When Chaucer said to his work at the end of *Troilus* 'Go, litel bok', he was acknowledging a fact of book production and readership that was true in his day and remains true in ours.[57] Books have always left their original sites of production and reception. The 'bokes duelle' indeed, but they dwell all over the world, under a range of conditions, and it is there that we must meet them.

Notes

1. John Holmes in 1836, quoted in A. Prescott, 'What's in a Number? The Physical Organisation of the Collections of the British Library', in A. N. Doane and K. Wolf, eds., *Beatus Vir: Studies in Early English and Norse Manuscripts in Memory of Phillip Pulsiano* (Tempe, AZ: ACMRS 2006), 512.
2. G. Meer, 'An Early Seventeenth-Century Catalogue of Cotton's Anglo-Saxon coins', in C. J. Wright, ed, *Sir Robert Cotton as Collector* (London: The British Library, 1997), 168–82; O. M. Dalton, 'Notes on Wax Discs used by Dr Dee', *Proceedings of the Society of Antiquaries of London*, 2nd series, 21 (1906–7), 380–3.
3. A. Tonnochy, *Catalogue of British Seal-Dies in the British Museum* (London: British Museum, 1952); T. C. Skeat, *British Museum: The Catalogues of the Manuscript Collection* (London: Trustees of the British Museum), 36–8; M. A. E. Nickson and J. Conway, *The British Library: Guide to the Catalogues and Indexes of the Department of Manuscripts*, 3rd edn (London: The British Library, 1998), 12.
4. L. Webster and J. Backhouse, eds., *The Making of England: Anglo-Saxon Art and Culture AD 600–90* (London: The British Museum and The British Library, 1991), 46–7.
5. T. J. Brown, G. M. Meredith-Owens, and D. H. Turner, 'Manuscripts from the Dyson Perrins Collection', *British Museum Quarterly*, 23 (1961), 27–38.
6. N. H. Nicolas, *Observations on the State of Historical Literature* (London: Pickering, 1830), 78–83.
7. H. Jenkinson, *A Manual of Archive Administration*, 2nd edn (London: Percy Lund, Humphries, 1966), 42.

263

8. G. Pollock, *Encounters in the Virtual Feminist Museum: Time, Space and the Archive* (London: Routledge, 2007), 10.

9. Ibid., 12.

10. G. C. Macaulay, ed., *The Complete Works of John Gower*, 4 vols. (Oxford: Clarendon Press, 1899–1902).

11. Oxford, All Souls College, MS 98; London, British Library, Cotton MS Tiberius A. iv; Glasgow, Hunterian Library, MS Hunter 59; London, British Library, MS Harley 6291; London, British Library, MS Additional 59495; Oxford, Bodleian Library, MS Bodley 294; San Marino, Huntington, MS HM 150; Oxford, Bodleian Library, MS Fairfax 3; London, British Library, MS Harley 3869; Geneva, Fondation Bodmer, MS Bodmer 178; Oxford, Bodleian Library, MS Hatton 92; Oxford, Bodleian Library, MS Laud 719; Lincoln Cathedral Library, MS A. 72; Dublin, Trinity College, MS D. 4. 6; Cambridge, Trinity College, MS R. 3. 2; and Nottingham, Wollaton Library Collection, MS WLC. LM. 8.

12. *Rex celi deus* 166r; *O recolende* 166v; *Carmen super multiplici vitiorum* 167r; *Quod patet ad limen* 167v; *Deficit in verbo sensus* 168v; *O sexus fragilis ex quo natura virilis* 169r; *Sunt duo cognati viciorum* 170v; *De lucis scrutinio* 171v; *Notula de libris* ... 173r; *Carmen, quod quidam philosophus* ... 173v; *Orantibus pro anima* ... 173v; *O deus immense* 173v; *Notula de Johannis Gower chronicis. Aliique, forsan ejusdem, versiculi* 175r; 1802 catalogue, 32. Note that these titles are not all the standard ones now used by Gower scholars; for example, Gower's colophon is traditionally referred to as the *Quia vnusquisque*, from its first words, adopted by G. C. Macaulay as the title in his 1899 edition. The Planta catalogue of course pre-dates Macaulay. The foliation used by Planta also differs from the current foliation of the manuscript, as discussed below.

13. Email communication from Catherine Angerson, 25 February 2013.

14. www.bl.uk/catalogues/illuminatedmanuscripts/aims.asp (accessed 14 February 2016). See A. Prescott, M. Brown, and R. Masters, 'The Survey of Illuminated Manuscripts', in L. Carpenter, S. Shaw, and A. Prescott, eds., *Towards the Digital Library: The British Library's Initiatives for Access Programme* (London: The British Library, 1998), 130–47.

15. A. Prescott, *The Function, Structure and Future of Catalogues*: http://digitalriffs .blogspot.co.uk/2013/01/the-function-structure-and-future-of.html (accessed 12 February 2016).

16. Cambridge, Trinity College, Wren Library: https://www.trin.cam.ac.uk/library/ wren-digital-library/

17. London, British Library, MS Additional 62002, fol. 74.

18. London, British Library, MS Additional 62577, fols. 6v–7.

19. C. G. C. Tite, *The Manuscript Library of Sir Robert Cotton* (London: The British Library, 1994), 79–99.

20. Prescott, 'What's in a Number?', 511.

21. Ibid., 513.

22. K. A. Manley, 'The Bodleian Classification of Manuscripts', *Journal of Librarianship* 10.1 (1978), 56–9.

23. A. Prescott, 'The Panizzi Touch: Panizzi's Successors as Principal Librarian', *British Library Journal*, 23 (1997), 194-236, at p. 225.

24. Prescott et al., 'Survey of Illuminated Manuscripts', 130–3.

Accessing and Disciplining the Medieval Manuscript

25. S. Echard, 'Containing the Book: The Institutional Afterlives of Medieval Manuscripts' in M. Johnston and M. van Dussen, eds., *The Medieval Manuscript Book: Cultural Approaches* (Cambridge: Cambridge University Press, 2015), 96–118.

26. Prescott, 'What's in a Number?', 516.

27. Ibid., 515.

28. See, for example, the description of London, British Library, MS Additional 15003, fol. 29 in the *Catalogue of Additions*.

29. D. Pearsall, 'The Manuscripts and Illustrations of Gower's Works', in S. Echard, ed., *A Companion to Gower* (Cambridge: D. S. Brewer, 2004), 78.

30. Skeat, 'Catalogues of the British Museum', 27; Nickson, *Guide*, 4.

31. www.irht.cnrs.fr/?q=fr/agenda/manuscript-ids-pour-un-identifiant-unique-des -manuscrits-2 (accessed 2 December 2018); T. Burrows, 'Towards Unique Identifiers for Medieval and Renaissance Manuscripts', https://tobyburrows .wordpress.com/2014/11/17/towards-unique-identifiers-for-medieval-and-renais sance-manuscripts/#comments (accessed 2 December 2018).

32. A. Prescott, 'Their Present Miserable State of Cremation: The Restoration of the Cotton Library', in Wright, ed., *Cotton as Collector*, 400.

33. K. Kiernan, ed., *Beowulf and the Beowulf Manuscript*, 2nd edn (Ann Arbor: University of Michigan Press, 1996), 68–9.

34. Prescott, 'What's in a Number?', 483.

35. Kiernan, *Beowulf*, xxi–xxiv, 65–169.

36. R. Beadle and P. Meredith, eds., *The York Play: A Facsimile of British Library MS Additional 35290*, Leeds Texts and Monographs, Medieval Drama Facsimiles 7 (Leeds, 1983), x–xi.

37. http://britishlibrary.typepad.co.uk/collectioncare/2013/09/a-guide-to-british- library-book-stamps.html (accessed 6 February 2016).

38. S. Keynes, 'The Reconstruction of a Burnt Cottonian Manuscript: The case of Cotton MS Otho A. I', *British Library Journal*, 22 (1996), 113–60.

39. J. Backhouse, 'Manuscripts on Display: Some Landmarks in the Exhibition and Popular Publication of Illuminated Books', in L. Dennison, ed., *The Legacy of M. R. James* (Donington: Shaun Tyas, 1995), 37–52, at 37.

40. W. A. Smith, *A Study of the Gospels in Codex Alexandrinus: Codicology, Palaeography, and Scribal Hands* (Leiden: Brill, 2014), 42.

41. Prescott, 'Panizzi Touch', 202–6.

42. L. Born, *British Manuscripts Project: A Checklist of Microfilms Prepared in England and Wales for the American Council of Learned Societies 1941–1945* (Washington: The Library of Congress, 1955), 16.

43. P. R. Harris, *A History of the British Museum Library 1753–1973* (London: The British Library, 1998), 522.

44. H. Jerman, 'Ultra-violet Photography', *National Library of Wales Journal*, 1 (1939), 45–6.

45. M. Pidd, E. Stubbs, and C. Thomson, 'The Hengwrt Canterbury Tales: Inadmissible Evidence?', *Canterbury Tales Project Occasional Papers*, 2 (1997), 61–8.

46. https://blogs.windows.com/msedgedev/2015/07/02/moving-to-html5-premium- media/ (accessed 12 February 2016).

47. London, British Library, MS Additional 12043; MS Additional 22139; MS Additional MS 59495; Cotton MS Titus A. xiii; MS Egerton 913; MS Egerton

265

1991; MS Harley 3490; MS Harley 3869; MS Harley 6291; MS Harley 7184; MS Royal 18 C. xxii; Stowe MS 950.

48. London, British Library, Cotton MS Tiberius A. viii; MSS Harley 1766, 2278, and 4826; MS Royal 18 D. II; and MS Yates Thompson 47. His work is also to be found in the digitized miscellany MS Additional 60577.

49. https://mss-cat.trin.cam.ac.uk/search.php?shelfmark=R.3.2

50. A. I. Doyle and M. B. Parkes, 'The Production of Copies of the *Canterbury Tales* and the *Confessio Amantis* in the Early Fifteenth Century', in M. B. Parkes and A. G. Watson, eds., *Medieval Scribes, Manuscripts and Libraries: Essays Presented to N. R. Ker* (London: Scolar Press, 1978), 163–210.

51. digital.bodleian.ox.ac.uk (accessed 2 December 2018).

52. Macaulay, ed., *The Complete Works of John Gower*, Book III, ll. 659–61.

53. Chaucer, Geoffrey, *The Book of the Duchess*, ed. by Larry D. Benson, *The Riverside Chaucer* (Oxford University Press, 1988), ll. 46–49.

54. See A. Taylor, 'Into His Secret Chamber: Reading and Privacy in Late Medieval England', in J. Raven, H. Small, and N. Tadmor, eds., *The Practice and Representation of Reading in England* (Cambridge: Cambridge University Press, 1996), 41–61.

55. Geoffrey Chaucer, 'The General Prologue', in *The Canterbury Tales*, *The Riverside Chaucer*, l. 294.

56. See J. Coleman, *Public Reading and the Reading Public in Late Medieval England and France* (Cambridge: Cambridge University Press, 2005); and 'Lay Readers and Hard Latin: How Gower May Have Intended the *Confessio Amantis* to Be Read', *Studies in the Age of Chaucer*, 24 (2002), 209–35.

57. Geoffrey Chaucer, *Troilus and Criseyde*, in *The Riverside Chaucer*, book V, l. 1786.

12

SUZANNE PAUL

The Curation and Display of Digital Medieval Manuscripts

Introduction

Accessing medieval manuscripts is not easy, as Echard and Prescott have shown in the previous chapter. Even as recently as 2014, undergraduates at the University of Cambridge were required to supply a letter of reference from their tutor to my predecessor as Keeper of Manuscripts in order to consult a medieval manuscript in the reading room of Cambridge University Library. Letters are no longer required and undergraduates are warmly welcomed into the reading room. Nevertheless, I am conscious that as a curator, I and my colleagues are still responsible to a considerable degree for mediating access to manuscripts by the decisions we make. In raising awareness of this mediation in this chapter, I want to focus on access via the availability of digital images which has transformed both the scholarly study and the popular awareness of medieval manuscripts. By and large, with a few exceptions, digital images are democratic; all users have equal access to the same resources,[1] though as Martin Foys comments: 'Improved access to at least the visual content of a medieval manuscript is undeniably significant, but the relationships digitality engenders between modern users and medieval sources are, as the expression on Facebook goes, complicated.'[2]

It barely needs to be said that access to digital images is not equivalent to access to the manuscripts themselves. In addition to being facsimiles, simulacra, avatars, or surrogates for the manuscripts,[3] digital images are objects in their own right which not only provide access to some aspects of medieval manuscripts but also possess properties of their own. In the first decade or so of widespread digitization, many manuscript scholars lamented the inadequacies of digital images and their inability to convey the physical characteristics of the 'real' manuscript;[4] increasingly, scholars are beginning to recognize the particular characteristics of digital images and the ways in which they can be used to address new scholarly questions. Understanding the qualities of digital images and the processes by which they are produced and displayed, and some of the numerous decisions made by curators, cataloguers, conservators, photographers, administrators, software developers, research councils, and grant-making trusts which go into those processes can be just as helpful for twenty-first-century manuscript scholars as understanding the work of parchmentmakers and scribes.

Digitization: Who Decides?

Although the creation of digital images of medieval manuscripts has been transformative, it is important to acknowledge that at this point in time, only a very small proportion of the medieval manuscripts that survive as a whole or in fragmentary form have been digitized. Why and how were these ones selected? The first point to understand is that very few institutions fund digitization of their collections from their core budget; by and large, the costs of digitization have to be met from external sources. The majority of manuscript digitization is done in the form of large-scale projects funded by trusts and foundations or by research councils. Thus, a manuscript is more likely to be digitized if it can be neatly packaged as part of a collection, if it is owned by an institution with existing digitization infrastructure, or if its contents are the object of active research interest. The Insular Manuscripts project led by Joanna Story has identified that of the circa 500 extant insular manuscripts created between the years 650 and 850, almost 50 per cent now have a digital presence online; the vast majority of these fall into all three categories.[5]

In institutions such as my own, early manuscripts, vernacular manuscripts, illuminated manuscripts, and those with illustrious provenance are at the front of the queue for digitization, as they are for loans and exhibitions. There have always been different levels of accessibility between manuscripts in large institutions, those in smaller collections, which are more likely to lack regular opening hours or staff, and those in private hands. While digital coverage remains uneven within and between institutions, there is a risk that this accessibility gap will continue to widen and a new digital canon will form, as those manuscripts that are available on screen become the only or primary objects of study while those that are hidden from digital view are ignored. In developing projects and funding applications, scholars and curators need to be mindful of the process of selection and seek to widen the pool of available digital resources.

Creating Digital Images

In the context of mass digitization enterprises such as Google Books, the creation of digital surrogates of medieval manuscripts can never be more than a small-scale endeavour.[6] It is unavoidably labour-intensive and many

The Curation and Display of Digital Medieval Manuscripts

times more expensive than the automated processes used to digitize nineteenth- and twentieth-century books. In discussing how digital images of medieval manuscripts are made, I am drawing on my own experience, first as a researcher on the Parker on the Web project at Corpus Christi College in Cambridge from 2007 to 2013 and then at Cambridge University Library from 2013 onwards.[7] Parker on the Web was perhaps the first large-scale project to complete the digitization of an entire manuscript library. It was admittedly a relatively small library of some 560 manuscripts, but it is regarded as an extremely significant one, particularly for its early British content.[8]

When the project started, there were few standard protocols for the production of digital images of manuscripts and many decisions had to be made; some of the choices we opted for have been superseded and some are now considered norms. The first decision was what we were trying to capture. The answer: every page of every manuscript, as far as possible. This was in contrast to many digital library sites launched earlier which only displayed a selection of images from each manuscript, such as Digital Scriptorium,[9] or which cherry-picked the choicest selection of manuscripts such as the British Library's Treasures collection.[10] This means that alongside the most significant manuscript of the Anglo-Saxon Chronicle and the sixth-century St Augustine gospels, Parker on the Web also displays every page of an obscure fourteenth-century writing manual.[11] As is now standard, the front and back covers, both inside and outside, and spine of each manuscript were also photographed. The project did not quite meet its aim of photographing every page of every manuscript; a small number of fourteenth- and fifteenth-century paper manuscripts from a Polish convent, not part of Matthew Parker's original bequest to his old college, were so water-damaged and fragile that it was not possible to photograph them completely.[12]

Before being photographed, two essential processes had to take place. First, every single manuscript was assessed by a conservator to ensure that it was physically suitable to undergo photography; and second, a curator checked that every page was uniquely foliated, including the flyleaves. Manuscript bindings, particularly early ones, can be fragile but many nineteenth- and twentieth-century bindings are even more challenging for digitization. Their rigid spines full of glue make it difficult to open the manuscripts sufficiently wide to capture a page image which includes the inner margins, where annotations often reside.

As in most major libraries, the photographic rigs for digitizing manuscripts at Corpus Christi College and at Cambridge University Library incorporate an adjustable cradle which supports the manuscripts at a consistent opening,

269

usually between 90 and 120 degrees, but less if the manuscript (or conservator) does not permit, although this does restrict the area of the page which can be imaged. The page being photographed is placed on a bar which exerts gentle suction to hold it taut and a red LED beam ensures that the page is flat and lined up parallel to the camera. The photographer shoots all the rectos first, one page at a time, and then turns the manuscript and shoots all the versos. The most time-consuming element of digitization is the set-up, which includes colour calibration, focus, and exposure. Once all the arrangements are in place, a skilled photographer can shoot on average 150–200 images per day, though considerably fewer if the manuscript is particularly fragile. In such cases, a conservator may be present to turn the pages. Conservators are closely involved in the digitization process; the original adjustable manuscript cradle was designed by Manfred Mayer, a conservator at the University of Graz, Austria.

Each image is saved as a separate file and the sequence of images then has to be matched against the folio or page numbers of the volume to ensure that the digital copy is complete and that the pages are displayed in the right order. The importance of unambiguous foliation for digital display can demand the numbering or renumbering of manuscript pages; in most cases, this just affects flyleaves but on occasion, the entire foliation of a manuscript may need to be added or changed. Composite manuscripts in which multiple works each have their own foliation, misbound manuscripts in which quires are misplaced, and manuscripts with lots of added slips or missing leaves may all need to be refoliated. If folios are renumbered, the old foliation must be recorded, not least so that references from earlier bibliography can be followed up.

After a manuscript has been photographed, the images undergo quality control checks. These ensure that all the pages have been photographed, that they are in focus and aligned, that the exposure is correct, and the white balance and colour profile are accurate. The images also undergo a certain amount of post-processing. The nature and extent of image processing varies from institution to institution. At Cambridge University Library, it is minimal: the images are rotated, cropped, and straightened; if more than two degrees of straightening is required, the image is reshot. Very large objects such as maps or plans can be photographed in sections and the images digitally stitched together, but the aim is always to provide, as far as possible, a faithful two-dimensional representation of the object.

Displaying Digital Images

When visiting libraries to consult medieval manuscripts in person, we accept that no two reading rooms are alike; each time we have to learn how to order

The Curation and Display of Digital Medieval Manuscripts

a manuscript, what type of rests are available, where the book snakes are kept, and which is the best seat in the room for optimal light and temperature. In the same way, we have become accustomed to adjusting to a huge variety of online viewing experiences. Whether as part of a project site or an institutional digital library, the way the manuscript appears onscreen and the options available for interacting with it are the result of numerous conscious and unconscious decisions and have a significant impact on our experience.

Even the basic modality of viewing varies: do you see one page or two? Early digital projects defaulted to two, consciously attempting to replicate the opening one would find in the reading room but often the two single images were awkwardly melded together and additional traces of facing pages remained in the gutter; the usual view now is single page. Other options, such as thumbnail or scroll views, allow the viewer to see all the pages of a manuscript in sequence which can be useful, for example, for gaining an overview of decorative initials or illustrations or for identifying the start of texts or scribal stints.

Almost all image viewers offer a variety of navigational controls – to make an image bigger or smaller, to zoom in, to move to the next page, or to jump to a new page – but there is little standardization across sites in the functionality offered, the icons used, or the location of these icons on the screen. Designers of institutional digital libraries do draw upon and conduct user-experience research to understand how users interact with their content but are often creating a platform for multiple types of digital objects. The complex non-standard layouts of medieval manuscripts with a different combination of scripts, texts, and decorative features on each page arguably invite a wider variety of forms of engagement with their digital surrogates than printed books or photographs do. To increase the challenge for site designers, users want to interact with digital images on a range of devices, including mobile and touch-screen devices. The screen size makes a big difference to how users experience digital images; even when the dimensions are given or a ruler is included in the photograph, it is still challenging for users to appreciate the actual size of the physical manuscript.[13]

The initial images on screen are generally accompanied by text but, once again, there is little standardization in the content or placement of text across portals. Most sites provide basic descriptive metadata under headings, akin to (and often derived from) an existing catalogue record. However, beyond author (if applicable), title (often supplied by a modern cataloguer), and date (often a range), there is no universally agreed set of fields for describing a medieval manuscript.[14] If the digitized images are part of a project site, the metadata may reflect the particular interests of the project and ignore other types of information. Decisions about what information to include are not straightforward; should items in the margins or non-medieval texts added later be listed? Should every prayer, recipe or letter in a collection be included in a list of contents? The decision made could determine whether it takes a day, a week, or a month to complete the description of an individual manuscript. In many cases, the decision depends on whether the cost implications were assessed before the original project funding application was made.

As mass digitization spread in the late 1990s and early 2000s and each institution and project developed its own portal, it became apparent that no platform was going to meet every user need and furthermore that the potential of digital images for scholarly and public uses could not be realized while they remained siloed in multiple repositories. This was the impetus behind the development of the community-driven International Image Interoperability Framework (IIIF).[15] If institutions adopt this framework, a set of shared application programming interface (API) specifications, the images they publish online can be easily reused by others. Rather than the images having to be downloaded and stored by users, they are served dynamically from the host institution which retains responsibility for storage and long-term preservation. Medieval manuscripts formed key use cases which helped to define the functionality required of IIIF and scholars and curators are still actively involved in its development.[16] Images of the work of an individual artist or scribe now held continents apart can be placed side by side on screen for comparison; disbound manuscripts can be digitally reconstructed from dispersed leaves; libraries of long-dissolved monasteries can be virtually reconstituted; virtual exhibitions can be assembled which would not be physically possible.

The IIIF offers a technical solution, enabling digital images to be reused and recontextualized in innumerable ways. It is an extremely valuable step forward and offers great opportunities for institutions to have their images shared more widely and in richer, more varied settings and for individuals to create their own new contexts for these images. However, many institutions and users are still grappling with complex issues around the use and reuse of digital images, only some of which can be solved by technical advances.

'Publishing' Digital Images

The majority of institutions have traditionally set conditions for the use of images of objects from their collections, distinguishing two categories: private research use and publication, whether commercial or not. This was relatively straightforward to administer when the only images users could obtain were those they purchased from the institution. It has been made

The Curation and Display of Digital Medieval Manuscripts

significantly more complicated, first by institutions publishing their own digital images in digital libraries and repositories, and second, by allowing users to take their own images for free in the reading room for private research use. Many institutions are unwilling to allow such images to be used for publication, whether to ensure that only high-quality images of their manuscripts are published or to preserve an income stream.

Rights and permissions with regard to digital objects are extremely complex; there are national variations in the legal frameworks around copyright and varying interpretations of those frameworks. The availability or otherwise of licences and permissions can have a significant impact on whether and how digital images are reused. Some organizations have made their images completely freely available and eloquent arguments have been made for this approach.[17] Most institutions retain some rights and restrictions over the digital reproduction of collection items, but terms can vary even within a single institution or collection.[18] Having discovered an image online, even on an institutionally hosted page, it can be challenging to track down the conditions of use, even before attempting to determine whether the use envisaged meets the conditions.[19]

Even the basic distinction between 'private use' and 'publication' is increasingly blurred in a digital age.[20] Scholars may once have circulated precious microfilm printouts of hard-to-access manuscripts within tight-knit circles and considered it 'private research use' but should tweeting images from the reading room be considered 'publication'? Social media is increasingly recognized as a fundamental platform for academic and public engagement; it has transformed the discovery, appreciation, and study of manuscripts, particularly by non-specialist audiences. Both institutions and individuals who are alert to this have used manuscript images strategically to build their profiles and promote their brands.[21] Adam Koszary, previously responsible for social media at the Bodleian Libraries in Oxford, describes this as 'old school curation for the digital age'; he emphasizes that it involves just as much work as traditional curation.[22] In an environment in which public impact is highly prized, tangible advantages and opportunities can result from a well-curated Twitter or Instagram feed or a viral meme that strikes a chord.

Social media platforms highlight the constant interplay between institutional and DIY digitization; it is often unclear whether the fragmented manuscript images we encounter on Twitter or Instagram are the product of an expensive high-quality professional process or a camera phone snap. Does it matter? As a curator, I am conscious of the enormous benefits of DIY digitization. It has allowed users to build their own digital archives, particularly of manuscripts not high up the queue for digitization for whatever reason; combined with social media, it has increased the number of opportunities for users to encounter manuscript images. I would argue that it has been at least as transformative of the field of medieval Manuscript Studies as the millions spent on high-quality institutional digitization. Not least, it has fundamentally reshaped the traditional reading room visit; what used to be an archetypal experience of slow looking or slow reading is often now replaced by the rapid rhythm of page turning and image capture.[23]

The two modes of digitization can coexist happily; more important from my perspective is that those sharing manuscript images online cite shelfmarks accurately and, where possible, link to fuller images or texts or other useful information to enable users to contextualize an image they find online. When reusing an image that ultimately derives from an institutional repository, it is helpful to cite its persistent URL, both to enable users to find it and to support the institution in tracking reuse. Curators are often asked to produce quantitative and qualitative evidence of use of digital images to justify internal and external support for digitization projects. This can be a challenge when there is still a degree of opacity about the use of digital images in some academic writing; scholars are not always open about the fact that aspects of their work rely on them. Occasionally errors are made based on the use of decontextualized digital images and scholars need to be alert to this possibility.[24] It is not the case that the physical manuscript needs to be consulted for each and every point made, but it is good practice to be explicit about the particular evidence and sources on which an argument is built. Keeping silent about the use of digitized manuscripts undermines rather than supports the credibility of scholarly work.

Working with Digital Images

Having acknowledged the complexities around the use and reuse of digital images of medieval manuscripts, it is only fair to outline some of the myriad opportunities created by the availability of such images. On a basic level, the availability of digital images enables more people to view and use more manuscripts; it has also fundamentally changed the ways in which scholars and the public 'view' and 'use' medieval manuscripts and makes us question what we mean by those terms. We have already established that digital images are not just facsimiles or surrogates for medieval manuscripts, but are also textual objects in their own right, not just images to be viewed but also data and, as such, raw material to be organized, analysed, annotated, aggregated, mined, linked, manipulated, and visualized. Working with digitized manuscripts, scholars are able to ask new research questions or test out new hypotheses to answer old questions.

The Curation and Display of Digital Medieval Manuscripts

To a large degree, working with digitized manuscripts also provides a fruitful opportunity for collaboration. They can simply be a higher resolution replacement for the grainy microfilm, allowing editors on different continents to work on texts together but they can also open the door to other forms of collaboration, notably between scholars and manuscript-owning institutions and between scholars from different disciplines. Institutions undertaking digitization projects increasingly seek out collaboration with scholars to enrich the curation and display of their digital medieval manuscripts through descriptions, transcriptions, online contextual essays, virtual exhibitions, and use cases. Scholars working on digital manuscript projects utilize the expertise of curators, photographers, conservators, and imaging scientists; many successful projects are genuinely collaborative from the moment of conception. Most of the more advanced imaging of medieval manuscripts is driven by specialist research questions and the full value of such images is only really evident in the context of scholarly selection and interpretation.

Some of the most exciting developments in the creation and use of manuscript images derive from collaborations between medievalists and heritage scientists that fully exploit their properties as digital objects.[25] Advanced imaging technologies and processing techniques are applied to reveal erased text and digitally 'restore' damaged manuscripts. The principal technology employed is multispectral imaging in which multiple images are captured of a single page at different wavelengths across the spectrum from near ultraviolet to near infrared. The data captured are then processed using statistical methods to produce enhanced images. In the case of the Great Parchment Book project, a combination of practical conservation and digital image manipulation rendered a distorted and fire-damaged seventeenth-century manuscript legible.[26]

Before mass digitization, scholars wanting to undertake research into a corpus of manuscripts faced many obstacles in assembling the raw material; they painstakingly compiled collections of microfilm printouts or photocopies of odd pages from facsimiles or reference books. Such activities may still be required; it is unlikely that *every* manuscript one wants to see will be digitized or able to be photographed but it is becoming possible to assemble large corpora of manuscript images. Although not 'big data' on the scale seen in the sciences, these images and their associated metadata are structured datasets and it is possible to conduct computational analysis of their script, layout, decoration, or other elements to compare features and identify patterns.[27] The success of this type of analysis depends on careful curation of the dataset, clear hypotheses to be tested and meaningful contextualization and presentation of results; the skills and experience of the manuscript scholar are just as essential here as in any more 'traditional' research project.

The availability of large quantities of digitized manuscript images is crucial to perhaps the most significant computational challenge relating to manuscripts: the development of machine learning tools for the automatic recognition and transcription of handwritten text. Intensive research is ongoing by several groups. As in optical character recognition for printed text, there are several pre-processing stages such as identifying non-textual elements on the page image and segmenting the text into individual lines. The software then needs to be trained to read a particular script; the Transkribus platform developed by the EU-funded READ project, for example, depends on high-quality images of manuscript pages and a significant quantity of training data, that is, at least 20,000 words of human-generated transcription. Once trained on a particular collection of documents, it can then be run on others of a similar type. Machine-generated transcriptions still require human editing but the error rates on a character level are currently less than 10 per cent. Such transcriptions are readable and, even uncorrected, offer opportunities for keyword searching.[28] The development and application of this technology has the potential to open up huge quantities of unedited manuscript books and documents, to create vast new datasets and to make possible new forms of analysis

Digital images not only facilitate research and engagement at the advanced scholarly level, but also enable individuals who would not normally be able to access manuscripts in person to learn about manuscripts and to contribute to research. Digital manuscript images feature heavily in online educational resources aimed at school or general audiences. Digital manuscripts have also been the focus of a number of MOOCs (Massive Online Open Courses). Crowdsourcing open to both specialist and general audiences has been used successfully by several institutions and projects to identify, tag, annotate, or transcribe manuscript images.[29] Tools such as Omeka enable institutions, individuals, or classes to create and curate impressive online exhibitions and resources, even with limited technical expertise.

Current and Future Challenges

Attempts to predict even the near future with regard to digital resources is always a risky undertaking. The following suggestions are necessarily selective and derive from my curatorial perspective. Before looking forward, it is instructive to reflect on where we are and how far we have come. In 2013, Elaine Treharne, commenting on the inability of 'flat, upright, floating' digital images to convey the qualities of a 'fleshy voluminous book', used the resonant phrase 'incunabula period' to describe the state of manuscript digitization.[30] Martin Foys used the same metaphor in 2015, commenting on

The Curation and Display of Digital Medieval Manuscripts

early digitization efforts which focused on selected, often illuminated folios divorced from their manuscript context.[31] In 2018, Bridget Whearty stated confidently that we are leaving the incunabula age.[32]

If this is the case, then the incunabula period of mass digitization of medieval manuscripts has lasted about 20–25 years. How can this period be characterized and what signifies that we are leaving it? Fifteenth-century printers in some sense sought to imitate and emulate medieval manuscripts, just as early digitization projects aimed to provide users with an experience as close as possible to turning the pages of the manuscript in the reading room.[33] It is notable that page-turning software was considered an essential element of the Parker on the Web digitization project (launched 2009) but was not included in Parker 2.0 (launched 2018). The incunable (literally 'cradle' or by extension 'infancy') period of printing was also characterized by the refining and sharing of techniques, tools, and equipment, by innovation and experimentation – for example, with colour printing – and by the development of norms and standards.

The same applies to the development of mass digitization in the late 1990s and early 2000s; institutions developed their own bespoke solutions to the challenges of holding a page taut, capturing gold illumination, handling scrolls, or displaying pages with foldout sections. These solutions were often copied or shared and standards have evolved. Whole volume digitization (including flyleaves, blank leaves, and covers) is now established as the norm; some institutions now digitize in full any item that is sent to the studio, even if a user only orders a few images. Imaging equipment (cameras, lights, cradles, image processing software) is now fairly standardized and it is likely that technical advances in these areas will provide only incremental improvements; the near future is unlikely to see any significant change in the processes for the capture of digital manuscript images.

There is a considerable appetite from scholars and institutions for more manuscripts to undergo advanced imaging techniques such as multispectral and 3D-imaging as part of what Andrew Prescott and Lorna Hughes term '"slow digitization", in which rapid access is less important than the use of technological and other tools to gradually excavate the complex layers that make up each manuscript'.[34] Other approaches may also be more widely adopted, such as multimedia or virtual reality. All these representations and contextualizations will need to be incorporated effectively into new display formats. Given the costs and time involved in the creation of such resources, in the near future at least, the flat representation of manuscript pages which has become the default will remain standard, for all its imperfections.

As the percentages of manuscripts digitized at large institutions creep up, the biggest challenge in terms of the creation of digital images will be the capture of manuscripts held in smaller institutions. Although we may be reaching a tipping point with some types of high-profile material, such as pre-1200 vernacular manuscripts, it must be remembered that there is a 'long tail' of medieval manuscripts in cathedral libraries, local record offices, public libraries, museums, smaller universities and colleges, independent schools, and historic houses, which collectively possess significant holdings; but many lack the resources or the will to undertake digitization. Ensuring that these manuscripts can be incorporated into the digital scholarly domain is a significant challenge but the creation of a comprehensive image dataset of British medieval manuscripts is fundamental to future research. Collaborations between larger and smaller institutions are one potential solution.

Perhaps the one sign that we are leaving the incunabula age is that there is considerably less discussion about what digitized manuscripts are *not* and more about what they *are*. Rather than focusing on what is lost through digitization, the past few years have seen a growing critical interest in the qualities, properties, contexts, creation histories, and metadata of digitized manuscripts. Scholars are beginning to undertake fruitful investigations into the relationships between digital manuscript images and physical manuscripts, between digital images and their users, and between digital images and their creators, drawing parallels between medieval scribes and the invisible labour of the digitization studio.[35]

As Martin Foys points out, crucial to developing the field of digital manuscript studies beyond the emulation of print are interoperability and the ability to link data.[36] The siloed datasets held in institutional digital libraries, project databases, and websites, whether images, transcriptions, translations, or descriptions, need to be harvestable and networked so that they can be found, combined, interrogated, and easily reused. The development of IIIF is hugely significant in providing a robust and scalable protocol for the use and reuse of images that has been widely implemented by cultural institutions.

It also incorporates the functionality for annotating digital images which, although not widely used in this field at present, has enormous potential. It is already possible for an individual or class or project team to curate their own personalized digital image collection and annotations allow them to contextualize, describe, transcribe, or tell stories with those images. Open source web annotations, which can be linked, shared, tracked, searched, discovered, and stored, are micro-publications; they can serve as teaching resources or research outputs. In addition to human-generated annotations, there is also great potential in automatic image annotation by computer vision for the analysis of large image datasets.

The Curation and Display of Digital Medieval Manuscripts

Interoperability largely relies on a critical mass of content creators consistently adhering to standard models and protocols. Although IIIF has made a big difference, much progress remains to be made in the area of standards relating to textual data. As Whearty points out, 'One of the largest challenges facing interoperability, and the creation of a single, universal digital manuscript hub, lies not in new technology but in old practice.'[37] As I noted earlier, there is no consistent format for describing manuscripts; in addition to the variations in terminology and levels of detail, institutions employ different metadata standards. Libraries, archives, and museums tend to use different formats and cataloguing rules. Libraries in the United States generally catalogue manuscripts in the same system as their printed books; libraries in the UK do not. Whearty's article explores some of the frustrations she encountered in trying to combine metadata about manuscripts from three different digital collections, 'working towards that dream of a single portal through which the digitized manuscripts of the world may be seen'.[38]

To someone embarking on the study of medieval manuscripts, it may seem surprising that such progress has been achieved in the creation of so many digital images and yet there exists no comprehensive cross-institutional method of searching and discovering them; it seems like a fundamental element of the digital landscape is lacking. Medieval British manuscripts are particularly ill served in this regard. Many European countries have developed national portals and promoted national metadata standards which bring together all the digitized manuscripts in their repositories and allow them to be searched; this has not been attempted in the UK.[39] Of course, to be truly effective, any portal must be global. Efforts are underway; international collaboration is surely the way to crack the problems of discoverability and searchability.

Perhaps the greatest challenge of all is ensuring the sustainability of digital manuscript resources. Barring fire, flood, and biblioclasm, medieval manuscripts are icons of survival. In contrast, digital resources are incredibly fragile and transient; online projects disappear as funding dries up, hardware and software become obsolete, storage media fail, digital objects decay. Preservation planning for digital materials needs to be built into every personal and institutional project from dissertation to mass digitization. Creating sustainable digital resources is not just about adhering to standards, producing open data, or keeping back-up copies, important though these are. It also means understanding, embracing, and being transparent about the inevitability of change for both physical and digital objects. As manuscript scholars, we are aware that very few medieval manuscripts preserve their 'original' form and appearance: they have new bindings, repairs, ownership inscriptions, bookplates, library stamps, annotations, manicules, lost leaves, and excised illuminations. We can mourn the loss of a pristine 'original' or we can be curious about what these changes tell us about the reception and use of medieval manuscripts at particular historical moments.

The creation of digital images marks and captures one particular historical moment in the life of a medieval manuscript.[40] Digitization can be a catalyst for physical change, such as conservation work or refoliation; it can provide evidence of the infinitesimally slow process of decay;[41] it can provide access to previous reproductions.[42] Digital images themselves are also subject to change; many institutions which were early adopters of digitization are currently engaged in a virtual rebinding process, transferring images from legacy websites and databases to new digital libraries. This provides additional functionality, ensures the images are more discoverable and reusable and may involve new or updated descriptive metadata, but it is often done without acknowledging the loss and change involved.[43]

The context in which those images were 'originally' published online reflected scholarly understanding and digital practice at that historical moment and is a legitimate object of study for understanding the reception and use of medieval manuscripts in the twentieth and twenty-first centuries. In addition to archiving old sites, institutions need to be explicit and transparent about the nature of the digital resources they are creating; a 'new' interface might incorporate a description from a catalogue written a hundred or more years ago and updated ten years ago alongside digital images taken twenty years ago, without crediting any of the individuals responsible or giving dates for the production of any of these elements. It is important for users now and in the future that institutions capture and present this information, the metadata about their metadata, as fully as possible.

The development of mass digitization and the availability of digital images has transformed how we view and use medieval manuscripts. As the most significant mediators between us and physical manuscripts and the objects of new forms of enquiry, it is crucial that we understand what we are seeing and are able to critically evaluate these sources in order to use them effectively. From my perspective as a curator, digitization has enabled access to manuscripts by a truly global audience and opened up opportunities for research collaboration with manuscript scholars, photographers, conservators, heritage scientists, and software developers. If we really are leaving the incunabula age, it has been an era of rapid change, of innovative experimentation and reactive problem-solving; many challenges are still outstanding. It is now up to institutions and scholars to work together to realize the full potential of digitized images both as chapters in the long histories of medieval manuscripts and as objects in their own right.

The Curation and Display of Digital Medieval Manuscripts

Notes

1. Parker on the Web (https://parker.stanford.edu/parker/) was originally a subscription-only service but Parker 2.0 was released in 2018 as a fully open resource. Perhaps the only remaining large-scale set of digitized images behind a paywall is the Codices Vossiani Latini Online collection hosted by Brill on behalf of Leiden University Library (https://brill.com/abstract/db/cvlo?rskey=4ixNoM&result=1).
2. M. Foys, 'The Remanence of Medieval Media', in J. E. Boyle and H. J. Burgess, eds., *The Routledge Research Companion to Digital Medieval Literature* (London: Routledge, 2018).
3. D. Porter, 'Is This Your Book? What We Call Digitized Manuscripts and Why It Matters', 12 June 2018, www.dotporterdigital.org/is-this-your-book-what-digitiza tion-does-to-manuscripts-and-what-we-can-do-about-it/ (accessed 30 July 2018).
4. See, for example, A. S. G. Edwards, 'Back to the Real?', *The Times Literary Supplement*, 7 June 2013, www.the-tls.co.uk/articles/public/back-to-the-real/ (accessed 20 December 2018).
5. 'Networks of Knowledge: Insular Manuscripts and Digital Potential', 27 June 2018, http://blogs.bl.uk/digitisedmanuscripts/2018/06/networks-of-knowledge-insular-manuscripts-and-digital-potential.html (accessed 30 July 2018).
6. See J. Howard, 'What Happened to Google's Effort to Scan Millions of University Library Books?', 10 August 2017, www.edsurge.com/news/2017-08-10-what-happened-to-google-s-effort-to-scan-millions-of-university-library-books (accessed 20 December 2018).
7. I am indebted to my colleague Amélie Deblauwe, senior digitization technician in the Digital Content Unit at Cambridge University Library, for confirming the details in this section.
8. https://parker.stanford.edu/parker/ (accessed 20 December 2018).
9. https://www.digital-scriptorium.org/ (accessed 20 December 2018).
10. https://www.bl.uk/british-library-treasures/collection-items (accessed 20 December 2018).
11. Respectively, Cambridge, Corpus Christi College, MSS 173, https://parker .stanford.edu/parker/catalog/wp146tq7625; 286 https://parker.stanford.edu /parker/catalog/mk707wk3350; and 445 https://parker.stanford.edu/parker/cat alog/wr530wf1030 (accessed 20 December 2018). The latter was revealed by Ben Albritton on Twitter to be the least-viewed manuscript on Parker on the Web between 2009 and 2018.
12. See, for example, Cambridge, Corpus Christi College, MS 526, https://parker .stanford.edu/parker/catalog/td896qm4276 (accessed 20 December 2018).
13. E. Treharne, 'Fleshing Out the Text: The Transcendent Manuscript in the Digital Age', *Postmedieval* 4.4 (2013), 465–78, at 475–6. Laure Miolo and Alison Hudson, 'Size Matters', British Library medieval manuscripts blog, 23 May 2016, http://blogs .bl.uk/digitisedmanuscripts/2016/05/size-matters.html (accessed 13 July 2018).
14. See Chapter 1 of this volume.
15. https://iiif.io/ (accessed 13 July 2018).
16. See https://iiif.io/community/groups/manuscripts/, 'About' (accessed 13 July 2018).
17. This is the approach followed at the Walters Art Gallery, Baltimore and the University of Pennsylvania. See T. Thoung-Ha, 'The Wide Open Future of the

Art Museum: Q & A with Will Noel', 29 May 2012, https://blog.ted.com/the-wide-open-future-of-the-art-museum-qa-with-william-noel/ (accessed 24 July 2018) and A. Mott, 'The Kislak Center Embraces Open Data', 2 April 2015, https://penntoday.upenn.edu/spotlights/kislak-center-embraces-open-data (accessed 24 July 2018).

18. See the British Library's digital images of medieval manuscripts, which are currently spread across several different services.

19. See M. Terras's series of blogposts on reusing digital content, beginning with https://melissaterras.org/2014/10/06/reuse-of-digitised-content-1-so-you-want-to-reuse-digital-heritage-content-in-a-creative-context-good-luck-with-that/ (accessed 24 July 2018).

20. This topic was discussed in a symposium on DIY digitization held at the Bodleian Libraries in January 2016. The collected papers, edited by Daniel Wakelin and Daryl Green, are in preparation for publication.

21. See, for example, the British Library's @BLMedieval Twitter account with almost 80,000 followers; Damien Kempf of the University of Liverpool (@DamienKempf; over 73,000 followers) and Erik Kwakkel of the University of British Columbia (@erik_kwakkel; over 27,000 followers). (All figures applicable in March 2020.)

22. A. Koszary, 'Lowering the Tone: Doing Social Media at Bodleian Libraries', 15 January 2017, https://artplusmarketing.com/lowering-the-tone-doing-social-media-at-bodleian-libraries-5c6c6d6287ca (accessed 13 July 2018).

23. S. Tishman, *Slow Looking: The Art and Practice of Learning through Observation* (New York: Routledge, 2017) and https://en.wikipedia.org/wiki/Slow_reading (accessed 24 July 2018). See also B. Whearty, 'Adam Scriveyn in Cyberspace: Loss, Labour, Ideology and Infrastructure in Interoperable Reuse of Digital Manuscript Metadata', in M. E. Davis, T. Mahoney-Steel, and E. Turnator, eds., *Meeting the Medieval in a Digital World* (Leeds: ARC Humanities Press, 2018), 157–202, at 159.

24. M. H. Green, K. Walker-Meikle, and W. P. Müller, 'Diagnosis of a "Plague" Image: A Digital Cautionary Tale', *The Medieval Globe* 1 (2014), 309–26, https://scholarworks.wmich.edu/tmg/vol1/iss1/13 (accessed 24 July 2018).

25. Institutions are increasingly realizing the value of heritage science and employing dedicated specialists to work on their collections, such as David Howell at Bodleian Libraries (https://www.bodleian.ox.ac.uk/our-work/heritage-science) and Christina Duffy at the British Library (https://nationalheritagescience forum.wordpress.com/2015/03/14/five-minutes-with-dr-christina-duffy-imaging-scientist-the-british-library/) (accessed 24 July 2018).

26. See www.greatparchmentbook.org.

27. See, for example, the DigiPal project www.digipal.eu.

28. https://read.transkribus.eu/category/success-stories/ (accessed 28 July 2018).

29. See M. Erwin, 'Fragments of Medieval Manuscripts in Printed Books: Crowdsourcing and Cataloging Medieval Manuscript Waste in the Book Collection of the Harry Ransom Center', *Manuscripta* 60 (2016), 188–247.

30. Treharne, 'Fleshing out the Text', 474.

31. M. Foys, 'Medieval Manuscripts: Media Archaeology and the Digital Incunable', in M. Van Dussen and M. Johnston, eds., *The Medieval Manuscript Book: Cultural Approaches* (Cambridge: Cambridge University Press: 2015), 119–39, at 131.

The Curation and Display of Digital Medieval Manuscripts

32. Whearty, 'Adam Scriveyn in Cyberspace', 196.

33. The proprietary 'Turning the Pages' software (http://ttp.onlineculture.co.uk) was designed with this aim.

34. See A. Prescott and L. Hughes, 'Why Do We Digitize? The Case for Slow Digitization', *Archive Journal* (September 2018), www.archivejournal.net/essays/why-do-we-digitize-the-case-for-slow-digitization/ (accessed 20 December 2018).

35. See J. Green, 'Textuality in Transition: Digital Manuscripts as Cultural Artefacts', in G. Hulsman and C. Whelan, eds., *Occupying Space in Medieval and Early Modern Britain and Ireland* (Oxford: Peter Lang, 2016); Whearty, 'Adam Scriveyn in Cyberspace'; B. Mak, *How the Page Matters* (Toronto: Toronto University Press, 2012).

36. Foys, 'Medieval Manuscripts', 133. See also Will Noel's principles around open data which state that it should SUCK – be sustainable, useable, complete, and known, for example, https://twitter.com/Purdom_L/status/294911371735355392, 25 January 2013 (accessed 20 December 2018) and B. Whearty, 'Adam Scriveyn in Cyberspace', 163–4.

37. Whearty, 'Adam Scriveyn in Cyberspace', 164.

38. Ibid., 160.

39. National portals include the French Biblissima (http://beta.biblissima.fr), the German Manuscripta Mediaevalia (www.manuscripta-mediaevalia.de), the Italian Manus Online (https://manus.iccu.sbn.it//), and the Swiss e-codices (www.e-codices.unifr.ch).

40. Whearty, 'Adam Scriveyn in Cyberspace', 196.

41. See A. Dunning, A. Hudson, and C. Duffy, 'Reconstructing Burnt Anglo-Saxon Fragments in the Cotton Collection at the British Library', *Fragmentology*, 1 (2018), 7–37, at 15.

42. Digital Bodleian includes digitized images of several 35 mm slide collections originally created in the 1980s, scanned in 2005 and published online in 2007. Emma Stanford discussed the challenges of creating metadata about a copy of a copy of a copy of a manuscript in an unpublished paper, 'Ethical End-of-Life Care for Digitised Manuscripts: A Case Study from the Bodleian Library', delivered at the Parker Library on the Web 2.0 symposium at Corpus Christi College, Cambridge on 16 March 2018.

43. To give just one example, Oxford, Merton College, MS 249 was originally digitized in 1998 and published on the 'Early Manuscripts at Oxford University' site (http://image.ox.ac.uk). In 2018 it was republished on Digital Bodleian (https://digital.bodleian.ox.ac.uk/inquire/p/ad6e13ec-e70a-4b54-8008-d124fd93a320). As the updated descriptive metadata points out, in the intervening twenty years, the manuscript has been refoliated; thus the page foliated in both modern and medieval hands as 109r is labelled digitally '108r [formerly 109r]'. There is no indication online as to whether the new foliation has been added to the physical manuscript.

13

A. S. G. EDWARDS

Medieval Manuscripts, the Collector, and the Trade

The materials for the study of the history of the commercial trade in medieval manuscripts are usually at best only obliquely reflected in the manuscripts themselves through shelfmarks, signatures, annotations, and bookseller's codes. The retrieval of such a history involves an understanding of the evidence of book lists, auction and bookseller's records, and the inventories of private collectors. Such material is often not easy of access; some of it is non-existent. Yet its potential value to the historian of the book cannot be overemphasized. The details of the movement of manuscripts from owner to owner and the records of prices paid offer evidence of collecting, of connoisseurship and of cultural commodification that has received little developed consideration. And the history of the economic structures that have surrounded the trade in manuscripts that such evidence reveals has yet to be written.

The nature of markets for manuscripts in the Middle Ages in England is generally not easy to understand. We know a certain amount about sites and costs of production, but very little about direct costs to the purchaser and about the market pressures that could shape such costs. And actual retail prices do not survive. Prices that are recorded are almost always for used books, as they were valued for some legal purpose, most often estate valuation, or confiscation, or for purposes of book pledging to loan chests, as was often the case in Oxford and Cambridge colleges,[1] or for annual elections in such colleges, where books were again valued.[2] Such a trade in used books must have been extensive, of course, and must have been to some degree categorized by specialist markets, such as those for university students and teachers, or for lawyers and doctors. But the mechanics of the organization of such selling and the associated costs remain unclear: we assume (by analogy with what has been established for the medieval Paris book trade) that the organization of the selling of secondhand manuscripts depended crucially on the shadowy figure of the stationer, the same figure posited as having a central role in the organization of the production of new manuscripts.[3] In

284

Medieval Manuscripts, the Collector, and the Trade

addition, it is clear that, at least by the fifteenth century, there was an import trade for manuscripts operating in England. Most obviously this included the importation of large numbers of Books of Hours from the Low Countries and parts of France, but it probably also extended to other kinds of books possibly bought speculatively abroad to meet English market demands.[4]

The emergence of a developed production of and trade in printed books in England from the end of the fifteenth century must have limited the demand for new manuscripts. But such a culture clearly continued to exist down to the end of the seventeenth century and must have had commercial underpinning.[5] The appetite for medieval manuscripts is harder to gauge in the sixteenth and seventeenth centuries, but there were evidently a number of collectors of them during this period. The dissolution of the monasteries in the 1530s must have both helped to stimulate such collecting and led to a market glut for medieval manuscripts that probably led to a general depreciation in prices. It also seems to have caused a devaluation of such manuscripts as artefacts, numbers of which were destroyed or used as waste paper (we have the testimony of Bishop John Bale, among others).[6] Some materials, particularly historical ones, were preserved by influential antiquaries and historians, as with those acquired by Matthew Parker and his circle. And such preservation can be linked to the apparent emergence of trade conduits to establish markets to manage this dispersal. Oxford stationer Garbrand Harkes, for example, is reported to have made 'considerable purchases at the sales of monastic libraries' some of which can be subsequently identified in the possession of collectors, but it is unclear where and in what circumstances such sales were held.[7]

It is also unclear whether there were specialist book dealers trading in medieval manuscripts in the later sixteenth and seventeenth century or the extent to which (if they did) they had an effect on value. But by the middle of the seventeenth century the distinctiveness of medieval manuscripts begins to be reflected in the compilation of catalogues. James Ware's *Librorum manuscriptorum in bibliotheca Jacobi Waraei equitis aurati catalogus* (Dublin, 1648) is the first printed catalogue of a private collection of medieval manuscripts. This is the first foreshadowing of Edward Bernard's great catalogue of manuscripts in both public and private libraries, his *Catalogus ... manuscriptorum Angliae et Hiberniae* (1697). Such attempts to organize and record information about individual holdings assembled information of importance to both collectors and dealers.

The interval between these publications saw the emergence in England of a new trade mechanism, the book auction. In 1676, William Cooper, a bookseller and publisher, sold by this means, for the first time in England, the library of Lazarus Seaman. By 1681 Cooper's auctions included

285

manuscripts. By December 1682 he was advertising 'many Curious Manuscripts on Vellam [*sic*]', including a Wycliffe Bible and two copies of Lydgate's *Fall of Princes*.[8] Medieval English manuscripts became a small but recurrent aspect of the early auction trade.[9] The auction provided both a new means of marketing and a potentially volatile element in establishing prices for such material.[10] Initially, even after the advent of the auction, important parts of the trade in manuscripts remained private. Humfrey Wanley, for example, although he made auction purchases for the Harley library, also bought much from individuals.[11] But auctions became an increasingly important element in sales. Of the surviving London auction houses, Sotheby's held its first book auction in 1745, Christie's in 1776, and numerous smaller and/or less long-lived houses appeared from the early eighteenth century onwards.

To mention Wanley and the Harleys is to point to another key factor in the evolution of the medieval manuscript trade, the systematic creation of the major library with a significant collection of manuscripts that was conceived as an enduring collection. This form of acquisition is adumbrated in the activities of sixteenth- and seventeenth-century collectors such as Matthew Parker, Robert Cotton, Thomas Bodley, and William Laud, all of whose libraries were not dispersed on their deaths but instead found permanent homes. The Harleys stand near the beginning of newer patterns of the dispersal and redistribution of smaller collections into larger ones, also seen in the activities of such important collectors as Richard and Thomas Rawlinson and Hans Sloane, which drew as well on the widening range of possibilities for acquisition that were signalled by the development of the auction house and the book dealer as means of acquisition.

For collectors of this kind, with the shaping vision of an enduring library, the relationship with the book trade was one way: the intention was to permanently remove manuscripts from commercial circulation. For other collectors, the scope of collecting ambition was not matched by such clarity of ultimate purpose. Most famously, the activities of Sir Thomas Phillipps, the dispersal of whose enormous library, including over 60,000 manuscripts (not all of them medieval), was not completed until more than 130 years after his death in 1872, show the ways in which individual collectors, sometimes operating in tension with the growing pressures created by institutional buyers, could become crucial factors in the book trade. The complexities of the commercial organization and disposal of such a mass of material has involved a clear understanding of the risks of creating a market glut, which would obviously push down prices, while maintaining a steady flow of new material for purchase.[12]

Medieval Manuscripts, the Collector, and the Trade

If Phillipps was exceptional in the range of his collecting appetite, other collectors have been motivated by a more focused desire to construct a manuscript collection around a particular topic or field. This is not the place to attempt any definition of the various forms such manuscript collecting has taken. But the patterns of acquisition and dispersal of such collections over time have been an important factor in the commercial growth of the trade in manuscripts. Particularly in the twentieth century, such collections as those of Chester Beatty, J. R. Abbey, Dyson Perrins, William and Christina Foyle, Ladislaus von Hoffman, Harry Bradfer-Lawrence, and Wilfred Merton have come back onto the market, usually at auction, but occasionally through dealers, often making available to new generations of collectors 'fresh' materials, that is, those of greatest potential value because they have not recently been on the market.

As it has evolved in modern times, the trade in medieval manuscripts involves the collector, the specialist dealer, and the auction house. The collector may be an individual or an institution, usually a library if the latter. In either case the collector is likely to have a relationship with a dealer or dealers, who may advise and bid on their behalf at auction, and, in the appropriate circumstances, arrange an export licence for items acquired on the collector's behalf.

Dealers may also acquire items on their own behalf at auction for their stock and subsequent resale, although such purchases may be made privately from either individuals or institutions, who themselves may choose to consign their property to an auction house for sale. Sometimes, groups of dealers form ad hoc consortia to either buy from individuals or at auction.

There are potentially different financial implications to either course of action. A dealer may buy outright at an agreed price from a vendor; or he may take manuscripts on consignment and sell them on behalf of the vendor for an agreed percentage. The financial prospects for the vendor are less clear-cut if manuscripts are sold at auction. Auction house do not normally guarantee a minimum price so there are elements of chance in what can happen at the time of the auction. To some extent a vendor is protected by establishing a reserve (see below) on items to be sold. This means that if an item does not achieve a specified minimum price in the sale, it is deemed unsold and the vendor will retain possession of it. If it does sell, the auction house will charge a vendor's premium (as well as a buyer's premium). The vendor may be liable for various charges (insurance and photography costs, for example) even if a lot does not actually sell at auction.

Both auction house and dealer share certain commonly acknowledged responsibilities to their clients as they engage in their business. The first is to establish the vendor's clear title to what is being sold. This will often

287

involve study of the provenance of a manuscript to establish details of its earlier ownership and sale history. Such evidence may form part of a published manuscript description (see below), but it need not. There is no necessity on the part of either dealer or auction house to publicly identify a vendor, or to give details of the ownership history of a manuscript unless there is a legal challenge to its title, though such information is generally likely to be divulged to at least some degree in a sale catalogue, particularly if the manuscript has been previously owned by prominent collectors or by other figures of historical interest; in such circumstances this information may potentially add to its value.

The establishing of title is an obvious aspect of due diligence on the part of any vendor's agent. Another part, equally crucial, is the accurate description of what is to be sold. Over time, sale catalogue descriptions of manuscripts have evolved from simple records of author and title (not always accurate) to detailed descriptions of the physical form and content of a manuscript. The amount of detail in a manuscript description is likely to reflect its potential profitability: those that are likely to be the most expensive will usually be described in the greatest detail. But any description of an item offered for sale has potential legal implications, and detailed descriptive accuracy is now a general feature of sale catalogues of any kind, often accompanied by illustration. Any description of a manuscript will normally include full details of its physical size and material(s), its collation, that is, the sequence of quires with details of any loss of leaves, description of its decoration, including illustration, a general statement about overall condition (the degree of damage it has suffered over time, from water or rodents, for example) as well as (very likely) some account of its provenance, the history of its earlier ownership (with the provisos noted above). Major auction houses and dealers draw on a specialist staff and often the services of consultants in drawing up descriptions. Such expertise means that manuscripts are catalogued to a high standard.

The final element of a manuscript description in a sale catalogue will be a statement about its price. In the case of a dealer's catalogue this will be an actual published price, although this may be higher than that which is actually paid by a client. Thus, regular clients of a dealer may reasonably expect to receive a discount on a purchase, as may customers making multiple purchases at one time. It is not unheard of for dealers to include items already sold in a catalogue at a higher price. In the case of an auction, the catalogue description price will be an estimate, within a range, indicating the lower and higher possibilities that a manuscript is felt likely realize in the sale. In the past such estimates were confidential, but now they are usually published with the catalogue description. The lower estimate often

Medieval Manuscripts, the Collector, and the Trade

constitutes the 'reserve', the price below which it will not be sold, at which it will be bought in by the auctioneer. In some instances, such reserves are not binding on the auction house and are intended only as a guide to the potential bidder; the auctioneer may have discretion to sell below the reserve. Not infrequently there may be what are termed 'post sale opportunities', whereby a dealer or other purchaser may be able to negotiate with the auction house a sale after the auction for an unsold item, with the approval of the vendor. Such procedures are standard auction practice.

The lower end of the reserve price provides security to the vendor, and also to the auction house. It ensures against either party suffering an unreasonable loss on an item. In the past it has also been a means of resisting the operation of any 'ring', an ad hoc consortium of dealers or individuals who by operating in concert in the auction room conspire to keep prices low in the sale. Any items acquired through such activity would then be privately resold among the members of the ring. 'Ringing' is illegal and it is unlikely that it now occurs at major auctions.[13]

How prices are established by auction houses or dealers depends on an experienced sense of markets for particular works or kinds of works about which it is not easy to generalize. But two factors are likely to play important parts in setting prices or (in the case of auction houses) reserves. These are condition and rarity. The latter is likely to be of the greater importance. Even small fragments in not particularly good condition may, at times, achieve high prices because they are of a kind that rarely appears on the market. For example, on 8 July 2014 Sotheby's (London) sold, as lot 1, two small strips (90 × 23 mm; 95 × 22 mm) from a tenth-century English Gospel Book. They fetched £105,000, the highest price in the sale (against an pre-sale estimate of £20,000–30,000). The price clearly reflected an appreciation of the infrequency with which manuscripts in Old English of any kind or size come up for sale.

On the other hand, it is possible to massively overestimate likely market prices. For example, the sale of the first part of the Arcana collection at Christie's on 7 July 2010 included (lot 30) a Psalter/Book of Hours produced in England in the fourteenth century for Elizabeth de Bohun. This was a lavish manuscript with a number of miniatures and high-quality decoration throughout. The catalogue described it as 'THE MOST SUMPTUOUS FOURTEENTH-CENTURY ENGLISH ILLUMINATED MANUSCRIPT LIKELY EVER TO APPEAR ON THE OPEN MARKET.' The pre-sale estimate was £2m–3m (it had previously made £1.54m when sold at Sotheby's, 21 June, 1988, lot 52). But bidding stopped at £1.5m and it was bought in. Clearly the market felt, for whatever reasons, that the reserve price overvalued it.

Prices themselves at auction sales are not simply unpredictable, but also difficult to interpret, since the final price is composed of a number of elements. The first of these is the 'hammer price'. This is the price the manuscript actually achieves in the saleroom. But this is not the final price, which will include the various vendor's and buyer's premiums that are added and in some situations the addition of local or national charges such as (in England) Valued Added Tax (VAT).

Until the quite recent past, some auction houses have been reluctant to identify publicly lots that failed to sell and have concealed the fact of such failure by giving these lots fictitious names and prices. This can create difficulties for anyone seeking to identify the present location of a particular item from earlier auction records, those, that is, up to the 1970s. Manuscripts that are unsold at auction are now explicitly identified as such by the auctioneer in the sale itself, generally by the word 'pass', and such unsold lots are not recorded in any published sale results. But identification of buyers in general is now more difficult in other respects because, since the mid-1980s, manuscripts have not sold to identified individuals or dealers but by numbered paddles to preserve buyer confidentiality. And much more bidding now takes place over the telephone or internet.

It is worth emphasizing that those involved in the commercial trade in manuscripts are not just concerned with commerce, as agents for vendors or buyers. As experts, both dealers and auction houses also have roles as consultants and advisors for individuals and institutions, often valuing manuscripts that are offered to the nation or to public institutions either for purchase or to offset inheritance tax liabilities. Members of the trade may also serve on the Waverley Committee that oversees the granting of export licences for manuscripts.

The study of the commercial trade in manuscripts is of relevance to the manuscript student in part because of the descriptive record sale catalogues provide of the physical form and content of particular manuscripts; such descriptions, and accompanying illustrations, often provide the only detailed descriptive record of such manuscripts. Modern sale catalogues often supply very reliable manuscript descriptions and are hence of considerable scholarly value.

These descriptions also offer the possibility of retrieving information about the history of their transmission from collection to collection, that is, their provenance. The study of such transmission can involve the history of individual collectors and libraries and the assemblage and dispersal of their collections, the histories of individual book dealers and of auction houses that have been involved in the sale of books, and the history of individual

Medieval Manuscripts, the Collector, and the Trade

manuscripts as they have passed through the hands of these persons and institutions.

This general concern with transmission from owner to owner achieves a particular urgency in some situations. The interplay of all these elements can become particularly relevant in circumstances where manuscripts have been subject to mutilation or breaking up and where consequently individual parts of the same manuscript, or even separate leaves, have been sold separately after it has been sold at auction.[14] For example, on 13 June 1983, in the sale of the Marquess of Bute's manuscripts, lot 32 was a previously unrecorded manuscript of Chaucer's *Treatise on the Astrolabe* together with other texts in verse and prose in Middle English and Latin. The manuscript was bought by New York dealer H. P. Kraus, who broke it into several parts, one of which was sold to a private collector in Japan, another to an American collector, Lawrence J. Schoenberg, his MS LJS 188, now in the University of Pennsylvania Library, and a third to the Huntington Library, in California, now MS 60320. The tracking of such processes of commercial fragmentation through the sale catalogues of individual dealers, libraries, and collectors can be a complex process. At times, however, the expertise of dealers can lead to the restoration of important fragments to their larger context, as with Richard Linenthal's recent discovery and identification of a single leaf from a very significant early manuscript of John Gower's *Confessio Amantis*.[15] At others, a wide-ranging knowledge of the commercial trade in fragments can make possible at least the partial reconstruction of manuscripts that have been broken up for commercial purposes.

Some understanding of the ways in which the book trade operates is necessary for students of manuscripts. There is no general overview of the whole subject of the buying and selling of manuscripts. John Carter's *Taste and Technique in Book Collecting* (Cambridge, 1948; 2nd edn, London, 1970) is still the best overview of the history of book collecting in general; hence his observations have applicability to the field of manuscript collecting. A. N. L. Munby's *Connoisseurs and Medieval Miniatures* (Oxford, 1972) has much valuable information about English manuscript collectors. There are various studies of individual collectors. Seymour de Ricci, *English Collectors of Books & Manuscripts (1530–1930)* (Cambridge and New York, 1930) contains useful information about specific sales and collectors. William Younger Fletcher, *English Book Collectors* (London, 1902) is less extensive in range but more detailed in its examination of those collectors it discusses. Bernard Quaritch, ed., *Contributions towards a Dictionary of English Book-Collectors* (1892; reprinted New York, 1968) contains useful, if uneven, information. The most detailed discussion of an individual English collector is A. N. L. Munby's five-volume *Phillipps*

Studies (Cambridge, 1951–60), an examination of the assemblage and dispersal of Sir Thomas Phillipps's library, the greatest ever assembled in this country. There are also useful biographical accounts of a number of (mainly American) collectors in the various biographies of members of the Grolier Club of New York, collected in *Grolier 75: A Biographical Retrospective to Celebrate the Seventy-Fifth Anniversary of the Grolier Club in New York* (New York, 1959) and *Grolier 2000: A Further Biographical Retrospective in Celebration of the Millenium* (New York, 2000), and in Donald C. Dickinson, *Directory of American Book Collectors* (New York, 1986). The journal the *Book Collector* (1952–) has two intermittent series, 'Portrait of a Bibliophile' and 'Contemporary Collectors', which discuss individual collectors of different periods and countries. Nicolas Barker's recent *The Roxburghe Club: A Bicentennial History* (London, 2012) has biographical accounts of members of this most exclusive society of book collectors from its beginnings in 1812.

Individual firms and book dealers are the subject of a rather shapeless literature. Some English dealers have found their way into the *Oxford Dictionary of National Biography* (2004–) but the field is generally underrepresented there. There is a small number of autobiographies or biographies of major dealers who were significantly involved with medieval manuscripts. These include H. P. Kraus's autobiography *A Rare Book Saga* (London, 1979), and Edwin Wolf and John Fleming, *Rosenbach* (London, 1960), the biography of Philadelphia dealer A. S. W. Rosenbach. Others figure in the *Oxford Companion to the Book*, ed. Henry Woudhuysen and Michael Suarez (Oxford, 2010).

There are few histories of firms involved in book dealing or of auction houses. On early book auctions, see John Lawler, *Book Auctions in England in the Seventeenth Century* (London, 1896). Frank Herrmann's *Sotheby's: Portrait of an Auction House* (London, 1980) includes useful information. There is no comparable history of Christie's, nor are there histories of such major dealers as Maggs and Quaritch, both of whom have been prominent in the trade in medieval manuscripts since the late nineteenth century. Some, but not all, of the records of both firms are deposited in the British Library, Department of Manuscripts, but information about sales by both firms is not always easy to recover. The annotated auctioneer's copies of the printed sale catalogues of Sotheby's up to 1970 have been placed in the British Library (SC Sotheby (1)). These include records of buyers and prices. It should be noted that this information is not always to be taken at face value, since up to this date and beyond efforts were made to conceal the fact that an item was unsold and bought in by the use of *noms de vente* and of spurious prices. Christie's sale records remain in the firm's possession.[16]

Medieval Manuscripts, the Collector, and the Trade

Locating specific sale catalogues can be a complicated and frustrating business. Much useful information about where such catalogues can be found is in David Pearson, *Provenance Research in Book History* (London, 1994, esp. pp. 132–69); a new edition was published by the Bodleian Library in 2019. There is also much valuable information in A. N. L. Munby and Lenore Coral, *British Book Sale Catalogues 1676–1800: A Union List* (London, 1977). The Schoenberg database, now housed at the University of Pennsylvania, contains much material on sales, but it is not always easy to search, is incomplete, and is not always accurate. It is, however, being regularly updated. For the period from 1987 to 2012 the publication *English Manuscript Studies, 1100–1700* had regular articles recording English manuscripts sold at auction or in dealer's catalogues. The Department of Manuscripts in the British Library has on open access a regularly updated file of 'Restricted Photographs'. The 'RP' file contains details of manuscripts that have been granted an export licence, with information about the purchaser; when such a licence is granted, the exporting purchaser is sometimes required to provide a facsimile of the manuscript, in part or in whole, as specified by the licence, which is deposited in the British Library. Access to these images is sometimes time-restricted. But 'RP' is a British Library shelfmark and such images of exported manuscripts can be called up under it by researchers. It is also relevant to note that the British Library's Department of Manuscripts has its own collection of sale catalogues, which does include catalogues that are not in the main collection. This collection is part of the British Library's holdings and readers are entitled to request catalogues from it. They sometimes contain useful annotations by members of the department about purchasers and prices.

Notes

I gratefully acknowledge advice and information on specific points from Christopher de Hamel, Margaret Lane Ford, and Richard Linenthal.

1. See, for example, G. Pollard, 'Medieval Loan Chests at Cambridge', *Bulletin of the Institute of Historical Research*, 17 (1939–40), 113–29; and R. Lovatt, 'Two Collegiate Loan Chests in Late Medieval Cambridge', in P. N. R. Zutshi, ed., *Medieval Cambridge: Essays on the Pre-reformation University* (Woodbridge: Boydell Press, 1993), 129–65. A pledged Bible was sold at Sotheby's, 18 June 1991, lot 74.
2. See E. Leedham-Green, 'University Libraries and Book-sellers', in L. Hellinga and J. B. Trapp, eds., *The History of the Book in Britain, Volume III: 1400–1457* (Cambridge: Cambridge University Press, 1999), 323–6.
3. See P. Christianson, 'The Rise of the London Book Trade,' in Hellinga and Trapp, eds., *The History of the Book in Britain, Volume III*, 128–47.

293

4. See, for example, J. D. Farquhar, *Creation and Imitation: The Work of a Fifteenth-century Manuscript Illuminator* (Fort Lauderdale, FL: Nova University Press, 1976).

5. See, for example, H. Woudhuysen, *Sir Philip Sydney and the Circulation of Manuscripts, 1558–1640* (Oxford: Clarendon Press, 1996); P. Beal, *In Praise of Scribes: Manuscripts and Their Makers in Seventeenth-century England* (Oxford: Clarendon Press, 1998).

6. See C. E. Wright, 'The Dispersal of the Libraries in the Sixteenth Century', in F. Wormald and C. E. Wright, eds., *The English Library before 1700* (London: Athlone Press, 1958), 148–75, at 153–4.

7. E. G. Duff, *A Century of the English Book Trade* (London: Bibliographical Society, 1905), 66.

8. J. Lawler, *Book Auctions in England in the Seventeenth Century* (London: Elliot Stock, 1896), 24.

9. R. Beadle, 'Medieval English Manuscripts at Auction 1676–c.1700', *The Book Collector*, 53 (2004), 46–63.

10. See F. Herrmann, 'The Emergence of the Book Auctioneer as a Professional', in R. Myers and R. Harris, eds., *The Property of a Gentleman: The Formation, Organization and Dispersal of the Private Library 1620–1920* (Winchester: St Paul's Bibliographies, 1991), 1–14.

11. See C. E. Wright and R. C. Wright, eds., *The Diary of Humfrey Wanley, 1715–1726*, 2 vols. (London: Bibliographical Society, 1966).

12. See A. Hobson, 'The Phillipps Sales', in G. Mandelbrote, ed., *Out of Print and into Profit: A History of the Rare and Secondhand Book Trade in Britain in the Twentieth Century* (London: British Library, 2006), 157–64.

13. See A. Freeman and J. Ing Freeman, *Anatomy of an Auction: Rare Books at Ruxley Lodge 1919* (London: Book Collector, 1990).

14. See C. de Hamel, *Cutting up Manuscripts for Pleasure and Profit* (Charlottesville, VA: Book Arts Press, 1996).

15. B. Quaritch, *Bookhands of the Middle Ages: VI. Medieval Manuscripts Leaves and Binding Fragments* (London: Bernard Quaritch, 2000), no. 55 (with plate); A. S. G. Edwards and T. Takamiya 'A New Fragment of Gower's *Confessio Amantis*', *Modern Language Review*, 96 (2001), 931–6.

16. See further, ' Appendix: Book Auctions at Christie's and Sotheby's', in R. Myers, M. Harris, and G. Mandelbrote, eds., *Under the Hammer: Book Auctions since the Seventeenth Century* (London: British Library Publications and Oak Knoll Press, 2001), 231–6.

GUIDE TO FURTHER READING

The contributors to this volume have used a wide array of sources, references to which can be found in the endnotes to each chapter. The following listed sources are of general use to manuscript scholars. References correspond to the three major sections of this volume – How, Why, and Where do we study the manuscript? Works which are applicable to more than one section have not been duplicated; readers are advised to scrutinize all recommended readings.

For technical terms, and for Glossaries to Manuscript Studies, see, in particular, M. B. Parkes, *Their Hands before our Eyes: A Closer Look at Scribes* (Aldershot: Ashgate, 2008); O. Da Rold, T. Kato, M. Swan, and E. Treharne, *The Production and Use of English Manuscripts, 1060–1220* (Leicester: University of Leicester, 2010), https:// em1060.stanford.edu; Denis Muzurelle, Vocabulaire codicologique: Répertoire méthodique des termes français relatifs aux manuscrits, avec leurs équivalents en anglais, italien, espagnol. Sous le patronage du comité international de paléographie latine. Edition hypertextuelle, Version 1.1, 2002–2003, http://vocabulaire.irht.cnrs.fr /pages/vocab2.htm; and David Burnley and Alison Wiggins, eds., 'Glossary of technical terms' in 'The Auchinleck Manuscript (NLS Adv MS 19.2.1), www.nls.uk/auchinleck/ editorial/glossary-nav.html.

Part I How Do We Study the Manuscript?

Alexander, J. J. G., *Medieval Illuminators and their Methods of Work* (New Haven and London: Yale University Press, 1992)
  ed., *A Survey of Manuscripts Illuminated in the British Isles*, 6 vols. (London: Harvey Miller, 1975–96)
Alexander, J. J. G. and P. Binski, eds., *Age of Chivalry: Art in Plantagenet England, 1200–1400* (London: Collins, 1987)
Badham, S., J. Blair, and R. Emmerson, *Specimens of Lettering of English Monumental Brasses* (London: Longman, 1976)
Barnet, S., *A Short Guide to Writing about Art* (orig. pub. Boston: Little & Brown, 1981)
Bat-Yehouda, M. Z., *Le Papier au Moyen Âge: Histoire et Techniques* (Turnhout: Brepols, 1999)
Bately, J., M. Brown, and J. Roberts, eds., *A Palaeographer's View: The Selected Writings of Julian Brown* (London: Harvey Miller, 1993)

295

FURTHER READING

Beadle, R., *Henry Bradshaw and the Foundations of Codicology: The Sandars Lectures 2015* (Cambridge: Langham Press, 2017)

Beadle, R. and A. J. Piper, eds., *New Science out of Old Books: Studies in Manuscripts and Early Printed Books in Honour of A. I. Doyle* (Aldershot: Scolar Press, 1995)

Beit-Arié, M., *Hebrew Manuscripts of East and West: Towards a Comparative Codicology* (London: British Library, 1992)

Bisagni, J., 'Prolegomena to the Study of Code-Switching in Old Irish Glosses', *Peritia*, 24–25 (2014), 1–58

Bishop, T. A. M., *English Caroline Minuscule* (Oxford: Clarendon Press, 1970)

Blockley, M., 'Addenda and Corrigenda to N. R. Ker's "A Supplement to *Catalogue of Manuscripts Containing Anglo-Saxon*"', *Notes and Queries*, 29 (1982), 1–3.

Breay, C. and J. Story, eds., *Anglo-Saxon Kingdoms: Art, Word, War* (London: British Library, 2018)

Briquet, C.-M., *Les Filigranes: Dictionaire Historique des Marques du Papier . . .*, ed. A. Stevenson, 4 vols. (Amsterdam: Paper Publications Society, 1968)

Brown, C. and R. H. Robbins, *Index of Middle English Verse* (New York: printed for the Index Society by Columbia University Press, 1943)

Brown, M. P., *Understanding Illuminated Manuscripts: A Guide to Technical Terms* (London: British Library, 1994)

Brown, M. P., I. H. Garipzanov, and B. C. Tilghman, eds., *Graphic Devices and the Early Decorated Book* (Woodbridge: Boydell, 2017)

Buridant, C., '*Translatio medievalis*: Théorie et pratique de la traduction médiévale', *Travaux de linguistique et de littérature*, 21 (1983), 81–136

Burnett, C., *The Introduction of Arabic Learning into England* (London: British Library, 1997)

Burnley, D. and A. Wiggins, eds., 'Glossary of technical terms', in 'The Auchinleck Manuscript (NLS Adv MS 19.2.1)', www.nls.uk/auchinleck/editorial/glossary-nav.html

Busby, K., *Codex and Context: Reading Old French Verse Narrative in Manuscript*, 2 vols. (Amsterdam: Rodopi, 2002)

Büttner, F. O. ed., *The Illuminated Psalter: Studies in the Content, Purpose and Placement of Its Images* (Turnhout: Brepols, 2004)

Cappelli, A., *Dizionario di Abbreviature latine ed italiane*, 6th edn (Milan: Hoepli, 1967)

Careri, M., C. Ruby, and I. Short, *Livres et écritures en français et en occitan au XIIe siècle: Catalogue illustré* (Rome: Viella, 2011)

Cherubini, P. and A. Pratesi, *Paleografia Latina: L'avventura grafica del mondo occidentale* (Vatican City: Scuola vaticana di paleografia, diplomatica e archivistica, 2010)

Cigni, F., ed. and Italian trans., *Il romanzo arturiano di Rustichello da Pisa* (Pisa: Pacini, 1994)

Clemens, R. and T. Graham, *Introduction to Manuscript Studies* (Ithaca and London: Cornell University Press, 2007)

Collins, R. L., *Anglo-Saxon Vernacular Manuscripts in America* (New York: Pierpont Morgan Library, 1976)

Conner, P. W., 'On the Nature of Matched Scribal Hands', in J. Wilcox, ed., *Scraped, Stroked and Bound: Materially Engaged Readings of Medieval Manuscripts* (Turnhout: Brepols, 2013), 39–73

FURTHER READING

Da Rold, O., 'Codicology', in S. Echard and R. Rouse, eds., *The Encyclopaedia of Medieval British Literature* (Oxford: Wiley-Blackwell, 2017)

Delaissé, L. M. J., 'Towards a History of the Mediaeval Book', *Miscellanea André Combes* (1967), 28–39

De la Mare, A. C., *Catalogue of the Collection of Medieval Manuscripts Bequeathed to the Bodleian Library, Oxford by James P. R. Lyell* (Oxford: Clarendon Press, 1971)

Delisle, J. and J. Wordsworth, eds., *Translators through History*, rev. edn (Amsterdam/Philadelphia: John Benjamins, 2012)

Denholm-Young, N., *Handwriting in England and Wales* (Cardiff: University of Wales Press, 1964)

Derolez, A., *The Handwriting of Gothic Manuscript Books* (Cambridge: Cambridge University Press, 2003)

Destrez, J., *La Pecia Dans les Manuscrits Universitaires du XIIIe et du XIVe siècle* (Paris: J. Vautrain, 1935)

Doyle, A. I., 'Book Production by the Monastic Orders in England (c.1375–1530): Assessing the Evidence', in L. L. Brownrigg, ed., *Medieval Book Production: Assessing the Evidence* (Los Altos Hills, CA: Anderson-Lovelace, 1990), 1–19

'Introduction to Neil Ker's Elements of Medieval English Codicology', *English Manuscript Studies*, 14 (2008), 244–5

Driver, M., '"Me fault faire": French Makers of Manuscripts for English Patrons', in J. Wogan-Browne et al., eds., *Language and Culture in Medieval Britain: The French of England c.1100–c.1500* (York: York Medieval Press, 2009), 420–43

Dumville, D. N., *English Caroline Script and Monastic History: Studies in Benedictinism, AD 950–1030* (Woodbridge: Boydell Press, 1993)

'English Square Minuscule Script: The Background and Earliest Phases', *Anglo-Saxon England*, 16 (1987), 147–79

'English Square Minuscule Script: The Mid-Century Phases', *Anglo-Saxon England*, 23 (1994), 133–64

A Palaeographer's Review: The Insular System of Scripts in the Early Middle Ages, Vol. 1 (Osaka: Institute of Oriental and Occidental Studies, Kansai University, 1999)

Duncan, E., *A History of Gaelic Script* (unpublished PhD thesis, University of Aberdeen, 2010)

Gameson, R., ed., *The Cambridge History of the Book in Britain, Volume I: c.400–1100* (Cambridge: Cambridge University Press, 2012)

Gaskell, P., *A New Introduction to Bibliography* (Oxford: Clarendon Press, 1972)

Gilissen, L., *Prolégomènes à la Codicologie: Recherches sur la construction des cahiers et la mise en page des manuscrits médiévaux* (Ghent: Éditions Scientifiques Story-Scientia, 1977)

Gillespie, A. and D. Wakelin, eds., *The Production of Books in England* (Cambridge: Cambridge University Press, 2011)

Gneuss, H. and M. Lapidge, *Anglo-Saxon Manuscripts: A Bibliographical Handlist of Manuscripts and Manuscript Fragments Written or Owned in England up to 1100* (Toronto: University of Toronto Press, 2014)

Griffiths, J. and D. Pearsall, eds., *Book Production and Publishing in Britain 1375–1475* (Cambridge: Cambridge University Press, 1989)

Gullick, M., ed., *Pen in Hand: Medieval Scribal Portraits, Colophons and Tools* (Walkern: Red Gull Press, 2006)

FURTHER READING

Gumbert, J. P., 'Ruling by Rake and Board: Notes on Some Late Medieval Ruling Techniques' in P. Ganz, ed., *The Role of the Book in Medieval Culture* (Turnhout: Brepols, 1986), 41–54

'Sizes and Formats', in M. Maniaci and P. F. Munafò, eds., *Ancient and Medieval Book Materials and Techniques* (Vatican City: Biblioteca apostolica vaticana, 1993), 227–63

'Skins, Sheets and Quires', in D. Pearsall, ed., *New Directions in Manuscript Studies* (Woodbridge: Boydell Press, 2000), 81–90

Hanna, R., 'Booklets in Medieval Manuscripts: Further Considerations', *Studies in Bibliography*, 39 (1986), 100–11

'Middle English Books and Middle English Literary History', *Modern Philology*, 102 (2004), 157–78

Pursuing History: Middle English Manuscripts and Their Texts (Stanford: Stanford University Press, 1996)

Heawood, E., 'Sources of Early English Paper Supply', *The Library*, 4th series, 10 (1929–30), 282–307, 427–54

Hector, L. C., *The Handwriting of English Documents* (London: E. Arnold, 1958)

Heimann, D. and R. Kay, *The Elements of Abbreviation in Medieval Latin Palaeography* (Lawrence, KA: University of Kansas Libraries, 1982)

Holcomb, M., *Pen and Parchment: Drawing in the Middle Ages* (New Haven and London: Yale University Press for the Metropolitan Museum of Art, New York, 2009)

Inghilleri, M., and C. Baker, 'Ethics', in M. Baker and G. Saldanha (eds.), *Routledge Encyclopedia of Translation Studies*, 2nd edition (Abingdon: Routledge, 2009), pp. 100–04

James, M. R., *A Descriptive Catalogue of the Manuscripts Other than Oriental in the Library of King's College, Cambridge* (Cambridge: Cambridge University Press, 1895)

Jolliffe, P. S., *A Check-List of Middle English Prose Writings of Spiritual Guidance* (Toronto: Pontifical Institute of Medieval Studies, 1974)

Jones, L. W., 'Pricking Manuscripts: The Instruments and Their Significance', *Speculum*, 21 (1946), 389–403

Karkov, C., *The Art of Anglo-Saxon England* (Woodbridge: Boydell Press, 2011)

Ker, N. R., *Catalogue of Manuscripts Containing Anglo-Saxon* (Oxford: Clarendon Press, 1957, repr., 1991)

'Elements of Medieval English Codicology (1944)', *English Manuscript Studies*, 14 (2008), 246–50

Medieval Libraries of Great Britain, 2nd edn (London: Offices of the Royal Historical Society, 1964)

'A Supplement to *Catalogue of Manuscripts Containing Anglo-Saxon*', *Anglo-Saxon England*, 5 (1976), 121–31

Ker, N. R. et al., *Medieval Manuscripts in British Libraries*, 5 vols. (Oxford: University Press, 1969–92)

Kwakkel, E., 'Biting, Kissing and the Treatment of Feet: The Transitional Script of the Long Twelfth Century', in E. Kwakkel, R. McKitterick, and R. M. Thomson, eds., *Turning over a New Leaf: Change and Development in the Medieval Manuscript* (Leiden: Leiden University Press, 2012), 79–125

FURTHER READING

Lees, C. A., ed., *The Cambridge History of Early Medieval Literature* (Cambridge: Cambridge University Press, 2013)

Lehmann, S., 'La Mise en scène du texte scientifique à la fin du moyen âge: propriétés macro- et microstructurelles', in O. Bertrand, ed., *Sciences et savoirs sous Charles V* (Paris: Champion, 2014), 87–112

Lieftinck, G. I., 'Pour une nomenclature de l'écriture livresque de la période dite gothique', in B. Bischoff, G.I. Lieftinck, and G. Batelli, eds., *Nomenclature des écritures livresques du IXe au XVIe siècle* (Paris : Centre National de la Recherche Scientifique, 1953)

Lindsay, W. M., *Notae Latinae: An Account of Abbreviation in Latin Manuscripts of the Early Minuscule Period, c. 700–850* (Cambridge: University Press, 1915)

Lowe, E. A., *The Beneventan Script: A History of the South Italian Minuscule* (Oxford: Clarendon Press, 1914)

English Uncial (Oxford: Clarendon Press, 1960)

Mallon, J., *De l'écriture: recueil d'études publiées de 1937 à 1981* (Paris: Editions du Centre national de la recherche scientifique, 1986)

Martin, H. J. and J. Vezin, *Mise-en-page et mise-en-texte du livre manuscrit* (Paris: Éditions du Cercle de la librairi–Promodis, 1990)

Matheson, L. M., *The Prose Brut: The Development of a Middle English Chronicle* (Tempe: Medieval and Renaissance Texts and Studies, 1998)

Mooney, L. R. and E. Stubbs, *Scribes and the City: London Guildhall Clerks and the Dissemination of Middle English Literature, 1375–1425* (York: York Medieval Press, 2013)

Morison, S., *'Black-Letter' Text* (Cambridge: Cambridge University Press, 1942)

Politics and Script: Aspects of Authority and Freedom in the Development of Graeco-Latin Script from the Sixth Century BC, ed. N. Barker (Oxford: Clarendon Press, 1972)

Murano, G., 'Zibaldoni (Commonplace Books)', *Scriptorium*, 67 (2013), 394–406

Muzurelle, D., Vocabulaire codicologique: Répertoire méthodique des termes français relatifs aux manuscripts, avec leurs équivalents en anglais, italien, espagnol. Sous le patronage du comité international de paléographie latine. Edition hypertextuelle, Version 1.1, 2002–3, http://vocabulaire.irht.cnrs.fr/pages/vocab2.htm

Mynors, R. A. B., *Catalogue of the Manuscripts of Balliol College, Oxford* (Oxford: Clarendon Press, 1963)

Nevalainen, T. and I. Tieken-Boon van Ostade, 'Standardisation', in R. Hogg and D. Denison, eds., *A History of the English Language* (Cambridge: Cambridge University Press, 2006), 271–311

Nichols, S. G. and S. Wenzel, eds., *The Whole Book: Cultural Perspectives of the Medieval Miscellany* (Ann Arbor: University of Michigan Press, 1996)

O'Neill, T., *The Irish Hand: Scribes and Their Manuscripts from the Earliest Times* (Cork: Cork University Press, 2014)

O'Sullivan, W., 'Insular Calligraphy: Current State and Problems', *Peritia*, 4 (1985), 346–59

Olszowy-Schlanger, J., *Les manuscrits hébreux dans l'Angleterre médiévale: Étude historique et paléographique* (Paris: Peeters, 2003)

Olszowy-Schlanger, J. et al., eds., *Dictionnaire hébreu-latin-français de la Bible hébraïque de l'Abbaye de Ramsey (XIIIe s.)* (Turnhout: Brepols, 2008)

FURTHER READING

Oresme, N., *Le Livre de Ethiques d'Aristote*, ed. A. D. Menut (New York: Stechert, 1940)

Pächt, O., *Book Illumination in the Middle Ages: An Introduction*, trans. Kay Davenport (London: Harvey Miller; Oxford and New York: Oxford University Press, 1986)

Pächt, O. and J. J. G. Alexander, *Illuminated Manuscripts in the Bodleian Library, Oxford*, 3 vols. (Oxford: Clarendon Press, 1966–73)

Parkes, M. B., *English Cursive Book Hands 1250–1500* (Oxford: Clarendon Press, 1969)

    'Handwriting in English books', in N. Morgan and R. M. Thomson, eds., *The Cambridge History of the Book in Britain. Volume II: 1100–1400* (Cambridge: Cambridge University Press, 2008), 110–35

    Pause and Effect: An Introduction to the History of Punctuation in the West (Aldershot: Ashgate, 1992)

    Their Hands Before our Eyes: A Closer Look at Scribes (Aldershot: Ashgate, 2008)

Parkes, M. B. and A. G. Watson, eds., *Medieval Scribes, Manuscripts and Libraries: Essays Presented to N.R. Ker* (London: Scolar Press, 1978)

Pearsall, D., 'The Whole Book: Late Medieval English Manuscript Miscellanies and Their Modern Interpreters', in S. Kelly and J. J. Thompson, eds., *Imagining the Book* (Turnhout: Brepols, 2005), 17–29

Pearson, D., *English Bookbinding Styles, 1450–1800: A Handbook* (London: British Library, 2005)

    Provenance Research in Book History: A Handbook (London: British Library, 2004)

Pelzer, A., *Abréviations latines médiévales: Supplément au Dizionario di Abbreviature Latine ed Italiane de Adriano Cappelli*, 2nd edn (Louvain: Publications Universitaires, 1966)

Petrucci, A., *La Descrizione del Manoscritto: Storia, Problemi, Modelli* (Rome: Carocci, 1984)

    Public Lettering: Script, Power and Writing, trans. L. Lappin (Chicago: University of Chicago Press, 1993)

Piper, A. J. and M. R. Foster, 'Evidence of the Oxford Booktrade, about 1300', *Viator*, 20 (1989), 155–60

Pollard, G., 'Describing Medieval Bookbindings', in J. J. G. Alexander and M. T. Gibson, eds., *Medieval Learning and Literature: Essays Presented to R. W. Hunt* (Oxford: Clarendon Press, 1976), 50–65

    'Notes on the Size of the Sheet', *The Library*, 4th series, 22 (1941), 105–37

Quenzer, J. B., S. Bondarev, and J.-U. Sobisch, eds., *Manuscript Cultures: Mapping the Field* (Berlin: De Gruyter, 2014)

Reed, R., *Ancient Skins, Parchments and Leathers* (London and New York: Seminar Press, 1972)

Resnick, I. M., '*Lingua Dei, lingua hominis*: Sacred Language and Medieval Texts', *Viator*, 21 (1990), 51–74

Rickert, M., *Painting in Britain: The Middle Ages*, 2nd edn (London: Penguin Books, 1965)

Roberts, J., *Guide to Scripts Used in English Writings up to 1500* (London: British Library, 2005)

FURTHER READING

Robinson, P. R., 'The "Booklet": A Self-contained Unit in Composite Manuscripts', *Codicologica: Essais typologiques*, 3 (1980), 46–69

Catalogue of Dated and Datable Manuscripts in Cambridge Libraries c. 737–1600, 2 vols. (Cambridge: D.S. Brewer, 1988)

Catalogue of Dated and Datable Manuscripts c.888–1600 in London Libraries, 2 vols. (London: British Library, 2003)

'Self-contained Units in Composite Manuscripts of the Anglo-Saxon Period', *Anglo-Saxon England*, 7 (1978), 231–8

Robinson, P. R., ed., *Teaching Writing, Learning to Write* (London: King's College London Centre for Late Antique & Medieval Studies, 2010)

Scott, K. L., *Dated and Datable English Manuscript Borders, c.1395–1499* (London: British Library, 2002)

Scott-Fleming, S., *The Analysis of Pen-Flourishing in Thirteenth-Century Manuscripts* (Leiden: Brill, 1989)

Shuttleworth, M. and M. Cowie, *Dictionary of Translation Studies* (Manchester: St Jerome, 1997; London: Routledge, 2014)

Sigurðsson, G. and V. Ólason, *Manuscripts of Iceland* (Reykjavík: Árni Magnússon Institute in Iceland, 2004)

Simpson, G. G., *Scottish Handwriting 1150–1650: An Introduction to the Reading of Documents* (Edinburgh: Bratton Publishing, 1973)

Sirat, C., *Writing as Handwork: A History of Handwriting in Mediterranean and Western Culture* (Turnhout: Brepols, 2006)

Spector, S., 'Symmetry in Watermark Sequences', *Studies in Bibliography*, 31 (1978), 162–77

Stevenson, A. H., 'Paper as Bibliographical Evidence', *The Library*, 5th series, 17 (1962), 197–212

'Watermarks are Twins', *Studies in Bibliography*, 4 (1951–2), 52–91

Stiennon, J., *Paléographie du Moyen Âge*, 2nd edn (Paris: A. Colin, 1991)

Stokes, P. A., 'The Problem of Grade in English Vernacular Minuscule, *c.* 1060 to 1220', *New Medieval Literatures*, 13 (2011), 23–47

English Vernacular Minuscule from Æthelred to Cnut, circa 990–circa 1035 (Cambridge: Cambridge University Press, 2014)

Szirmai, J. A., *The Archaeology of Medieval Bookbinding* (Aldershot: Ashgate, 1999)

Tanselle, G. T., 'The Bibliographical Description of Paper', *Studies in Bibliography*, 24 (1971), 27–67

Tedeschi, C., 'Some Observations on the Palaeography of Early Christian Inscriptions in Britain', in J. Higgitt, K. Forsyth and D. Parsons, eds., *Roman, Runes and Ogham: Medieval Inscriptions in the Insular World and on the Continent* (Donington: Shaun Tyas, 2001), 16–25

Thompson, D. V., *The Materials and Techniques of Medieval Painting* (New York: Dover, 1956)

Trachsler, R., 'Le Visage et la voix: L'Auteur, le narrateur et l'enlumineur dans la littérature narrative médiévale', *Bibliographical Bulletin of the International Arthurian Society*, 57 (2005), 349–71

Treharne, E., 'Manuscript Studies', in S. Echard and R. Rouse, eds., *The Encyclopaedia of Medieval British Literature* (Oxford: Wiley-Blackwell, 2017)

'The Production and Script of Manuscripts containing English Religious Texts in the First Half of the Twelfth Century', in M. Swan and E. M. Treharne, eds.,

FURTHER READING

Rewriting Old English in the Twelfth Century (Cambridge: Cambridge University Press, 2000), 11–40

Ullmann, B. L., *Ancient Writing and Its Influence*, Medieval Academy Reprints for Teaching (Toronto: University of Toronto Press, 1980)

Ustick, W. L., '"Parchment" and "Vellum"', *The Library*, 4th series, 16 (1936), 439–43

Vezin, J., 'Observations sur l'Emploi des Réclames dans les Manuscrits Latins', *Bibliothèque de l'Ecole des Chartes*, 125 (1967), 5–33

Wakelin, D., 'Palaeography', in S. Echard and R. Rouse, eds., *The Encyclopaedia of Medieval British Literature* (Oxford: Wiley-Blackwell, 2017)
  Scribal Correction and Literary Craft: English Manuscripts 1375–1510 (Cambridge: Cambridge University Press, 2014)

Warner, L., *Chaucer's Scribes: London Textual Production 1384–1432* (Cambridge: Cambridge University Press, 2018)

Watson, A. G., *Medieval Manuscripts in Post-medieval England* (Aldershot: Ashgate, 2004)

Webster, L., *Anglo-Saxon Art: A New History* (Ithaca: Cornell University Press, 2012)
  'Encrypted Visions: Style and Sense in the Anglo-Saxon Minor Arts A.D. 400–900', in G. Hardin Brown and C. E. Karkov, eds., *Anglo-Saxon Styles* (Albany, NY: State University of New York, 2003), 11–30

Willoughby, J., 'The *Secundo Folio* and Its Uses, Medieval and Modern', *The Library*, 7th series, 12 (2011), 237–58

Wormald, F., *English Drawings of the Tenth and Eleventh Centuries* (London: Faber & Faber, 1952)

Part II   Why Do We Study the Manuscript?

Ball, R. M., *Thomas Gascoigne, Libraries and Scholarship* (Cambridge: Cambridge Bibliographical Society, 2006)

Beadle, R., 'Dated and Datable Manuscripts in Cambridge Libraries', *English Manuscript Studies 1100–1700*, 3 (1992), 238–45

Bell, D. N., ed., *The Libraries of the Cistercians, Gilbertines and Premonstratensians*, CBMLC 3 (London: British Library, 1992)

Bischoff, B., *Latin Palaeography: Antiquity and the Middle Ages*, trans. D. Ó Cróinín and D. Ganz (Cambridge: Cambridge University Press, 1990)

Cavanaugh, S. H., 'A Study of Books Privately Owned in England, 1300–1450' (unpublished PhD thesis, University of Pennsylvania, 1980)

Clarke, P. D., *The University and College Libraries of Cambridge*, CBMLC 10 (London: British Library, 2002)

Cowan, Y., 'Reading Material Bibliography and Digital Editions: The Case of the Early English Text Society', in D. Cullen, ed., *Editors, Scholars and the Social Text* (Toronto: University of Toronto Press, 2012), 279–99

Da Rold, O., 'Codicology, Localization, and Oxford, Bodleian Library, MS Laud Misc. 108', in C. M. Meale and D. Pearsall, eds., *Makers and Users of Medieval Books: Essays in Honour of A. S. G. Edwards* (Cambridge: D. S. Brewer, 2014), 48–59

FURTHER READING

Davis, T., 'The Practice of Handwriting Identification', *The Library*, 7th series, 8 (2007), 251–76

Doyle, A. I., 'Book Production by the Monastic Orders in England (c.1375–1530): Assessing the Evidence', in L. L. Brownrigg, ed., *Medieval Book Production: Assessing the Evidence* (Los Altos Hills, CA: Anderson-Lovelace, 1990), 1–19

'The English Provincial Book Trade before Printing', in P. Isaac, ed., *Six Centuries of the Provincial Book Trade in Britain* (Winchester, St Paul's Bibliographies, 1990), 13–29

du Bouveret, B., *Colophons de manuscrits occidentaux des origines aux XVIe siècle*, 6 vols. (Fribourg: Editions Universitaires, 1965–82)

Edwards, A. S. G., 'A.I. Doyle, a Tribute at 90', *The Book Collector*, 64 (2015), 583–90

'Editing and the Teaching of Alliterative Verse', in V. P. McCarren and D. Moffat, eds., *A Guide to Editing Middle English* (Ann Arbor: University of Michigan Press, 1998), 95–106

Favier, J. and J. Dufour, *Recueil des rouleaux des morts (VIIIe siècle-vers 1536)* (Paris: Diffusion de Boccard, 2005–8)

Foster Evans, D. et al., ed., *Gwalch Cywyddau Gwŷr: Essays on Guto'r Glyn and Fifteenth-Century Wales* (Aberystwyth: Centre for Advanced Welsh and Celtic Studies, 2013)

Foucault, M., 'What Is an Author?', in D. F. Bourchard, ed., *Language, Counter-Memory, Practice: Selected Essays and Interviews*, trans. D. F. Bourchard and S. Simon (Oxford: Blackwell, 1977), 113–18

Fulton, H., 'The Editor as Author: Re-producing the Text. A Case Study of Parry's *Gwaith Dafydd ap Gwilym*', *Bulletin of the Bibliographical Society of Australia and New Zealand*, 19.2 (1995), 67–78

'Punctuation as a Semiotic Code: The Case of the Medieval Welsh *Cywydd*', *Parergon*, 13.2 (1996), 2–17

Ganz, D., 'Can a Scriptorium Always Be Identified by Its Products?', in A. Nievergelt et al., eds., *Scriptorium: Wesen, Funktion, Eigenheiten* (Munich: Bayerische Akademie der Wissenschaften, 2015), 51–62

Gillespie, V. and A. Hudson, eds., *Probable Truth: Editing Medieval Texts from Britain* (Turnhout: Brepols, 2013)

Hanna, R., 'Problems of "Best-Text" Editing and the Hengwrt Manuscript of *The Canterbury Tales*', in D. Pearsall, ed., *Manuscripts and Texts: Editorial Problems in Later Middle English Literature* (Cambridge: D. S. Brewer, 1987), 87–94

Hellinga, L. and J. B. Trapp, eds., *The Cambridge History of the Book in Britain, Volume III, 1400–1557* (Cambridge: Cambridge University Press, 1999)

Ker, N. R., *English Manuscripts in the Century after the Norman Conquest* (Oxford: Clarendon Press, 1960)

Leedham-Green, E. and T. Webber, eds., *The Cambridge History of Libraries in Britain and Ireland to 1640, Volume I* (Cambridge: Cambridge University Press, 2006)

Machan, T. W., *Textual Criticism and Middle English Texts* (Charlottesville, VA: University Press of Virginia, 1994)

Matthews, D., *The Making of Middle English, 1765–1910* (Minneapolis and London: University of Minnesota Press, 1999)

FURTHER READING

Michael, M. A., 'English Illuminators *c.*1190–1450: A Survey from Documentary Sources', *English Manuscript Studies 1100–1700*, 4 (1993), 62–113

'Oxford, Cambridge and London: Towards a Theory for Grouping Gothic Manuscripts', *Burlington Magazine*, 130 (1988), 107–15

Moffat, D. with V. P. McCarren, 'A Bibliographical Essay on Editing Methods and Authorial and Scribal Intention', in V. P. McCarren and D. Moffat, eds., *A Guide to Editing Middle English* (Ann Arbor: University of Michigan Press, 1998), 25–57

Moorman, C., 'One Hundred Years of Editing *The Canterbury Tales*', *Chaucer Review*, 24 (1989), 99–114

Morgan, N. J. and R. M. Thomson, eds., *The Cambridge History of the Book in Britain, Volume II, 1100–1400* (Cambridge: Cambridge University Press, 2008)

Ouy, G., 'Les bibliothèques', *L'histoire et ses methodes*, ed. C. Samaran (Paris: Gallimard, 1961)

Parkes, M. B., 'The Provision of Books', in J. I. Catto and T. A. R. Evans, eds., *The History of the University of Oxford, Volume II: Late Medieval Oxford* (Oxford: Oxford University Press, 1992), 407–83

Roberts, J., 'On Giving Scribe B a Name and a Clutch of London Books from *c.*1400', *Medium Ævum*, 80 (2011), 247–70

Rosenthal, J. T., 'Aristocratic Cultural Patronage and Book Bequests, 1350–1500', *Bulletin of the John Rylands Library*, 64 (1982), 522–48

Rouse, R. H. and M. A. Rouse, eds., *Registrum Anglie de libris doctorum et auctorum veterum*, CBMLC 2 (London: British Library, 1991)

Rudy, K. M., *Piety in Pieces: How Medieval Readers Customized Their Manuscripts* (Cambridge: Open Book Publishers, 2016)

Sahle, P., 'What Is a Scholarly Digital Edition?', in M. J. Driscoll and E. Pierazzo, eds., *Digital Scholarly Editing: Theories and Practices* (Cambridge: Open Book Publishers, 2016)

Scott, K. L., 'Past Ownership: Evidence of Book Ownership by English Merchants in the Later Middle Ages', in C. M. Meale and D. Pearsall, eds., *Makers and Users of Medieval Books: Essays in Honour of A.S.G. Edwards* (Cambridge: D. S. Brewer, 2014), 150–77

Sharpe, R., 'Accession, Classification or Location: Pressmarks in Medieval Libraries', *Scriptorium*, 50 (1996), 279–87

'The Medieval Librarian', in E. Leedham-Green and T. Webber, eds., *The Cambridge History of Libraries in Britain and Ireland, Volume I, to 1640* (Cambridge: Cambridge University Press, 2006), 218–41

Singleton, A., 'The Early English Text Society in the Nineteenth Century: An Organizational History', *Review of English Studies*, 56 (2005), 90–118

Solopova, E., *Manuscripts of the Wycliffite Bible in the Bodleian and Oxford College Libraries* (Liverpool: University of Liverpool Press, 2016)

ed., *The Wycliffite Bible: Origin, History and Interpretation* (Leiden: Brill, 2017)

Steinmann, M., *Handschriften im Mittelalter: Eine Quellensammlung* (Basel: Schwabe Verlag, 2013)

Venuti, L., *The Translator's Invisibility: A History of Translation*, 2nd edn (London: Routledge, 2008)

Watson, A. G., *Catalogue of Dated and Datable Manuscripts c.435–1600 in Oxford Libraries*, 2 vols. (Oxford: Clarendon Press, 1984)

FURTHER READING

Catalogue of Dated and Datable Manuscripts c.700–1600 in the Department of Manuscripts, The British Library, 2 vols. (London: British Library, 1979)

ed., *Medieval Libraries of Great Britain: A List of Surviving Books. Supplement to the Second Edition* (London: Royal Historical Society, 1987)

Webber, T., 'English Manuscripts in the Century after the Norman Conquest: Continuity and Change in the Palaeography of Books and Book Collections', in E. Kwakkel, ed., *Writing in Context: Insular Manuscript Culture 500–1200* (Leiden: Leiden University Press, 2013), 185–228

'The Libraries of Religious Houses', in E. Kwakkel and R. M. Thomson, eds., *The European Book in the Long Twelfth Century* (Cambridge: University Press, 2018), 103–21

Scribes and Scholars at Salisbury Cathedral, c.1075–c.1125 (Oxford: Oxford University Press, 1992)

Willoughby, J. M. W., ed., *The Libraries of Collegiate Churches*, 2 vols., CBMLC 15 (London: British Library, 2013)

Willoughby, J. M. W. and N. Ramsay, eds., *Secular Cathedrals*, CBMLC 17 (London: British Library, forthcoming)

Wogan-Browne, J. et al., eds., *The Idea of the Vernacular: An Anthology of Middle English Literary Theory, 1280–1520* (Exeter: University of Exeter Press, 1999)

Worley, M., 'Using the *Ormulum* to Redefine Vernacularity', in F. Somerset and N. Watson, eds., *The Vulgar Tongue: Medieval and Postmedieval Vernacularity* (University Park, PA: Pennsylvania State University Press, 2003), 19–42

Wright, L., *Sources of London English: Medieval Thames Vocabulary* (Oxford: Clarendon Press, 1996)

Zink, G., *Le Moyen Français (XIVe et XVe siècles)* (Paris: Presses Universitaires de France, 1990)

Part III   Where Do We Study the Manuscript?

Backhouse, J. 'Manuscripts on Display: Some Landmarks in the Exhibition and Popular Publication of Illuminated Books', in L. Dennison, ed., *The Legacy of M. R. James* (Donington: Shaun Tyas, 1995), 37–52

Beadle, R., 'Medieval English Manuscripts at Auction 1676–c.1700', *The Book Collector*, 53 (2004), 46–63

Borrie, M., 'Panizzi and Madden', *British Library Journal*, 5 (1979), 18–36

Craven, L., *What Are Archives? Cultural and Theoretical Perspectives: A Reader* (Aldershot: Ashgate, 2008)

de Hamel, C., *Cutting up Manuscripts for Pleasure and Profit* (Charlottesville, VA: Book Arts Press, 1996)

Duff, E. G., *A Century of the English Book Trade* (London: Bibliographical Society, 1905)

Dunning, A., A. Hudson, and C. Duffy, 'Reconstructing Burnt Anglo-Saxon Fragments in the Cotton Collection at the British Library', *Fragmentology*, 1 (2018), 7–37

Echard, S., 'Containing the Book: The Institutional Afterlives of Medieval Manuscripts' in M. Johnston and M. van Dussen, eds., *The Medieval Manuscript Book: Cultural Approaches* (Cambridge: Cambridge University Press, 2015), 96–118

'House Arrest: Modern Archives, Medieval Manuscripts', *Journal of Medieval and Early Modern Studies*, 30 (2000), 185–210

Printing the Middle Ages (Philadelphia: University of Pennsylvania Press, 2008)

Edwards, A. S. G., 'Back to the Real?', *The Times Literary Supplement*, 7 June 2013, www.the-tls.co.uk/articles/public/back-to-the-real/

Edwards, A. S. G. and T. Takamiya, 'A New Fragment of Gower's *Confessio Amantis*', *Modern Language Review*, 96 (2001), 931–6

Erwin, M., 'Fragments of Medieval Manuscripts in Printed Books: Crowdsourcing and Cataloging Medieval Manuscript Waste in the Book Collection of the Harry Ransom Center', *Manuscripta*, 60 (2016), 188–247

Farquhar, J. D., *Creation and Imitation: The Work of a Fifteenth-century Manuscript Illuminator* (Fort Lauderdale, FL: Nova University Press, 1976)

Foys, M., 'Medieval Manuscripts: Media Archaeology and the Digital Incunable', in M. Van Dussen and M. Johnston, eds., *The Medieval Manuscript Book: Cultural Approaches* (Cambridge: Cambridge University Press: 2015), 119–39

'The Remanence of Medieval Media', in J. E. Boyle and H. J. Burgess, eds., *The Routledge Research Companion to Digital Medieval Literature* (London: Routledge, 2018)

Freeman, A. and J. Ing Freeman, *Anatomy of an Auction: Rare Books at Ruxley Lodge 1919* (London: Book Collector, 1990)

Green, J., 'Textuality in Transition: Digital Manuscripts as Cultural Artefacts', in G. Hulsman and C. Whelan, eds., *Occupying Space in Medieval and Early Modern Britain and Ireland* (Oxford: Peter Lang, 2016), 65–86

Green, M. H., K. Walker-Meikle, and W. P. Müller, 'Diagnosis of a "Plague" Image: A Digital Cautionary Tale', in *The Medieval Globe*, 1 (2014), 309–26

Hanna, R., 'Manuscript Catalogues and Book History', *The Library*, 18 (2017), 45–61

Harris, P. R., *A History of the British Museum Library 1753–1973* (London: British Library, 1998)

Hellinga, L. and J. B. Trapp, eds., *The History of the Book in Britain, Volume III: 1400–1457* (Cambridge: Cambridge University Press, 1999)

Herrmann, F., 'The Emergence of the Book Auctioneer as a Professional', in R. Myers and R. Harris, eds., *The Property of a Gentleman: The Formation, Organization and Dispersal of the Private Library 1620–1920* (Winchester: St Paul's Bibliographies, 1991)

Hobson, A., 'The Phillipps Sales', in G. Mandelbrote, ed., *Out of Print and Into Profit: A History of the Rare and Secondhand Book Trade in Britain in the Twentieth Century* (London: British Library, 2006), 157–64

Howard, J., 'What Happened to Google's Effort to Scan Millions of University Library Books?', August 2017, www.edsurge.com/news/2017–08–10-what-happened-to-google-s-effort-to-scan-millions-of-university-library-books

Ker, N. R., 'Introduction', *Medieval Manuscripts in British Libraries*, Vol. 1 (Oxford: Clarendon Press, 1969), vii–xiii

Keskiaho, J., *The Appendix to His Dreams and Visions in the Early Middle Ages* (Cambridge: Cambridge University Press, 2015)

Koszary, A., 'Look at This Absolute Unit', 10 April 2018, https://medium.com/@adamkoszary/look-at-this-absolute-unit-763207207917

FURTHER READING

'Lowering the Tone: Doing Social Media at Bodleian Libraries', 15 January 2017, https://artplusmarketing.com/lowering-the-tone-doing-social-media-at-bodleian-libraries-5c6c6d6287ca

Lawler, J., *Book Auctions in England in the Seventeenth Century* (London: Elliot Stock, 1896)

Liberman Cuenca, E. and M. Kowaleski, 'Omeka and Other Digital Platforms for Undergraduate Research Projects on the Middle Ages', *Digital Medievalist*, 11.1, http://doi.org/10.16995/dm.69

Manley. K. A. 'The Bodleian Classification of Manuscripts', *Journal of Librarianship*, 10.1 (1978), 56–9

McKitterick, D., *Old Books, New Technologies: The Representation, Conservation and Transformation of Books since 1700* (Cambridge: Cambridge University Press, 2013)

Porter, D., 'Is This Your Book? What We Call Digitized Manuscripts and Why It Matters', 12 June 2018, www.dotporterdigital.org/is-this-your-book-what-digitization-does-to-manuscripts-and-what-we-can-do-about-it/

Prescott, A., 'The Function, Structure and Future of Catalogues', http://digitalriffs.blogspot.co.uk/2013/01/the-function-structure-and-future-of.html

'What's in a Number? The Physical Organisation of the Collections of the British Library', in A. N. Doane and K. Wolf, eds., *Beatus Vir: Studies in Early English and Norse Manuscripts in Memory of Phillip Pulsiano* (Tempe, AZ: ACMRS, 2006), 471–525

Prescott, A. and E. Treharne, 'The Origin and Context of the Salisbury Magna Carta', June 2015, http://historyoftexttechnologies.blogspot.com/2015/06/the-origin-and-context-of-salisbury.html

Prescott, A. and L. Hughes, 'Why Do We Digitize? The Case for Slow Digitization', *Archive Journal* (September 2018), www.archivejournal.net/essays/why-do-we-digitize-the-case-for-slow-digitization/

Schubert, K., *The Curator's Egg: The Evolution of the Museum Concept from the French Revolution to the Present Day*, 3rd edn (London: Ridinghouse, 2009)

Tishman, S., *Slow Looking: The Art and Practice of Learning through Observation* (New York: Routledge, 2017)

Tite, C. G. C., *The Manuscript Library of Sir Robert Cotton* (London: British Library, 1994)

Treharne, E., 'Fleshing out the Text: The Transcendent Manuscript in the Digital Age', *Postmedieval*, 4.4 (2013), 465–78

Whearty, B., 'Adam Scriveyn in Cyberspace: Loss, Labour, Ideology and Infrastructure in Interoperable Reuse of Digital Manuscript Metadata', in M. Evan Davis, T. Mahoney-Steel, and E. Turnator, eds., *Meeting the Medieval in a Digital World* (Leeds: ARC Humanities Press, 2018), 157–202

INDEX

Aberystwyth, National Library of Wales
  21248D, 108 v–109 r, 201
  3021 F, 201
  3049D, 201–6
  8497B, 201–6

Bangor, Bangor University Library
  Gwyneddon 4, 201–7
Belfast, Queen's University
  Brett 3/12B, 123

Cambridge, Corpus Christi College
  41, 134
  173, 115–16, 118, 136
    fols. 1 r–32 r, 137,
      138, 141
  198, 111
  199, 59
  419, 45, 46
  421, 45, 46
Cambridge, St John's College
  E. 2, 122
Cambridge, Trinity College
  B. 1. 37, 216–18
  O. 9. 1, 143
  R. 3. 2, 68, 114, 245, 260, 264n
  R. 15. 18, 216
  R. 17, 159, 166–8, 174
Cambridge, University Library
  Dd. 14. 30, fol. 10 r, 65
  Dd. 3. 53, 169–72, 174
  Ff. 6. 31, 110
  Gg. 4. 27, fol. 457 v, 70
  Ii. 3. 26, 69
  Kk. 3. 18, 134
  Kk. 5. 16, 131
Cologny, Bodmer
  178, 261, 264n

Columbia University Library
  Plimpton 265, 261

Dartmouth College, Rauner Special Collections
    Library
  003183, 110
Dublin, Trinity College
  58, 52
  490, 117
  1339, 261
  D. 4. 6, 261, 264n

Glasgow, Hunterian Library
  Hunter 59, 264n

Lincoln Cathedral Library
  91, 112
  A. 72, 264n
London, British Library
  Additional 12043, 265n
  Additional 15003, fol. 29, 265n
  Additional 22139, 265n
  Additional 23211, 240
  Additional 24193, 51, 122
  Additional 31042, 112
  Additional 35290, 255
  Additional 40542, 249–50
  Additional 47967, 136
    fols. 2–87, 135
  Additional 59495, 248, 264n,
    265n
  Additional 60577, 266n
  Additional 62002, fol. 74, 264n
  Additional 62577, fols. 6 v-7, 264n
  Arundel 60, 79–100, 103–5
    fol. 5 v, 90
    fol. 12 v, 82, 92
    fol. 13 r, 91, 92
    fol. 52 v, 83, 94

INDEX

fol. 53, 94
fol. 85 r, 100
Cotton Domitian A. ix, fol. 9rv, 138
Cotton Domitian A. viii, fols. 30 r–70 v, 137
Cotton Domitian ix, fol. 11 r, 134
Cotton Faustina A. x, 44
Cotton Otho A. xii, 249, 254
Cotton Otho B. xi, 134, 138
Cotton Tiberius A. ii, 58
Cotton Tiberius A. iv, 237–8, 239, 242–3,
    244, 245–7, 248–52, 253–5, 257, 259,
    260, 262
Cotton Tiberius A. vi, fols. 1 r–35 v, 137, 142
Cotton Tiberius A. viii, 266n
Cotton Tiberius B. i
    fols. 3 r–111 v, 136
    fols. 115 v–164 r, 137
Cotton Tiberius B. iv, fols. 3 r–9 v, 19 r–86
    v, 137, 141
Cotton Tiberius C. i, 52
Cotton Tiberius C. vi, 97–100, 103
    fols. 2 v–5 v, 100
    fol. 13 r, 99
Cotton Titus A. xiii, 265n
Cotton Vitellius A. xv, 255
Egerton 617/618, 180
Egerton 913, 265n
Egerton 1991, 266n
Harley 266, 123
Harley 1758, 260
Harley 1766, 266n
Harley 2253, 61, 209
Harley 2278, 266n
Harley 3490, 266n
Harley 3869, 243–4, 259, 264n
Harley 4826, 266n
Harley 6291, 243–4, 264n, 266n
Harley 7184, 266n
Harley 7334, 260
Lansdowne 5, 254
Otho E. xiv, 247
Royal 16 E. viii, 248
Royal 18 C. xxii, 266n
Royal 18 D. II, 266n
Sloane 2400, 101–3
Stowe 950, 266n
Yates Thompson 47, 266n

Manchester, John Rylands Library
    Eng. 895, 106, 108

Nottingham, Wollaton
    WLC LM 8, 264n

Oxford, All Souls College
    98, 260, 262, 264n
Oxford, Bodleian Library
    Ashmole 328, 161
    Bodley 183, 184
    Bodley 264, 172–4
    fol. 67 r, 63
    Bodley 294, 264n
    Bodley 340, 151–3, 156
    Bodley 938, 121
    Digby 86, 61
    Douce 369, 179
    Fairfax 3, 264n
    Fairfax 11, 184
    Hatton 115, 39–45, 46–7, 111
    Junius 1, 161–3
    Laud 719, 264n
    Laud Misc. 23, 120–1
    Laud Misc. 636, fols. 1 r–91 v, 137, 138–9,
        141–2
    Laud Misc. 656, 194
    Rawl. Poet. 163, 68
    Tanner 10, 134, 136
Oxford, Corpus Christi College
    279B, 134
Oxford, New College
    320, 181

Paris, Bibliothèque nationale
        de France
    français 1463, 175–6
    hébreu 113, 156, 158–9, 166

Salisbury Cathedral Library
    11, 227
San Marino, Huntington Library
    60320, 291
    EL 26 A 13, 261
    HM 150, 264n
St Petersburg, National Library of Russia
    lat.Q.v. I. 18, 131

University of Pennsylvania Library
    LJS 188, 291
Utrecht, Universiteitsbibliotheek
    32, 103

Vatican, Vatican Library
    Ottobonianus Latinus 1474, 163–5
Vercelli, Biblioteca Capitolare
    CXVII, 43
Vienna, Österreichische Nationalbibliothek
    Cod. 1861, 101

GENERAL INDEX

Abbey, R., 287
abbreviation, 31, 149
Ælfric, 41, 42–4, 46, 134–5, 151, 190
   Lives of Saints, 134
Æthelberht, king of Kent, lawcode of, 55
Æthelthryth, 134
Alexander and Dindimus (Alexander
   Fragment B), 172–4
Alexander the Great, 172–4
Alexandre de Paris
   Roman d'Alexandre, 172
Alfred, King, 109–10, 115–16, 134, 136,
   139
   Laws of Alfred, 58, 116
All Souls College descriptive catalogue, 245
alteration, 32
American Council of Learned Societies, 257
Anglo-American Cataloguing Rules, 245
Anglo-Catalan Psalter, 103
Anglo-Saxon Chronicle, 58, 133, 136, 138,
   139–42, 269
   Abingdon Chronicle, 136, 137
   Battle of Brunanburh, 140–1
   Cynewulf and Cyneheard, 140
   Parker Chronicle, 115–16, 118, 136, 137,
    138, 141
   Peterborough Chronicle, 138–9, 141
   Worcester Chronicle, 137, 141
Anglo-Saxons, historical writing, 133–4
annotations, 151
   as evidence of use, 227–8
   digital, 278
anonymity, 130, 190
Aphelisa, Prioress, 129
Arabic, 40, 155, 169, 171
Aramaic, 168
archivists, 241, 256
Aristotle, *Ethics* and *Politics*, 169

armorial stamps, 246
Arthur, King, 143
Arthurian texts, 175–6
Arts and Humanities Research Board
   (AHRB), 200
Arts and Humanities Research Council
   (AHRC), 200
Arundel Psalter, illuminations, 5, 79
   composition, 79–85
   disparities in style and techinque, 103–5
   generic context, 97–100
   intellectual context, 86–7
   internal composition, 87–8
   manuscript context, 88–97
Arundel, Thomas, Archbishop of
   Canterbury, 179
Ashburnham House fire (1731), 238,
   252–3, 256
Asser, *Life of King Alfred*, 109–10
Athanasian Creed, 257
Athelstan, 140–1
Augustine
   De ciuitate Dei, 116
   De contemptu mundi, 120
   De Trinitate, 59
author, 189–92
   known vs. anonymous, 130

Bald's Leechbook, 58
Bale, Bishop John, 285
Barker, Nicolas, *The Roxburghe Club:*
   A Bicentennial History, 292
Barnicle, Mary Elizabeth's, *Seege or Batayle*
   of Troye, The (EETS edition), 195
Barthes, Roland, 191
   'The Death of the Author', 190
Beadle, Richard, 255
Beatty, Chester, 287

GENERAL INDEX

Bede, *Historia ecclesiastica gentis Anglorum*, 57, 130–1, 163
  Malmesbury's testimonial, 131–4
  Old English version, 134–5, 136
Beinecke Library (Yale University), 261
Beowulf, 255
Bernard, Edward, *Catalogus ... manuscriptorum Angliae et Hiberniae*, 285
Beryn scribe, 115
Bibles. *See also* Vulgate Bible; Wycliffite Bible
  language of, 155
  Northumbrian, 57
  scripts, 64
bifolia, 109, 122, 123
binding, 22, 27, 33–4, 106, 209
  as evidence of origin and provenance, 215–16
  decoration, 100–2
  difficulties in digitization of, 269
  flyleaves as a component of, 21
  for visual effect, 251
  limp bindings, 110–11
  manuscripts reused in, 106, 108
  Opus anglicanum ('English work'), 101
  rebinding, 245–6, 253–4
    virtual, 279–80
  treasure bindings, 100
Bischoff, Bernhard, 215
Bodleian Library, 239, 247, 260
  digitized catalogues, 261
Bodley, Thomas, 286
Bohun, Elizabeth de, 289
Bond, Edward Augustus, 251
book collections, 143, 225, 228–9, 239
  acquisition of, 286–7, 291
Book Collector (journal), 292
book languages, 154–65
Book of Kells, 52
Book of Leinster, 261
Book of Nunnaminster, 57
book production
  collaborative, 220, 223
  early English, 109
  evidence of
    handwriting, 223–4
    in religious or ecclesiastical settings, 220–2
    in secular contexts, 220
    projects which have assembled, 218–20
  late medieval, 110–11
  sources of information, 214–15
book trade, 284–5
  auctions, 285–6

collectors role in and relationship with, 286–7
establishment of prices at auction, 289–90
establishment of title, 287–8
identification of manuscripts unsold at auction, 290
manuscript descriptions in sale catalogues, 288–9, 290–1
sources of information on, 291–3
booklets, 27–9, 41–5, 47, 111–13, 120–1
booklists, 225–6, 228, 284
Books of Hours, 238
bookstands, 238
borrowing, 149
boxing (of manuscripts), 245
boxing (of texts), 29
Bradfer-Lawrence, Harry, 287
Bradshaw, Henry, 14, 22
Breton, 150
Briquet, C.-M., 19
British Academy, 200
British Library, 7
  'Anglo-Saxon Kingdoms' exhibition, 1
  accessing manuscripts, 259–60, 292–3
  Additional Manuscripts/Additional Charters series, 241
  Catalogue of Illuminated Manuscripts, 244
  Department of Manuscripts, 248, 255, 292–3
  Digital Catalogue of Illuminated Manuscripts, 259
  'Explore Archives and Manuscripts' catalogue, 242–5, 259–60
  institutional framework, 239–42
  Manuscripts Reading Room, 237, 239
  ordering system, 242, 250
  Treasures collection, 269
  Turning the Pages animations, 258
British Manuscripts Project, 257
British Museum, 239–40, 246–7, 249, 252, 256–8, 260
  Antiquities Department, 240
  Department of Manuscripts, 239, 249
  foliation rules, 255
  King's Library, 250
  Manuscript Saloon, 250–2
Brittonic languages, 163–5
Brittonic manuscripts, 59
Brut, 108, 110–11, 114–15, 116–17, 123, 143–4
Bury, Richard de, 143
  Philobiblon, 143
Bute, Marquis of, 291
Byrhtferth, *Enchiridion*, 159–61

311

GENERAL INDEX

Cædmon, 130
calendar years, 15–16
calendars, 79, 89, 101, 182, 183
Cambridge History of Libraries in Britain and Ireland, 214
Cambridge History of the Book in Britain, 214
Canolfan Uwchefrydiau Cymreig a Cheltaidd (Centre for Advanced Welsh and Celtic Studies), 188
Canterbury Tales Project, 188, 198
capitulum marks, 29
Carter, John, *Taste and Technique in Book Collecting*, 291
Casley, David, 247, 252, 253
Catalogue of Additions, 249
catalogues
  development of, 285
  interpreting manuscripts from, 39–47
  online, 245, 259–61
  Planta's Cotton manuscript catalogue, 243, 253
  sale catalogues, 288–9, 290–1, 292–3
  sourcing documents in, 242–5
cataloguing, 1, 237
catchwords, 20, 23, 25–6, 27
Cavanaugh, Susan, 228
Caxton, William, 117
Ceolwulf, King of Northumbria, 132
chained books, 33
chain-line patterns, 25
Charlemagne, 101
Chaucer, Geoffrey, 66, 69, 143, 190, 250, 260
  Book of the Duchess, 262
  Canterbury Tales, 114
    digital edition, 198
    Ellesmere manuscript, 194
    Hengwrt manuscript, 194, 258
    Manly Rickert edition, 189
  The Parliament of Fowls, 69–71
  Treatise on the Astrolabe, 6, 122, 169–72, 291
  Troilus, 263
Christ Church Cathedral, Canterbury, 166
Christian tradition, 53
Christie's, 286, 289, 292
chronicles, 137–9
classification and shelving systems, 246–7
code-switching, 149
Codex Alexandrinus, 257
codicology, 1, 2, 16
  structural, 106–8, 109, 113
collaborative work, 275

collation, 22–5, 40–1, 42, 209
Collette, C. P., 143
Colop, John, 'Common Profit Book', 110
colophon, 15, 16, 179
colour touching, 29
columns, 16
Comité Internationale de Paléographie Latine, 15, 218
'common-profit' books, 229
'commonplace books', 118
composite manuscripts, 108, 111
Conner, Patrick, 67
Connolly, Margaret, 120
Cooper, William, 285
copying, 18, 22, 25, 131, 150, 220
  from exemplars, 29, 51–2, 66
  incorporation of abbreviations, 31
  Latin diplomas, 58
Cornish, 150, 165
Corpus of British Medieval Library Catalogues, 219, 225
correction, 32–3
'Corrigitur', 113
Cotton collection, 237, 239, 247, 249, 250, 257
  arrangement, 246
  catalogue, 243, 253
  exhibition, 252
  foliation, 254–5
  numbering, 250
  restoration after fire damage, 252–4
Cotton family, 239
Cotton, Sir Robert, 239, 241, 246, 252, 256, 258, 286
Counsels of Isidore, 120
curatorial systems, 238
curators, 241–2, 254–5
  difficulties in digital imaging, 273–4
Cyfres Beirdd yr Uchelwyr ('The Poets of the Nobility Series'), 187, 192, 194, 195, 198, 210
  Gwaith Hywel (digital edition), 200

D'Ewes, Sir Simon, 123
Dafydd ap Gwilym, 188, 190, 197
Dafydd ap Gwilym.net, 188, 199
Dagulf Psalter, 101
Danish language, 150
dating, 15–16
  using watermarks, 19
De Brailes Hours, 240
decoration, 15, 27, 29, 30, 149, *See also* images
  in the Wycliffite Bible, 180

312

GENERAL INDEX

of covers, 33
Dee, John, 239
descriptions, 13–14
  dimensions of leaves, 20–1
  headings and preliminary information,
    14–16
  identifying the script, 30–1
  interpreting manuscripts from catalogues,
    39–47
  number of leaves, 21
  of binding, 33–4
  of contents, 16–17
  of decoration, 30
  of materials, 17–20
Dickinson, Donald C., *Directory of American
  Book Collectors*, 292
Digital Bodleian, 261
digital images
  accessing, 267–8
  citation of, 274
  creation of, 268–70
  displaying, 270–2
  preservation of, 279–80
  publishing of, 272–4
  selection of, 268
  working with, 274–6
Digital Scriptorium, 261, 269
digitization
  future trends and challenges, 278–80
  incunabula period, 276–8
  projects, 258–62
digitized manuscripts, 78, 188, 198–200
diglossia, 154
donation lists, 226, 228
Douce, Francis, 241
Doyle, A. I., 14, 114, 184, 215, 261
  'Some English Scribes and Scriptoria of the
    Later Middle Ages' (Lyell
    Lectures), 219
drawing, 76, 89, 98, 103
Dutch language, 153

Eadwine Psalter, 159, 166–9, 174
Earls of Oxford, 239, 241
early English texts, 111
Early English Text Society (EETS) series, 187,
    192, 193, 198, 210, 255
  Guidelines for Editors, 197
e-Codices project, 261
editorial methodologies, 188–92
editorial practices
  apparatus, 206–7
  base texts, 201

choosing a base text, 193–5
choosing apparatus, 197–8
digital, 198–200
economic limitations, 210
emendations, 196, 207
future trends, 208–10
noting variants, 195–6, 202–6
punctuation, 196–7, 202–6
sorting the manuscripts, 192–3, 201
transparency, 210
Edward I, 117, 123
Edward III, 117, 143, 144
Edward the Elder, 116
Edward, Prince of Wales, 143
Edwards, A. S. G., 196
Egerton collection, 246
Ellis, Sir Henry, 241
Emden, A. B., 228
Encoded Archival Description (EAD), 245
Encomium Emmae reginae, 142
endleaves, 151, 228
English Manuscript Studies, 293
English Wycliffite Sermons, 184
Epistles of Clement, 257
erasures, 32, 35
'Erthe upon Erthe', 120
Eulalia, abbess of Shaftesbury, 217
evolution of books, 121–4
ex dono inscriptions, 227
ex libris inscriptions, 7, 215, 227
exemplar poverty, 118
exemplars, 29, 51–2, 113–14, 135
Exeter scribes, 45, 46
exhibiting and display, 251–2
expunctions, 32

Faddan More Psalter, 55
fascicles, 27–9
Felbrigge Psalter, 101–3
Fenton, Roger, 257
Ferguson, Charles, 154
'Findern Anthology', 228
Flemish, 150
Fletcher, William Younger, *English Book
  Collectors*, 291
Floretum, 184
flourishers, 29, 30
flyleaves, 21, 33, 122
  notices of possession, 35
foliation, 237, 254–6, 270
Fondation Bodmer, 261
fonds, 15, 240
Forshall, Josiah, 246–7, 253

313

Foucault, Michel, 'What is an Author?', 189, 190–1
Foyle, William and Christina, 287
Foys, Martin, 267, 276, 278
Fragmenta Manuscripta, 122
fragments, 108, 122–3
  commercial trade in, 291
Franciscus, Ricardus, 67
Franco-Italian language, 175
French, 149–50, 158–9, 162, 166–9, 172–4
French cultural theory, 189–90
Frithustan, bishop of Winchester, 141
Furnivall, F. J., 187

Gaelic, 53, 54, 150
Gaimar, Geoffrey, 190
  Lestorie des Engleis, 139–40
Gascoigne, Thomas, 228
Gatfield, George, 255
'Gawain-poet' ('Pearl-poet'), 190
Geoffrey of Monmouth, *History of the Kings of Britain*, 163
George III, library of, 240
Gervase of Canterbury, 138, 139
Getty Foundation, 244
Gildas, 53, 130
gilding, 30
Glossed Gospels, 179, 184, 185
glosses, 151, 153, 156, 158–9, 165, 166–8, 183
Google Books, 268
Gorleston Psalter, 240
Gough, Henry, 253–4
Gower, John, 66, 190, 223, 224, 237, 238, 242, 243–4, 249, 252, 262–3
  Chronica Tripertita, 242
  Clinkante Balades, 248
  Confessio Amantis, 68, 114, 252, 261, 262, 291
  digitized manuscripts, 259–62
  Traitié, 248
  Vox Clamantis, 242, 248
grading systems, 247–50
Great Parchment Book project, 275
Greek, 155, 168, 169
Gregory the Great, 56
Grenville, Thomas, library of, 240
Grolier 2000: A Further Biographical Retrospective in Celebration of the Millenium, 292
Grolier 75: A Biographical Retrospective to Celebrate the Seventy-Fifth

Anniversary of the Grolier Club in New York, 292
Grolier Club, 292
group-copying, 28
Guto'r Glyn, 188, 200–1
  'In Praise of Hywel', 200–8
Guto'r Glyn.net, 199, 201, 202

Hadrian, Pope, 101
Halidon, Battle of, 117
handwriting, 15, 19, 27, 29, 30–1, 49–50
  as evidence of book production, 223–4
  calligraphic, 64
  cursive, 31
  development of, 251
  'house style', 67
  reform in, 68
Hanna, Ralph, 108, 112, 118–19, 193, 194
Harkes, Garbrand, 285
Harley collection, 243–4, 246, 253, 259–60, 286
Harley Lyrics, 209
Harris, Kate, 228
Hebrew language, 150, 155, 156–8, 168, 169
Hebrew Psalms (*Gallicanum, Romanum,* and *Hebraicum*), 166
Hebrew Psalter, 156–9
Hebrew scripture, 97, 101
Heidelberg University Press, 188
Henry III, 123, 143
Henry IV, 180
Henry V, 117
Henry VI, 180
Henry VII, 180
heraldic devices, 30
Hereford, Nicholas, 179
Hermann, Frank, *Sotheby's: Portrait of an Auction House*, 292
Hilton, Walter, *Scale of Perfection*, 208
historical texts, 135–7
  intertextual connections, 131–3
  production and dissemination, 129–31
Hoccleve, Thomas, 114, 190–1, 210
Hoffman, Ladislaus von, 287
Horobin, Simon, 66
Hugh of St Victor, 247
Hughes, Lorna, 277
hybridization, 149
Hywel ap Dai of Northop, Sir, 200

Iceland, 67
iconography, 30, 80, 85, 86, 87, 89, 97, 103

314

GENERAL INDEX

Ieuan ap Llywelyn Fychan, 194
Ieuan ap Sulien, 59
illumination. *See* decoration; images
illuminators, 29, 30, 77, 104, 143
Image Interoperability Framework (IIIF), 259,
    272, 278, 279
images, 76–7
  art historical component, 102–5
  composition, 79–85
    colour and graphic technique, 84
    figural and ornamental, 79–80
    relationships, 85
    representation, 81–4
  contextualization, 85–6
    generic context, 97–100
    intellectual history, 86–7
    internal composition, 87–8
    manuscript context, 88–97
  iconography, 85
  materials and techniques, 77–9
    limitations of digital and facsimile
      editions, 78
  on covers, 100–2
  understanding colour, 87–8
indexing letters, 182, 184
inking, 29, 30
inks, 209
inscriptions of ownership, 34–5, 214, 215,
    218, 227, 228, 258
insertions, 32
Insular Manuscripts project, 268
International Standard of Archive Description
    (ISAD-G), 245
Iolo Goch, 190
Irish Script on Screen initiative, 261
Italian, 150

James, M. R., catalogue of, 14,
    245, 260
Jenkinson, Sir Hilary, 241
John of Cornwall, 163–5
John of Gaunt, 180
John of Salisbury, 163
Johnston, Dafydd, 188, 197
Journeys of Ohthere and Wulfstan,
    136
Joursanvault, Baron de, 241
Julian of Norwich, 190

Kempe, Margery, 190
Ker, N. R., 218, 219, 249
  Catalogue of Manuscripts Containing
    Anglo-Saxon, 39–47

Medieval Manuscripts in British Libraries,
    14, 16
Keynes, S., 110, 139
Kidd, Peter, 104
Kiernan, Kevin, 253, 255
  Electronic Beowulf, 259
King Horn, 209
Koszary, Adam, 273
Kraus, H. P., 291
  A Rare Book Saga, 292
Kwakkel, Erik, 60

Lake, Cynfael, 200
Langland, William, 66, 190
language knowledge, 150
Lansdowne collection, 246
Lapidge, M., 110
late Middle Age texts, 112
Latin, 133, 149–50, 151,
    155–165
Laud, William, 286
Lawler, John, *Book Auctions in England in*
    the Seventeenth Century, 292
Lawton, David, 193, 194
lawyers, 60
Le Voyage au paradis terrestre, 172
leaf signatures, 25, 27
leaves
  dimensions of, 20–1
  number of, 21
  reuse of, 122–3
Les Vœux du paon, 172
Liber Aureus and Gospel of
    Nichodemus, 123
library management, 225
Library of Congress, 257
library, definition, 225
Lindisfarne Gospels, 249
line fillers, 29
Linenthal, Richard, 291
liturgical books, reuse of, 121–3
Livingston, Michael, 193
Lollards, 180, 184–5
Longleat House, 256
Lumley, John, first Baron, 243
Luttrell Psalter, 249
Lyall, J. R., 'paper revolution', 18
Lydgate, John, 190, 260
  Fall of Princes, 286

Macaulay, G. C., 242, 260, 262
Machan, Tim William, 191
machine learning tools, 276

GENERAL INDEX

Mackney, Frederick, 255
Madden, Sir Frederic, 240, 246, 248, 249, 251, 253–4, 256, 257
Maggs, book dealers, 292
Magna Carta, 252, 256
Manley, John, 258
MARC (MAchine Readable Catalogue), 245
Marchaunt, John, 114
marginalia, 34, 209
Matheson, L. M., 114, 115, 116–17, 144
Mathilda, Empress, 139
Matilda, abbess of Wilton, 217
Maty, Matthew, 252, 253
Mayer, Manfred, 270
McGann, Jerome J., 191
Medieval Libraries of Great Britain, 218, 226
Meditaciones de Passione Christi, 120
membrane, 17–18
  images produced on, 77
Meredith, Peter, 255
Merlin's prophecies, 123, 163–5
Merton, Wilfred, 287
Michael, M. A., 215
microfilm, 78, 257–8, 275
Microsoft Silverlight, 259
Middle English, 162, 172–4, 195, 291
Middle English texts, 188, 192, 194, 198–9, 209, 261, *See also Brut*
  transmission of, 144
Middle Welsh, 188, 192, 198, 200–8
Mirador, 259
miscellanies, 118–20
mise-en-page, 4, 15, 29–30, 135, 149, 150, 165, 168, 210
mise-en-texte, 149, 162
MLGB3 (online digital resource), 226
Moffat, Douglas, 189, 193
MOOCs (Massive Online Open Courses), 276
Mooney, L. R., 114, 115, 210
Morte d'Arthure, 112
mortuary rolls, 129–30
Mosser, D., 114, 115
Mountford, Sir William, 144
mouvance, 208
multilingualism, 149, 153
Munby, A. N. L.
  British Book Sale Catalogues 1676–1800: A Union List, 293
  Connoisseurs and Medieval Miniatures, 291
  Phillipps Studies, 291
Murano, Giovanna, 111

Murphy, Patrick J., 112
Myers, R., Harris, M., and Mandelbrote, G., eds., *Under the Hammer: Book Auctions since the Seventeenth Century*, 292

National Archives, 239, 240
National Gallery, 239
National Library of Wales, 248, 258
Natural History Museum, 239
networks of knowledge, 142–4
Neville, Cecily, will of, 122–3
New Catalogue, 261
New Palaeographical Society, 251, 257
New Testament, 155
Nickson, M. A. E., 249
Nicolas, Sir Nicholas Harris, 241
nodes, 108, 119–20, 121
non-book languages, 155, 156, 159
Norse language, 150
Norwich Cathedral, 101
numbering, 237, 247, 249–50

Old Dutch literature, 151
Old English, 45, 46, 52, 134–5, 151, 153, 161–2
  Standard, 159
  vernacular, 151
Old French, 159
Old Testament, 155
Old Welsh, 52
Older Scots, 68
Omeka, 276
Open Access, 259
Oresme, Nicole, 169–71
origin, establishing, 215–18
original text, 189–90, 191
Orosius, Paulus, *Historiarum adversum Paganos libri septem*, 135–6
Orrm, 6, 161–3
Orrmulum, 161–3
Oscott Psalter, 240
Oswald, king of Northumbria, 132
Owen, Ann Parry, 199
owner's marks, 156
ownership, establishing, 224–9
Oxford Dictionary of National Biography, 292

painting, 30, 76–7, 78, 84, 89–91, 100
palaeography, 1, 2, 49, 71, 215
palimpsest, 122
paper, 18–20

paraphs, 29
parcheminers (parchmentmakers), 18
parchment, 17, 19, 20, 43, 46, 52, 84, 106
  bindings, 110
parent texts, 113
Parker Library, Corpus Christi College,
  Cambridge, 239
Parker on the Web project, 258, 259, 269, 277
Parker, Matthew, 46, 116, 241, 256, 258,
  269, 285, 286
Parkes, M. B., 14, 23, 29, 31, 60, 114, 115,
  219, 260
Parry, Thomas, 197
Paulus Orosius' *Historiarum adversum*
  Paganos libri septem (*History against*
  the Pagans in Seven Books), 135
Pearsall, Derek, 118, 249, 250
Pearson, David, *Provenance Research in*
  Book History, 293
pecia system, 113–14
Peel, Sir Robert, 250
Penda, king of Mercia, 132
Pentateuch, 100
pen-trials, 34, 122, 151, 156, 228
Perrins, Charles Dyson, 240, 287
Perryman, Judith
  King of Tars, The, 194
Petrarch, 143
Phillipps, Sir Thomas, 256, 286, 292
photographic facsimiles, 251, 256–7,
  275
photomicroscopy, 78
Piccard, G., 19
Piers Plowman Electronic Archive, 198
Piers Plowman, Skeat's edition, 193
Pinkhurst, Adam, 210
Pipe Rolls, 240
Planta, Joseph, 243, 247, 249, 253,
  254–255
Pollard, Graham, 113, 219
Pope, John, 41
Porcheddu, Fred, 112
Prescott, A., 277
pressmarks, 255
pricking, 26–7
proofreading, 32
Prophecies of Merlin, 6
provenance, 14, 27, 34–6, 192, 209, 215–18,
  223, 228, 229, 288, 290
psalters (genre), 97–100
punctuation, 31–2, 202–6
Pynkhurst, Adam, 250

Quaritch, Bernard, 292
  Contributions towards a Dictionary of
    English Book Collectors, 291
Quarto Catalogues, 261
quire signatures, 25, 27, 117
quires, 18
  collation of, 22–5
quotation, 149
Quran, 155

Ralph II, 227
Raman microscopes, 78
Rawlinson, Richard, 241, 286
Rawlinson, Thomas, 286
READ project, 276
reading stands, 238
recto, 16
restoration, 252–4
Revised Psalter Commentary, 184, 185
Rhigyfarch, *Lament*, 59
rhizomorphic editions, 208–9
rhyme brackets, 29
Ricci, Seymour de, *English Collectors of*
  Books & Manuscripts, 291
Rimius, Henry, 252, 253
Robinson, F. N., 189
Robinson, P. R., 27, 41, 42, 111
Rochester Cathedral Priory, 151
Roman alphabet, 155, 218
Rosarium, 184
Rosenbach, A. S. W., 292
Rouse, Richard and Mary, 220
Royal Bible, 57
Royal manuscripts, 246
rubricators, 29
Rule of St Benedict, 56
ruling, 26–7, 29
Rustichello da Pisa, 175

Sahle, Patrick, 198
St Alban, 41
St Anselm, letters of, 216–18
St Augustine gospels, 269
St Boniface, 131
St Erkenwald, 183
St Jerome, 166
St Patrick, 53, 55
Salesbury, William, 201
Salisbury Cathedral, 217, 227
Salisbury, Eurig, 201, 202
Sargent, Michael G., 208
Scase, Wendy, 229

317

GENERAL INDEX

Schoenberg Database (University of
    Pennsylvania), 293
Schoenberg, Laurence J., 291
scribes, 60–2, 66–9, 209–10
    'hooked g', 68
    identification of, 217
    professional, 114–15
    skills of, 51–2
scriptorium, 220, 225
scripts, 49, 53
    anglicana, 184
    anglicana formata, 61, 66, 68, 69, 117
    Anglo-Caroline minuscule, 161
    Arabic-based, 50
    Ashkenazi square, 158
    bastard *anglicana*, 61
    bastard secretary, 61
    Caroline minuscule, 50, 55, 57–9, 68, 131,
        153, 161
    Continental, 56–7
    difference between typeface and, 49–50
    Gothic cursives, 64–71
    Gothic *textualis* (*textura*), 50, 59–64, 66,
        67, 69, 180, 184
    half-uncial, 55–6, 57, 59
    Insular minuscule, 53–5,
        57, 65
        reconfiguration of, 57–9
        Square minuscule, 58, 59
    Irish, 55–6
    Roman cursive, 53, 55
    Roman influence, 52–3
    Rustic capitals, 57
    secretary, 61, 67–9
    uncial, 56, 68
    Welsh minuscule, 188
scriveners
    legal, 60
    urban, 67
Seaman, Lazarus, 285
Sedulius, *Carmen Paschale*, 116
sermons, 64, 151, 153
Seymour, M. C., 122
Shaw, Henry, 256
shelfmarks, 15, 247, 274
shelving, 237
Siege of Jerusalem, The, 193, 194, 198
Skeat, Theodore C., 249, 255
Skeat, Walter W., 193
Sloane Charters, 249
Sloane collection, 246
Sloane, Sir Hans, 239, 241, 249, 286
Smirke, Robert, 250

Smith, Thomas, 249
social media platforms, 273–4
Sotheby's, 286, 289, 292
South Kensington Museum (Victoria and
    Albert Museum, 256
Springmount Bog tablets, 55
stamping, 237, 256
stemmata, 192, 199, 208
stemmatics (recension), 189
Stephen, king of England, 139
Story, Joanna, 268
structured indeterminacy, 108–11
Stubbs, E., 114
Sulien, bishop of St. David's, 59
Summary Catalogue, 261
superimpositions, 32

Talbot, Henry Fox, 256–7
    The Pencil of Nature, 257
TEAMS Middle English Texts series, 188,
    193, 198–9, 209, 210
TEI (Text Encoding Initiative), 199
terminus ante quem non, 15
terminus post quem non, 15
textual structuring, 117–20
textual transmission, 144
textual transmission, 129, 130, 141, 193, 209,
    290–1
themes, 118, 120
Thomas of Erceldoune's prophecy, 209
Thomas of Lancaster, Duke of Clarence,
    144, 180
Thomas of Woodstock, Duke of Gloucester,
    180, 181
Thompson, Edward Maunde, 246
Thompson, Henry Yates, 240
Thornton, Robert, 110, 112
Tiberius Psalter, 97–100, 103
Tollemache Orosius, 135
Transkribus platform, 276
translatio studii, 166
translatio studii et imperii, 166
translation, 154, 158–9, 163–165
    knowledge transfer and, 165–75
Treharne, Elaine, 276
Trevisa, John, 66, 179
Trinity College Dublin, 261
Tuckett, Charles, 246, 253–4
Tyler, E. M., 142
typeface, 49–50

underdrawing, 78
underlining, 29

318

GENERAL INDEX

Unicode, 199
Universal Viewer, 259
University of Kansas Library, 42
Utrecht Psalter, 168, 257

Vaughan of Hengwrt, Robert, 241
vellum, 17, 238, 247, 253, 255
Venantius Fortunatus, 122
Venuti, Laurence, 171
Vercelli Book, 43
vernacular, 149, 155–9, 161–5, 184, 224
   'national', 153
   translations, 165–72, 181
versals, 29
verso, 16
Victoria and Albert Museum, 258, 259
Virtual Manuscript Library of
   Switzerland, 261
Voigts, Linda, 122
Vulgate Bible, 155, 179, 181

Wanley, Humfrey, 256, 286
Ware, James, *Librorum manuscriptorum in
   bibliotheca Jacobi Waraei equitis
   aurati catalogus*, 285
Warner, Sir George, 251
watermarks, 15, 19, 25, 209
Waverley Committee, 290
wax tablets, 52
Wealdhere, Bishop of London, 57

Welsh, 150, 165
Western Manuscripts Card Catalogues, 261
Whearty, Bridget, 277, 279
Whitgift, John, 111, 216, 218
Wiliems, Thomas, 201
William of Malmesbury, 131–4, 135,
   137, 139
   Gesta Regum Anglorum, 132, 133
   Historia Regum Anglorum, 131
wills, evidence of book ownership in,
   225, 228
Wolf, E. and Fleming, J., *Rosenbach*, 292
workshop concept, 220, 223, 225
Woudhuysen, H. and Suarez, M.,
   *Oxford Companion to the
   Book*, 292
Wyclif, John, 179
Wycliffite Bible, 64, 179–85, 286
   chronology and patterns of production,
   180–1
   glosses, 183
   liturgical aids, 182
   ownership, 180
   production, 183–4
   provenance, 183
   translation, 181–2

York Play, 255

Zumthor, Paul, 208

319

Cambridge Companions To ...

AUTHORS

Edward Albee edited by Stephen J. Bottoms

Margaret Atwood edited by Coral Ann Howells

W. H. Auden edited by Stan Smith

Jane Austen edited by Edward Copeland and Juliet McMaster (second edition)

Balzac edited by Owen Heathcote and Andrew Watts

Beckett edited by John Pilling

Bede edited by Scott DeGregorio

Aphra Behn edited by Derek Hughes and Janet Todd

Saul Bellow edited by Victoria Aarons

Walter Benjamin edited by David S. Ferris

William Blake edited by Morris Eaves

James Baldwin edited by Michele Elam

Boccaccio edited by Guyda Armstrong, Rhiannon Daniels, and Stephen J. Milner

Jorge Luis Borges edited by Edwin Williamson

Brecht edited by Peter Thomson and Glendyr Sacks (second edition)

The Brontës edited by Heather Glen

Bunyan edited by Anne Dunan-Page

Frances Burney edited by Peter Sabor

Byron edited by Drummond Bone

Albert Camus edited by Edward J. Hughes

Willa Cather edited by Marilee Lindemann

Cervantes edited by Anthony J. Cascardi

Chaucer edited by Piero Boitani and Jill Mann (second edition)

Chekhov edited by Vera Gottlieb and Paul Allain

Kate Chopin edited by Janet Beer

Caryl Churchill edited by Elaine Aston and Elin Diamond

Cicero edited by Catherine Steel

J. M. Coetzee edited by Jarad Zimbler

Coleridge edited by Lucy Newlyn

Wilkie Collins edited by Jenny Bourne Taylor

Joseph Conrad edited by J. H. Stape

H. D. edited by Nephie J. Christodoulides and Polina Mackay

Dante edited by Rachel Jacoff (second edition)

Daniel Defoe edited by John Richetti

Don DeLillo edited by John N. Duvall

Charles Dickens edited by John O. Jordan

Emily Dickinson edited by Wendy Martin

John Donne edited by Achsah Guibbory

Dostoevskii edited by W. J. Leatherbarrow

Theodore Dreiser edited by Leonard Cassuto and Claire Virginia Eby

John Dryden edited by Steven N. Zwicker

W. E. B. Du Bois edited by Shamoon Zamir

George Eliot edited by George Levine and Nancy Henry (second edition)

T. S. Eliot edited by A. David Moody

Ralph Ellison edited by Ross Posnock

Ralph Waldo Emerson edited by Joel Porte and Saundra Morris

William Faulkner edited by Philip M. Weinstein

Henry Fielding edited by Claude Rawson

F. Scott Fitzgerald edited by Ruth Prigozy

Flaubert edited by Timothy Unwin

E. M. Forster edited by David Bradshaw

Benjamin Franklin edited by Carla Mulford

Brian Friel edited by Anthony Roche

Robert Frost edited by Robert Faggen

Gabriel García Márquez edited by Philip Swanson

Elizabeth Gaskell edited by Jill L. Matus

Edward Gibbon edited by Karen O'Brien and Brian Young

Goethe edited by Lesley Sharpe

Günter Grass edited by Stuart Taberner

Thomas Hardy edited by Dale Kramer

David Hare edited by Richard Boon

Nathaniel Hawthorne edited by Richard Millington

Seamus Heaney edited by Bernard O'Donoghue

Ernest Hemingway edited by Scott Donaldson

Homer edited by Robert Fowler

Horace edited by Stephen Harrison

Ted Hughes edited by Terry Gifford

Ibsen edited by James McFarlane

Henry James edited by Jonathan Freedman

Samuel Johnson edited by Greg Clingham

Ben Jonson edited by Richard Harp and Stanley Stewart

James Joyce edited by Derek Attridge (second edition)

Kafka edited by Julian Preece
Keats edited by Susan J. Wolfson
Rudyard Kipling edited by Howard J. Booth
Lacan edited by Jean-Michel Rabaté
D. H. Lawrence edited by Anne Fernihough
Primo Levi edited by Robert Gordon
Lucretius edited by Stuart Gillespie and Philip Hardie
Machiavelli edited by John M. Najemy
David Mamet edited by Christopher Bigsby
Thomas Mann edited by Ritchie Robertson
Christopher Marlowe edited by Patrick Cheney
Andrew Marvell edited by Derek Hirst and Steven N. Zwicker
Ian McEwan edited by Dominic Head
Herman Melville edited by Robert S. Levine
Arthur Miller edited by Christopher Bigsby (second edition)
Milton edited by Dennis Danielson (second edition)
Molière edited by David Bradby and Andrew Calder
Toni Morrison edited by Justine Tally
Alice Munro edited by David Staines
Nabokov edited by Julian W. Connolly
Eugene O'Neill edited by Michael Manheim
George Orwell edited by John Rodden
Ovid edited by Philip Hardie
Petrarch edited by Albert Russell Ascoli and Unn Falkeid
Harold Pinter edited by Peter Raby (second edition)
Sylvia Plath edited by Jo Gill
Edgar Allan Poe edited by Kevin J. Hayes
Alexander Pope edited by Pat Rogers
Ezra Pound edited by Ira B. Nadel
Proust edited by Richard Bales
Pushkin edited by Andrew Kahn
Thomas Pynchon edited by Inger H. Dalsgaard, Luc Herman and Brian McHale
Rabelais edited by John O'Brien
Rilke edited by Karen Leeder and Robert Vilain
Philip Roth edited by Timothy Parrish
Salman Rushdie edited by Abdulrazak Gurnah
John Ruskin edited by Francis O'Gorman
Sappho edited by P. J. Finglass and Adrian Kelly
Seneca edited by Shadi Bartsch and Alessandro Schiesaro

Shakespeare edited by Margareta de Grazia and Stanley Wells (second edition)
George Bernard Shaw edited by Christopher Innes
Shelley edited by Timothy Morton
Mary Shelley edited by Esther Schor
Sam Shepard edited by Matthew C. Roudané
Spenser edited by Andrew Hadfield
Laurence Sterne edited by Thomas Keymer
Wallace Stevens edited by John N. Serio
Tom Stoppard edited by Katherine E. Kelly
Harriet Beecher Stowe edited by Cindy Weinstein
August Strindberg edited by Michael Robinson
Jonathan Swift edited by Christopher Fox
J. M. Synge edited by P. J. Mathews
Tacitus edited by A. J. Woodman
Henry David Thoreau edited by Joel Myerson
Tolstoy edited by Donna Tussing Orwin
Anthony Trollope edited by Carolyn Dever and Lisa Niles
Mark Twain edited by Forrest G. Robinson
John Updike edited by Stacey Olster
Mario Vargas Llosa edited by Efrain Kristal and John King
Virgil edited by Fiachra Mac Góráin and Charles Martindale (second edition)
Voltaire edited by Nicholas Cronk
David Foster Wallace edited by Ralph Clare
Edith Wharton edited by Millicent Bell
Walt Whitman edited by Ezra Greenspan
Oscar Wilde edited by Peter Raby
Tennessee Williams edited by Matthew C. Roudané
William Carlos Williams edited by Christopher MacGowan
August Wilson edited by Christopher Bigsby
Mary Wollstonecraft edited by Claudia L. Johnson
Virginia Woolf edited by Susan Sellers (second edition)
Wordsworth edited by Stephen Gill
Richard Wright edited by Glenda R. Carpio
W. B. Yeats edited by Marjorie Howes and John Kelly
Xenophon edited by Michael A. Flower
Zola edited by Brian Nelson

TOPICS

The Actress edited by Maggie B. Gale and John Stokes

The African American Novel edited by Maryemma Graham

The African American Slave Narrative edited by Audrey A. Fisch

African American Theatre by Harvey Young

Allegory edited by Rita Copeland and Peter Struck

American Crime Fiction edited by Catherine Ross Nickerson

American Gothic edited by Jeffrey Andrew Weinstock

American Literature of the 1930s edited by William Solomon

American Modernism edited by Walter Kalaidjian

American Poetry since 1945 edited by Jennifer Ashton

American Realism and Naturalism edited by Donald Pizer

American Travel Writing edited by Alfred Bendixen and Judith Hamera

American Women Playwrights edited by Brenda Murphy

Ancient Rhetoric edited by Erik Gunderson

Arthurian Legend edited by Elizabeth Archibald and Ad Putter

Australian Literature edited by Elizabeth Webby

The Beats edited by Stephen Belletto

Boxing edited by Gerald Early

British Black and Asian Literature (1945–2010) edited by Deirdre Osborne

British Fiction: 1980–2018 edited by Peter Boxall

British Fiction since 1945 edited by David James

British Literature of the 1930s edited by James Smith

British Literature of the French Revolution edited by Pamela Clemit

British Romantic Poetry edited by James Chandler and Maureen N. McLane

British Romanticism edited by Stuart Curran (second edition)

British Theatre, 1730–1830, edited by Jane Moody and Daniel O'Quinn

Canadian Literature edited by Eva-Marie Kröller (second edition)

The Canterbury Tales edited by Frank Grady

Children's Literature edited by M. O. Grenby and Andrea Immel

The Classic Russian Novel edited by Malcolm V. Jones and Robin Feuer Miller

Contemporary Irish Poetry edited by Matthew Campbell

Creative Writing edited by David Morley and Philip Neilsen

Crime Fiction edited by Martin Priestman

Dante's 'Commedia' edited by Zygmunt G. Barański and Simon Gilson

Dracula edited by Roger Luckhurst

Early Modern Women's Writing edited by Laura Lunger Knoppers

The Eighteenth-Century Novel edited by John Richetti

Eighteenth-Century Poetry edited by John Sitter

Emma edited by Peter Sabor

English Dictionaries edited by Sarah Ogilvie

English Literature, 1500–1600 edited by Arthur F. Kinney

English Literature, 1650–1740 edited by Steven N. Zwicker

English Literature, 1740–1830 edited by Thomas Keymer and Jon Mee

English Literature, 1830–1914 edited by Joanne Shattock

English Melodrama edited by Carolyn Williams

English Novelists edited by Adrian Poole

English Poetry, Donne to Marvell edited by Thomas N. Corns

English Poets edited by Claude Rawson

English Renaissance Drama, second edition edited by A. R. Braunmuller and Michael Hattaway

English Renaissance Tragedy edited by Emma Smith and Garrett A. Sullivan Jr.

English Restoration Theatre edited by Deborah C. Payne Fisk

The Epic edited by Catherine Bates

Erotic Literature edited by Bradford Mudge

European Modernism edited by Pericles Lewis

European Novelists edited by Michael Bell

Fairy Tales edited by Maria Tatar

Fantasy Literature edited by Edward James and Farah Mendlesohn

Feminist Literary Theory edited by Ellen Rooney

Fiction in the Romantic Period edited by Richard Maxwell and Katie Trumpener

The Fin de Siècle edited by Gail Marshall

Frankenstein edited by Andrew Smith

The French Enlightenment edited by Daniel Brewer

French Literature edited by John D. Lyons

The French Novel: from 1800 to the Present edited by Timothy Unwin

Gay and Lesbian Writing edited by Hugh Stevens

German Romanticism edited by Nicholas Saul

Gothic Fiction edited by Jerrold E. Hogle

The Graphic Novel edited by Stephen Tabachnick

The Greek and Roman Novel edited by Tim Whitmarsh

Greek and Roman Theatre edited by Marianne McDonald and J. Michael Walton

Greek Comedy edited by Martin Revermann

Greek Lyric edited by Felix Budelmann

Greek Mythology edited by Roger D. Woodard

Greek Tragedy edited by P. E. Easterling

The Harlem Renaissance edited by George Hutchinson

The History of the Book edited by Leslie Howsam

Human Rights and Literature edited by Crystal Parikh

The Irish Novel edited by John Wilson Foster

Irish Poets edited by Gerald Dawe

The Italian Novel edited by Peter Bondanella and Andrea Ciccarelli

The Italian Renaissance edited by Michael Wyatt

Jewish American Literature edited by Hana Wirth-Nesher and Michael P. Kramer

The Latin American Novel edited by Efraín Kristal

Latin American Poetry edited by Stephen Hart

Latina/o American Literature edited by John Morán González

Latin Love Elegy edited by Thea S. Thorsen

Literature and Disability edited by Clare Barker and Stuart Murray

Literature and Food edited by J. Michelle Coghlan

Literature and the Posthuman edited by Bruce Clarke and Manuela Rossini

Literature and Religion edited by Susan M. Felch

Literature and Science edited by Steven Meyer

The Literature of the American Renaissance edited by Christopher N. Phillips

The Literature of Berlin edited by Andrew J. Webber

The Literature of the Crusades, Volume 1, edited by Anthony Bale

The Literature of the First World War edited by Vincent Sherry

The Literature of London edited by Lawrence Manley

The Literature of Los Angeles edited by Kevin R. McNamara

The Literature of New York edited by Cyrus Patell and Bryan Waterman

The Literature of Paris edited by Anna-Louise Milne

The Literature of World War II edited by Marina MacKay

Literature on Screen edited by Deborah Cartmell and Imelda Whelehan

Lyrical Ballads edited by Sally Bushell

Medieval British Manuscripts edited by Orietta Da Rold and Elaine Treharne

Medieval English Culture edited by Andrew Galloway

Medieval English Law and Literature edited by Candace Barrington and Sebastian Sobecki

Medieval English Literature edited by Larry Scanlon

Medieval English Mysticism edited by Samuel Fanous and Vincent Gillespie

Medieval English Theatre edited by Richard Beadle and Alan J. Fletcher (second edition)

Medieval French Literature edited by Simon Gaunt and Sarah Kay

Medieval Romance edited by Roberta L. Krueger

Medieval Women's Writing edited by Carolyn Dinshaw and David Wallace

Modern American Culture edited by Christopher Bigsby

Modern British Women Playwrights edited by Elaine Aston and Janelle Reinelt

Modern French Culture edited by Nicholas Hewitt

Modern German Culture edited by Eva Kolinsky and Wilfried van der Will

The Modern German Novel edited by Graham Bartram

The Modern Gothic edited by Jerrold E. Hogle

Modern Irish Culture edited by Joe Cleary and Claire Connolly

Modern Italian Culture edited by Zygmunt G. Baranski and Rebecca J. West

Modern Latin American Culture edited by John King

Modern Russian Culture edited by Nicholas Rzhevsky

Modern Spanish Culture edited by David T. Gies

Modernism edited by Michael Levenson (second edition)

The Modernist Novel edited by Morag Shiach

Modernist Poetry edited by Alex Davis and Lee M. Jenkins

Modernist Women Writers edited by Maren Tova Linett

Narrative edited by David Herman

Narrative Theory edited by Matthew Garrett

Native American Literature edited by Joy Porter and Kenneth M. Roemer

Nineteen Eighty-Four edited by Nathan Waddell

Nineteenth-Century American Poetry edited by Kerry Larson

Nineteenth-Century American Women's Writing edited by Dale M. Bauer and Philip Gould

Nineteenth Century Thought edited by Gregory Claeys

The Novel edited by Eric Bulson

Old English Literature edited by Malcolm Godden and Michael Lapidge (second edition)

Performance Studies edited by Tracy C. Davis

Piers Plowman by Andrew Cole and Andrew Galloway

The Poetry of the First World War edited by Santanu Das

Popular Fiction edited by David Glover and Scott McCracken

Postcolonial Literary Studies edited by Neil Lazarus

Postcolonial Poetry edited by Jahan Ramazani

Postcolonial Travel Writing edited by Robert Clarke

Postmodern American Fiction edited by Paula Geyh

Postmodernism edited by Steven Connor

The Pre-Raphaelites edited by Elizabeth Prettejohn

Pride and Prejudice edited by Janet Todd

Queer Studies edited by Siobhan B. Somerville

Renaissance Humanism edited by Jill Kraye

Robinson Crusoe edited by John Richetti

Roman Comedy edited by Martin T. Dinter

The Roman Historians edited by Andrew Feldherr

Roman Satire edited by Kirk Freudenburg

Science Fiction edited by Edward James and Farah Mendlesohn

Scottish Literature edited by Gerald Carruthers and Liam McIlvanney

Sensation Fiction edited by Andrew Mangham

Shakespeare and Contemporary Dramatists edited by Ton Hoenselaars

Shakespeare and Popular Culture edited by Robert Shaughnessy

Shakespeare and Religion edited by Hannibal Hamlin

Shakespeare on Film edited by Russell Jackson (second edition)

Shakespeare on Screen edited by Russell Jackson

Shakespeare on Stage edited by Stanley Wells and Sarah Stanton

Shakespearean Comedy edited by Alexander Leggatt

Shakespearean Tragedy edited by Claire McEachern (second edition)

Shakespeare's First Folio edited by Emma Smith

Shakespeare's History Plays edited by Michael Hattaway

Shakespeare's Language edited by Lynne Magnusson with David Schalkwyk

Shakespeare's Last Plays edited by Catherine M. S. Alexander

Shakespeare's Poetry edited by Patrick Cheney

Sherlock Holmes edited by Janice M. Allan and Christopher Pittard

The Sonnet edited by A. D. Cousins and Peter Howarth

The Spanish Novel: from 1600 to the Present edited by Harriet Turner and Adelaida López de Martínez

Textual Scholarship edited by Neil Fraistat and Julia Flanders

Theatre and Science edited by Kristen E. Shepherd-Barr

Theatre History by David Wiles and Christine Dymkowski

Transnational American Literature edited by Yogita Goyal

Travel Writing edited by Peter Hulme and Tim Youngs

Twentieth-Century British and Irish Women's Poetry edited by Jane Dowson

The Twentieth-Century English Novel edited by Robert L. Caserio

Twentieth-Century English Poetry edited by Neil Corcoran

Twentieth-Century Irish Drama edited by Shaun Richards

Twentieth-Century Russian Literature edited by Marina Balina and Evgeny Dobrenko

Utopian Literature edited by Gregory Claeys

Victorian and Edwardian Theatre edited by Kerry Powell

The Victorian Novel edited by Deirdre David (second edition)

Victorian Poetry edited by Joseph Bristow

Victorian Women's Poetry edited by Linda K. Hughes

Victorian Women's Writing edited by Linda H. Peterson

War Writing edited by Kate McLoughlin

Women's Writing in Britain, 1660–1789 edited by Catherine Ingrassia

Women's Writing in the Romantic Period edited by Devoney Looser

World Literature edited by Ben Etherington and Jarad Zimbler

Writing of the English Revolution edited by N. H. Keeble

The Writings of Julius Caesar edited by Christopher Krebs and Luca Grillo

Printed in the United States
By Bookmasters